ABLE ARCHER 83

ABLE ARCHER 83

The Secret History of the NATO Exercise That Almost Triggered Nuclear War

Edited by Nate Jones

With a foreword by Tom Blanton

THE NEW PRESS

NEW YORK
LONDON

Published in the United States by The New Press, New York, 2016
Distributed by Two Rivers Distribution

LIBRARY OF CONGRESS CATALOGING-IN-PUBLICATION DATA

Names: Jones, Nate, author.
Title: Able Archer 83 : the secret history of the NATO exercise that almost triggered nuclear war / Nate Jones ; with a foreword by Thomas S. Blanton.
Other titles: Secret history of the NATO exercise that almost triggered nuclear war
Description: New York : The New Press, [2016] | Includes bibliographical references and index.
Identifiers: LCCN 2016023458 (print) | LCCN 2016032122 (ebook) | ISBN 9781620972618 (hc : alk. paper) | ISBN 9781620972625 (e-book)
Subjects: LCSH: Europe—History, Military—20th century. | Military maneuvers—Europe—History—20th century. | Nuclear crisis control—History—20th century. | United States—History, Military—20th century—Sources. | Nuclear weapons—Government policy—United States—History—20th century. | North Atlantic Treaty Organization—History—20th century. | Europe, Western—Defenses—History—20th century. | Soviet Union—Foreign relations—United States—Sources. | United States—Foreign relations—Soviet Union—Sources. | Cold War—Sources.
Classification: LCC UA646 .J656 2016 (print) | LCC UA646 (ebook) | DDC 355.5/209409048—dc23
LC record available at https://lccn.loc.gov/2016023458

The New Press publishes books that promote and enrich public discussion and understanding of the issues vital to our democracy and to a more equitable world. These books are made possible by the enthusiasm of our readers; the support of a committed group of donors, large and small; the collaboration of our many partners in the independent media and the not-for-profit sector; booksellers, who often hand-sell New Press books; librarians; and above all by our authors.

www.thenewpress.com

Book design and composition by Bookbright Media
This book was set in URW Palladio

For my family, Durl, Wendy, Ben, and Eric

CONTENTS

FOREWORD

READ THIS BOOK AND YOU will make the world a safer place. Read these former secrets—many of them classified above Top Secret—and you will see how truly scary the War Scare of 1983 was. Read this book and you will understand how the Cold War dangers that flared in 1983—and could have produced a nuclear war through miscalculation and misperception—are still with us today.

You don't have to take the author's word for it. Nate Jones has personally led the cutting edge of scholarship, breaking loose the primary sources, the classified contemporaneous notes, the highest-level intelligence assessments, from all sides, through the U.S. Freedom of Information Act and through archival research in collections ranging from the East German Stasi to the Soviet Politburo to the CIA's database of declassified records. Here in this book, Nate shows you the actual documents, along with his own narrative and analysis, so you can judge for yourself.

This book effectively resolves a heated controversy that divided the CIA in the 1980s and has led to sharp exchanges between scholars ever since. The debate over the 1983 War Scare secretly raged for years inside the classified conference rooms of U.S. and British spy agencies, and inside the closed briefing sessions with presidents and prime ministers. Word of the War Scare of 1983 only reached the public domain in the 1990s, and scholars took up cudgels on both sides of the debate, some expressing serious alarm and others pooh-poohing the fright factor, but all lacking the firsthand evidence that you will read about in this book.

Here's how President Ronald Reagan summed up the key question about the 1983 War Scare (in a query to his ambassador to Moscow, Arthur Hartman, in ink Soviet leaders really fear us, or is all the huffing and r propaganda?" In other words, did the Soviet leadership vorry in 1983 that the United States might be planning a e, a nuclear blitzkrieg, or were the Soviet public statements just PR meant for the court of public opinion?

the documents, President Reagan himself was getting contradictory s core question in 1983. On the one hand, the KGB station chief in London, Oleg Gordievsky—who had defected in place to British intelligence—was providing truly alarming evidence of Soviet paranoia: a massive intel collection effort that assumed a U.S. first strike was in the works and focused on indicators of imminent attack.

On the other hand, the top CIA analysts of the Soviet Union assured the president there was no such danger. In their view, the Gordievsky information just showed how dysfunctional the communist system was, and since we knew we wouldn't launch such an attack, all the Soviet statements were just propaganda, meant to keep the Soviet population mobilized, the European peace movement energized, and the Americans blamed for warmongering. This became the official position of the CIA in their highly classified National Intelligence Estimates, which argued that training exercises like Able Archer were so routine that the Soviets couldn't have been really scared.

Years later, this line of argument showed up in the scholarly debate over the 1983 War Scare as the position adopted by scholars most critical of the Soviet Union and least worried about nuclear accidents or misperception. One scholar even titled his conference paper "The Able Archer Non-Crisis."

Interestingly, President Reagan did not share the CIA view. Nate Jones quotes a Reagan diary entry from December 1983—after Gordievsky's initial warnings—to the effect that Reagan had learned something new, something he should have realized before: that despite all good American intentions, the Soviets were genuinely scared of us, and that made it even more important for Reagan to get them in the same room and convince them to work with us to get rid of nuclear weapons.

"Huffing and puffing" or real fear? This book concludes that the answer is "both." Just because the Soviets turned U.S. and NATO actions into propaganda does not eliminate the likelihood they were also scared—and that fear could have led to a ratcheting up of alarm and alert and mobilization to the brink of war.

This book presents extraordinary evidence from the "other side" of the Cold War in 1983 to make these points. For example, in the Averell Harriman papers at the Library of Congress, Nate Jones found Harriman's own notes from the meeting with Soviet general secretary Yuri Andropov in July 1983 where the Soviet leader expressed his fear that nuclear war would come not from either side attacking the other, but from miscalculation or inadvertence. This volume includes the interview evidence from conversations with Marshal Sergei Akhromeyev and other Soviet generals about the dangers inherent in the "masking" effect created by NATO exercises—such as the big Autumn Forge package, of which the Able Archer nuclear command exercise was a small part—that could hide preparations for an actual attack.

The genius of this book is the combination of all source information, Soviet, U.S., East and West German, NATO, and after-action reporting. Together with the first-hand Andropov and Akhromeyev quotations, Nate Jones presents detailed comparisons with other "routine" exercises that prove, for the first time, how unusual many elements of Able Archer turned out to be, well beyond previous maneuvers, in ways that could indeed look more dangerous than the planners intended.

Perhaps most chilling of all are the documents showing how the Able Archer exercise ramped up right into pretend nuclear war, in a matter of days, when "Blue's use of nuclear weapons did not stop Orange's aggression." This is the way the world ends.

Old intelligence hands will complain that Nate Jones does not have all the inside scoop, that there are reams of sources not yet declassified—and indeed, most of the signals intelligence and overhead photography from the fall of 1983, both American and Soviet, remains in classified vaults today. But this book publishes the next-best thing to having it all: the one retrospective study that did have access to the all-source intelligence, years later, in 1990, when President George H.W. Bush's Foreign Intelligence Advisory Board (PFIAB) made its own sober assessment of how well U.S. spy agencies had performed in 1983, and concluded, not so well. But the study itself stayed under wraps for twenty-five years, labeled Top Secret UMBRA GAMMA WNINTEL NOFORN NOCONTRACT ORCON.

When Nate Jones got this PFIAB study declassified in 2015, it proved to be a blockbuster. The *Washington Post* put the study's conclusions on the front page, under the headline "In 1983 'War Scare,' Soviet Leadership Feared Nuclear Surprise Attack by U.S."

In this book, you will finally read the Top Secret assessment for yourself. With access to all the intelligence and lots of hindsight, the president's board concluded that the CIA was wrong and the United States "may have inadvertently placed our relations with the Soviet Union on a hair trigger" during Able Archer 83.

Fortunately, as the PFIAB found, "the military officers in charge of the Able Archer exercise minimized this risk by doing nothing in the face of evidence that parts of the Soviet armed forces were moving to an unusual level of alert." So you will find some heroes in this book, like the Air Force lieutenant general Leonard Perroots, who just decided to do "nothing."

Nate Jones draws important lessons for today from this previously secret history. At the top of the list is the continuing danger posed by nuclear weapons in the hands of fallible humans. We can reduce that danger by knowing our own history, getting rid of the hair triggers, and controlling those nukes and the fissile material in them. That's where reading this book will help make the world a safer place.

The final lesson is about empathy. The U.S. intelligence community went wrong on the 1983 War Scare because it mirror-imaged the enemy—well, we Americans are never going to launch a Pearl Harbor–style surprise attack, especially not a nuclear attack, so that Soviet "huffing and puffing" can't reflect real fear!

This book will teach us, if we let it, to put ourselves in the shoes of our adversaries—what do our actions look like to them? What motivations must they have? What fears do they feel? Empathy doesn't mean identifying with the adversary, no indeed, but understanding them. And ourselves.

Tom Blanton
Director, National Security Archive
George Washington University, Washington, D.C.
July 4, 2016

ABLE ARCHER 83

Introduction: "Two Spiders in a Bottle"

THE COLD WAR TURNED HOT in 1983. The impetus was a sudden change of leadership in the Kremlin, which had taken place the previous year. A new Kremlin faction aimed to reverse recent Western geopolitical and economic gains by asserting greater Soviet power in the petroleum-rich Gulf States. By March, Moscow was fighting proxy wars against the United States in the Middle East by providing political support as well as arms to Iran, Syria, and South Yemen.[1]

By June, conflict spread from the Middle East to Europe. The fledgling Soviet leadership was unable to continue providing its usual levels of aid to its satellites in Eastern Europe. Despite Moscow's desperate efforts to utilize planted political parties, pressure groups, and propaganda campaigns to quell dissatisfaction and unrest throughout its Eastern European sphere of influence, the region's economic situation continued to worsen. The East's military preparedness, however, improved. Warsaw Pact forces conducted frequent field training exercises, stockpiled equipment, and increased activity in naval dockyards, while factories producing materiel went on round-the-clock schedules.

Then, in August, nonaligned Yugoslavia shifted toward the West, formally requesting economic and military assistance from several NATO countries. Moscow, fearing Yugoslavia's shift could herald the further defection of its Eastern European allies and buffer states, dooming the worldwide communist movement, chose to invade. After a month of mobilization exercises and forward deployments, Soviet and Warsaw Pact forces entered Yugoslavia.

On October 31, the ground war broadened. Soviet forces invaded Finland

and, the next day, Norway. The Soviets commenced massive air and naval attacks against NATO's European forces and bases. In southern Europe, Soviet ground forces invaded Greece while its navy carried out attacks in the Adriatic, Mediterranean, and Black Seas.

By November 4, Soviet and Warsaw Pact forces crossed through the Fulda Gap while bombarding the entire eastern border of West Germany with air attacks. Because NATO forces provided strong resistance to these Soviet invasions, conventional war turned unconventional; by November 6, Soviet forces had launched chemical attacks. The next day, NATO forces responded in kind.

The war soon spread to Britain. On November 10, "attacks on UK airfields disrupted B-52 and KC-135 operations as well as destroy[ed] some aircraft." Eight KC-135 Stratotankers in the United Kingdom were "launched for survival"; they would later be available to refuel nuclear bombers.[2] Under attack, NATO headquarters was forced to relocate its Mons, Belgium, headquarters to an Alternate War Headquarters at the Heinrich Hertz Kaserne in Birkenfeld.[3]

Unable to repel the Soviets' ground advance, NATO attempted to send a message to the Warsaw Pact via nuclear signaling—the nuclear destruction of one city in the hope of averting total nuclear war. On the morning of November 8 NATO requested permission from its members for "initial limited use of nuclear weapons against pre-selected fixed targets" on the morning of November 9.[4] The Western capitals granted NATO permission to destroy Eastern European cities with nuclear attacks.

But this did not stop the Warsaw Pact. As a result, the next day the leader of NATO's military, the Supreme Allied Commander Europe (SACEUR), requested a "follow-on use of nuclear weapons." Washington—and the other capitals—approved this request within twenty-four hours, and on November 11 the follow-on attack was executed. A full-scale nuclear war had broken out.

Then, with nothing left to destroy, Able Archer 83, a NATO war-gaming exercise designed to practice the release of nuclear weapons during wartime conditions, came to an end.

While NATO was staging its Able Archer 83 exercise—simulating a slow escalation from a conventional military response to a chemical and limited nuclear strike and finally into full nuclear war—the Soviet Union was not practicing. It feared that Able Archer 83 was not just a war game, but could potentially be an actual planned nuclear attack.

For a variety of reasons—including the end of détente, the Reagan administration's strident rhetoric, and the impending deployment of nuclear-armed, "decapitating" Pershing II intermediate range missiles and Gryphon cruise missiles to Europe—the Soviets were so worried about U.S. and NATO intentions that they were actively preparing for an actual surprise nuclear missile attack by the West during Able Archer 83.

On November 8, as NATO was simulating a launch of its nuclear arsenal at "preselected fixed targets," Oleg Gordievsky,[5] a London-based KGB colonel turned double agent for the British MI6 intelligence service, reported to his British controllers that KGB and GRU (military intelligence) residencies in Western Europe received flash telegrams reporting "an alert on U.S. bases."[6] These telegrams, part of Soviet intelligence's Operation RYaN (the Russian acronym for *Raketno-Yadernoe Napadenie,* or, in English, a nuclear missile attack), an intelligence-gathering operation to detect and possibly preempt a Western nuclear attack on the Soviet Union, implied that one explanation for the reported Western alert was that the countdown to a nuclear first strike had actually begun.[7]

A declassified British Ministry of Defence document from a few months later confirms the "unprecedented Soviet reaction to Able Archer 83."[8] A retrospective, highly classified all-source American review conducted in 1990 by the President's Foreign Intelligence Advisory Board concluded that Able Archer 83 "may have inadvertently placed our relations with the Soviet Union on a hair trigger."[9]

When President Reagan read a report on the Soviet reaction to Able Archer 83 in June of 1984, he "expressed surprise" and "described the events as 'really scary.'"[10]

Reagan's counterpart, Yuri Andropov, the general secretary of the Soviet Union, understood the increased and unacceptable risks of nuclear war through miscalculation even before Able Archer 83. In a key June 1983 discussion in the Kremlin, Andropov told Averell Harriman—the longtime U.S. envoy to Moscow who had negotiated with Stalin during World War II—that although an awareness of the danger of inadvertent nuclear war should be "precisely the common denominator with which statesmen of both countries would exercise restraint and seek mutual understanding to strengthen confidence, to avoid the irreparable," the superpowers had been "moving toward the dangerous 'red line'" of nuclear war in the early 1980s.[11]

Reagan also understood the most important lesson of Able Archer 83: that war—including inadvertent war—between the United States and Soviet Union would have been "two spiders in a bottle locked in a suicidal fight until both were dead."[12]

"Do you think Soviet leaders really fear us, or is all the huffing and puffing just part of their propaganda?" President Reagan asked his ambassador to the Soviet Union, Arthur Hartman, in early 1984.[13] He had pinpointed a question central to the 1983 War Scare. That question is key to the real-time intelligence reporting, the retroactive intelligence estimates and analyses, and today's continuing debate between historians over the danger and lessons of the Able Archer 83 War Scare.

Robert Gates, who was the CIA's deputy director for intelligence during the War Scare, has concluded that the fear was real. "After going through the experience at the time, then through the postmortems, and now through the documents, I don't think the Soviets were crying wolf. They may not have believed a NATO attack was imminent in November 1983, but they did seem to believe that the situation was very dangerous."[13] The CIA's national intelligence officer for the Soviet Union, Fritz Ermarth, takes a different view. He argued in the CIA's first analysis of the War Scare that because the CIA had "many [Soviet] military cook books" it could "judge confidently the difference between when they might be brewing up for a real military confrontation or . . . just rattling their pots and pans." Their response to Able Archer 83, he concluded, was just pot-rattling.[14]

"Huffing and puffing"? "Crying wolf"? "Just rattling their pots and pans"? While real-time analysts, actors re-inspecting events, and the historical community may be at odds as to how dangerous the War Scare was, all agree that the dearth of available evidence has until now made firm conclusions harder to arrive at. Some historians have even characterized the study of the 1983 War Scare as "an echo chamber of inadequate research and misguided analysis" and "circle reference dependency," with an overreliance upon "the same scanty evidence."[15]

This book presents the evidence that has previously been hidden from the public debate. It is based upon more than a thousand pages of declassified documents on Able Archer 83 and Operation RYaN pried loose from secret files around the world in conjunction with the National Security Archive.[16] These include Freedom of Information Act releases by the Central Intelligence Agency, the National Security Agency, the Department of Defense, the Department of State and the Ronald Reagan and George H.W. Bush presidential libraries; research findings from American and British archives; and previously classified Soviet Politburo and KGB files, interviews with former Soviet generals, and records from other former communist states.[17] This book contains the best, most interesting, and latest exposed secrets about Able Archer 83 and Operation RYaN. Now, readers can assess for themselves the causes, risks, and lessons of the once-classified 1983 War Scare.

Part I: "Standing Tall," the "Mirror-Image," and Operation RYaN

THE NATIONAL SECURITY AGENCY'S TOP SECRET internal history *American Cryptology During the Cold War* states that the period from 1982 until 1984 "marked the most dangerous Soviet-American confrontation since the Cuban Missile Crisis."[1] In other words, the 1983 War Scare stood at the center of one of the two most risky moments of the Cold War—yet its danger has largely been hidden from the public.

The NSA's assertion is accurate. President Jimmy Carter, attempting to counter Soviet domestic human rights abuses, communist expansion in the Third World, the December 1979 invasion of Afghanistan, and the placement of medium-range SS-20 missiles in Europe, took steps that ended the U.S. policy of détente that had been crafted between Presidents Nixon and Ford and General Secretary Brezhnev. He increased U.S. military spending, imposed embargos on the USSR, continued America's diplomatic tilt toward China, pulled back from SALT II, the Strategic Arms Limitation Treaty that had been signed in 1979, and boycotted the 1980 Moscow Olympics. This superpower hostility and competition mirrored the beginning of the Cold War, leading one historian to note that "the early 1980s had a feeling of déjà vu."[2] Ronald Reagan's assumption of office in January 1981 hastened the deterioration of relations. The relative parity and cordiality achieved by the two powers during the twenty years since the Missiles of October—the Cuban Missile Crisis had disappeared by 1983, paving the way for the Missiles of November.

Upon entering office, Reagan's tactical goal was to reverse what he viewed as

American geopolitical decline during the Carter years and get America to "stand tall" politically, economically, and militarily against the Soviet Union.[3] The pursuit of this aim, evidenced in his early speeches and actions, startled the Politburo, which had predicted that the rhetoric he had deployed during the election campaign would dissipate once he took office and that U.S.-Soviet relations would return to Nixon's pragmatic approach. In fact, Reagan showed the Soviet Union immediately that "times had changed" by sharply curtailing both formal and backchannel contacts. This changed attitude further manifested itself in Reagan's abandonment of Senate ratification of SALT II, the sluggish pursuit of START (Strategic Arms Reduction Talks), and the refusal to compromise on INF (Intermediate Nuclear Forces) limitation and reduction treaties. Reagan's first secretary of state, Alexander Haig, later justified this decline in dialogue by saying, "at this early stage there was nothing substantive to talk about, nothing to negotiate, until the USSR began to demonstrate its willingness to behave like a responsible power. That was the basis of our early policy toward Moscow."[4]

But while Reagan's tactical goal was to achieve "peace through strength," remedy perceived American weakness, and attack the immoralities of Soviet Union, he had a larger ultimate strategic aim. This aim was to achieve reductions in worldwide nuclear armaments—possibly even their abolition!—which would foster peaceful coexistence between the United States and Soviet Union. Speaking to the Japanese Diet on the day Able Archer 83 ended, Reagan proclaimed, "I know I speak for people everywhere when I say, our dream is to see the day when nuclear weapons will be banished from the face of this Earth."[5]

Reagan did work toward this goal, and ultimately made remarkable strides in accomplishing it. But during his first three years, his policies and words toward the Soviets clearly undercut his ultimate objective.

As Soviet Ambassador to the United States Anatoly Dobrynin masterfully explained, the "Paradox of Ronald Reagan"[6] was that the president "saw nothing contradictory in publicly—and I think sincerely—attacking the Soviet Union as the evil empire and describing its leadership in rather uncomplimentary terms, while in the next moment writing personal letters in his own hand to the general secretary of the Soviet Communist Party very privately expressing his desire for a nonnuclear world, better Soviet-American relations, and a summit meeting with the world's chief communist and atheist." Reagan's "vision of nuclear apocalypse and his deeply rooted but almost hidden conviction that nuclear weapons should ultimately be abolished . . . would ultimately prove more powerful than his visceral anticommunism,"[7] though not until after the 1983 War Scare had shown him the brink.

Correspondence Between Statesmen

Reagan's quip that he was unable to make diplomatic progress because "the Soviet leaders kept dying on me"[8] has often been cited, along with his handwritten letters to General Secretaries Brezhnev and Andropov, as evidence that he was determined to work with the Soviet Union from his inauguration, but the Soviet side had proved either unwilling or unable to cooperate. But Ambassador Jack Matlock, perhaps Reagan's most trusted Soviet advisor, explains in his memoirs that during Reagan's first two years in office he eschewed efforts to improve relations with the Soviet Union through increased dialogue. According to Matlock, the president's policies toward the Soviet Union were "interrelated but distinct: telling the truth about the Soviet Union, restoring U.S. and allied strength, deterring aggression, and establishing reciprocity."[9] His administration pursued these goals at the cost of engagement with the Soviet Union.

At the first meeting between Soviet Ambassador Dobrynin and Secretary of State Haig, the former repeatedly asked how both governments could "begin to develop a dialogue." Haig replied that "there could be no business as usual" until the Soviet Union showed "restraint" regarding, among other things, "control of its client, Cuba."[10]

A week after Reagan was discharged from George Washington University Hospital following John Hinckley's March 30 assassination attempt, he wrote a reply to a letter he had received from Brezhnev before the shooting. In that letter, Brezhnev had indicated willingness for a summit meeting as well as "dialogue that is active at all levels."[11] Reagan's response included two letters. The first, personal and cordial, recalled a 1973 meeting between the two leaders at San Clemente at a summit between Nixon and Brezhnev that "had captured the imagination of all the world." Reagan told Brezhnev that he had lifted a grain embargo, allowing American farmers to sell their products to the Soviet Union. He explained that he hoped what some viewed as a move driven by domestic politics would "contribute to creating the circumstances which will lead to the meaningful and constructive dialogue which will assist us in fulfilling our joint obligation to find lasting peace."[12] But this constructive letter, which could have led to improved relations between the superpowers, was accompanied by another more official missive, also signed by the president, but likely drafted by Haig's State Department. This letter condemned the "USSR's unremitting and comprehensive military build up over the past fifteen years, a build up which . . . carries disturbing implications for a search for military superiority." It also accused the Soviet Union of violating the Helsinki Pact and pursuing "unilateral advantage in various parts of the globe."[13] Given all this, the second letter continued, "I do not believe [the conditions for a meeting] exist at present, and so my preference would be for postponing a meeting of such importance to a later date."[14] The statesmen's personal correspondence ended, likely owing to the contradictory tones of the two letters.[15]

This bizarre strategy of communication—reminiscent of the schizoid telegrams sent from Khrushchev to Kennedy at the height of the Cuban Missile Crisis—exemplifies a deep and continuing conflict in the actions of Reagan and his administration: Engage with the Soviets? Or attempt to defeat them? Throughout its first two years, the Reagan administration provided glimpses of both strategies, but the embrace of confrontation generally won out. Reagan sent one heartfelt letter pleading for dialogue, yet signed another spurning Brezhnev's advances toward improved relations.

After Brezhnev's death in November 1982, the new Soviet leader, Yuri Andropov, resumed substantive correspondence with Reagan. On June 22, 1983, he pledged to Reagan "an unbending commitment to the cause of peace, the elimination of the nuclear threat, and the development of relations based on mutual benefit and equality with all nations" and "welcome[d] practical steps of your government in this direction."[16]

Reagan again drafted a personal reply to Andropov, telling the general secretary, "Let me assure you the govt & the people of the United States are dedicated to the cause of peace & the elimination of the nuclear threat." He even made the extraordinary suggestion that "verifiable reductions in the number of nuclear weapons we both hold could . . . be a first step toward the elimination of all such weapons."[17]

But Reagan's offer to end the nuclear arms race was removed at the behest of his subordinates. According to Don Oberdorfer's account in *The Turn*, Reagan gave his handwritten draft to National Security Advisor William P. Clark, who shared it with foreign policy advisors on the White House staff. Their response to Reagan's proposal was not favorable. They "were horrified by the idea of eliminating the nuclear weapons," and Clark wrote a memo to Reagan recommending that the president remove this phrase. The president acquiesced and wrote a more tepid letter in his own hand on White House stationery.[18]

Though the president wrote that he and Andropov "shared an enormous responsibility for the preservation of stability in the world" and recommended the two leaders communicate through "private and candid" channels, because of intervention from those in his administration his letter to Andropov was again much less ambitions (and more confusing[19]) than what he had initially drafted.

American Defense: Catch Up or Build Up?

Notwithstanding Reagan's vague overtures in his letters to Soviet leaders, his early defense buildup and rhetoric toward the USSR were unquestionably hardline. From his inauguration, President Reagan extended the Carter administration's trend of increased military spending; Reagan implemented and oversaw the largest peacetime military buildup in American history. He proposed a $2.7 trillion defense budget for 1982–1989, with an 18.1 percent increase for military spending in 1983 alone.[20] Despite the president's justification for this spending—that "the Soviet Union does have a definite margin of superiority"—the CIA, in a September 1983 congressional hearing, testified that Soviet military expenditures, both absolute and relative to GDP, had been declining since 1976.[21]

Reagan's push for increased military spending—even beyond Carter's increases—was embraced and encouraged by his cabinet. Thirty-two of his advisors were members of the Committee on the Present Danger, a hawkish foreign policy interest group that staunchly opposed START II and other weapons reductions.[22] Disregarding evidence of American superiority, Reagan's secretary of defense, Caspar Weinberger, declared that his first priority was "to rearm America."[23]

Reagan's early National Security Decision Directives 32 and 75 exemplified the United States' aggressive military and geopolitical posture toward the Soviet Union. NSDD 32 stated that U.S. policy was to weaken the Soviet Union's alliances (especially in Poland) by fostering nationalism in the Soviet satellite states, to force the USSR to "bear the brunt of its economic shortcomings," and "to limit Soviet military capabilities by strengthening the U.S. military."[24] NSDD 75, signed January 17, 1983, reflected the administration's ambivalence toward U.S.-Soviet policy. On the one hand, it declared that U.S. policy toward the USSR would consist of "external resistance to Soviet imperialism [and] internal pressure on the USSR to weaken the sources of Soviet imperialism." On the other, it embraced "negotiations to eliminate, on the basis of strict reciprocity, outstanding disagreements."[25] Despite these contradictions, and its lukewarm embrace of engagement with the Soviets to further U.S. goals, the national security policy of the early Reagan administration hearkened to the more hard-line "rollback" strategy of the Eisenhower administration.

Reagan's decision to continue the deployment of Pershing II and long-range cruise missiles in Western Europe was a key pillar of his early policy toward the Soviet Union.[26] While the decision to deploy intermediate range missiles in Europe was presented as an attempt to preserve nuclear parity with the Soviet Union, the Strategic Defense Initiative (SDI), defined by NSDD 85 on March 25, 1983, as a space-based missile defense shield,[27] was viewed by the Soviets as an expansion of the arms race into space and an attempt to seek offensive nuclear superiority.

The motivation behind Reagan's decision to attempt to build SDI was likely as altruistic as he described it; he believed SDI offered the possibility to end the phenomenon of "both of us sitting here with these horrible missiles aimed at each other and the only thing preventing a holocaust is just so long as no one pulls the trigger."[28]

But the Soviets did not believe him. On March 27, Andropov personally and harshly responded to Reagan's Strategic Defense Initiative in an interview with *Pravda*. He accused the United States of attempting "to achieve military superiority over the Soviet Union," and warned that SDI could "open the floodgates of a runaway race of all types of strategic arms, both offensive and defensive."[29]

SDI caused the Soviets to question the viability of missile-reduction treaties with the United States and it—along with the pending introduction of intermediate range nuclear weapons in Europe—was cited as a key factor for their walkout from the INF and START talks on November 23, 1983.[30]

Pershing IIs, Launch on Warning, and Operation RYaN

While the Soviets feared that SDI reflected a clear, long-term plan to disrupt nuclear parity, it was the imminent deployment of Gryphon and Pershing II missiles that played the largest role in shaping the Soviet response during the 1983 War Scare. Even though the range of the Pershing IIs was classified, the United States publicly announced their range as 1,800 kilometers, long enough to reach eastern Russia and its forward-deployed forces from West Germany in less than ten minutes.[31] But Soviet specialists feared that the missiles were even more dangerous, estimating that they had a range of 2,500 kilometers, posing a direct threat to Soviet leadership in Moscow. Mikhail Gorbachev described the weapons as "a gun pressed to our temple."[32]

There was no question that the Gryphon cruise missiles—though slower—could reach Moscow; they could also fly low enough to avoid Soviet radar.[33] Anatoly Chernyaev, deputy director of the International Department of the Central Committee, described the Gryphons as "amazing . . . missiles that, like in a cartoon, could be guided through a canyon and hit a target 10 meters in diameter from 2,500 kilometers away."[34]

The correct belief among experts in the USSR was that the new missiles would render Moscow, including the Soviet nuclear command, vulnerable to a decapitating first strike.[35] On August 4, 1983, the Politburo resolved to actively try to block the deployment of intermediate range missiles. Andropov outlined three pillars of this opposition to his colleagues:

1. We must not lose time setting in motion all the levers which could impact the governments and parliaments of the NATO countries in an attempt to create the most possible opposition towards the deployment of American missiles in Europe.

2. It is essential to specifically and overarchingly coordinate all opposition; diplomatic action and propaganda must complement and reinforce each other.
3. Steps should not be formal, but specifically designed to produce the effect [of aborted deployment].[36]

Soviet opposition to NATO's missile deployments involved a careful propaganda campaign filtered through the Communist parties of the West. The Soviet Union also attempted to broadcast its anti-INF message by utilizing its robust foreign broadcasting information services. It also created and attempted to control international councils and organizations—most prominently the World Peace Council—that were sympathetic to its message. *Time* magazine quoted a State Department official who estimated that the KGB may have spent as much as $600 million attempting to control the peace movement. Despite this expenditure, Western intelligence experts, cited in the same article, concluded that the worldwide peace movement was in all likelihood organic and too robust to be Soviet-controlled.[37]

Some have argued that the fear of war within the Soviet Union during Able Archer 83 was "engineered" by Soviet leadership for "its campaign against NATO's 'Euromissiles,'" and was "called off" after the West German Bundestag's crucial November 23, 1983, vote for deployment.[38] But according to the bulk of the evidence now available, the Soviet fear of war during Able Archer 83 was real, not manufactured, and the deployment of Pershing II missiles was a contributing factor to, not an end result of, the War Scare.[39] After the Cold War's end, Soviet defense advisor Vitalii Kataev recounted: "We in the Central Committee's Defense Department considered the early 1980s to be a crisis period, a pre-wartime period. We organized night shifts so that there was always someone on duty in the Central Committee." The Pershing IIs "were extremely destabilizing . . . the only possible targets of these missiles was our leadership in Moscow because Pershings could not reach most of our missiles."[40]

Valentin Falin, a high-ranking official in the Soviet Foreign Ministry, explained the reason behind this anxiety in *Kommunist,* the Central Committee's journal. With the deployment of Pershing II missiles, he argued, "imperialism has decided to limit both the time and the space of the USSR and for all the world of socialism, to just five minutes for contemplation in a crisis situation."[41] Indeed, this new minutes-long window to launch a successful nuclear counterstrike put the very theory of Mutually Assured Destruction into question.

A great irony of the Cold War is that despite the central role the theories of deterrence and Mutually Assured Destruction played, as the Cold War progressed both superpowers perceived themselves as increasingly vulnerable to a decapitating nuclear strike. A preemptive nuclear strike could—both sides feared—cut communication between the central command of a superpower and its arsenals, making it impossible to launch a counterattack and thus incapacitating the vast nuclear stockpiles each side had built up to deter the other. To protect against a decapitating first strike, each side began to rely upon the doctrine of Launch on Warning (LOW); since only a few minutes would be available to counter a nuclear strike, early detection and preemption became the strategy nuclear planners chose to ensure that their vast arsenals of nuclear weapons would not be rendered moot in a war.[42]

At the Cold War's end, Viktor Surikov, who had more than thirty years' experience building, testing, and analyzing missiles and related systems for the Soviet Union, explained that a shift toward preemption had occurred. In one 1993 interview conducted for a study commissioned by the U.S. Department of Defense, Surikov challenged his U.S. interviewer, John Hines, contending that U.S. strategy and posture was to strike first in a crisis in order to minimize damage to the United States. Surikov stated he believed that U.S. nuclear policymakers were well aware that there were tremendous differences in levels of damage to the United States under conditions where the United States succeeded in preemptively striking Soviet missiles and control systems before they launched versus under conditions of a simultaneous exchange or U.S. retaliation. According to the account, Surikov said, "John, if you deny that, then either you're ignorant about your own posture or you're lying to me." Hines acknowledged to Surikov that the United States "certainly had done such analysis" of a preemptive first strike against the Soviet Union.[43]

Surikov admitted that the basic Soviet nuclear position and posture was also preemption. Soviet general Valentin Varennikov, who served on the General Staff, corroborates this dangerous shift in nuclear war planning. He recounts that in 1983, the Soviet military conducted its own exercise, Zapad [West] 83, which "prepared (for the first time since the Second World War) for a situation where our armed forces obtained reliable data of [an adversary's] decision made by highest military and political leadership to launch a surprise attack, using all possible firepower (artillery, aviation, etc.) against us. In response, we conducted offensive operations to disrupt the enemy attack and defeat its troops. That is, a preemptive strike."[44]

The prospective introduction of new, "decapitating"[45] Pershing II missiles further increased pressure on Soviet leaders to adopt a Launch on Warning (LOW) doctrine.

While the core of LOW was the detection of actual missile launches, one key consequence of the doctrine was the increased reliance Moscow placed upon human intelligence (as opposed to radar and satellite technology) to monitor planning and mobilization for a nuclear attack.

In 1979 the Institute for Intelligence Problems, coordinated by the KGB's First Chief Directorate, was tasked to work on "the development of new intelligence concepts" that could provide preliminary warning of Western preparations for a first strike. The result of this work was the creation of Operation RYaN, which was announced in May of 1981.[46] At a major KGB conference in Moscow, General Secretary Leonid Brezhnev and Yuri Andropov, then chairman of the KGB, justified the creation of Operation RYaN. The United States was, they claimed, "actively preparing for nuclear war" against the Soviet Union and its allies.[47] According to an East German Stasi report on the conference, the primary "Chekist work" discussed there was the "demand to allow for 'no surprise.'"[48]

The establishment of Operation RYaN is corroborated by KGB annual reports from 1981 and 1982. The 1981 annual report states that the KGB had "implemented measures to strengthen intelligence work in order to prevent a possible sudden outbreak of war by the enemy." To do this, the KGB "actively obtained information on military and strategic issues, and the aggressive military and political plans of imperialism [the United States] and its accomplices," and "enhanced the relevance and effectiveness of its active intelligence abilities."[49]

The 1982 annual report confirmed Soviet fears of Western encirclement, and noted the challenges of countering "U.S. and NATO aspirations to change the existing military-strategic balance," spurred by the pending November 1983 deployment of Pershing II and Gryphon missiles, which threatened to decapitate Soviet nuclear command and control. Therefore, "primary attention was paid to military and strategic issues related to the danger of the enemy's thermonuclear attack."[50]

East German documents on Operation RYaN, recently disclosed by the Cold War International History Project, reveal that within the KGB, three hundred positions were created so that RYaN operatives could report on and monitor incoming intelligence and implement the real-time "transmission and evaluation" of reported indicators showing the likelihood of a Western first strike. By July of 1984, KGB chairman Viktor Chebrikov expanded Operation RYaN by creating a new division within the First Department (Information) of the KGB's First Main Directorate (responsible for foreign intelligence and operations) to implement Operation RYaN throughout the KGB and the world. This coordinating division was composed of fifty KGB officers.[51] The documents also contain references to the primitive computer system that the Soviet Union was attempting to use to track and calculate the "correlation of world forces"—the relative international strength of the Soviet Union—including the risk of nuclear war. The KGB reported to the Stasi that it had "revised its planning for scientific-technological research and industrial procurement" of new "reliably working technology."[52] Oleg Gordievsky had reported to the British on "a large computer model in the Min[istry] of Defense to calculate and monitor the correlation of forces, including mili[tary], economy, [and] psychological factors, to assign numbers and relative weights."[53] On November 23, 1983, U.S. Defense and Intelligence officials circulated an article entitled "In Pursuit of the

Essence of War" that described a Soviet computer system that "cataloged and computerized" the world's "correlation of forces." The results, it claimed, were "highly objective, empirically provable and readily adaptable to modern data processing."[54] The East Germans, however, were much more skeptical of Soviet computing prowess: past "Soviet experiences show us that a danger exists of computer application concepts not getting implemented," wrote intelligence head Markus Wolf in a rather snide declassified memo. He did not believe the Soviets could build such a computer.[55]

Computer analysis was likely desired because the amount of information captured during Operation RYaN was massive. Newly released Stasi documents provide great detail about the precise indicators that human intelligence collectors were compiling and analyzing (including activity at defense installations, the location of prominent political officials, and even the disposition of "the most important government documents at the U.S. National Archives," including the U.S. Declaration of Independence and Constitution). In October 1983 Deputy KGB Chairman Vladimir Kryuchkov reported that the First Main Directorate's Institute for Intelligence Problems had compiled seven binders full of possible RYaN indicators.[56] By May of 1986, these binders had evolved into a catalogue of 292 indicators of "signs of tension."[57] The Stasi reported that 226 indicators (77 percent) were able to be "covered, though to varying degree." The indicators were organized into five main categories: Political, Military, Intelligence Services, Civil Defense Agencies, and the Economic sector. A read through the newly released full catalogue of RYaN indicators (as opposed to the truncated list published by Gordievsky) makes the program appear more rational and effective than has previously been portrayed.[58] In one telling example, RYaN watchers had sniffed out the U.S. Continuity of Government program, discovering and surveilling "two presidential planes . . . equipped with accelerated speed [and] electronic apparatuses which work under conditions of nuclear weapons use."[59] These planes were where the president and his emergency cabinet would exercise command during a nuclear war.

RYaN watchers were also instructed to monitor the "preparation and conduct of large-scale exercises," because they increased "the level of combat-readiness of U.S. strategic forces," and hence could indicate intentions for a "surprise nuclear missile attack."[60]

In February 1983 the KGB headquarters in Moscow sent its London residency a Top Secret telegram that contained instructions on how to report on indicators pointing toward a nuclear sneak attack. This document, "Permanent Operational Assignment to Uncover NATO Preparations for a Nuclear Missile Attack on the USSR," was published in full in 1991 by Soviet double agent Oleg Gordievsky and British intelligence historian Christopher Andrew in *Comrade Kryuchkov's Instructions: Top Secret Files on KGB Foreign Operations, 1975–1985*. It revealed in precise terms the instructions given to KGB agents during Operation RYaN. In theory, RYaN used Soviet political and military intelligence to put the USSR's nuclear arsenal on hair-trigger alert. Reagan's aggressive buildup had placed the Soviet Union in a "hyper-defensive" state, and Soviet agents were tasked with detecting, in order to preempt, a (nonexistent) nuclear attack.

War of Words

President Reagan's anti-Soviet public statements increased after the May 1981 launch of Operation RYaN, creating more fear in the Soviet Union. From his first press conference, Reagan established his opposition to détente and implied the impossibility of coexistence, declaring that "détente's been a one-way street that the Soviet Union has used to pursue its own aims . . . of world revolution and a one-world Socialist or Communist state, whichever word you want to use."[61] This statement directly clashed with Brezhnev's appeal two months earlier for cooperation, in which he had pledged that "any constructive steps by the United States administration in the sphere of Soviet-American relations and pressing world problems will be met with a positive response on our part."[62] When Reagan was elected, the Soviets were hopeful and willing to engage in dialogue; but the new American administration believed that compromise through dialogue favored only the Soviet Union, and rebuffed overtures for increased conversation.

In June 1982, Reagan renewed his call for the end of the Soviet Union. Addressing the British Parliament, he described

> a plan and a hope for the long term—the march of freedom and democracy which will leave Marxism-Leninism on the ash-heap of history as it has left other tyrannies which stifle the freedom and muzzle the self-expression of the people. . . . Let us now begin a major effort to secure . . . a crusade for freedom that will engage the faith and fortitude of the next generation.[63]

Six months later, in his State of the Union address, Reagan declared that to achieve peace, "the Soviet Union must show by deeds as well as words a sincere commitment to respect the rights and sovereignty of the family of nations."[64]

When Reagan assumed the presidency, the Soviets were ready and hopeful for mutual cooperation with the United States. In fact, Reagan likely privately hoped to work with the Soviets for the reduction of nuclear armaments and other endeavors; as he told reporters in December of 1981, "I've always recognized that ultimately there's got to be a settlement, a solution."[65] But his public actions—including increased military spending and confrontational rhetoric—precluded this from happening. As Soviet ambassador Anatoly Dobrynin wrote in his memoirs, it was "most difficult for us to fathom [his] vehement public attacks on the Soviet Union while he was secretly sending—orally or through his private letters—quite different signals seeking more normal relations."[66]

As Secretary of State Alexander Haig explained in a 1984 interview, these early Soviet-American hostilities were not

> a tit-for-tat response. The Soviets stayed very, very moderate, very, very responsible during the first three years of this administration. I was mind-boggled with their patience. They were genuinely trying. What they hadn't faced up to was what it would really take to convince us.[67]

In November 1982, Brezhnev publicly announced an end to the Soviet Union's attempt to achieve mutual cooperation with the United States. "We know well," Brezhnev said, "that peace with the imperialists is not for the asking. It can be safeguarded only by relying on the invincible might of the Soviet Armed Forces."[68] Reagan's rhetoric had convinced the Soviets that improvement of diplomatic relations was unrealistic and stoked their fear of war and the belief in the possible necessity of nuclear preemption.

The Reagan administration's rhetoric reached its most inflammatory and threatening point on March 8, 1983, when Reagan declared to the National Association of Evangelicals in Orlando, Florida, that the Soviet Union was "the focus of evil in the modern world." In this speech, to a conservative evangelical Christian group—a speech that had not been vetted by Secretary of State George Shultz, the State Department, or anyone outside the White House—Reagan instructed his followers "to resist the attempts of those who would have you withhold your support for our efforts"—that is, those advocating a policy of rapprochement or a nuclear freeze. Reagan ended his speech by asserting that the struggle against communism was "a spiritual one; at root, it is a test of moral will and faith," explaining that communism was not born in nineteenth-century Germany, but "in the Garden of Eden with the words of temptation, 'Ye shall be as gods.'"[69] While this was a speech primarily to his conservative base and not a declaration of policy, Reagan nonetheless evoked and embraced the image of a religious war to defeat communism. The president's rhetoric and military expansion may have bolstered his domestic support, but they also exacerbated fears of war between the superpowers: 47 percent of Americans polled by Gallup on December 22, 1983, felt that the Reagan administration's defense policies had brought the United States "closer to war."[70]

Perplexingly, these condemnations of the Soviet Union were made while Reagan himself had been pondering beginning a dialogue attempting to thaw relations with the very country he had denounced as the epicenter of evil in the modern world. Secretary of State Shultz attributes the beginning of the end of the Cold War at least partially to a freak February 12, 1983, snowstorm that covered Washington, D.C., with as much as twenty inches of snow and shut down the government.[71] That snow forced the president and first lady to cancel their planned trip to Camp David; instead, they invited the secretary of state and his wife to the White House for dinner. The president quizzed Shultz about the secretary's recent trip to China, asked about his meetings with Chinese leader Deng Xiaoping, and—encouraged by Nancy—asked how he could arrange his own trips to China and the Soviet Union. Coyly, Shultz responded that it could be "a great idea if it comes about in the right way."[72] In the meantime, he suggested, Reagan should meet with Ambassador Dobrynin.

Three days later, the ambassador arrived at the White House for his first meeting with the president. During the meeting, which spanned two hours—very long for the president—Reagan and Dobrynin spoke about arms control, the plight of seven Pentecostal Christians from Siberia who had been barred from leaving the USSR, other human rights issues, and the general state of relations between the superpowers. The president also asked Dobrynin the key, recurring question of the Era of Renewed Confrontation: did "the Soviet Union indeed believe the United States posed a threat to the Soviet Union—could the United States attack the Soviet Union and start a nuclear war?"[73]

President Reagan continued to privately maintain his aspirations for improved relations with the Soviet Union after his speeches to the British Parliament and the National Association of Evangelicals. On April 6, he wrote in his diary of his anger at members of the National Security Council who he believed were "undercutting [Shultz] on plans he & I discussed for quiet diplomacy approach to the Soviets. . . . Some of the NSC staff are too hard line and don't think any approach should be made to the Soviets. I think I'm hard line and will never appease. But I do want to try and let them see there is a better world if they show by deed that they want to get along with the free world."[74]

But his rhetoric was also to blame for the "undercutting." As the National Security Agency's internal history correctly noted, "the rhetoric on both sides, especially during the first Reagan administration, drove the hysteria" of the War Scare.[75]

"A Mirror-Image of Reagan's Own Policy"

Reagan's rhetoric, combined with his downgrading of diplomatic efforts and his vast military buildup, worked almost diametrically against what he hoped to achieve: cooperation with the Soviet Union to abolish, or short of that, to reduce nuclear weapons.

The core of this discrepancy was Reagan's belief that domination of, rather than negotiation with, the Soviet Union was the only way to achieve arms reduction. He wrote in his memoirs: "at the foundation of my foreign policy, I decided we had to send as powerful message as we could to the Russians. . . . Our policy was to be one based on strength and realism. I wanted peace through strength, not peace through a piece of paper."[76]

What Reagan viewed as "peace through strength," the Soviets regarded as warmongering, and they responded in kind. In his memoirs, Ambassador Dobrynin reports that the effect of Reagan's early foreign policy "was exactly the opposite from the one intended by Washington."

> It strengthened those in the Politburo, the Central Committee, and the security apparatus who had been pressing for a mirror-image of Reagan's own policy. Ronald Reagan managed to create a solid front of hostility among our leaders. Nobody trusted him. Any of his proposals almost automatically were considered with suspicion. This unique situation in our relations threatened dangerous consequences.[77]

On January 4, 1983, Andropov, now general secretary of the CPSU, gave a speech in Prague to the Political Consultative Committee, the controlling organ of the Warsaw Pact countries. Andropov condemned the deployment of Gryphon and Pershing II missiles in Europe. He said that the Warsaw Pact's only option was to continue striving to maintain parity but warned:

> The new round of the arms race, which is being imposed by the United States, has principal qualitative features that distinguish it from the previous ones. If in the past the Americans, when speaking about their nuclear weapons, preferred to emphasize the fact that those were, first of all, means of "deterrence," now, by creating the improved missile systems, they are not trying to conceal the fact that those are realistically designed for a future war. This is where the doctrines of a "rational" or "limited" nuclear war come from, this is the source of the arguments about the possibility to survive and to win in a protracted nuclear conflict.[78]

Andropov, believing Reagan may have calculated that a nuclear war could be won, bolstered the Warsaw Pact security establishment. Following the general secretary's remarks, KGB agents abroad received an Operation RYaN telegram entitled "Permanent Operations Assignment to Uncover NATO Preparations for a Nuclear Missile Attack on the USSR."[79] It was addressed to each station chief by name, labeled "strictly personal," and was designated to be kept in a special file. The telegram stated:

> The objective of the assignment is to see that the residency works systematically to uncover any plans in preparation by the main adversary [USA] for RY[a]N and to organize a continual watch to be kept for indications of a decision being taken to use nuclear weapons against the USSR or immediate preparations being made for a nuclear missile attack.

Attached to the telegram was a list of seven "immediate" and thirteen "prospective" tasks for the agents to complete and report back. These included: the collection of data on potential places of evacuation and shelter, an appraisal of the level of blood held in blood banks, observation of places where nuclear decisions were made and nuclear weapons were stored, observation of key nuclear decision makers, observation of lines of communication, reconnaissance of the heads of churches and banks, and surveillance of security services and military installations.[80]

Many of the assigned observations—including the blood bank supply levels and the movement of high-level church officials—would have been very poor indicators of a nuclear attack. Others, including communications lines, nuclear decision makers, and—most significantly—missile depots, would have accurately shown whether a nuclear attack was imminent.[81]

Also attached to the telegram was a thorough and accurate description of the likely methods by which the United States or NATO would launch nuclear war. This attachment emphasized that once the West had decided to launch a nuclear attack, a substantial preparatory period would be required. These preparations included nuclear consultations through secret channels, transportation of nuclear weapons, and preparation of civil defense institutions.

"Whither the Soviet Leadership"

The Soviet leadership was in a fluid state during the 1983 War Scare. At the shifting center of power was Yuri Andropov. Oleg Kalugin, head of KGB operations in the United States until 1980, has confirmed that Reagan's early policies and rhetoric "scared the wits out of our leadership, and Andropov notified KGB stations around the world to be on the lookout for signs of an imminent American attack. A brand new program [Operation RYaN] was created to gather information on a potential American first nuclear strike."[82] Ambassador Dobrynin acknowledged that the KGB resident in Washington had informed him of Operation RYaN. He also wrote that none of the general secretaries for whom he served—Khrushchev, Brezhnev, Chernenko, and Gorbachev—believed "an attack could take place unexpectedly at any moment." Andropov proved the "probable exception" to this. "While still head of the KGB, Andropov did believe that the Reagan administration was actively preparing for war," he wrote, recalling a "very private" conversation with Andropov in which he cautioned that "Reagan is unpredictable. You should expect anything from him."[83]

Secretary Shultz had met Andropov himself briefly during November 1982 at Brezhnev's funeral. Shultz reported to the CIA's deputy director that the new general secretary "appeared adroit—with the facility to react at a moment's notice" and that he "could escalate a situation very quickly and 'take us on.'" Andropov, Shultz reported, "still had a great deal of energy about him" even after shaking some two thousand hands.[84]

The CIA also had a laudatory opinion about the new Soviet leader. A biographical sketch of Andropov, in all likelihood read by Shultz before his trip, described him as "complicated and puzzling" yet "probably better informed on foreign affairs, and on at least some domestic matters, than any other Soviet party chief since Lenin."[85]

In early 1983, Andropov's kidneys began to fail. A special room was set up in a Moscow hospital to provide him treatment, including dialysis. By November Andropov had become critically ill and dropped out of public view; his grasp on power appeared to be slipping but he was still in control.[86] CIA analysts at the time speculated—and it has since been confirmed—that during this period the Politburo was steered by the triumvirate of Foreign Minister Andrei Gromyko, Andropov, and Defense Minister Dmitry Ustinov. Of the three, Gromyko was the most "moderate." Due to his familiarity to the West, he was doubtful of a Western first strike. According to Reagan's national security advisor Robert McFarlane, Gromyko was the "ultimate guarantor" against miscalculation. "He had been in Washington many, many years, and understood our processes and the consultative process between Congress and the Presidency about any significant escalation of the use of force."[87]

Accounts of the Soviet political elite generally place Defense Minister Ustinov to the right of Andropov. Oleg Gordievsky speculates that Ustinov advocated the creation of Operation RYaN to Andropov in 1981; in December 1982, Ustinov condemned military doctrines "which stem from the strategy of 'direct confrontation' proclaimed by Washington and are directed at achieving military superiority over the Soviet Union and establishing U.S. world supremacy."[88]

But in 1983 power in the Soviet Union was not wholly centered in the Politburo; the military's grasp on power was expanding too. A December 12 National

Intelligence Council document entitled "Whither the Soviet Leadership" noted that "the military's influence appears to have expanded over the past several years and especially since the advent of Andropov."[89] Ustinov, the most hawkish of the triumvirate, appears to have been more reasonable than the military leadership. Take, for example, the issue of nuclear war fighting: in January of 1982, Marshal Nikolai Ogarkov, chief of staff of the Soviet military, published a pamphlet entitled "Always in Readiness for Defense of the Fatherland." In it he glorified "the cult of the offensive," the importance of surprise in military operations, and alluded to the possibility of a Soviet preemptive strike. He stated that nuclear weapons would give Soviet commanders "the increased ability to achieve war aims."[90]

Ustinov released a pamphlet in May 1982, entitled "Serving the Country," which strongly contradicted Ogarkov's assertions about the viability of nuclear war, writing that "to count on victory in the arms race and in the nuclear war is madness." Such a war, he wrote, would cause "irreplaceable losses," destroying "entire peoples and their civilizations."[91]

While it is clear that Andropov and Ustinov were fearful of a possible Western first strike, it is also clear that leaders of the military were more likely to suspect, attempt to preempt, and believe they could win a nuclear war with the West. Ustinov, although usually depicted as the most hard-line member of the Politburo, was clearly more moderate than the generals and he used his powerful position to solidify control over the military during the "succession crisis."

Intelligence Collection During Operation RYaN

Although Operation RYaN originated at the highest levels of the Soviet government, intelligence collection was carried out by Soviet domestic intelligence (the KGB) and military intelligence (the GRU), as well as by the intelligence agencies of its Warsaw Pact allies. The German Democratic Republic (GDR) provided an immense amount of intelligence to the Soviet Union, with its highly capable Hauptverwaltung Aufklärung (HVA), Main Reconnaissance Administration, playing a large role in Operation RYaN. Markus Wolf, known as "the man without a face," who served for decades as East Germany's spymaster, later wrote that "our Soviet partners had become obsessed with the danger of a nuclear missile attack." Consequently, the HVA's most important priority became the surveillance of Pershing II and cruise missile sites.[92]

Karl Koecher, a Czechoslovakian spy working illegally in the United States in the early 1980s, confirms the existence of Operation RYaN and justifies it. In *Novosti razvedki i kontrrazvedki*, he asserts that Operation RYaN acted as an effective counter to the increased risk of nuclear war under Reagan.[93]

Documents from other Warsaw Pact countries corroborate Soviet descriptions of Operation RYaN. A Top Secret 1984 Bulgarian intelligence document provided instructions to its agents to monitor underground networks, diplomatic representatives from NATO, combat readiness in neighboring countries, and radio-electronic intelligence.[94] Sources from Czechoslovakian intelligence also confirm the existence of Operation RYaN and state that compiling an "index of sudden aggression" was the primary mission of Warsaw Pact intelligence agencies.[95]

Gordievsky, Kalugin, and Wolf—it is important to note—were extremely skeptical of the idea of a NATO first strike. Wolf recalls that "like most intelligent people, I found these war games a burdensome waste of time."[96] But despite his skepticism, Wolf forwarded his agency's Operation RYaN surveillance to Soviet allies who were more persuaded by these "indicators" of possible nuclear war. Dobrynin and Gordievsky believed that the drive for Operation RYaN came from the leadership of Andropov, Ustinov, and KGB chief of foreign operations Vladimir Kryuchkov, whom they described as the last guards of the Stalinist mentality.

Although most agents did not believe an attack was imminent, they were ordered to report their raw observations of events, not their assessment of what the observations meant. This critical flaw in the Soviet intelligence system—for which Gordievsky coined the term the "intelligence cycle"—played a key role in exacerbating the Soviet leadership's fear of a U.S. nuclear strike. One American official may have correctly believed Soviet intelligence agents abroad were "just going through the motions"—but Soviet intelligence analysts in Moscow used this reporting to relay an incorrect scenario of a possible nuclear first strike.[97]

"Is All the Huffing and Puffing Just Part of Their Propaganda?"

At a June 2, 1983, meeting with Andropov, Averell Harriman, a veteran foreign policy expert and Democratic Party elder who had been the U.S. ambassador to the USSR during World War II, glimpsed the Soviet leadership's fear of an American attack.[98] During the conversations, which the Soviets viewed as "the first real meeting between the United States and the Soviet Union since the start of the [Reagan] administration," Andropov opened by saying that "there are indeed grounds for alarm." He bemoaned the harsh anti-Soviet tone of the president[99] and warned that "the previous experience of relations between the Soviet Union and the United States cautions beyond all doubt that such a policy can merely lead to aggravation, complexity and danger." Andropov alluded to nuclear war four times during his short statement; most ominously, he morosely warned,

> It would seem that awareness of this danger should be precisely the common denominator with which statesmen of both countries would exercise restraint and seek mutual understanding to strengthen confidence, to avoid the irreparable. However, I must say that I do not see it on the part of the current administration and they may be moving toward the dangerous "red line."[100]

Harriman concluded that "the principal point which the General Secretary appeared to be trying to get across . . . was a genuine concern over the state of U.S.-Soviet relations and his desire to see them at least 'normalized,' if not improved. He seemed to have a real worry that we could come into conflict through miscalculation."[101]

While Harriman believed Andropov's fear to be genuine, others thought he was slyly using "accidental nuclear blackmail" to improve the Soviet strategic position vis-à-vis the United States. The acting director of central intelligence, John McMahon, asserted in a February 3, 1984, letter to National Security Advisor Robert McFarlane that "clearly, Andropov has a stake in the 'appearance' of bilateral tension as long as it appears that the United States is the offending party. This would not be the first time that Soviet leaders have used international tensions to mobilize their population."[102]

The two views were neatly summarized in a secret November 1983 intelligence memorandum entitled "The View from Moscow." After presenting a bleak view of the future of the Soviet Union, the memo's author, Herbert Meyer, vice chairman of the National Intelligence Council, predicted that its leadership would either "make necessary sacrifices to stay in the game, get their licks in whenever and wherever they can, and count on new successes to come" or, less likely, "might consider themselves backed into a corner and lash out dangerously."[103]

This intelligence battle—and the entire War Scare debate—was accurately summed up by the question Reagan posed to his ambassador to the Soviet Union, Arthur Hartman: "Do you think the Soviet leaders really fear us, or is all the huffing and puffing just part of their propaganda?"[104] In 1983, U.S. intelligence errantly believed the Soviet Union was just "huffing and puffing."

Any lingering hopes Andropov had for normalized relations with the United States were lost on September 1, 1983, when the Soviet Union shot down a Korean civilian airliner, KAL 007, after it had flown into Soviet airspace.[105] To Reagan, the attack represented everything wrong with the Soviet Union; he decried the Soviet action as "barbaric" and a "crime against humanity."[106] KAL 007 illustrated the

Soviet Union's increased fear of U.S. aggression, low confidence in its air detection systems, and hair-trigger mindset. In his memoirs, Reagan considered the danger posed by this mindset: "If, as some people speculated, the Soviet pilots simply mistook the airliner for a military plane, what kind of imagination did it take to think of a Soviet military man with his finger close to a nuclear push button making an even more tragic mistake?"

Part II: "Thoroughly White Hot," Able Archer 83, and the Crux of the War Scare

THE UNITED STATES AND ITS allies had no plans to launch a preemptive nuclear attack in November 1983. However, in the nuclear era, fear of a nonexistent attack still presents a genuine danger. The Soviet intelligence assessment of NATO actions was not mistaken; it correctly assessed that from November 7 through 11, 1983,[1] the United States and NATO were conducting exercises related to nuclear weapons that spanned the continent of Europe, involved more than forty thousand American, Dutch, German, British, and Canadian soldiers, and "emphasized the transition from conventional to chemical and nuclear operations."[2] But Soviet intelligence was direly wrong about what these actions meant. President Reagan, the West, and NATO were not planning to launch a bolt from the blue at the Soviet Union in 1983.

Able Archer 83 was a NATO command post exercise sponsored by the NATO Supreme Allied Commander in Europe (SACEUR) conducted annually[3] as the final phase of a much larger, months-long series of NATO maneuvers known as Autumn Forge 83. Autumn Forge 83 consisted of more than a dozen exercises, each with its own unique name, conducted by some forty thousand troops from NATO countries.[4] The largest of these exercises was known as Reforger 83, which occurred during the final phases of Autumn Forge; it included a momentous "show of resolve" in the face of a hypothetical Soviet invasion, airlifting 19,000 troops and 1,500 tons of cargo from the United States to Europe to simulate a response to a conventional war. Able Archer simulated the shift from this conventional war to a chemical and nuclear war. The objectives of Able Archer 83 were to "conduct military operations in Europe with necessary command, control, and communications (C3) Systems,"[5] and to "exercise a scenario of decision-making that involved conventional attack in Europe that escalated to possible use of nuclear weapons."[6] The exercise ended after Blue (NATO) launched a massive nuclear attack against Orange (the Soviet Union and its Warsaw Pact allies).[7]

Contrary to descriptions of Able Archer 83 as an exercise so routine that it could not have alarmed the Soviet military and political leadership, the declassified evidence reveals multiple non-routine elements—including radio silences, the loading of warheads, reports of "nuclear strikes" on open radio frequencies, and a countdown through all DEFCON phases to "general alert"—that were very similar to actual preparations for a nuclear war.[8] These variations, seen through the fog of nuclear exercises, did in fact match official Soviet intelligence-defined indicators for "possible operations by the USA and its allies on British territory in preparation for RYaN"—the KGB term for a feared Western nuclear missile attack (*Raketno-Yadernoe Napadenie*).[9]

PSYOPs, False Alarms, and "Canopy Wing"

Since the early years of the Reagan administration, the United States military had conducted a number of secret psychological military operations (PSYOPs) that activated Soviet radar and even penetrated Soviet territory. According to the National Security Agency's declassified history, "these actions were calculated to induce paranoia, and they did."[10] This "psychological military warfare" by the U.S. Air Force and Navy had the effect of distorting Soviet perceptions of actual U.S. geopolitical intentions. The PSYOPs confirmed to Soviet intelligence, military, and political leadership that the Soviet Union was vulnerable to a U.S. first strike—and convinced them that there was an increased possibility that the West could actually be planning one.

The conductors of U.S. military policy explained these operations as a means "to keep [the Soviets] guessing what might come next." They justified the PSYOPs as elements "designed to roll back and weaken Soviet power."[11] Like many other elements of the War Scare, this "silent campaign" of military aggression was secret—even within the U.S. government. According to Undersecretary of Defense Fred Iklé, "it was very sensitive . . . nothing was written down about it so that there would be no paper trail."[12]

U.S. warships penetrated the far northern and eastern regions of the Soviet Union, areas where they had never before operated. In August and September of 1981, a U.S., British, Canadian, and Norwegian naval armada sailed through the strategically important Greenland–Iceland–United Kingdom (GUIK) gap in the

North Atlantic undetected by the Soviets. During that period, U.S. naval ships began operating in "forward areas" such as the Baltic, Black, and Barents Seas. In April and May of 1983, forty ships, including three aircraft carrier battle groups, sailed within 450 miles of Petropavlovsk, on the Kamchatka peninsula, in the Soviet Union's far east. Navy aircraft even carried out a simulated bombing run over a Soviet military site on the Pacific island of Zeleny.[13]

The Navy's newfound stealth was as important as its projection of force. U.S. ships maintained radio silence, utilized emission controls, jammed radar, and transmitted false signals. The armada, according to a CIA history, was even able to avoid detection by a Soviet satellite launched specifically to detect it.[14]

Even more startling to the Soviets, it was during this period that the U.S. Navy reversed the advantage that the Soviets had gained from the John Walker spy ring. Walker and his ring had provided one of two elements that the Soviets needed to crack the KW-7 cipher machine, the primary cipher machine used by the U.S. military to send encrypted communications. Beginning in 1968, Walker's ring provided a steady supply of stolen physical KW-7 crypto keys to the Soviets. The other element needed to crack this secret communication channel was access to an actual working KW-7 cipher machine. The North Koreans captured one onboard the USS *Pueblo* in 1968 and provided the Soviets with access to it, allowing Soviet intelligence to intercept some U.S. military communications almost immediately after they were sent. According to the NSA, it was "almost certainly the most lucrative espionage operation the Soviets ever had."[15] But in the years preceding the War Scare, currently available evidence suggests that it had come to an end.[16] The U.S. Navy—likely fearful that it had been infiltrated—began using new technology to undermine the Soviets' ability to spy on the communications and movements of its ships and submarines. At the same time that the U.S. Navy was increasing its aggressiveness the Soviets were losing the capacity to keep abreast of its maneuvers.

U.S. planes also probed Soviet air defense near the USSR's borders. These PSYOPs "exposed gaping holes in Soviet ocean surveillance and early warning systems." "Sometimes," according to General Jack Chain of the U.S. Strategic Air Command, "we would send bombers over the North Pole and their radars would click on. . . . Other times fighter-bombers would probe their Asian or European periphery."[17] According to a Soviet démarche condemning the intrusion, Navy aircraft flew twenty miles into Soviet-claimed territory on the Kuril Islands and remained there for up to twenty minutes.[18]

These aggressions and vulnerabilities alarmed Soviet leadership to an extreme never seen during the Cold War. A former U.S. official with knowledge of the PSYOPs told the journalist Peter Schweizer, "It really got to them. . . . They didn't know what it all meant. A squadron would fly straight at Soviet airspace, and other radars would light up and units would go on alert. Then at the last minute the squadron would peel off and return home."[19]

Following the April 1983 Navy bombing runs, the NSA history reports, "Soviet concern for border security had escalated into a paranoid intensity." Soviet reactions to U.S. reconnaissance flights reached their apogee. Andropov himself responded to the PSYOPs by issuing a "shoot-to-kill" order for border intrusions that led directly to the deaths of all those aboard the civilian Korean airliner KAL 007 when it was shot down in the Sea of Japan. The provocative American PSYOPs contributed to this atmosphere of panic, and they would also greatly contribute to the nuclear danger of Able Archer 83.

Soviet early warning systems not only failed to detect incursions, they also produced false alarms. At 12:15 a.m. on September 27, 1983, Serpukhov-15, the Soviets' early warning station monitoring for a potential nuclear attack from the West, reported the detection of an incoming Minuteman intercontinental missile from the United States. Two minutes later, four more missile launches were reported. The Soviet reports came from one of seven orbiting Soviet Oko [Eye] satellites that had been put into service in 1982—over a dozen Oko satellites had already failed.[20]

After a few terrifying minutes, the on-duty officer Colonel Stanislav Petrov reported, "this is a false alarm." Petrov came to this decision because he calculated that there was not yet enough corroborating radar or telescopic data, and because his "gut instinct" told him that the United States would not launch a sudden nuclear attack against the Soviet Union. He knew Serpukhov-15's warnings would be sent automatically up the Soviet military chain, perhaps to the General Staff, which, within minutes, would have to decide in conjunction with the minister of defense and general secretary whether the alert was real and the Soviet Union should launch its own missiles before they were destroyed.[21] Petrov did not want to take this chance. He insisted that this was a false alarm. The message was relayed to his superiors.[22] It was later determined that what the Soviet satellite had detected that had caused such alarm was rays of sunlight reflecting off of high-altitude clouds.[23]

"Gut instinct" would later play a role during Able Archer 83, this time on the American side.

It is possible that the secret American program codenamed "Canopy Wing" may have made the Soviets even more concerned about their nuclear vulnerability. According to a review by former CIA historian Benjamin Fischer, Canopy Wing was a secret American program that could possibly exploit and terminate the Soviets' high frequency command and control frequencies and leave them even more vulnerable to a nuclear "decapitation" or "surgical strike" that would prevent them from retaliating against the West. The discovery of this program by the Stasi—likely revealed by James W. Hall III, a U.S. signals intelligence analyst stationed in

Berlin—"sent ice-cold shivers down our spines," according to East German analyst Klaus Eichner. "We had never seen this type of official material regarding active preparations for war, for the consideration of aggression against the Warsaw Pact."[24]

There is evidence from the Soviet archives that General Secretary Andropov thought much about the risk of accidental nuclear war—though he only spoke about the risk of an American finger beginning Armageddon. During a meeting on January 11, 1983, with Hans-Jochen Vogel, the former mayor of West Berlin and a leader of the Social Democratic Party of the Federal Republic of Germany, Andropov emphatically warned, "I don't want to speak such banal truths, but the fact of the matter is that we have an accumulation of dangerous weapons. . . . When it comes to the accumulation of nuclear weapons, it is even more dangerous. After all, at the button that activates the nuclear weapon could be a drunken American sergeant or a drug addict. There were also occasions when the Americans fired rockets at flocks of geese. And if these rockets fell in our territory, it could lead to war. It could further slide towards the brink of war. It would be better to move away from this reality. After all, it is about the life of nations."[25]

Able Archer 83 Declassified

On November 7, 1983, Exercise Able Archer 83 began. Recently declassified documents reveal details of the nuclear release exercise that many—including Gordievsky, the British Ministry of Defence, NSA and CIA histories, CIA National Intelligence Estimates, and, finally, a retroactive all-source review by the President's Foreign Intelligence Advisory Board—have described as the peak of the 1983 War Scare.

One of the declassified reports—an Air Force after-action report—makes clear that Able Archer was not an isolated exercise. It was the finale of a simulated land war in Europe, including as many as 40,000 troops (19,000 of them American), the "culmination" of both Autumn Forge 83 (which began on August 9, 1983, and ended November 11[26]) and Reforger 83 (which began on September 19 and ended on September 30[27]). While the majority of NATO troops and units did not participate in the Able Archer 83 simulated nuclear release that ended the war games, the majority of deployed troops did participate in the Autumn Forge 83 war games, which simulated a land war against the Warsaw Pact in Europe leading up to nuclear war.[28]

The after-action report reveals just how involved the simulation was. War gamers took special steps at NATO headquarters in Brussels to simulate a nuclear release during Able Archer 83. The scripted pathway to nuclear war (see pages 1–2) mirrored real world events. It was chaotic, fast-paced, and covered all of Europe.[29] The Air Force attempted to overcome the East's conventional advance by utilizing actual plans for war in Europe[30] and, when these didn't work, tried unconventional tactics such as "unconventional warfare personnel"—saboteurs.[31]

Attempts to Signal

The Air Force's account also clears up disputes about the exercise that have arisen from previous published accounts. First, it recounts "a SACEUR decision" before the beginning of the exercise "to reduce the level of nuclear exchange between Blue and Orange"—that is, between NATO and the Warsaw Pact. The summary written by Supreme Headquarters Allied Powers in Europe (SHAPE) states that "because the exercise scenario began at a low crisis level, there was actually less nuclear play than in previous years." It's possible that planners may have attempted to scale back the exercise given the tensions between the superpowers.

Despite the drawdown indicated by the U.S. Air Force account, the UK's Ministry of Defence reported afterwards "an unprecedented Soviet reaction to Able Archer 83."[32] If NATO was attempting to "reduce the level of nuclear exchange" to signal to the Soviets that Able Archer 83 was an exercise and not an actual (or masked) attack, the Soviets did not get the signal.

Many accounts of Able Archer 83, including the NSA's and CIA's, erroneously report that upon the advice of National Security Advisor Robert McFarlane, high-level U.S., West German, and British officials who were scheduled to participate in the exercise dropped out.[33] This, according to NATO documents, was not the case. The simulated nuclear attack was conducted only by "small response cells" from the United States Joint Chiefs of Staff, the Ministry of Defence in the United Kingdom, and the Exercise Directing Staff within NATO.[34] According to Gregory Pedlow, chief SHAPE historian, "There was . . . no involvement of national leaders in the exercise, and no such involvement was ever planned, despite some recent allegations to this effect."[35]

While no national U.S. leader participated in Able Archer 83, the chairman of the U.S. Joint Chiefs of Staff, General William Vessey Jr., was aware of the activities of the JCS response cell. According to the JCS after-action report, "the Nuclear Contingency Branch, Strategic Operations Division, J-3, provided a 24 hour-a-day Joint Staff Nuclear Response Cell to process requests for selective nuclear release. Joint Operations Division, J-3, provided an officer, when required, to action requests for chemical release."[36] According to a letter from Vessey to the SACEUR, General Bernard Rodgers, "From our perspective, the exercise proceeded smoothly and joint staff participation added realism while providing valuable training in nuclear release procedures for our participants."[37]

The Soviet View

The Soviets had multiple reasons for their "unprecedented" response to Able Archer 83. In addition to Reagan's rhetoric, the PSYOPs, and the recent missile-detection malfunctions, a series of world events likely led Soviet agents abroad to report further "indicators" of a Western nuclear attack. U.S. military bases had heightened their security following the October 11 bombing of the Marine barracks in Beirut in which 220 service members were killed. The October 25 U.S. invasion of the former British colony of Grenada, ostensibly to prevent harm to U.S. medical students, triggered an influx of ciphered communications between the United States and Britain, which objected to the invasion.[38]

Two other reasons, both arising from the fog of nuclear exercises, additionally alarmed the Soviets during Able Archer 83. The first was Soviet military doctrine that held that a nuclear attack could be effectively obscured by war games or military exercises. Though Secretary of Defense Caspar Weinberger considered Able Archer 83 a "standard exercise," he did empathize with the concerns about American *maskirovka*, or deception, that were felt by the Soviet military.[39] "I do remember—and I do know, because I felt the same way on our side—that it is sometimes quite difficult to tell the difference between an exercise and the beginning—the raising of indicators that we watch all the time every day, every hour."[40] He cited his anxiety watching a previous North Korean exercise. "They were moving a hell of a lot of stuff in position and everybody knew it was just a maneuver and it was an annual exercise, but I got quite alarmed, because I kept saying 'What if it isn't? We've lost about five days of time.' So the difference between a realistic exercise or maneuver and what could be preparations for an attack, that line is sometimes quite blurred."[41]

The second, and more dangerous, reason for the Soviet reaction was reporting from Operation RYaN. On November 5, two days before Able Archer 83 began, KGB headquarters in Moscow sent the London residency a telegram: "In response to your request we are sending you the information which the Centre has regarding possible Operations by the USA and its allies on British territory in preparations for RYaN [a nuclear strike]."[42]

The telegram continued, "Surprise is the key element in the main adversary's [the United States'] plans and preparations for war in today's conditions. As a result it can be assumed that the period of time from the moment when the preliminary decision for RYaN [a nuclear strike] is taken, up to the order to deliver the strike will be of very short duration, possibly 7–10 days." The center instructed agents to monitor "possible contacts and consultations between the United States government and British leadership" (including at thirteen specific UK Ministry of Defence buildings), and warned them to watch for "announcements of military alert in units and at bases" and the "appearance of new channels of communications." The beginning of Able Archer 83 included at least some of these indicators. Presumably an alert intelligence officer would have concluded, as did Gordievsky, that despite these indicators Able Archer 83 was in all likelihood a nuclear drill. An intelligence officer caught in what Gordievsky termed "the vicious circle of intelligence," however, would have reported what his superiors ordered him to report, not what he himself actually believed.[43]

On November 7, the day Able Archer 83 began, an East German major general, Willi Damm, who was responsible for liaising with the KGB, received a summary of earlier discussions between Stasi head of foreign intelligence Markus Wolf and deputy KGB chairman Vladimir Kryuchkov. The discussions covered a range of topics but included an ominous statement that "currently strategic nuclear weapons can be used in less than 24 hours." There was also a substantial section on the collection and analysis, including "the studying of war preparations," and the need to determine and analyze "characteristics, phenomena, and indicators" of a possible NATO attack.[44]

Then, Gordievsky wrote, on either November 8 or 9, flash telegrams were sent to KGB and GRU residencies in Western Europe reporting "an alert on U.S. bases."[45] The flash telegrams "clearly implied that one of several possible explanations for the (non-existent) alert was that the countdown to a nuclear first strike had actually begun."[46]

According to the SHAPE summary, the morning of November 8 was when NATO's Supreme Allied Commander Europe requested "initial limited use of nuclear weapons against pre-selected fixed targets." The request was approved by "small cells" in the United States and the UK simulating political authorities in the evening, and the weapons were employed on the morning of 9 November.

Beyond the Soviet doctrinal concerns, the danger was further magnified because Able Archer 83 included new, non-routine elements that would have likely alarmed the Soviets even if they were not being watched and reported by intelligence agents working on Operation RYaN. These included a 170-flight, radio-silent airlift of nineteen thousand U.S. soldiers to Europe; the shifting of command from "Permanent War Headquarters to the Alternate War Headquarters"; the practice of "new nuclear weapons release procedures," including consultations with cells in Washington and London and a simulated move through all DEFCON levels to "general alert"; U.S. aircraft practicing nuclear warhead handling procedures, including taxiing out of hangars carrying "realistic-looking dummy warheads"; and the "sensitive, political issue" of numerous "slips of the tongue" over open interceptible radio communications in which B-52 sorties were referred to as nuclear "strikes."[47]

Taking these wrinkles into consideration, a retrospective review of the war game warned of a "tendency for most to describe the annual Able Archer exercise simply as 'a command and control' exercise, and thus, clearly nonthreatening to the Warsaw Pact. Not only was Able Archer 83 unique in some significant ways from earlier ones, it also incorporated live mobilization exercises from some U.S. military forces in Europe."[48]

One participant has recounted that the primary purpose of Able Archer 83 was to practice the new nuclear release procedures that had just been presented at an Allied Command Europe Officers' Nuclear Weapons Release Procedures Course that was held October 17 to 21 at the NATO School in Oberammergau, Germany, and attended by more than fifty officers from NATO countries.[49]

Another officer who participated in Able Archer at the platoon level said, "it was more certainly than that [a 'command post exercise']. For the European based nuclear forces it was a full blown Field Exercise. For military personnel the distinction between the two is significant." According to his account, "During Able Archer 83, we actually deployed the 'non-warload' (non-operational) systems to dispersal sites in the woods around Ulm, Schwäbisch Günd, and Heilbronn [West Germany]. There were a number of simulated radio transmissions during the exercise that were 'novel.'" Additionally, according to his account the U.S. troops took the missiles, erector-launchers, C2, and transload vehicles off the Combat Alert Sites and the caserns at Neu-Ulm, Stuttgart, and Waldheide. He believes with certainty that Soviet military liaison personnel and other Warsaw Pact agents noticed this anomaly. This, coupled with their communications and signals intelligence, "must have caused paranoia to a greater degree than in other situations."[50]

These variations did in fact match official Soviet intelligence-defined indicators for "possible operations by the USA and its allies on British territory in preparation" for a feared Western nuclear missile attack.

Of course, the West had no plans for a first strike. But as General Secretary Yuri Andropov had warned the U.S. envoy Averell Harriman a few months earlier, the tense relations between superpowers (and nuclear response times of just minutes) meant that the miscalculation of a nonexistent attack could still present a genuine danger.

A third NATO officer who was assigned to NATO's HQ Allied Forces Northern Europe during Able Archer 83 described working the torn tape relay—a form of teletype messaging—inside a bunker outside of Oslo, Norway. There, he spent eleven to twelve hours each day of the exercise receiving messages from headquarters and preparing responses that simulated how NATO would fight a nuclear war. According to the officer, "As the exercise progressed over a few days we began to settle into our routines and have conversations about the exercise and what we were seeing. Eventually we began doing the what if questions . . . 'What if the Soviets actually think we're going to launch nuclear weapons and we're disguising it as an exercise?' 'What if they launch against us?' 'What if, what if, what if . . .' It was a pretty crazy time."[51]

Weeks before Able Archer 83, President Reagan received a briefing on SIOP-6, the sixth generation of the United States' Single Integrated Operational Plan for nuclear war, which was based upon a target database of some fifty thousand Soviet targets.[52] In his memoirs, he derided the very notion of general plan for nuclear war: "there were still some people at the Pentagon who claimed a nuclear war was 'winnable.' I thought they were crazy. Worse, it appeared there were also Soviet generals who thought in terms of winning a nuclear war."[53] Days after Able Archer 83, Reagan attended a session in the White House situation room where he received "a briefing on our complete plan in the event of a nuclear attack" and simulated his role as commander in chief giving the order to unleash Armageddon. In his diary he described the event as "a most sobering experience."[54]

A "Non Crisis"?

We now know from U.S. and British intelligence that the Soviets reacted to Able Archer 83 by placing nuclear forces on alert, something there is no evidence of the Soviets having done during previous exercises. The Soviet Union, which believed its only chance of surviving a NATO strike was to preempt it, readied its nuclear arsenal.

What remains unknown—or secret—is exactly which Soviet forces went on alert or how close the Soviets came to launching a nuclear attack to preempt a feared NATO strike. Former Eastern Bloc spies have described the danger in stark terms. The double agent Gordievsky's description blames Operation RYaN for causing significant danger of unintended nuclear war: "In the tense atmosphere generated by the crises and rhetoric of the past few months, the KGB concluded that American forces had been placed on alert—and might even have begun the countdown to war. . . . The world did not quite reach the edge of the nuclear abyss during Operation RYaN. But during Able Archer 83 it had, without realizing it, come frighteningly close—certainly closer than at any time since the Cuban missile crisis of 1962."[55]

A declassified CIA history also establishes—for the first time—that another CIA source was at least partially corroborating Gordievsky's reporting. This Czechoslovakian intelligence officer—who worked closely with the KGB on RYaN—"noted that his counterparts were obsessed with the historical parallel between 1941 [when Operation Barbarossa, Hitler's successful sneak attack on the Soviet Union, was executed] and 1983. He believed this feeling was almost visceral, not intellectual, and deeply affected Soviet thinking."[56]

Rainer Rupp, a former East German spy within NATO, claims that as head of

NATO's Current Intelligence Group, the "nerve center of NATO," he had access to "all information on the situation of the enemy [the Soviet Union] and their own [NATO]." Rupp describes the danger of Able Archer 83 even more starkly—and portrays himself as playing a central role in ending the danger. Rupp, who was imprisoned for spying after German reunification, recounted in an interview for a 2008 British television documentary that during Able Archer 83, a courier delivered him a message that read, "'High alert, the Russians are really scared and they want to know if . . . NATO is preparing for war and so on.' I was really upset, I was thinking where is this leading?" To allay Moscow's fears during Able Archer 83, he provided all of the "officially numbered" documents that he had access to so that the intelligence services "could clearly see that nothing was missing and that nothing important had been overlooked." He also transmitted daily messages to East Berlin, his final one declaring that "there was no indication that NATO was preparing for war at this time."[57]

But because there has not been any Eastern Bloc military documentary evidence to corroborate the spies' claims, some historians have suggested that the Soviet leadership did not actually receive the warnings from Operation RYaN during Able Archer 83; therefore the War Scare was not significantly dangerous. The historian Vojtech Mastny asserts that neither East German nor Soviet intelligence agents, either "out of common sense or because of incompetence," passed on intelligence about Able Archer 83 to the Soviet Defense Ministry or Politburo, and that the War Scare was thus solely a Soviet propaganda ploy to stop the deployment of Pershing II and Gryphon cruise missiles into Western Europe, which ultimately "remained unaffected by . . . 'Able Archer.'"[58]

Mark Kramer has written that the "purported crisis" of 1983 "did not exist at all." His conclusion, however, relies primarily upon an analysis of Politburo minutes from 1983 and early 1984, which do not mention "Able Archer 83 or the specific threat of imminent nuclear war, and upon conversations with some high-ranking Soviet officials who were in power during the War Scare and did not recall the exercise."[59]

However, historians do not yet have access to the minutes of every Politburo meeting from that period.[60] Furthermore, many of the key discussions during Andropov's tenure as general secretary did not occur in formal Politburo meetings, but at his hospital bedside. According to historian Roy Medvedev's biography, it was there that Andropov would summon his advisors, generals, and Politburo members to govern the Soviet Union. Despite his illness, Andropov was "fully engaged in the leadership of the country and the army, and the defense of the country," said Marshal Nikolai Ogarkov.[61] As such, an examination of sources broader than select Politburo minutes is required to attain a full picture of the Soviet leadership's views on the 1983 War Scare.

Other evidence suggests that senior Soviet military leadership did monitor and were worried about a potential preemptive nuclear attack during Able Archer 83. A 1990 interview between *Washington Post* journalist Don Oberdorfer and Marshal Sergei Akhromeyev, the former head of the Soviet General Staff, exposes a key historiographical problem in the study of the "Able Archer 83" War Scare: the NATO exercise was not known as "Able Archer 83" to Soviet intelligence as it was being conducted. Soviet analysts have referred to it as "Autumn Forge 83," the name for the larger, months-long, umbrella exercise of which Able Archer was the conclusion.[62]

The name "Able Archer 83" only came into the public realm with the first public exposé of the incident in an article in the *Sunday Telegraph* from October 16, 1988, "Brink of World War III: When the World Almost Went to War." Hence, "Able Archer 83," the term most used by the historical community, was not the term most commonly used by actors as the event transpired.

In the key exchange of the interview, Akhromeyev told Oberdorfer that he did not remember "Able Archer 83" but that "we believed the most dangerous military exercises [were] Autumn Forge and Reforger. These [were] the NATO exercise[s] in Europe." While Akhromeyev states that he felt no "immediate threat of war," he adds: "I must tell you that I personally and many of the people that I know had a different opinion of the United States in 1983 than I have today [1990]. I considered that the United States [was] pressing for world supremacy . . . and I considered that as a result of this situation there [could] be a war between the Soviet Union and the United States on the initiative of the United States."[63]

Commander Victor Tkachenko, stationed at a Soviet missile silo during Able Archer 83, described the attentiveness of the Soviet military leadership and the high tensions that arose: "When we reached the command bunker that night, we received a special order. We were told to immediately go to raised combat alert. It was so serious that there was a third man there with us, to maintain uninterrupted communications."[64] As Tkachenko's silo went on heightened alert, he "was waiting for one last order—the order to open the . . . top secret envelope—your hands always shake . . . if we received an order to open such envelope . . . what followed suit was that you had to turn the key and launch the missiles."[65]

According to the former head of Soviet Strategic Rocket Forces Colonel-General Viktor Yesin, Soviet forces were on "combat alert" during Able Archer 83. He also stated that he could say "with a high degree of confidence" that the chief of the General Staff of the USSR, Marshal Nikolai Ogarkov, participated in the alert from a central control bunker near Moscow.[66]

Though the exact Soviet military reaction still remains a Russian secret, recent American and British declassification of the Soviets' actions in response to Able Archer 83 and its "special wrinkles" make it very clear that the danger of war through miscalculation increased during November of 1983. Moscow conducted an "unprecedented technical collection foray against Able Archer 83," including more than thirty-six Soviet intelligence flights, significantly more than any previous exercises. These were conducted over the Norwegian, North, Baltic, and Barents Seas, "probably to determine whether U.S. naval forces were deploying forward in support of Able Archer."[67]

Warsaw Pact military reactions to Able Archer 83 were also "unparalleled in scale" and included "transporting nuclear weapons from storage sites to delivery units by helicopter," and suspension of all flight operations except intelligence collection flights from November 4 to 10, "probably to have available as may aircraft as possible for combat."[68]

The CIA reported Warsaw Pact military activity in the Baltic Military District and Czechoslovakia, and that nuclear-capable aircraft in Poland and Germany were placed "on high alert status with readying of nuclear strike forces."[69] Peter Vincent Pry, a former CIA analyst, suspects that the aircraft were merely the tip of the iceberg; he hypothesizes that—in accordance with Soviet military procedure and history—ICBM silos, already at a high state of alert and difficult for the United States to detect, were also prepared for a launch.[70]

The NSA's internal history discloses that during Able Archer 83, U.S. reconnaissance forces could not track the location of the Soviet Union's mobile SS-20 missiles, which could be assembled or torn down within an hour and crawled along the USSR's western front undetected and possibly ready to launch. When one of the Soviet's 405 SS-20 launchers was detected by the NSA's overhead photography, it was "an occasional lucky accident."[71]

Several other Soviet nuclear responses remain redacted by American authorities. Though hidden, at least two of these likely involve further Soviet preparations for nuclear war as they include the phrase "30-minute, around-the-clock readiness time and assigning priority targets." The definitive, all-source, retroactive President's Foreign Intelligence Advisory Board report authored in 1990 concludes that the Soviet response "strongly suggests to us that Soviet military leaders may have been seriously concerned that the U.S. would use Able Archer 83 as a cover of launching a real attack."[72]

On November 5, the eve of Able Archer 83, Politburo member Grigory Romanov delivered an official speech to the Soviet population celebrating the Bolshevik Revolution. During his speech, Romanov declared that "perhaps never before in the postwar decades has the atmosphere in the world been as tense as it is now." "Comrades," he went on to say, "the international situation is at present white hot, thoroughly white hot."[73] The declassified evidence suggests why Romanov felt this way.

We now know that the "white hot" danger of Able Archer 83 began to subside when Lieutenant General Leonard Perroots—a deputy chief of staff for intelligence at the U.S. Air Force's European headquarters at Ramstein Air Base, West Germany—chose to do "nothing in the face of evidence that parts of the Soviet armed forces were moving to an unusual level of alert." Had Perroots mirrored the Soviets and escalated the situation, the War Scare could conceivably have become a war.

Like Stanislav Petrov months earlier, Perroots and other U.S. officers in the U.S. Air Force's Europe intelligence staff "acted correctly out of instinct, not informed guidance." Leading up to Able Archer 83, Perroots and the rest of the U.S. military had received no indication or training that the Soviet Union now viewed it as possible that the West could launch a nuclear first strike against them. Fortunately, Perroots trusted his gut, and Able Archer 83 ended without nuclear incident. More than a decade later, a review described Perroots's non-actions as "fortuitous, if ill-informed"—worlds that could perhaps describe the entire Cold War.

Part III: Aftermath, "One Misstep Could Trigger a Great War"

Intelligence Battle

DAYS AFTER ABLE ARCHER BEGAN, the U.S. Army's spies, the Intelligence and Security Command, produced a well-circulated raw intelligence summary based on information from a German "military staff agency which consistently provides reliable assessment information, detailed intelligence studies, and current intelligence." The document reported "continued [Soviet] sigint missions to monitor NATO" exercise Able Archer 83. These SIGINT (signals intelligence collection) missions supported Warsaw Pact military activities in the USSR and in the forward area, including the inner German border. The Soviet and East German Baltic fleet was deployed and "targeted against the NATO CPX [command post exercise] Able Archer 83." According to the military's raw intelligence, Soviet and Warsaw Pact air forces in the forward area conducted flight operations at a low level. This first known U.S. intelligence report about the Warsaw Pact reaction to Able Archer 83 stated—incorrectly—that "the continued low level of [Warsaw Pact] ground, air, and naval forces overall renders no intelligence indicating any change in the substance of the threat."[1]

Despite Soviet preparations for a potential NATO first strike, American intelligence continued to incorrectly report that there was no genuine Soviet fear of a U.S. attack. A December 30, 1983, CIA report entitled "Soviet Thinking on the Possibility of Armed Confrontation with the United States" built on the initial reporting to reach this conclusion: "Contrary to the impression conveyed by Soviet propaganda, Moscow does not appear to anticipate a near-term military confrontation with the United States." Rather, the CIA's directorate of intelligence believed, Moscow was "playing up the 'war danger'" to stop the deployment of intermediate range nuclear missiles to Western Europe, deepen cleavages within the Atlantic alliance, and increase pressure for a more conciliatory U.S. policy posture toward the USSR.[2]

While concluding that the Soviets did not genuinely believe a Western attack was possible, this report did contain intelligence that there was a palpable fear—genuine or ginned up—gripping the Soviet Union in 1983. One Western visitor reported to the CIA "that Andropov had sent a letter to all party organizations in October forcefully declaring that the fatherland was truly in danger." Another reported "an obsessive fear of war, an emotionalism, and a paranoia . . . that had not been present earlier."

These conclusions were reinforced in a May 1984 Special National Intelligence Estimate entitled "Implications of Recent Soviet Military-Political Activities," which was specifically written to examine the Soviet reaction to Able Archer 83. This SNIE concluded, "We believe strongly that Soviet actions are not inspired by, and Soviet leaders do not perceive, a genuine danger of imminent conflict with the United States."[3]

Despite its conclusion, the SNIE included several indicators that the Soviet Union may have actually feared a Western strike. "Since November 1983 there has been a high level of Soviet military activity, with new deployments of weapons and strike forces," at least partially in response to Able Archer 83 (the SNIE does not mention the nineteen thousand troops transported to Europe during Reforger 83 and Autumn Forge 83). The SNIE also stated that Able Archer 83 "was larger than previous 'Able Archer' exercises and included new command, control, and communications procedures for authorizing use of nuclear weapons."

Strangely, the SNIE reported an "elaborate" Soviet reaction to Able Archer 83 including "increased intelligence collection flights, and the placing of Soviet air units in East Germany and Poland on heightened readiness in what was declared to be a threat of possible aggression against the USSR and Warsaw Pact countries" but did not allow that these reactions could have represented genuine Soviet fear during the NATO nuclear release exercise.[4]

The SNIE hypothesized that the Soviets may have been using the alarm to "desensitize the United States to higher levels of Soviet military activity—thus masking intended future moves and reducing U.S. warning time." The SNIE also did not consider the possibility—embraced by American and Soviet defense heads, including Secretary of Defense Weinberger and Marshal Akhromeyev—that it was possible the Soviet Union feared that Able Archer 83 could itself have masked a "ruse of war." An article in the February 1984 edition of the most prominent Soviet military theory journal, *Voennaya Mysl*, warned that during Autumn Forge (and hence Able Archer), "it was more and more difficult to tell the difference between work on military drills and real preparations for wide-scale aggression," a possibility not explored by the SNIE.[5]

Although the SNIE professed to present airtight evidence that U.S. policy makers should in no way be worried about war with the Soviet Union through miscalculation, the final page of the SNIE did acknowledge that the CIA had "inadequate information about . . . the Soviet reading of our own military operations [and] current reconnaissance and exercises." Nonetheless, the U.S. intelligence community boldly affirmed that the Soviets did not fear "an imminent military clash."

This SNIE was also contradicted by evidence from human sources. It asserted that "in private diplomatic exchanges with Moscow over the past six months the Soviets have neither made any direct threats connected with regional or other issues nor betrayed any fear of a U.S. attack." This claim did not square with Andropov's plea to Averell Harriman months earlier that the Reagan administration "may be moving toward the dangerous 'red line'" of nuclear war.[6]

It also contradicted two sources that had warned the Soviet expert Jack Matlock, a National Security Council staffer, of dangerous tensions. On October 11, 1983, a Soviet journalist from *Pravda*, Sergei Vishnevsky, told Matlock that he was personally fearful: "The state of U.S.-Soviet relations has deteriorated to a dangerous point. Many in the Soviet public are asking if war is imminent."[7] Intelligence documents report that a second, unnamed source who had traveled to Moscow reported to Matlock that "fear of war seemed to affect the elite as well as the man on the street," and that the source "perceiv[ed] a growing paranoia among Soviet officials, and [could] see them literally obsessed by fear of war." Because of these factors, the source claimed that he could "not discount the possibility of irrational elements in Soviet decision-making."[8]

Robert McFarlane recalls that throughout 1983, "we had been receiving reports from [assets in] European capitals based on their interviews with Russian attachés and ambassadors that there was fear, alarm, among Russians and Soviets about the American intentions and whether we might even be planning an attack of our own."[9] Another of McFarlane's sources was Suzanne Massie, the Russian scholar who, though far outside of U.S. government bureaucracy, was one of President Reagan's most influential advisors on the Soviet Union.[10] At a Moscow meeting in September 1983, Massie met with Radomir Bogdanov, the deputy director of the Institute of the U.S.A. and Canada, who in all likelihood had ties to the KGB. During the meeting, Bogdanov warned Massie, "You don't know how close war is." After attempting and failing to relay this danger to the White House via the famed cellist Mstislav Rostropovich, she was eventually able to relay Bogdanov's warning to National Security Advisor McFarlane, fresh on the job after replacing William Clark on October 17.[11]

The British Role

The policy makers who wrote the Special National Intelligence Estimate "Implications of Recent Soviet Military-Political Activities" did not just misinterpret intelligence, they also omitted it. The declassified cover memo for the Department of State copy of the SNIE reveals that it was British intelligence—from their asset, Oleg Gordievsky—rather than American intelligence that first reported the Soviet response to Able Archer 83: "You will recall that in response to British concerns, the intelligence community undertook a detailed review of recent Soviet military and political moves beginning with exercise Able Archer 83."[12]

Declassified British Ministry of Defence documents further confirm that British intelligence observed "an unprecedented Soviet reaction to Able Archer 83 and other reports of alleged concern about a surprise NATO attack."[13] Prime Minister Margaret Thatcher discussed the danger of the War Scare with her senior cabinet members and intelligence heads on April 10, 1984. According to notes of the meeting, Thatcher instructed the government to "consider what could be done to remove the danger that, by mis-calculating Western intentions, the Soviet Union would over-react," and she also noted the need to "urgently consider how to approach the Americans on the question of possible Soviet misapprehensions about a surprise NATO attack."[14]

According to Michael Herman, head of the Soviet Division of Britain's Government Communications Headquarters (GCHQ) from 1977 to 1982, this "unprecedented Soviet reaction" was primarily reported by an analyst working for the Ministry of Defence and Joint Intelligence Committee (JIC) named Harry Burke. Burke, aware of Gordievsky's reports on Operation RYaN, corroborated this reporting with "unusual activities described in some of the Sigint reports," but not at the time highlighted by the British SIGINT agencies. "He put this together with Gordievsky's evidence to argue for the evidence of Soviet fears of Able Archer," and produced the subsequent JIC report that eventually reached Washington.[15]

When the British conveyed this information to the Americans in March of 1984, it "was not well received in the U.S. intelligence community." British Ambassador Oliver Wright presented the danger to Under Secretary for Political Affairs Lawrence Eagleburger, but Eagleburger, backed by the Department of State's Bureau of Intelligence and Research (INR), refuted the ambassador's warnings, arguing that the Soviets were simply "pursuing a massive propaganda campaign." The INR briefer later revealed that he had presented Eagleburger "a skeptical version of events, designed, in his [the reviewer's] words, to 'discourage the British.'" Other American officials even questioned the British motives for warning of the War Scare, believing the Foreign Office was "simply capitalizing on a good political occasion to force President Reagan to tone down his rhetoric and delay deployments of the INF missiles."[16]

Misleading NATO

The Department of State's cover letter, which revealed that the British had first detected and warned of the danger of Able Archer 83, also revealed that the United States appears to have attempted to hide its true danger from its NATO allies. The letter's author, Director of the Bureau of Intelligence and Research Hugh Montgomery, reported that a sanitized version of the SNIE had been produced for release to the British and other NATO ministerial colleagues. The attached "sanitized version"—which is marked "Secret" rather than "Top Secret"—removed all references to Able Archer 83 and the Soviet response to it, despite the fact that the British first reported it.[17]

Removing all mentions of "Able Archer 83"—the very reason the intelligence estimate was created—before providing it to NATO raises the disturbing possibility that the U.S. classification system hid the danger of accidental nuclear war from allies who participated in the exercise that caused it. This may have been done for two reasons. The first, possibly legitimate, was to protect Oleg Gordievsky, the UK's double agent within the KGB, from spies at NATO headquarters. The second, more nefarious, was to ensure that NATO countries (most pressingly West Germany) would not waver in their decision to host the newly deployed U.S. Pershing II nuclear missiles, which could reach the Soviet Union in minutes—upsetting the previous nuclear strategic balance in Europe and leading directly to hair-trigger alerts, Operation RYaN, and the danger of Able Archer 83. If an account of this nuclear danger reached the public, it likely would have further bolstered the already powerful antinuclear movement.

Eventually, differing views of the Able Archer 83 War Scare emerged within the intelligence community, even reaching President Reagan (as discussed below). But these differing opinions of the danger were produced late—in two cases five and seven years after the War Scare had ended. They were also bureaucratically hidden. According to the PFIAB, "The last, most definitive intelligence community word on the Soviet war scare" was buried "in an annex to a [1988] National Intelligence Estimate on Soviet intelligence capabilities that was unintended for policymakers' eyes."[18]

A thorough U.S. intelligence community analysis of the dangers of nuclear miscalculation present during the 1983 War Scare may have never occurred were it not for Lieutenant General Leonard Perroots. Perroots, the officer who acted on instinct and chose to do "nothing in the face of evidence that parts of the Soviet armed forces were moving to an unusual level of alert" during Able Archer 83, wrote a letter to CIA Director William Webster and the President's Foreign Intelligence Advisory Board that outlined his disquiet over inadequate treatment of the Soviet War Scare.[19]

DCI Webster consulted with his National Intelligence Council, in-house advisors supporting the director of the Central Intelligence Agency (the PFIAB supported and advised the president). The NIC analysis reached the strange conclusion that while in 1983 "the Soviets had concern that the West might decide to attack the USSR without warning during a time of vulnerability," and they "consider[ed] a preemptive strike at the first sign of U.S. preparations for a nuclear strike," nonetheless any failing by the intelligence community analyzing the War Scare "was not grave."[20]

The PFIAB reviewed the evidence and came to a markedly different conclusion. It reported to the president that it was "deeply disturbed by the U.S. handling of the war scare, both at the time and since." Its response was to draft the definitive account of the War Scare, based off of hundreds of all-source intelligence documents and more than seventy-five interviews with American and British officials.

That ninety-four-page "above Top Secret" report, the only study written with access to all U.S. intelligence files on Able Archer 83 and the Soviet response, concludes that in 1983 the United States "may have inadvertently placed our relations with the Soviet Union on a hair trigger." "There is little doubt in our minds that the Soviets were genuinely worried by Able Archer," the study continued, declaring that "it appears that at least some Soviet forces were preparing to preempt or counterattack a NATO strike launched under cover of Able Archer" and that "the President was given assessments of Soviet attitudes and actions that understated the risks to the United States." According to the PFIAB, the U.S. intelligence community's erroneous reporting made the "especially grave error to assume that since we know the U.S. is not going to start World War III, the next leaders of the Kremlin will also believe that."[21]

According to the report, "In the early stages of the war scare period, when evidence was thin, little effort was made to examine the various possible Soviet motivations behind some very anomalous events. . . . When written, the 1984 SNIE's [assessments] were overconfident."[22]

Rather than shy away from discussing and analyzing the danger of nuclear war through miscalculation, the board,[23] chaired by Anne Armstrong, and the report's primary author, Nina Stewart, wrote that they hoped the "TOP SECRET UMBRA GAMMA WNINTEL NOFORN NOCONTRACT ORCON" report would prompt "renewed interest, vigorous dialogue, and rigorous analyses of the [War Scare]"—at least by the few cleared to read it!

The National Security Archive fought tirelessly for more than twelve years to win the release of this report. When it was finally declassified, a member of the Information Security Oversight Office—the ultimate arbiter of classification in the U.S. government—described it to the editor as "probably the most interesting document ever to have come across our desks." Now, more than three decades after Able Archer 83's end, the public can read and decide for themselves about the danger of the 1983 War Scare.[24]

Reagan's Reaction

In 1990, President Reagan was asked why he thought relations between the Soviet Union and the United States had improved so dramatically. Reagan answered that it was due to mutual interest: Gorbachev's interest in dealing with the economic emergency in the Soviet Union, and Reagan's belief that "it was a danger to have a world so heavily armed that one misstep could trigger a great war."[25] Reagan acted on his interests and fears thirteen months before Gorbachev rose to power, extending a hand to the Soviet leadership, and eventually meeting Gorbachev in Geneva to negotiate.

It is clear that after Able Archer 83, Reagan moved away from a confrontational U.S. policy toward the Soviet Union. In his journal, Reagan wrote of two events that profoundly affected him in the weeks leading up to Able Archer 83. The first was his October 10 viewing of the film *The Day After,* a realistic portrayal of nuclear war described by the *Washington Post* as a "horrific vision of nuclear holocaust." Reagan wrote in his diary that the film was "very effective and left me greatly depressed."[26] This glimpse of nuclear war psychologically primed Reagan for information about the War Scare, giving him a very specific picture of what could have occurred had the situation escalated further. Days after Able Archer 83, McFarlane shared intelligence reports describing the Soviets' nuclear activity after Able Archer. The president read the reports and responded with "genuine anxiety" and disbelief that his actions could have led to an armed attack; according to McFarlane, "It did bother him that they [the Soviets] could even take seriously the very idea [of a U.S. strike]."[27] Other officials, including Shultz, considered it "incredible, at least to us," that the Soviets would believe the United States would launch a genuine attack.[28] Reagan did not share the belief that cooler heads would prevail:

> We had many contingency plans for responding to a nuclear attack. But everything would happen so fast that I wondered how much planning or reason could be applied in such a crisis. . . . *Six minutes* to decide how to respond to a blip on a radar scope and decide whether to unleash Armageddon! How could anyone apply reason at a time like that?[29]

The impetus for Reagan's early 1984 change in policy has previously been variously explained as a seizure of power by the moderates in his administration, as simply election-year politics, or that Reagan in 1984 was simply ready to negotiate.[30] Of the three explanations the third seems the most plausible. The unprecedented tensions and nuclear fear of 1983 led Reagan, who believed the prophecy of Armageddon would be fulfilled by a nuclear apocalypse, who stated that "MAD policy was madness," and who wrote of civilization's regression due to nuclear weapons, to seek a policy toward the USSR that reduced, rather than increased, the risk of nuclear war.[31]

Reagan, who had vocally opposed communism since his days as an actor and trade union leader in Hollywood, did not sit idly as his underlings pivoted his policy towards Moscow after the War Scare; the decision came from the top. It is equally unlikely that Reagan's warming to the Soviet Union simply amounted to an election year ploy; Reagan took positions on abortion, the support of the Nicaraguan Contras, and the nuclear freeze[32] that were (sometimes drastically) out of step with public opinion. The most generally accepted conclusion, presented by Reagan's conservative base and the president himself, is that "the United States was in its strongest position in two decades to negotiate with the Russians from strength."[33] But even if Reagan used this rationalization as justification for his change in policy toward the Soviet Union, the United States did not hold a significantly stronger position in 1984 than it had in 1981.[34]

While each of the above reasons likely had some impact on Reagan as he changed the course of his presidency, so did his realization of the danger of nuclear war through miscalculation encapsulated by the Soviet reaction to Able Archer 83. To date there is no document definitively describing when exactly Reagan learned of Able Archer 83 or its potential danger. According to National Security Advisor McFarlane, Able Archer 83 was on the president's mind as he traveled throughout Asia from November 8 to 14. The two spoke about the situation several times, "on Air Force One and elsewhere."[35] According to the PFIAB report, no President's Daily Brief mentioned Able Archer 83 or the Soviet response while it was being conducted. During and immediately after Able Archer 83, the president participated in several National Security Planning Group meetings. Though stored at the Reagan Presidential Library, the pre-briefing notes from most of these remain classified, and generally no notes of the exact conversations exist at the presidential level, meaning that if Reagan's national security principals spoke of Able Archer or the Soviet reaction to it during a meeting on another subject, no White House record is available.[36]

The earliest definitive document available showing that Reagan was told about the Soviet Union's reaction to Able Archer 83 is a June 19, 1984, memorandum from Central Intelligence Agency Director William Casey to the president, vice president, secretary of state, secretary of defense, assistant to the president for national security affairs, and chairman of the Joint Chiefs of Staff entitled "US/Soviet Tension." This striking memo warned of "a rather stunning array of indicators [primarily drawn from the May 1984 SNIE drafted in response to Able Archer 83] of an increasing aggressiveness in Soviet policy and activities."[37]

Casey's conclusion warns the president:

> The behavior of the armed forces is perhaps the most disturbing. From the operational deployment of submarines to the termination of harvest support to the delayed troop rotation there is a central theme of not being strategically vulnerable, even if it means taking some risks. It is important to distinguish in this category those acts which are political blustering and those which may be, but also carry large costs. The point of blustering is to do something that makes the opponent pay high costs while the blusterer pays none or little. The military behaviors we have observed involve high military costs . . . adding thereby a dimension of genuineness to the Soviet expressions of concern that is often not reflected in intelligence issuances.

In other words, the Soviets may not have been bluffing.[38]

After reading this report, the president "expressed surprise" and "described the events as 'really scary.'"[39] But the president seemed to know of this danger of the Soviets misperceiving the U.S. aggression even before his CIA director warned him. On June 14, 1984, five days before the memo from Casey, he wrote, "A meeting with Geo. S & Bud [Secretary of State George Shultz and National Security Advisor Robert McFarlane]. We dug into the subject of a meeting with [new Soviet General Secretary Konstantin] Chernenko. I have a gut feeling we should do this. His reply to my letter is in hand and it lends support to my idea that while we go on believing, & with some good reason, that the Soviets are plotting against us & mean us harm, maybe they are scared of us & think we are a threat. I'd like to go face to face & explore this with them."[40]

Reagan kept a continued interest in reports about the War Scare, and their source, Oleg Gordievsky. According to a British journalist with an intelligence background, "In September and October 1985, British's officials passed Gordievsk[y]'s information on the Ryan exercise to the Americans, including his detailed 50-page analysis not merely of the Kremlin's strategy but of the Kremlin's psychology as it affected that strategy. . . . President Reagan was said to have read these Gordievsk[y] reports from beginning to end, which was far from being his standard practice."[41]

Reagan also kept tabs on Gordievsky's well-being and plied him for knowledge about the Soviet system. In May of 1985, the KGB—likely tipped off by Aldrich

Ames—correctly suspected Gordievsky was working as a double agent and he was abruptly recalled to Moscow and placed under surveillance. That September, he escaped across the Finnish border and defected to the United Kingdom. On July 21, 1987, President Reagan met with him. According to Reagan's journal, "this morning had a meeting with Col. Oleg Antonvich Gordiyevskiy—the Soviet K.G.B. officer who defected to Eng. His wife & 2 little girls were left behind. We've been trying to get them out to join him." Two weeks later, Gordievsky again appears in the president's journal. "Then [I read] a report on Col. Oleg Gordiaskiy—the K.G.B. defector to Eng. Margaret Thatcher is working on the Soviets as we are. We're going to hold back & see if she can get his wife & 2 children out of Russia." Gordievsky was reunited with his wife and daughters in September 1991.[42]

It is also possible, as McFarlane has described, that Reagan learned of the Soviet reaction to Able Archer 83 soon after it occurred. It certainly appears that this may have been the case from an entry in his diary on November 18, 1983, seven days after the conclusion of Able Archer 83:[43]

> George Shultz & I had a talk mainly about setting up a little in house group of experts on the Soviet U. to help us in setting up some channels. I feel the Soviets are so defense minded, so paranoid about being attacked that without being soft on them we ought to tell them no one here has any intention of doing anything like that. What the h--l have they got that anyone would want . . .[44]

This "in house group" included Shultz, McFarlane, Weinberger, Casey, and Bush, and was chaired by Matlock. The discussions were confidential and took place on Saturday mornings. Notes from the first meeting of November 19 reveal that the group's policy agenda was to:

1. Reduce use and threat of force in international disputes
2. Lower high levels of armaments by equitable and verifiable agreements; and
3. Establish minimal level of trust to facilitate the first two objectives, including
    a. Compliance with past agreements;
    b. Human rights performance;
    c. Specific confidence-building measures;
    d. Bilateral ties when mutually beneficial.[45]

The notes also stated that to achieve these goals, the Reagan administration would use realism, strength, and negotiation. U.S. policy would not challenge the legitimacy of the Soviet system, work toward military superiority, or attempt to force the collapse of the Soviet system. The notes to the meeting end with a list of "specific steps" that should be taken to "maximize success" toward the Soviet Union. These steps included more dialogue (including "informal and unofficial means of communication"), a letter from Reagan to Andropov offering to resume negotiations on intermediate range missiles, and a major speech by the president on U.S.-Soviet relations.[46]

Attempts to establish backchannel contacts with Soviet leaders were quickly implemented. In December 1983, Matlock drafted a memo entitled "Can a Private Channel [with the USSR] Be Useful?" In it, he wrote that "if it is handled properly" it could be. Matlock concluded that a private channel was important because "we need informal communications most during periods of tension. . . . We lose nothing from talking privately (so long as we are reasonably careful about what we say). And refusal to do so only encourages a Soviet stonewall—and perhaps worse."[47] A back channel with the Soviet Union was quickly established, with Reagan's advisor Brent Scowcroft serving as the link.

After the first Saturday breakfast meeting, Matlock and McFarlane began drafting a public pronouncement of Reagan's change in policy toward the Soviet Union.[48] According to Matlock, this shift in policy was driven by Reagan's "aspirations for his record as president." McFarlane recounts that Able Archer had a "big influence" on Reagan's thinking.[49] On January 16, Reagan delivered the pivotal speech he had tasked Matlock and McFarlane with drafting a month earlier. In the speech, given at a special time and utilizing new broadcasting technology that allowed his address to be heard live in the Soviet Union, Reagan no longer stressed the irresolvable differences between American capitalism and Soviet communism; instead he emphasized the necessity of working together to protect their common interests:

> If the Soviet Government wants peace, then there will be peace. Together we can strengthen peace, reduce the level of arms, and know in doing so that we have helped fulfill the hopes and dreams of those we represent and, indeed, of people everywhere. Let us begin now.[50]

Reagan drafted a late handwritten addition to his speech that explained this newfound logic of coexistence with a vintage Reaganesque parable:

> Just suppose with me for a moment that an Ivan and an Anya could find themselves, oh, say, in a waiting room, or sharing a shelter from the rain or a storm with a Jim and Sally, and there was no language barrier to keep them from getting acquainted. Would they then debate

> the differences between their respective governments? Or would they find themselves comparing notes about their children and what each other did for a living?
>
> Before they parted company, they would probably have touched on ambitions and hobbies and what they wanted for their children and problems of making ends meet. And as they went their separate ways, maybe Anya would be saying to Ivan, "Wasn't she nice? She also teaches music." Or Jim would be telling Sally what Ivan did or didn't like about his boss. They might even have decided they were all going to get together for dinner some evening soon. Above all, they would have proven that people don't make wars.[51]

Immediately following Reagan's speech, Shultz drafted an earnest message to Gromyko which began by stating:

> We have a problem, you and I. And we must do better than we have to date in dealing with it. The problem is how to manage the US-Soviet relationship in a manner which eliminates the risk of direct conflict, reduces the present dangerous level of confrontation, and turns our energies to peaceful competition and, where possible cooperation.[52]

Shultz stated that the United States and USSR were "at a point of genuine opportunity in [their] foreign policy." And then—echoing Andropov's June 1983 plea to Harriman—he called for an end to the existential danger each side posed to the other:

> The central issue between us is the avoidance of war. If we do not agree, at least tacitly, on that issue, the remainder of our agenda and yours is irrelevant. We must face this question openly or, if you prefer, privately. But there must be some minimum level of understanding about what you consider essential to your national security and what we consider essential for ours.[53]

In his memoirs, Reagan—without specifically mentioning Able Archer 83, as he stated earlier that he could not mention classified information—wrote of his realization:

> Three years had taught me something surprising about the Russians: Many people at the top of the Soviet hierarchy were genuinely afraid of America and Americans. Perhaps this shouldn't have surprised me, but it did. . . .

> During my first years in Washington, I think many of us in the administration took it for granted that the Russians, like ourselves, considered it unthinkable that the United States would launch a first strike against them. But the more experience I had with Soviet leaders and other heads of state who knew them, the more I began to realize that many Soviet officials feared us not only as adversaries but as potential aggressors who might hurl nuclear weapons at them in a first strike.[54]

Soviet Ripples

How Able Archer 83 shaped the Soviet leadership and its policy is more difficult to ascertain. On December 15, 1983, Ustinov gave a prominent speech addressed to Soviet war veterans in which he spoke of the tension between the United States and Soviet Union. He stated:

> The Soviet people well remember the lessons of the last war and draw the necessary conclusions. . . . As you can see, comrades, the situation in the world is extremely tense. But no matter how complicated the political-military situation, there is no point in overdramatizing it. . . . Soberly appraising the full seriousness of the current situation, one must see that imperialism is not all powerful. And its threats do not frighten us. The Soviet people have strong nerves.[55]

American intelligence officers paid close attention to Ustinov's speech.[56] The minister of defense had warned American policy makers about the danger of miscalculation. Yet he also appeared to call for a "sober appraisal" from within the Soviet Union, signaling to Soviet leadership that America was not truly planning to win a nuclear war.

The Soviet Ministry of Foreign Affairs was unsure of what to make of Reagan's call for rapprochement. According to Ambassador Dobrynin, "When we at the embassy heard the speech . . . we could not decide whether it was genuine or mere campaign oratory." Once again Moscow could not comprehend the "contradiction between words and deeds . . . the more so because Reagan himself never seemed to see it. In his mind such incompatibilities could coexist in perfect harmony, but Moscow regarded such behavior at the same time as a sign of deliberate duplicity and hostility."[57]

On January 28, 1984, a sickly Andropov wrote his final letter to Reagan. Responding to Reagan's offer to resume negotiations on intermediate range missiles, the general secretary first criticized the president for his previous aggressive policies, stating that he could not "fail to draw a conclusion that the U.S. pursued a goal . . . to challenge the security of our country and its allies." Andropov then listed mutual issues for the two superpowers to improve, including: general and European nuclear arms reduction, demilitarization in space, and limiting conventional arms sales to third world countries. He then coolly stated his willingness for renewed dialogue.[58]

Another possible consequence of Able Archer 83, according to Roy Medvedev, was Andropov's 1983 implementation of the "nuclear briefcase," in effect placing civilian control of the Soviet Union's nuclear arsenal in the hands of one political leader.[59]

After Able Archer 83, the Soviet Union and United States were also able to complete an upgrade to the communications "hotline" between Moscow and Washington. The upgraded hotline, based on facsimile and satellite technology, allowed leaders to transfer much higher quantities of information, including maps and pictures, to each other. A 1983 DOD report to Congress on direct communications links specifically rejected voice and video conference capabilities as the DOD believed they were more subject to misinterpretation and could result in "rash or instantaneous responses."[60]

Operation RYaN died down, but did not end. In fact (illustrating the inertia of Soviet bureaucracy) the operation lasted until the end of the Soviet Union. However, after Able Archer 83, the reports of preparations for U.S. nuclear attack passed along by Soviet agents abroad slowed to a trickle.[61] A Bulgarian document reported that in early 1984 units within Bulgarian intelligence held a meeting to coordinate "the necessary working contacts between information-analytical units on nuclear-attack [RYaN] problems." One can only hope Bulgarian intelligence decided greater collaboration was needed to avoid future false alarms.[62]

East German documents reveal a persistent undercurrent of skepticism and concern about the effectiveness of Operation RYaN. In August of 1984, Lev Shapkin, deputy director of the KGB for foreign intelligence, told Markus Wolf that reforms to Operation RYaN were underway. Though no faulty reporting by Operation RYaN during Able Archer 83 was mentioned in the meeting, the two intelligence officials were clearly worried that false alarms regarding an imminent Western nuclear first strike could lead to preemptive actions by Soviet nuclear forces. According to a summary of the meeting, Shapkin told Wolf that the indicators that agents were observing and reporting "must be complemented, revised, and made more precise," and bemoaned "the problem of not getting deceived" by faulty indicators. He reiterated that "clear-headedness about the entire RYaN complex" was a "mandatory requirement."[63] Markus Wolf included his concerns in an addendum to the summary of the meetings, stressing the need to know the "actual situation" rather than the picture presented by Operation RYaN's indicators. "Constant and ongoing assessments," he sensibly wrote, "have to be made whether certain developments actually constitute a crisis or not."[64]

Though the threat of nuclear war between East and West ebbed, Operation RYaN reporting continued until at least April 1989. But rather than accurately portraying the threat of nuclear war, these RYaN reports now serve as an invaluable resource for historians: monthly Soviet intelligence summaries (translated from Russian into German, and now into English) span from August 1986 to April 1989. The monthly summaries, serving a purpose likely never imagined by their drafters, allow us to see how Soviet intelligence witnessed and reported the peaceful conclusion of the Cold War.

The summaries include reports on the operational readiness of Pershing II, MX, and Trident missiles at specific bases and accounts of U.S. military activities in Nicaragua, Panama, Iran, and Iraq. They also include comprehensive reporting on NATO drills and maneuvers, including Able Archer 87, a later incarnation of the war game. Fortunately, this time the reporting was much more accurate, and the reports much more careful: NATO "simulated" the transition from peace to wartime; nuclear consultations were practiced only "in the context of the exercise."[65]

These monthly RYaN reports on the Cold War's peaceful resolution reflect the strangeness of the nuclear superpower rivalry itself. The absurd logic of the Cold War becomes evident when one reads about the NATO "elimination of intermediate and tactical nuclear missiles"—the missiles that were the primary cause of the War Scare—in a September 1987 report from KGB watchers incongruently entitled "On the Results of Intelligence Activities to Report Indicators for a Sudden Nuclear Missile Attack."[66]

Conclusion: "Why Is the World So Dangerous?"

ON NOVEMBER 30, 1983, A MEMORANDUM entitled "Why Is the World So Dangerous?" circulated among intelligence principals in the Reagan administration.[1] In it, Herbert Meyer, the missive's author and the vice chairman of the National Intelligence Council, argued that the Soviet Union's collapse was imminent and urged the United States to stay its foreign policy course. He conceded the "worrisome enough," but in his estimation low, possibility that the Soviets "could decide to go for it" and possibly even launch "a conventional or nuclear bolt-from-the-blue first strike on Western Europe or perhaps on the US." But the memorandum concluded that the danger of the current moment arose from the fact that the Soviet Union was "running out of time" and on a "shattering descent into history." It did not mention any U.S. contribution to the danger. Had, however, the principals honestly answered the question "why is the world so dangerous" in 1983, they would have acknowledged that the dangers posed by the War Scare were due, in part, to U.S. policies.

Answering honestly, they would have admitted that the world was so dangerous in 1983 because of the continued breakneck acceleration of the Cold War nuclear arms race between the United States and the Soviet Union. Despite mutually facing the brink of nuclear war during the Cuban Missile Crisis twenty-one years earlier, both countries eagerly churned out world-obliterating quantities—an estimated 58,958 warheads[2]—and destabilizing new designs—including MIRV-capped SS-20s and decapitating Pershing IIs and Gryphons—of nuclear weapons. As a result of this buildup, at the time of Able Archer 83 the Soviet Union and United States threatened each other with the largest, most destructive, and quickest-striking nuclear arsenal in the history of the world.

American intelligence agencies also bore responsibility for this danger because they failed to believe the obvious: that some Soviet leaders feared a Western nuclear strike was a genuine possibility. Downgrading real Soviet fear led the Reagan administration to continue its belligerent posture, which only increased the risk that an alarmed, desperate Soviet Union would lash out against the West. American intelligence believed there was virtually no chance of nuclear war and refused to conceive that its adversary could think otherwise. The U.S. intelligence community's erroneous assumption—"that since we know the U.S. is not going to start World War III, the next leaders of the Kremlin will also believe that"—invited nuclear disaster.[3] The United States' lack of formal and informal contacts with the Soviets, its introduction of newer balance-shifting nuclear weapons and defense systems, and its frequent rhetorical pledges to destroy communism heightened Soviet fears of a U.S. nuclear attack, pushing the world closer to the brink of nuclear Armageddon.

So in the dangerous year of 1983, exactly how close did the world come to nuclear war during the War Scare? The answer remains elusive, though perhaps a comparison to the risk of nuclear war present during the Cuban Missile Crisis in 1962 can give perspective. We now know that during the Cuban Missile Crisis the United States increased its readiness level to DEFCON 2, just short of full readiness for nuclear war. Sixty-six bombers were flying on continuous airborne alert, 912 bombers were on fifteen-minute ground alert, 182 intercontinental ballistic missiles and 112 submarine launched Polaris missiles were ready to fire. In total, nearly three thousand U.S. nuclear weapons were prepared for imminent launch.[4] While the Soviet Union placed its strategic forces on an "extraordinarily high state of alert," its "offensive forces avoided assuming the highest readiness stage, as if to insure that Kennedy understood that the USSR would not launch first."[5]

The precise state of alert of the Soviet nuclear forces during Able Archer 83 is less well known, though certainly stunning. Multiple high-level Soviet officers have confirmed in interviews that Soviet nuclear missile forces were placed on "raised combat alert" during the War Scare. At least one account claimed that the alert reached the highest levels of the Soviet military and that Marshal Nikolai Orgakov, chief of the General Staff, monitored events from a bunker outside of Moscow. During Able Archer 83, U.S. intelligence agencies reported that the Warsaw Pact suspended all flights other than those collecting intelligence in order to have as many planes as possible for combat. Forward deployed, nuclear-capable aircraft in Poland and East Germany were placed on alert along with other nuclear strike forces. Nuclear weapons were also transported from their storage sites to their delivery vehicles.

These nuclear preparations increased the likelihood of nuclear war through miscalculation to an unacceptable degree during both the Cuban Missile Crisis and the 1983 War Scare. In his seminal history of the Cuban Missile Crisis, Michael Dobbs wrote that the greatest causes of danger were "chance events, such as an airplane going astray, the misidentification of a missile, or a soldier losing his temper. Statesmen try to bend the chaotic forces of history to their will, with varying degrees of success. The likelihood of an unpredictable event occurring that can change the course of history is always greater at times of war and crisis, when everything is in flux."[6]

At the height of the 1962 crisis, there were many uncontrollable events that could have spiraled to disaster. On Black Saturday, October 27, Soviet air defense in Cuba shot down an American U-2 reconnaissance jet without General Secretary Khrushchev's authorization; minutes later another U-2 flew off course and breached Soviet airspace for more than an hour and was nearly intercepted, unbeknownst to President Kennedy. That evening, three U.S. Navy destroyers encircled the Soviet submarine *B-59* and attempted to force it to the surface by dropping depth charge explosives. The captain of the submarine was so distraught, he gave the order to arm a nuclear torpedo to attack the U.S. Navy destroyers.[7]

As Dobbs wrote, these unpredictable events in such circumstances created a situation where "the real danger no longer arose from a clash of wills between Kennedy and Khrushchev, but over whether the two of them jointly could gain control of the war machine they themselves had unleashed. . . . The crisis had gained a momentum of its own."[8]

These uncertain and unstable conditions were present again in 1983. There was a genuine risk that the Soviet leadership could have believed false RYaN reports of a Western nuclear strike and preempted it, leading to general nuclear war. This risk was what General Secretary Andropov feared when he warned Averell Harriman that the superpowers were approaching "the dangerous 'red line'" of nuclear war through "miscalculation."[9] The misidentification of dummy nuclear warheads, a "slip of the tongue" about nuclear strikes over open radio, an overreaction to massive troop movements, or a mistaken belief in reports that simulated DEFCON escalation to general alert and nuclear war all could have turned Able Archer 83 into a catastrophe.

Of course, chance events did not spin out of control during Able Archer 83. One key reason for this is likely the instinctual decision made by Lieutenant General Leonard Perroots, the officer in charge of Able Archer 83. Perroots monitored the Soviet air force's nuclear escalation and was alarmed by it, but he chose not to respond in kind. Perroots or a different officer could have very easily decided to follow standard procedure and escalate U.S. forces. After being informed that an American U-2 had blundered into Soviet airspace during the Cuban Missile

Crisis, further inflaming the risk of nuclear war, Kennedy—a former naval officer himself—vented, "There's always some sonofabitch that doesn't get the word."[10] During Able Archer 83, it was the "sonofabitch that didn't get the word" that acted on his gut to deescalate, rather than escalate, the nuclear tension and likely ended the "last paroxysm"[11] of the Cold War.

The study of the previously secret history of the 1983 War Scare forces the reevaluation of one of the core claims of Cold War historiography: that the Cold War slowly wound down after the Cuban Missile Crisis. Actually, the danger of nuclear confrontation remained constant and at times—including during Able Archer 83—escalated.

The world was so dangerous in 1983 because the leaders of both superpowers allowed it to be so. Despite some empty words on both sides, both Reagan and Andropov acquiesced to the status quo of the Era of Renewed Confrontation and operated as if governing a world a hair trigger away from nuclear war was "the new normal." To return to Reagan's analogy, the two spiders were in the bottle, preparing to fight and cultivating their venom, rather than attempting to escape through the open lid.[12]

The fact that an unacceptably high risk of nuclear war continued to exist during Able Archer 83—twenty-one years after the Cuban Missile Crisis—undermines the theory of nuclear deterrence and the idea that because World War III was avoided, the Cold War was actually the "long peace."[13] As both sides continued to increase the lethality of nuclear weapons, their own vulnerability increased. In 1983, Soviet and American leaders had just a *window of minutes* to decide whether to launch a preemptive nuclear strike and possibly survive a nuclear attack. Despite the protestations of advocates of so-called nuclear learning and treatises explaining how nuclear "game theories" ameliorated the risk of actual war, both of the superpowers became more unsafe as the Cold War progressed. While the United States and the Soviet Union maintained relative nuclear parity, each lacked nuclear security. The explanation to this nuclear paradox is simple: theories don't shape the course of human events; people do.

And so, while Andropov and Reagan deserve blame for their roles in causing the 1983 War Scare, they also deserve credit for avoiding war, and ultimately ending the Cold War. General Secretary Andropov once quipped to his ambassador Anatoly Dobrynin: "I am unlucky to get exactly this American president to deal with. Just my bad luck."[14] After Andropov's death and the Chernenko interregnum, the new general secretary, Mikhail Gorbachev, engaged with a seemingly new American president. Reagan was changed by the War Scare and ready for rapprochement. The president, in tandem with Gorbachev, a Soviet leader he "could do business with," eliminated the entire class of intermediate range nuclear weapons, including Pershing IIs, Gryphons, and SS-20s. Next, the two negotiated on the Strategic Arms

Reduction Treaty (START I), signed by Gorbachev and George H.W. Bush, which reduced the nuclear warheads and intercontinental ballistic missiles held by each side to 6,000 and 1,600, respectively. The mutual trust generated by these nuclear reductions was key to helping the two leaders eventually attain the peaceful end of the Cold War. The 1983 War Scare served as the fulcrum that pivoted U.S.-Soviet relations from the worst days of the Cold War to their best cooperation since World War II.

Within a year of becoming the president of Russia, Vladimir Putin dedicated a plaque to Yuri Andropov at Lubyanka, the headquarters of Russia's state security service and the former home of the KGB. Putin, a former KGB officer, lauded his old boss as an "outstanding political figure." He has also overseen the deterioration of relations between Russia and the United States.[15] In the twenty-first century, Russia and the United States have backed opposite sides of the wars in Iraq, Syria, Georgia, and Ukraine. In 2015 a Russian Buk surface-to-air missile shot down a passenger jet flying from Amsterdam to Kuala Lumpur, killing all 298 aboard; Cold Warriors were quick to evoke the KAL 007 tragedy. The recent provocative "buzzing" of American destroyers in the Baltic Sea by Russian fighter jets is reminiscent of American PSYOPs against Soviet forces in the early 1980s. Even Russian prime minister Dmitri Medvedev has warned that we may have "slid back to a new Cold War."[16]

But despite today's increased tensions, the efforts of Reagan and his Soviet counterparts continue to pay dividends. The world is markedly safer from the risk of nuclear war than it was during the "old" Cold War, including in 1983. Today, there is no "fear of war [that] seemed to affect the elite as well as the man on the street" in Russia.[17] Notwithstanding some legitimate concerns over compliance,[18] Reagan and Gorbachev's 1987 INF treaty has proven a strategic success as there are no longer any decapitating nuclear weapons in Europe. Even amid the United States' and Russia's regional power struggles, the New START treaty was signed in 2010, limiting each side's deployed nuclear warheads to 1,550 and intercontinental ballistic missiles to 700. Reagan's 1984 State of the Union pronouncement that a "nuclear war cannot be won and must never be fought" remains the entrenched doctrine of both superpowers.[19] Despite the many simmering geopolitical conflicts between the United States and Russia, the two countries are not threatened by the risk of nuclear war by miscalculation.[20]

The best way to ensure that the danger of nuclear war continues to decrease is to not hide it. Andropov and Reagan relied upon classified information unavailable to the public to realize the untenable nature of the nuclear arms race in the early 1980s. It is difficult to justify the initial concealment of how potentially lethal Able Archer 83 was, much less now, thirty-three years after the fact. Finally, after many long Freedom of Information Act battles fought by the National Security Archive, most—but not all—of the U.S. documents have been declassified and other countries' are trickling out to the public. The continued study of the 1983 War Scare will help to avert current and future nuclear standoffs, reduce the probability of nuclear war through miscalculation, and help battle against the dangerous ideas held by some of the "keepers of the keys." As one Soviet analyst on the General Staff explained:

> Among politicians as well as the military, there were a lot of crazy people who would not consider the consequences of a nuclear strike. They just wanted to respond to a certain action without dealing with the "cause and effect" problems. They were not seeking any reasonable explanations, but used one selective response to whatever an option was. I know many military people who look like normal people, but it was difficult to explain to them that waging nuclear war was not feasible. We had a lot of arguments in this respect. Unfortunately, as far as I know, there are a lot of stupid people both in NATO and our country.[21]

Nuclear secrecy should not be an accomplice to nuclear "stupidity."

The Soviet SS-20s and American Pershing IIs and Gryphons have been removed and retired, the Cold War has ended, and the Soviet Union no longer exists. Thirty years later, a fuller picture of the dangers of Able Archer 83 has finally emerged, and the lesson is soberingly clear: throughout the Cold War, "one misstep could trigger a great war."[22]

ACKNOWLEDGMENTS AND NOTES ON SOURCES

MOST CURRENT HISTORIES OF RONALD REAGAN, the Cold War, or the nuclear arms race now include mention of Able Archer 83 and the 1983 War Scare. But few have promulgated new evidence. If readers follow the footnotes, they will find that most treatments of the War Scare are based primarily upon Oleg Gordievsky and Christopher Andrew's initial account in *KGB: The Inside Story*, Benjamin Fischer's "A Cold War Conundrum" from the CIA's *Studies in Intelligence*, and, most recently, David Hoffman's *The Dead Hand*.

The goals of this book are to further the study of the 1983 War Scare by showcasing declassified primary sources—long secret and now public—and to use these documents to craft a precise, accurate, and readable narrative of events surrounding Able Archer 83. This account establishes what we now know, and indicates what we must further study.

Like all histories, this one was written on top of "the shoulders of giants" who have previously chronicled the era. Perhaps the most important giant is the late *Washington Post* journalist Don Oberdorfer. His 1998 book *From the Cold War to a New Era: The United States and the Soviet Union, 1983–1991* included a key footnote that tipped the public off to the existence of the President's Foreign Intelligence Advisory Board's comprehensive review of the War Scare. The best account of U.S.-Soviet relations during the post-détente era remains Raymond Garthoff's *The Great Transition: American-Soviet Relations and the End of the Cold War.* Beth Fischer first argued that the War Scare altered President Reagan and his policies in *The Reagan Reversal: Foreign Policy and the End of the Cold War.* In his biographical sketch of Reagan in *The*

Rebellion of Ronald Reagan: A History of the End of the Cold War, James Mann detailed how the president's reaction to Able Archer 83 impacted Reagan's turn from confrontation to cooperation. *The Triumph of Improvisation: Gorbachev's Adaptability, Reagan's Engagement, and the End of the Cold War* by James Graham Wilson uses the newest available evidence to place the War Scare in the context of the American and Soviet bureaucratic battles occurring at the Cold War's end. Wilson continues to heroically churn out documents related to the Era of Renewed Confrontation: he edits the Department of State's Foreign Relations of the United States series, including its recent volume on U.S.-Soviet relations from January 1981 to January 1983. Former CIA analyst Peter Vincent Pry's book *War Scare: Russia and America on the Nuclear Brink* produced a key account from the perspective of an intelligence analyst. In "The War Scare of 1983," my colleague John Prados has woven a captivating narrative of Able Archer 83 and its effect on the Reagan cabinet. James Hershberg, in "Reconsidering the Nuclear Arms Race: The Past as Prelude?" analyzed Operation RYaN and Able Archer 83 as part of his survey of nuclear history, concluding: "Historians who have drawn comforting lessons from the outcome of nuclear crises over the past half-century have overlooked or downplayed some ominous trends."[1]

President Reagan's speeches, memoirs, and diary present his changing opinions of the Soviet Union and the effect that Able Archer 83 had upon him. The public record of Reagan's speeches can be found in *Public Papers of the Presidents: Ronald Reagan, 1981–1989.* Perhaps most illuminating is Reagan's own description of the evolution of his policy, which can be found within the day-by-day accounts of his diaries and—with hindsight—in his autobiography, *An American Life.* Members of his administration have also published memoirs that comment on Able Archer 83 and its aftermath. These include Secretary of State Alexander Haig's *Caveat: Realism, Reagan and Foreign Policy,* his successor George Shultz's *Turmoil and Triumph,* Secretary of Defense Caspar Weinberger's *Fighting for Peace,* Soviet Advisor Jack Matlock's *Reagan and Gorbachev,* and National Security Advisor Robert McFarlane's *Special Trust.*

The view from the Soviet side is far more fragmentary. The best sources include the memoirs written by Soviet officials, including Ambassador to the United States Anatoly Dobrynin's *In Confidence: Moscow's Ambassador to America's Six Cold War Presidents (1962–1986),* Minister of Foreign Affairs Andrei Gromyko's *Memories,* and American specialist Georgi Arbatov's *The System: An Insider's Life in Soviet Politics.* Historian Vladislav Zubok presents the best available survey of Soviet decision-making in *A Failed Empire: The Soviet Union in the Cold War from Stalin to Gorbachev.* Russian language sources include the semi-official haliography of Soviet and Russian Intelligence Services, *Vneshnaya razvedka Rossii* (The Foreign Intelligence Service of Russia); *Glazami marshala i diplomata: kriticheskii vzgliad na vneshniuiu politiku SSSR do i posle 1985 goda* (With the eyes of a marshal and diplomat: A critical look at the international politics of the USSR through 1985), an analysis by Marshal Sergei Akhromeyev and foreign affairs specialist Georgy Kornienko; and Arbatov's *Delo: Iastreby i Golubi Kholodnoi Voiny* (Politics: Hawks and doves of the Cold War). Roy A. Medvedev's biography of Andropov, *Neizvestnii Andropov* (The unknown Andropov) chronicles the broader dynamics of the 1983 War Scare.

Both contemporary and modern films have contributed to the study of the War Scare. The films *WarGames* and *The Day After*—both viewed by President Reagan—documented the overriding fear held by the general public about the risk of nuclear war with the Soviet Union in 1983. *Threads*, released in September 1984 by the BBC, remains the most realistic portrayal of what the aftermath of a nuclear war would be. Today, television series including *Deutschland 83* and *The Americans* ensure that the nuclear danger of the late Cold War is not forgotten.

This history could not have been written without the diligent work of America's archivists and declassifiers. The bulk of the documents used and presented in this book were obtained from the holdings of the Ronald Reagan and George H.W. Bush Presidential Libraries, the U.S. National Archives and Records Administration, the Library of Congress, and Freedom of Information Act and Mandatory Declassification Review requests to the declassified document repositories of the Department of State, the Office of the Secretary of Defense, the Joint Staff, the U.S. Air Force, the Defense Intelligence Agency, and the Central Intelligence Agency. Special thanks are due to Kelly Barton and Whitney Ross at the Ronald Reagan Presidential Libary, Robert Holzweiss and Douglas Campbell at the George H.W. Bush Presidential Library, and to John Fitzpatrick, William Carpenter, Neena Sachdeva, and the rest of the Interagency Security Classification Appeals Panel at the National Archives who finally broke the twelve-year bureaucratic logjam and declassified the PFIAB's seminal report on the 1983 War Scare.

This book also relies upon interviews with Reagan administration officials. I am grateful I was able to conduct interviews with Reagan's national security advisor Robert McFarlane and his ambassador to NATO David Abshire. I am also indebted to a number of participants who shared their "on the ground" knowledge of Able Archer 83. I gleaned a wealth of information from interviews conducted by journalist and author Don Oberdorfer with key Soviet and American officials. These interviews were once "on background," but are now available to the public at Princeton University's Mudd Manuscript Library. Another invaluable source is the transcripts of the interviews conducted for Flashback Television's "Soviet War Scare 1983," copies of which were kindly provided to the National Security Archive by Taylor Downing.

Because the history of the Cold War is an international history, it was imperative to find Russian, Czech, Bulgarian, and German documents to show how the War Scare was viewed from behind the Iron Curtain. Though the documentary record from the Warsaw Pact is sparser than from the West, progress is being made. Key contributions can be found in Mark Kramer's "The Able Archer 83 Non-Crisis: Did Soviet Leaders Really Fear an Imminent Nuclear Attack in 1983?" and Vojtech Mastny's "How Able Was 'Able Archer'?: Nuclear Trigger and Intelligence in Perspective." I remain indebted to the Cold War International History Project, where I was fortunate enough to land my first Washington, D.C., internship, annotating and cataloguing, among other things, Averell Harriman's conversations with Stalin. Today, thanks go to its director Christian Ostermann, Evan Pikulski, Douglas Selvage, and Bernd Schaefer for continuing to supply trove after trove of formerly forbidden Cold War sources, including key Stasi, Bulgarian, and Czechoslovakian documentation on Operation RYaN. Many thanks to Ivan Pavlov, Jen Gaspar, and the fearless information fighters at the Freedom of Information Foundation for providing me with an incredible base to conduct a summer of research while in Russia.

My research was immeasurably helped by a series of forums that I was fortunate enough to attend along with the best minds in the field. The two-week Nuclear Boot Camp hosted by the Nuclear Proliferation International History Project at a former NATO base in Allumiere, Italy, and instructed by Leopoldo Nuti, Christian Ostermann, David Holloway, Joseph Pilat, and Martin Sherwin was an intellectual bliss. I benefited immensely by discussing the War Scare on a panel with Mark Kramer hosted in Blaubeuren, Germany, by Georg Schild, Martin Deuerlein, and Roman Krawielicki of the Universität Tübingen. The colloquium "1983: The Most Dangerous Year of the Cold War?" convened by Bernd Greiner and Klaas Voss on behalf of the Hamburg Institute for Social Research and the Einstein Forum Potsdam presented another tremendous opportunity to discuss the War Scare with the foremost experts. Each year, I look forward to teaching and learning the most effective archival techniques at The Summer Institute on Conducting Archival Research. Thank you to the Brenn Foundation for providing a wonderful refuge at Musgrove that allowed me the solitude to finally put all of the ideas I had gleaned from these remarkable individuals together.

There is no better place for a historian to work than at the National Security Archive in Washington, D.C. I am grateful every day for the leadership of our Executive Director Tom Blanton and Deputy Director Malcolm Byrne. Thanks to all my fellow archivistas, especially the old hands Bill Burr, John Prados, Svetlana Savranskaya, and Peter Kornbluh, for showing me the ropes and demonstrating how to win the release of history. Thanks to Lisa Thompson for compiling the index. Thanks to all my tenacious research assistants: Dan Jenkins, Seth Maddox, Bernie Horowitz, Tamar Gurchiani, Diana Bancheva, Jacob Lorber, Elena Burger, Michael Barclay, Clay Katsky, and Soraya Manar Haddad. Thanks to Sue Bechtel, Mary Curry, Veronica Franklin, Rinat Bikineyev, and Steve Paschke for keeping the Archive running.

Just next door to the Archive is George Washington University and its venerated Cold War History program. Many thanks to my graduate thesis advisor James Hershberg and to my readers Hope Harrison and Garret Martin for steering me down the correct path. Going further back, thanks to my Lewis and Clark College history and Russian professors and advisors Matthew Levinger, Tatiana Osipovich, and Donna Seifer for introducing me over a decade ago to the mystery that was the Able Archer 83 War Scare.

Thanks to Marc Ambinder for the stimulating correspondence and work we've shared on the War Scare; hopefully more to come!

Thanks to everyone at The New Press, including executive director Diane Wachtell, senior managing editor Maury Botton, managing editor Emily Albarillo, copy editor Angus Johnston, marketing manager Maredith Sheridan, and especially my absolutely ace editor Carl Bromley. Thanks to Tom Blanton, Svetlana Savranskaya, and Bill Burr for providing documents and graciously reading, commenting on, and immeasurably improving my early drafts. Thanks to Lauren Harper and her eagle eye for her magnificent edits to all my work for the past years. And thanks to Kyla Sommers for her comments, as well as her help and support to finally get this thing done. Of course, all errors are mine alone.

Let's keep fighting to get the documents out of the vaults!

CIA image displaying Warsaw Pact airbases during peacetime from National Intelligence Estimate, "Warsaw Pact Nonnuclear Threat to NATO Airbases in Central Europe," October 25, 1985, U.S. National Archives.

President Reagan and General Secretary Andropov were named "men of the year" in 1983 by *Time* magazine. The Central Intelligence Agency included an image of this cover in its history of the 1983 War Scare.

MEETING WITH AMBASSADOR HARTMAN

-- GLAD WE HAVE CHANCE TO MEET WHILE YOU ARE IN TOWN. WHY DO YOU THINK RUSSIANS STILL SEEM TO BE GIVING US COLD SHOULDER?

-- WHAT SORT OF TACTICS SHOULD WE BE FOLLOWING OVER COMING MONTHS? HAVE THEY REALLY DECIDED FINALLY THEY WILL NOT DEAL THIS YEAR, AS SOME ARE SAYING?

-- DO YOU THINK SOVIET LEADERS REALLY FEAR US, OR IS ALL THE HUFFING AND PUFFING JUST PART OF THEIR PROPAGANDA?

One of Ronald Reagan's two index cards containing questions for his March 28, 1984, meeting with Ambassador Hartman.

DOCID: 3471506

Approved for Release by NSA on 12-17-2008, FOIA Case # 5674[illegible]

Able Archer 83

From Wikipedia, the free encyclopedia

Able Archer 83 was a ten-day NATO exercise starting on November 2, 1983 that spanned the continent of Europe and simulated a coordinated nuclear release.[1] It incorporated a new, unique format of coded communication, radio silences, participation by heads of state, and a simulated DEFCON 1 nuclear alert. The realistic nature of the exercise, coupled with deteriorating relations between the United States and the Soviet Union and the anticipated arrival of Pershing II nuclear missiles in Europe, led some in the USSR to believe that Able Archer 83 was a genuine nuclear first strike.[1][2][3][4] In response, the Soviets readied their nuclear forces and placed air units in East Germany and Poland on alert.[5][6] This relatively obscure incident is considered by many historians to be the closest the world has come to nuclear war since the Cuban Missile Crisis of 1962.[7] The threat of nuclear war abruptly ended with the conclusion of the Able Archer 83 exercise on November 11, which, coincidentally, was also Armistice Day (alternatively called

The National Security Agency responded to one 2008 FOIA request on the War Scare by reviewing, approving for release, stamping, and mailing a printout of a Wikipedia article. It also denied eighty-one other relevant documents.

(U) Yuri Andropov

A photo of Soviet leader Yuri Andropov from the National Security Agency's *American Cryptology During the Cold War, 1945–1989, Book IV: Cryptologic Rebirth, 1981–1989.*

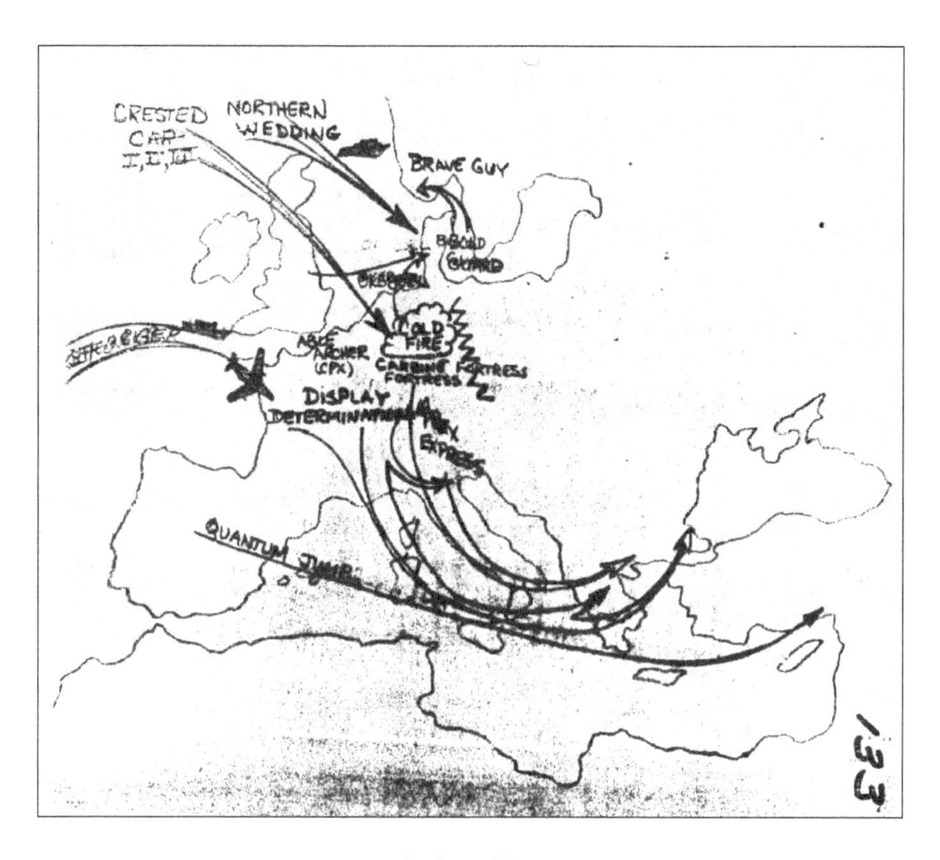

Above: A slide from a 1983 briefing shows the Europe-wide "footprint" of the Autumn Forge war games.
Left: A soldier takes a rest break during Autumn Forge 83—in a gas mask. From *Airman*.

(U) Briefing President Reagan. Clockwise: President Reagan, George Shultz, Robert McFarlane, William Casey, and Caspar Weinberger.

From the National Security Agency's *American Cryptology During the Cold War, 1945–1989, Book IV: Cryptologic Rebirth, 1981–1989.*

President Reagan meets Oleg Gordievsky on July 21, 1987. From the Ronald Reagan Presidential Library.

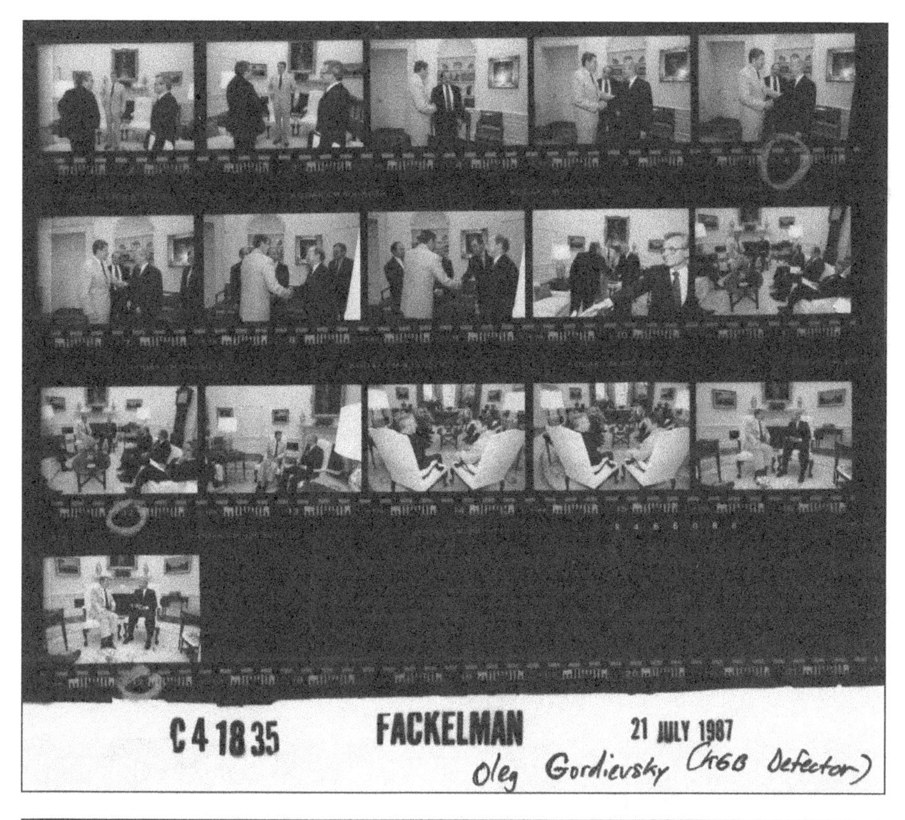

Top: The negatives of the photographs from Reagan and Gordievsky's meeting. Note that the photograph identifies Gordievsky as "KGB defector." **Above:** Artist's rendition of a mobile SS-20 launch in the field. According to the National Security Agency's internal history, the NSA's overhead photography was only able to spot SS-20s during "an occasional lucky accident." U.S. National Archives.

Artist's rendition of SS-20s in launch position. U.S. National Archives.

A Pershing II is fired at White Sands Missile Test Range on November 19, 1982. U.S. National Archives.

Soviet inspectors and their American escorts inspect several dismantled Pershing II missiles that were destroyed in accordance with the Intermediate-Range Nuclear Forces Treaty. January 14, 1989. U.S. National Archives.

Plaque commemorating Yuri Andropov at Lubyanka, the headquarters of Russian State Security, dedicated by Vladimir Putin. Courtesy Iain Kimm.

Document 1: President's Foreign Intelligence Advisory Board Report, "The Soviet 'War Scare,'" February 15, 1990, Top Secret, UMBRA GAMMA WNINTEL NOFORN NOCONTRACT ORCON

Source: Interagency Security Classification Appeals Panel release; document held at George H.W. Bush Presidential Library

The declassified retrospective President's Foreign Intelligence Advisory Board (PFIAB) report on the 1983 War Scare—the only study written with access to all U.S. intelligence files on U.S./NATO actions and the Soviet response—provides the most comprehensive account of the 1983 War Scare. It concludes that the danger of the 1983 War Scare was real, and the United States "may have inadvertently placed our relations with the Soviet Union on a hair trigger" during the 1983 NATO nuclear release exercise, Able Archer 83.

The report describes how the "Soviets had concern that the West might decide to attack the USSR without warning during a time of vulnerability . . . thus compelling the Soviets to consider a preemptive strike at the first sign of U.S. preparations for a nuclear strike." To counter this strike (which the West never intended to launch), Soviet leader Yuri Andropov initiated Operation RYaN, the Soviet human intelligence effort to detect and preempt a Western "surprise nuclear missile attack."

Fortunately "the military officers in charge of the Able Archer exercise minimized this risk by doing nothing in the face of evidence that parts of the Soviet armed forces were moving to an unusual level of alert." The decision not to elevate the alert of Western military assets in response was made by Lieutenant General Leonard Perroots while serving as assistant chief of staff for intelligence, U.S. Air Forces Europe. The report describes Perroots's decision as "fortuitous, if ill-informed" and states that "these officers acted correctly out of instinct, not informed guidance, for in the years leading up to Able Archer they had received no guidance as to the possible significance of apparent changes in Soviet military and political thinking."

Perroots's instinctual decision not to respond to the Soviet escalation in kind—an act until now unknown—may have been what ended the "last paroxysm of the Cold War," the 1983 War Scare.

According to the PFIAB, after learning of the War Scare, President Reagan "expressed surprise" and "described the events as 'really scary.'"

The ninety-four-page PFIAB report's striking conclusion—based on hundreds of documents and more than seventy-five interviews with American and British officials—is this: "There is little doubt in our minds that the Soviets were genuinely worried by Able Archer . . . it appears that at least some Soviet forces were preparing to preempt or counterattack a NATO strike launched under cover of Able Archer" and that "the President was given assessments of Soviet attitudes and actions that understated the risks to the United States." The U.S. intelligence community's erroneous reporting made the "especially grave error to assume that since we know the U.S. is not going to start World War III, the next leaders of the Kremlin will also believe that."

"The Board is deeply disturbed by the U.S. handling of the war scare, both at the time and since. In the early stages of the war scare period, when evidence was thin, little effort was made to examine the various possible Soviet motivations behind some very anomalous events. . . . When written, the 1984 SNIE's [assessments] were overconfident."

The existence of this PFIAB report was first revealed by Don Oberdorfer in his book *The Turn: From the Cold War to a New Era.* The National Security Archive fought twelve years for the declassification of this report before winning its release in October 2015.

~~TOP SECRET~~ UMBRA GAMMA
WNINTEL NOFORN NOCONTRACT ORCON

The Soviet "War Scare"

President's Foreign Intelligence Advisory Board

February 15, 1990

Classified by Multiple Sources
Declassify OADR

PFIAB Control # 1-90
Copy # 5

DECLASSIFIED IN PART
PER E.O. 13526
2012-0238-MR
SCS 10/14/15

WNINTEL NOFORN NOCONTRACT ORCON
~~TOP SECRET~~ UMBRA GAMMA

~~TOP SECRET~~ UMBRA GAMMA
WNINTEL NOFORN NOCONTRACT ORCON

Never, perhaps, in the postwar decades has the situation in the world been as explosive and, hence, more difficult and unfavorable as in the first half of the 1980's.

Mikhail Gorbachev
February 1986

WNINTEL NOFORN NOCONTRACT ORCON
~~TOP SECRET~~ UMBRA GAMMA

~~TOP SECRET~~ UMBRA GAMMA
WNINTEL NOFORN NOCONTRACT ORCON

CONTENTS

~~TOP SECRET~~ UMBRA GAMMA
WNINTEL NOFORN NOCONTRACT ORCON

This document is classified ~~TOP SECRET~~/UMBRA/GAMMA/WNINTEL/NOFORN/NOCONTRACT/ORCON in its entirety.

WNINTEL NOFORN NOCONTRACT ORCON
~~TOP SECRET~~ UMBRA GAMMA

Executive Summary

From the late 1970's to the mid-1980's, the military forces and intelligence services of the Soviet Union were redirected in ways that suggested that the Soviet leadership was seriously concerned about the possibility of a sudden strike launched by the United States and its NATO allies. These changes were accompanied by leadership statements -- some public, but many made in secret meetings -- arguing that the US was seeking strategic superiority in order to be able to launch a nuclear first strike. These actions and statements are often referred to as the period of the "war scare."

The changes in Soviet military and intelligence arrangements included: improvements of Warsaw Pact combat readiness (by recalling reservists, lengthening service times, increasing draft ages, and abolishing many draft deferments), an unprecedented emphasis on civil defense exercises, an end of military support for gathering the harvest (last seen prior to the 1968 Czech invasion), the forward deployment of unusual numbers of SPETSNAZ forces, increased readiness of Soviet ballistic missile submarines and forward deployed nuclear capable aircraft, massive military exercises that for the first time emphasized surviving and responding to a sudden enemy strike, a new agreement among Warsaw Pact countries that gave Soviet leaders authority in the event of an attack to unilaterally commit Pact forces, creation within the GRU of a new directorate to run networks of illegal agents abroad, an urgent KGB (and some satellite services') requirement that gave the highest priority the gathering of politico-military indicators of US/NATO preparations for a sudden nuclear attack, establishment of a special warning condition to alert Soviet forces that a surprise enemy strike using weapons of mass destruction was in progress, and the creation of a special KGB unit to manage a computer program (the VRYAN model) that would objectively measure the correlation of forces and warn when Soviet relative strength had declined to the point that a preemptive Soviet attack might be justified.

During the November 1983 NATO "Able Archer" nuclear release exercise, the Soviets implemented military and intelligence activities that previously were seen only during actual crises. These included: placing Soviet air forces in Germany and Poland on heightened alert, 3.3(b)(3); (b)(3)

3.3(b)(3); (b)(3)

The meaning of these events obviously was of crucial importance to American and NATO policymakers. If they were simply parts of a Soviet propaganda campaign designed to intimidate the US, deter it from deploying improved weapons, and arouse US domestic opposition to foreign policy initiatives, then they would not be of crucial significance. If they reflected an internal Soviet power struggle -- for example, a contest between conservatives and pragmatists, or an effort to avoid blame for Soviet economic failures by pointing to (exaggerated) military threats -- then they could not be ignored, but they would not imply a fundamental change in Soviet strategy. But if these events were expressions of a genuine belief on the part of Soviet leaders that the US was planning a nuclear first strike, causing the Soviet military to prepare for such an eventuality -- by, for example, readying itself for a preemptive strike of its own -- then the "war scare" was a cause for real concern.

During the past year, the President's Foreign Intelligence

Advisory Board has carefully reviewed the events of that period to learn what we (the U.S. intelligence community) knew, when we knew it, and how we interpreted it. The Board has read hundreds of documents, conducted more than 75 interviews with American and British officials, and studied the series of National Intelligence Estimates (NIE's) and other intelligence assessments that have attempted over the last six years to interpret the war scare data. Additionally, we have offered our own interpretation of the war scare events.

We believe that the Soviets perceived that the correlation of forces had turned against the USSR, that the US was seeking military superiority, and that the chances of the US launching a nuclear first strike -- perhaps under cover of a routine training exercise -- were growing. We also believe that the US intelligence community did not at the time, and for several years afterwards, attach sufficient weight to the possibility that the war scare was real. As a result, the President was given assessments of Soviet attitudes and actions that understated the risks to the United States. Moreover, these assessments did not lead us to reevaluate our own military and intelligence actions that might be perceived by the Soviets as signaling war preparations.

In two separate Special National Intelligence Estimates (SNIE's) in May and August of 1984, the intelligence community said: "We believe strongly that Soviet actions are not inspired by, and Soviet leaders do not perceive, a genuine danger of imminent conflict or confrontation with the United States." Soviet statements to the contrary were judged to be "propaganda."

The Board believes that the evidence then did not, and certainly does not now, support such categoric conclusions. Even without the benefit of subsequent reporting and looking at the 1984 analysis of then available information, the tone of the intelligence judgments was not adequate to the needs of the President.

~~TOP SECRET~~ UMBRA GAMMA
WNINTEL NOFORN NOCONTRACT ORCON

A strongly stated interpretation was defended by explaining away facts inconsistent with it and by failing to subject that interpretation to a comparative risk assessment. In time, analysts' views changed. In an annex to a February 1988 NIE, analysts declared: "During the late 1970's and early 1980's there were increasing Soviet concerns about the drift in superpower relations, which some in the Soviet leadership felt indicated an increased threat of war and increased likelihood of the use of nuclear weapons. These concerns were shaped in part by a Soviet perception that the correlation of forces was shifting against the Soviet Union and that the United States was taking steps to achieve military superiority." The Soviets' VRYAN program was evaluated as part of an effort to collect data and subject it to computer analysis in a way that would warn the USSR when the US had achieved decisive military superiority.

Reporting from a variety of [3.3(b)(1)] sources, including Oleg Gordiyevskiy (a senior KGB officer who once served as second in command in the London Residency and who has since defected to Great Britain), taken as a whole, strongly indicates that there was in fact a genuine belief among key members of the Soviet leadership that the United States had embarked on a program of achieving decisive military superiority that might prompt a sudden nuclear missile attack on the USSR.

Although some details of that belief became known only recently, there was at the time evidence -- from secret directives and speeches by Soviet authorities -- that a major change in Soviet political and strategic thinking had probably occurred. For example, we knew by 1984 at the latest that a Soviet general had interpreted President Carter's PD-59 as preparing US strategic forces for a preemptive strike, that the Head of the KGB's First Chief Directorate, General Kryuchkov had told key subordinates that the KGB must work to prevent the US from launching a surprise attack, that KGB and Czechoslovak intelligence Residencies had been

WNINTEL NOFORN NOCONTRACT ORCON
~~TOP SECRET~~ UMBRA GAMMA

tasked to gather information on US preparations for war, and that missile submarines had been placed on shortened readiness times.

Many of these facts were summarized in a memorandum from the National Intelligence Officer for Warning (NIO/W) to DCI William Casey in June 1984, a memo that Casey then forwarded to the President. 3.3(b)(1) 3.3(b)(1) Neither the NIO/W nor the altered the official position of the intelligence community as expressed in the May 1984 SNIE and as reasserted, in almost identical language, in the August 1984 SNIE.

Analysts will always have legitimate disagreements over the meaning of inevitably incomplete and uncertain intelligence reports. Moreover, part of the confidence that PFIAB has in its own assessment of the war scare derives from information not known at the time. Our purpose in presenting this report is not so much to criticize the conclusions of the 1984 SNIE's as to raise questions about the ways these estimates were made and subsequently reassessed.

In cases of great importance to the survival of our nation, and especially where there is important contradictory evidence, the Board believes that intelligence estimates must be cast in terms of alternative scenarios that are subjected to comparative risk assessments. This is the critical defect in the war scare episode. By "alternative scenarios," we mean a full statement of each major, possible interpretation of a set of intelligence indicators. In this case, these scenarios might have included the following:

1. Soviet leaders had not changed their strategic thinking but were attempting by means of propaganda and intelligence deceptions to slow the US military build-up, prevent the deployment of

new weapons, and isolate the US from its allies.

2. Soviet leaders may or may not have changed their strategic thinking, but a power struggle among Kremlin factions and the need to deflect blame for poor economic conditions made it useful to exaggerate the military intentions and capabilities of the US.

3. Soviet leaders had changed their strategic thinking and, in fact, believed that the US was attempting to gain decisive strategic superiority in order, possibly, to launch a nuclear first strike.

By "comparative risk assessment," we mean assigning two kinds of weights to each scenario: one that estimates the probability that the scenario is correct and another that assesses the risk to the United States if it wrongly rejects a scenario that is, in fact, correct.

In 1984, one might reasonably have given the highest probability of being correct to the first or second scenario (even though, as we argue in this report, we believe that would have been an error). But having done this, it would surely have been clear even then that if the third scenario was in fact correct and we acted as if it were wrong, the risks to the United States would have been very great -- greater than if we had rejected a correct first or second scenario. As it happened, the military officers in charge of the Able Archer exercise minimized this risk by doing nothing in the face of evidence that parts of the Soviet armed forces were moving to an unusual level of alert. But these officers acted correctly out of instinct, not informed guidance, for in the years leading up to Able Archer they had received no guidance as to the possible significance of apparent changes in Soviet military and political thinking.

By urging that some major estimates be based on a comparative assessment of fully developed alternative scenarios, we are not arguing for "competitive analyses" or greater use of dissenting opinions. An intelligence estimate is not the product of a governmental debating society in which institutional rivals try to outdo one another in their display of advocacy skills. We are arguing instead for adopting the view that since it is very hard to understand the present, much less predict the future, it is a mistake to act as if we can. On the most important issues, it is difficult if not impossible to say with confidence that we know what is happening or will happen. We can, however, say that there are a small number of possibilities, each of which has a (rough) probability and each of which presents to the policymaker likely risks and opportunities.

When analysts attempt to arrive at a single strong conclusion, they not only run the risk of being wrong, they run two additional and perhaps more worrisome risks. They are likely to underestimate the possibility of change (the safest prediction is always that tomorrow will be like today) and they are likely to rely on mirror-imaging (our adversaries think the way we do). In this era of unprecedented, breakneck change, the first error grows in importance. And since we cannot know what individuals will next hold power in the USSR or when, it is an especially grave error to assume that since we know the US is not going to start World War III, the next leaders of the Kremlin will also believe that -- and act on that belief.

In short, our criticism of the 1984 SNIE's, though in part substantive, is in larger part procedural. We do not think there is any simple organizational change that will correct that procedure. If strategic intelligence estimates are to give policymakers a better sense of risks and opportunities, it will only happen if policymakers insist that that is what they want and refuse to accept anything less.

~~TOP SECRET~~ UMBRA GAMMA
WNINTEL NOFORN NOCONTRACT ORCON

This review of the war scare period also suggests another lesson. It is quite clear to the Board that during the critical years when the Kremlin was reassessing US intentions, the US intelligence community did not react quickly to or think deeply about the early signs of that change. The war scare indicators began appearing in the early 1980's; the first estimate to address this was not written until 1984. At the time it was written, the US knew very little about Kremlin decisionmaking. [3.3(b)(1)] the SNIE authors wrote confidently about "Soviet leadership intentions."

We recommend that the National Security Council oversee a reassessment of the intelligence community's understanding of Soviet military and political decisionmaking, both in general terms and in light of the judgments made in the 1984 estimates. Our own leadership needs far better intelligence reporting on and assessments of the mindset of the Soviet leadership -- its ideological/political instincts and perceptions. As part of this reassessment, it should exploit the current opening in the Iron Curtain to interview past and present East Bloc and Soviet officials about the sources and consequences of the war scare in order to obtain a better understanding of the perceptions and inner conflicts of Soviet decisionmakers.

Finally, we suggest that the US review the way in which it manages military exercises, its own intelligence collection efforts, [3.3(b)(1)] [3.3(b)(1)] to insure that these are carried out in a way that is responsive to indications and warning for war.

In 1983 we may have inadvertently placed our relations with the Soviet Union on a hair trigger. Though the current thaw in US-Soviet relations suggests that neither side is likely in the near

WNINTEL NOFORN NOCONTRACT ORCON
~~TOP SECRET~~ UMBRA GAMMA

term to reach for that trigger, events are moving so fast that it would be unwise to assume that Soviet leaders will not in the future act, from misunderstanding or malevolence, in ways that puts the peace in jeopardy.

PART I US HANDLING OF THE "WAR SCARE": THE ESTIMATIVE PROCESS

INTRODUCTION

The Board has divided its presentation into two parts. The first (Part One) deals with a review of what the US (and the British) thought about the war scare both at the time and subsequently. It also summarizes some of the key characteristics of the estimative process and offers our conclusions for improvement. The second half (Part Two) summarizes the evidence that leads to the conclusion that the Soviet leadership genuinely developed a "war scare" in the early 1980's. We believe this to be a plausible version of events based upon new information as well as a reconsideration of evidence known then. Inevitably, there is some duplication between the two parts, but this is necessary in order to tell the story in an orderly way.

Part One, then, is a summation of what we knew, when we knew it, and how we interpreted it. It is not a competitive estimate. Rather than catalog the actual events in detail, we chose to summarize them and to focus instead on how the intelligence community reacted, as manifested in its analysis. Our conclusions mirror our profound dismay at what we believe to be the intelligence community's single largest failing -- the failure to provide policymakers with an adequate understanding of the risks and consequences associated with alternate scenarios involving uncertain events of grave import.

There were many other directions that we, given unlimited time, would have liked to embark. Intelligence issues that impacted upon our review of the war scare are identified in the

~~TOP SECRET~~ UMBRA GAMMA
WNINTEL NOFORN NOCONTRACT ORCON

final section of Part One. We regret that these important issues received short shrift; we encourage a complete review of them so that US indications and warning might be improved as we enter into the evermore complex, polycentric, and uncertain 1990's.

EARLY PERCEPTIONS OF THE SOVIET "WAR SCARE"

As the Carter years wound to a close, America's bilateral relationship with the USSR was on the downswing from the earlier detente. The Soviet Union's invasion of Afghanistan brought bitter NATO condemnation, and SALT II languished unratified. As the new Republican Administration took up the reins, President Reagan announced in his State of the Union speech a major peacetime military buildup. By May 1981, the "era of self-doubt," personified by the failed Iran hostage rescue attempt, had ended. United States foreign policy took on a new assertiveness: President Reagan declared that arms control treaties were no substitute for military preparedness and characterized the Soviet Union as an "evil force," the antithesis of the US. Soviet meddling in Afghanistan, Poland, Central America, and elsewhere increasingly proved a constant irritant to the new Administration, and seemed only to reinforce its "get tough" posture.

Recriminations flew between Moscow and Washington, and relations continued to slide. As the Administration settled into its first term, an intense "war scare" theme began to emerge in the Soviet media and in private fora, accompanied by anomalous and often provocative USSR behavior.

At first, such activity was easily dismissed as predictable Soviet responses to US efforts to deploy INF missiles in Europe in order to counter Soviet SS-20's and to modernize its strategic and conventional forces. United States officials understandably were suspicious of Soviet motivations as Washington struggled to gain public support in Western Europe and in the US for these force

WNINTEL NOFORN NOCONTRACT ORCON
~~TOP SECRET~~ UMBRA GAMMA

~~TOP SECRET~~ UMBRA GAMMA
WNINTEL NOFORN NOCONTRACT ORCON

improvements.[1]

In 1983, Soviet rhetoric had sharpened. Moscow had accused President Reagan and his advisors of "madness," "extremism," and "criminality" in the conduct of relations with the USSR. The United States was portrayed as a nation singularly pursuing a first-strike nuclear capability as a prelude to eradicating communism. Westerners, including some well-known experts on the Soviet Union, reported alarming conversations with Soviet citizens and officials that indicated a large portion of the Soviet population believed nuclear war was dangerously close. As diplomatic relations ebbed to near a postwar low, US analysts attributed Soviet anxieties and belligerence to a number of factors: initiation of INF deployments; a strong US posture in the START talks; US action in Grenada; deployment of Marines in Lebanon; US aid to insurgencies against Soviet client regimes; the Reagan Administration's perceived political "exploitation" of the KAL shootdown; and the Administration's perceived unwillingness to acknowledge the legitimacy of the Soviet regime or to treat the Kremlin with the "superpower" deference it desired.[2]

Moreover, US analysts concluded that certain developments could have heightened Moscow's uncertainties about its long-term geostrategic position:

o A possible adverse shift in the overall strategic balance, precipitated by resolute US moves to significantly bolster its strategic posture as well as its conventional capabilities.

---

[1]US officials detected a vigorous Soviet "active measures" campaign intended to thwart US strategic objectives.

[2]Grey Hodnett's memorandum of Dec. 22, 1983, entitled "Soviet Thinking on the Possibility of Armed Confrontation with the United States," Foreign Policy Issues Branch, Policy Analysis Division, Office of Soviet Analysis, Central Intelligence Agency.

~~TOP SECRET~~ UMBRA GAMMA
WNINTEL NOFORN NOCONTRACT ORCON

o The perceived lower priority accorded by the Reagan Administration to arms control negotiations, as "evidenced" by its unwillingness to accommodate Soviet interests and its apparent intention to proceed with weapons programs Moscow may have thought were on hold.

o The end of the "Vietnam syndrome" and readiness of Washington to use force once again in the Third World, either by supporting insurgencies against Soviet client regimes, as in Nicaragua, or acting directly, as in Lebanon and Grenada.[3]

Although US analysts aptly identified signs of emotional and paranoid Soviet behavior and offered an analysis of the potential causes, they reasoned that Moscow was fundamentally concerned not about any hypothetical near-term US nuclear attack, but about possible shifts in the strategic balance five-to-ten years hence. It was easy to distrust the USSR, they reasoned, because Soviet leaders had many plausible motives for trying to cleverly manipulate Western perceptions:

o To foster the "peace movement" in Western Europe so as to derail INF deployments and encourage neutrality within NATO.

o To portray President Reagan as an incompetent warmonger so as to deepen cleavages among nations in the West.

o To increase public pressure in the United States for providing a more conciliatory posture toward the USSR via lower defense spending, arms control concessions, and less "interventionist" policies.

Analysts also estimated that, for the Soviets, the Reagan Administration was the "least loved of any US Administration since

[3]Ibid.

WNINTEL NOFORN NOCONTRACT ORCON
~~TOP SECRET~~ UMBRA GAMMA

that of President Truman." It would be just like them to try to "undercut the President's reelection prospects."[4] Thus, the abnormal, emotional Soviet behavior could be, and was, viewed essentially in political terms in minor analytical products.

At the same time, US analysts often tended to characterize Soviet leadership decisionmaking as rational, even omnipotent. United States intelligence clearly did not have sufficient sources to derive a precise picture of the Kremlin's decisionmaking process, nor did it have a thorough understanding of the aging leadership's strengths and weaknesses. United States analysts, nevertheless, described Soviet policy as "driven by prudent calculation of interests and dogged pursuit of long-term objectives, even in the face of great adversity, rather than by sudden swells of fear or anger." Furthermore, analysts concluded that, "However disturbed Soviet policymakers might be by the Reagan Administration, they also have a sense of the USSR's strengths and of [US] vulnerabilities . . . the perception from the Kremlin is by no means one of unrelieved gloom." Moscow's economic problems, while described as "taut," were judged not likely to deter them from accelerating the pace of military spending to challenge the US.[5]

Undeterred by what was termed the "Soviet propaganda campaign" and very concerned about the threat posed by the large numbers of SS-20 deployments, America continued to firm up her defenses by, for example, deploying cruise missiles and Pershings in Europe, adopting a forward-based military strategy, embarking on a path of force modernization and improved readiness, and invigorating a strong "continuity in government" strategy designed to protect US leadership during a nuclear exchange.

---

[4]Ibid.

[5]Ibid.

~~TOP SECRET~~ UMBRA GAMMA
WNINTEL NOFORN NOCONTRACT ORCON

As the second Reagan/Bush campaign swung into high gear, US intelligence analysts began to compile solid evidence from within the Soviet bureaucracy of growing concern about nuclear war:

o In a briefing to Soviet and East European officials in the fall of 1983, a Soviet diplomat warned that the world was on the brink of war.

o Immediately following Brezhnev's death, KGB and GRU Residencies in Soviet missions abroad received orders to monitor US installations for indications of US military mobilization.

o Shortly after the second inauguration, Moscow enjoined KGB Residencies worldwide to work to detect any sign that the United States and its allies were about to unleash a first strike on the USSR. Already in mid-1981, reporting on possible US preparations to launch a first strike had been added to KGB collection requirements worldwide. In early 1983, Moscow warned KGB residencies that the United States was positioning itself for war.

o In early 1983, Soviet military intelligence, the GRU, created a new directorate to organize and manage "illegal" agent networks worldwide. The urgency of this move reportedly reflected perceptions of an increased threat of war. 3.3(b)(1) 3.3(b)(1) working-level officers treated the subject of wartime confrontation seriously, because they believed war could break out at any moment. 3.3(b)(1) 3.3(b)(1) while preparedness for war was not a new notion, it had taken on a sense of urgency not seen in the past. Directives from GRU Headquarters constantly reminded field elements to prepare for war. As a result, all Residency operations were geared to work under both peacetime and wartime conditions.

o 3.3(b)(1)

WNINTEL NOFORN NOCONTRACT ORCON
~~TOP SECRET~~ UMBRA GAMMA

3.3(b)(1) had been tasked with obtaining information on a major NATO exercise (believed to be Able Archer 83). This order reportedly followed from a high-priority requirement 3.3(b)(1) by Moscow a year before to look for any indication of US preparations for a nuclear first strike. Warsaw Pact leaders reportedly were convinced that the Reagan Administration was actively preparing for nuclear war and was capable of launching such an attack. 3.3(b)(1)

By the fall of 1983, the beat of Soviet "war scare" drums was almost lost in the cacophony of the international thunderstorm. Massive demonstrations erupted in Germany and other NATO countries to protest the INF deployments. The Soviets shot down KAL-007; the Marine barracks in Beirut was bombed; and the US invaded Grenada.

Against this backdrop, NATO held its annual command post exercise to practice nuclear release procedures in early November, 1983. This recurring exercise, known as Able Archer, included NATO forces from Turkey to England. Although past Able Archer exercises were monitored by Soviet intelligence, the reaction by Warsaw Pact military forces and intelligence services to the 1983 exercise was unprecedented. Air armies in East Germany and Poland were placed on alert. 3.3(b)(3); (b)(3) 3.3(b)(3); (b)(3) At the same time, the Soviets conducted significantly more reconnaissance flights than in previous years, and sent special intelligence requirements to KGB

~~TOP SECRET~~ UMBRA GAMMA
WNINTEL NOFORN NOCONTRACT ORCON

and GRU Residencies in western countries to report any unusual military activity that might signal an impending NATO surprise attack.

This abnormal Soviet behavior to the annual, announced Able Archer 83 exercise sounded no alarm bells in the US Indications and Warning system. United States commanders on the scene were not aware of any pronounced superpower tension, and the Soviet activities were not seen in their totality until long after the exercise was over. For example, while the US detected a "heightened readiness" among some Soviet air force divisions, the extent of the alert as well 3.3(b)(3); (b)(3) 3.3(b)(3); (b)(3) was not known until two weeks had passed after the completion of the exercise. The Soviet air force standdown had been in effect for nearly a week before fully armed MIG-23 aircraft were noted on air defense alert in East Germany.

There were plenty of reasons why the Soviet military response to Able Archer was missed; there was no context by which to judge the behavior. First, Moscow's "war scare" activity was not yet the focus of intelligence or policy attention. Additionally, Soviet intelligence requirements against the exercise, 3.3(b)(1) 3.3(b)(1) were not learned until long Moreover, the air standdown was not at first perceived abnormally because it occurred during the Soviet Revolution holiday; about midway through the exercise, 3.3(b)(3); (b)(3) Despite the late-developing information, the intelligence community evaluated the Soviet response as unusual but not militarily significant. Analysts reasoned that more indicators should have been detected if the Soviets were seriously concerned about a NATO

WNINTEL NOFORN NOCONTRACT ORCON
~~TOP SECRET~~ UMBRA GAMMA

attack.[6]

But beyond the puzzling Soviet reaction to the Able Archer 83 exercise, US analysts, by spring of 1984, had also detected a clear trend: Soviet forces, over the past decade, had "made an effort to respond more rapidly to the threat of war and to develop the capability to manage all aspects of a nuclear war."[7] In fact, Soviet exercise activity in 1983 highlighted "the continued testing of concepts necessary for avoiding surprise attack . . . . ." Common to all these exercises were the themes of continued concern over force readiness and vulnerability to attack; ensuring that dispersal and launch orders were complied with; and testing what previously had been paper or small-scale wartime concepts under actual operational conditions using larger numbers of forces. Analysts estimated that the attainment of the above objectives could increase the Soviet military's capability to respond quickly to an enemy surprise attack or launch an attack of their own.

<u>BRITISH ASSESSMENT</u>

By March, 1984, the issue of the war scare broke into Allied relationships. 3.3(b)(1)

[6]In fact, a potentially dangerous analytic assumption was also apparently at work. Despite indications of increased readiness with some units, other units upon which no positive intelligence existed regarding readiness were assumed to have <u>not</u> increased readiness.

[7]SNIE 11-10-84 "Implications of Recent Military-Political Activities."

~~TOP SECRET~~ UMBRA GAMMA
WNINTEL NOFORN NOCONTRACT ORCON

Despite -- or perhaps because of -- its disturbing message,

WNINTEL NOFORN NOCONTRACT ORCON
~~TOP SECRET~~ UMBRA GAMMA

the 3.3(b)(1) report was not well received in the US intelligence community 3.3(b)(1) 3.3(b)(1) Additionally, some officials in the British Ministry of Defense were also skeptical.

The British Foreign Ministry, however, was sure that something was amiss. The British Ambassador to the US paid a visit to the State Department's Under Secretary for Political Affairs, Lawrence Eagleburger, to discuss the issue. But according to the responsible briefing official from State's Bureau of Intelligence and Research (INR), INR's position at the time (and thus State's position) was that the Soviets were pursuing a massive propaganda campaign. The INR officer presented to Eagleburger a skeptical version of events, designed, in his words, to "discourage the British." The British case apparently was not helped by the Ambassador's presentation; he was not entirely clear about events, and his intelligence aide most familiar with the war scare was out of country. There was even suspicion in some American quarters that the Foreign Office was simply capitalizing on a good political occasion to force President Reagan to tone down his rhetoric and delay deployments of the INF missiles. Thus, the Foreign Office's expressions of worry fell on deaf ears.

US PERCEPTIONS ENTRENCHED

In May 1984, US intelligence addressed for the first time in a national estimate the possibility that the Soviets were fearful of a preemptive first US nuclear strike -- a full six months after the Able Archer NATO exercise. Despite the evidence of secret directives and speeches by Soviet authorities to prepare for sudden nuclear attack and of unique Soviet military activities,

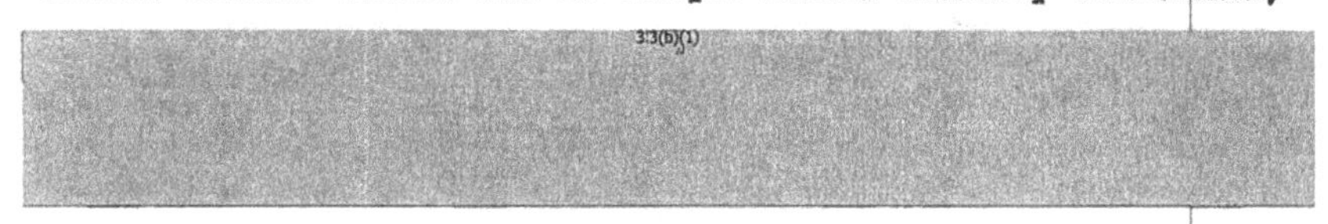

the issue was not treated as an evolutionary process. In fact, several intelligence officers told the Board that the estimate was undertaken essentially to explain a series of short-term abnormal events, rather than to examine the accumulated long-term reporting on the war scare. In the estimate's "Key Judgments," the intelligence community noted, "During the past several months, a number of coincident Soviet activities have created concern that they reflect abnormal Soviet fear of conflict with the United States, belligerent intent that might risk conflict, or some other underlying Soviet purpose." The "coincident" activities consisted of:

o Large-scale military exercises -- including a major naval exercise in the Norwegian Sea, unprecedented SS-20 launch activity, and large-scale SSBN dispersal;

o Preparations for air operations against Afghanistan;

o Attempts to change the air corridor regime in Berlin;

o New military measures described as responsive to NATO INF deployments; and

o Shrill propaganda attributing a heightened danger of war to US behavior.

United States analysts categorically concluded: <u>"We believe strongly that Soviet actions are not inspired by, and Soviet leaders do not perceive, a genuine danger of imminent conflict or confrontation with the United States.</u> This judgment is based on the absence of force-wide combat readiness or other war preparation moves in the USSR, and the absence of a tone of fear or belligerence [3.3(b)(3); (b)(3)]

(Underlining added.)[9] The estimate boldly declared that "Recent Soviet war scare propaganda . . . is aimed primarily at discrediting US policies and mobilizing 'peace' pressures among various audiences abroad." In a more piecemeal fashion, it was judged that "Each Soviet action has its own military or political purpose sufficient to explain it." The accelerated tempo of Soviet live exercise activity was explained simply as a reflection of "long-term Soviet military objectives."

The Soviet reaction to Able Archer 83 was dismissed as a "counterexercise," but analysts acknowledged that the "elaborate Soviet reaction" was "somewhat greater than usual." 3.3(b)(1) 3.3(b)(1) the Warsaw Pact intelligence services, especially the KGB, were admonished "to look for any indication that the United States was about to launch a first nuclear strike," analysts concluded that "by confining heightened readiness to selected air units, Moscow clearly revealed that it did not, in fact, think there was a possibility at this time of a NATO attack." The assessment, however, was not specific about what type of defensive or precautionary Soviet activity might be expected -- and detected -- were they preparing for an offensive NATO move. (Some intelligence officials have since told us that the West could very well have been witnessing a careful, deliberate Soviet defensive posturing designed to achieve improved readiness for attack, while not simultaneously escalating tensions.)

As for leadership instability, again analysts rejected the hypothesis that weak central leadership could account for Soviet actions. While acknowledging that either a Soviet military or

---

[9]The commentary did note that 3.3(b)(1); 3.3(b)(3); (b)(3) 3.3(b)(1); 3.3(b)(3); (b)(3) but neglected to explain that we had not seen a "force-wide" Soviet alert since World War II.

~~TOP SECRET~~ UMBRA GAMMA
WNINTEL NOFORN NOCONTRACT ORCON

hard-line foreign policy faction could possibly exert more influence on a weak Chernenko, the experts concluded that this was not, in fact, happening. It is unclear what evidence for this conclusion was used, since the estimate admitted that there was inadequate information on "the current mind-set of the Soviet political leadership" and on "the ways in which military operations and foreign policy tactics may be influenced by political differences and the policy process in the Kremlin."

Finally, analysts dismissed [3.3(b)(1)] [3.3(b)(1)] on the war scare, including the KGB's formal tasking to its Residencies. "This war scare propaganda has reverberated in Soviet security bureaucracies and emanated through other channels [3.3(b)(1)] We do not believe it reflects authentic leadership fears of imminent conflict." Instead, analysts viewed the Soviet talk about increased likelihood of nuclear war, as well as military actions, as designed to speak "with a louder voice" and show "firmness through a controlled display of muscle." Such judgments were made even though the analysis was tempered "by some uncertainty as to current Soviet leadership perceptions of the United States, by continued uncertainty about the Politburo decisionmaking processes, and by our inability at this point to conduct a detailed examination of how the Soviets might have assessed recent US/NATO military exercises and reconnaissance operations" -- which, of course, included the previous Able Archer exercise. In other words, US analysts were unsure of what the Kremlin leadership thought or how it made decisions, nor had they adequately assessed the Soviet reaction to Able Archer 83. This notwithstanding, the estimate concluded: "We are confident that, as of now, the Soviets see not an imminent military clash but a costly and -- to some extent -- more perilous strategic and political struggle over the rest of the decade."

But these bets were hedged. Deep in the body of the assess-

WNINTEL NOFORN NOCONTRACT ORCON
~~TOP SECRET~~ UMBRA GAMMA

ment, analysts conceded: "It is conceivable that the stridency of Soviet 'war scare' propaganda reflects a genuine Soviet worry about a near-future attack on them. This concern could be inspired by Soviet views about the depth of anti-Soviet intentions in Washington combined with elements of their own military doctrine projected onto the United States, such as the virtues of surprise, striking first, and masking hostile initiatives in exercises. Some political and military leaders have stressed the danger of war more forcefully than others, suggesting that there may have been differences on this score -- or at least how to talk about the issue -- over the past half year."

AN ALTERNATIVE OPINION

One month later, in June 1984, DCI Casey sent to the President a memorandum with a differing view of events. Uncertain whether the Soviets were preparing for a crisis or merely trying to influence events in the United States, Casey attached "a rather stunning array of indicators" of an "increasing aggressiveness in Soviet policy and activities." Prepared by the DCI's National Warning Staff, the events studied were described as "longer term" than those considered in the May NIE. In the Warning Staff's view, "the Soviets have concluded that the danger of war is greater and will grow with additional INF emplacements and that the reduced warning time inherent in Pershing II has lowered Soviet confidence in their ability to warn of sudden attack. These perceptions, perhaps driven by a building US defense budget, new initiatives in continental defense, improvements in force readiness, and a potentially massive space defense program may be propelling the USSR to take national readiness measures at a deliberate pace."

The indicators of abnormal Soviet behavior ranged in scope from domestic to international. They included:

~~TOP SECRET~~ UMBRA GAMMA
WNINTEL NOFORN NOCONTRACT ORCON

o Preparing Soviet citizens for war through civil defense activities and media broadcasts;

o Tightening of security procedures against Westerners, such as increased travel restrictions and isolation from the Bloc populace;

o Conducting political harassment;

o Improving military logistic systems;

o Shifting the economy more toward a wartime footing, such as terminating military support to the harvest, converting farm tractor plants to tank production, and reducing commercial aircraft production in favor of military transports;

o Conducting out-of-the-ordinary military activities, such as delaying troop rotations, increasing deployments of SPETSNAZ forces, and expanding reservist call-ups, as well as extending active duty tours; and

o Promulgating extraordinary intelligence directives for the purpose of warning.

Casey advised: "It is important to distinguish in this category those acts which are political blustering and those which may be, but also carry large costs . . . The military behaviors we have observed involve high military costs in terms of vulnerability of resources for the sake of improved national military power, or enhanced readiness at the price of consumer discontent, or enhanced readiness at the price of troop dissatisfaction. None of these are trivial costs, adding thereby a dimension of genuineness to the Soviet expressions of concern that is often not reflected in intelligence issuances."

WNINTEL NOFORN NOCONTRACT ORCON
~~TOP SECRET~~ UMBRA GAMMA

According to former National Security Advisor Robert McFarlane, President Reagan expressed surprise upon reading the Casey memorandum and described the events as "really scary." However, McFarlane himself was less convinced. He questioned Soviet motivations and wondered if their actions were part of an effort to drive a wedge in Europe to counter the Administration's SDI objectives. He also found it difficult to believe that the Soviets could actually fear a nuclear strike from the US, since he knew how preposterous that was. McFarlane wondered, if the war scare was real, why had the Soviets not raised it through diplomatic channels in Washington? (Yet, even the President's own personal emissary dispatched to Moscow months earlier with a message for Chernenko was frozen out of the Kremlin.)

On the other hand, McFarlane was "concerned" about reporting he had received from US citizens returning from the Soviet Union during the early 1980's. Many of them told of extreme Soviet paranoia over US intentions. In fact, one close friend who had visited Moscow said that the Soviets spoke of "going to general quarters" during the 1983 to 1984 time frame. McFarlane expressed surprise to us about the November 1983 Able Archer exercise; he could remember hearing nothing about it, including the Soviet 3.3(b)(3); (b)(3) during his tenure at the National Security Council. (No President's Daily Brief during this period mentioned it either.)

In a memorandum to Director Casey in June 1984, McFarlane called for a new intelligence estimate that would develop hypotheses to "anticipate potential Soviet political or military challenges during the coming six months." Clearly, the Administration viewed the indicators of unusual Soviet activity in the context of "the utility to the Soviets of interfering in various geographic trouble spots." One month later, the Casey memorandum of indicators was leaked to the Washington Times. It was fully reported as "Russia at high level of battle readiness."

~~TOP SECRET~~ UMBRA GAMMA
WNINTEL NOFORN NOCONTRACT ORCON

The following day, the Washington Times reported on a controversial split of opinion within military and intelligence circles over the significance of the Soviet behavior, saying CIA officials tended to downplay it.

THE REBUTTAL

Some officials on the National Intelligence Council were upset over the Casey memorandum. After all, they had just addressed the war scare in May through a fully coordinated SNIE that determined it was purely "propaganda." The Casey memorandum was not coordinated, refuted the SNIE, and yet had received Presidential attention.

By August 1984, the estimate called for by McFarlane was completed. Entitled "Soviet Policy Toward the United States in 1984," it was far more comprehensive than he initially requested. A "central concern" of the estimate was "the possibility of major Soviet initiatives to influence the November election," since "the motivation for Soviet policy . . . lies in the perception that the . . . current [US] Administration is a more consistently hostile opponent of the USSR's interests and aspirations than it has faced in many years." Thus, the Soviets could be expected to "combat and, if possible, deflect US policies, and create a more permissive environment in which Soviet relative military power and world influence can continue to grow."

The war scare, characterized in the SNIE as "hostile propaganda, which blames the United States for an increased danger of war and for diplomatic rigidity . . . is used to put the US Administration on the defensive where possible and to excite opposition to Washington's policies." In fact, such hostility toward the West was judged to serve Soviet leaders conveniently for "exhorting greater discipline, sacrifice, and vigilance on the Soviet home front . . . ." Analysts were, again, categoric in

WNINTEL NOFORN NOCONTRACT ORCON
~~TOP SECRET~~ UMBRA GAMMA

their conclusion: "<u>We strongly believe that Soviet actions are not inspired by, and Soviet leaders do not perceive, a genuine danger of imminent conflict or confrontation with the United States.</u> Also, we do not believe that Soviet war talk and other actions 'mask' Soviet preparations for an imminent move toward confrontation on the part of the USSR." (Underlining added.)

While acknowledging that "there may be debates among Soviet leaders about tactics toward the United States," analysts asserted that "current Soviet policy . . . is based on consensus in the Politburo." In fact, there was "indirect evidence of Soviet leadership debate over future policy direction, largely in the form of varying lines on the danger of war. . . ." The estimate admonished that such debates should not be taken to indicate sharp controversy in the Politburo because "showdown situations" were avoided in order to protect the Kremlin's hold on power. Gorbachev was lumped with Romanov, Ogarkov, and Ligachev as differing "from their elders only in the belief that they can pursue traditional Soviet aims more skillfully and successfully at home and abroad."

Analysts readily acknowledged that the previous six months had seen extraordinary, unprecedented Soviet activities. Large scale military exercises, "anomalous behavior" during the troop rotation, withdrawn military support for the harvest (last seen prior to the 1968 Czech invasion), new, deployed weapons systems (termed "in response to INF deployments"), and heightened internal vigilance and security activities were noted. These events, however, were judged to be "in line with long-evolving plans and patterns, rather than with sharp acceleration of preparations for a major war."

The NIE authors professed high confidence in the intelligence community's ability to detect widespread logistics, supply, and defense-economic preparations obligated by Soviet war doctrine and operational requirements. Such indicators, they insisted, were noteworthy by their absence. In seeming contradiction, however, the authors pointed out that US strategic warning indicators and methodologies are oriented toward providing "warning of war within a short period of time; at most, one to two months." But, "because we give less emphasis to defense-economic and other home front measures that might provide strategic warning . . . and because a pattern of such activities is inherently difficult to detect in their early stages . . . we have less confidence in longer range warning based on military and defense-related activities alone." Nonetheless, the authors asserted that, even without the capability to detect such indicators, the developments in Soviet foreign and domestic affairs made it "very unlikely" that they were preparing for a war. Both NSA and National Warning Staff officials confirmed to us recently that US technical systems in particular were not, in fact, tuned to long-range military, economic, and defense-related activities at the time.

The estimate concluded with a list of indicators detected at the time that strongly suggested unusual Pact military activity. Nearly all of them were dismissed as explainable for ordinary reasons. The Board did not conduct a retrospective of each indicator but we believe that such a review would prove useful to the continued validation of the assessment. We believe that some of the explanations given at the time will be found to be mistaken. For example, the estimate explained the appearance of high-level Warsaw Pact command posts in 1984 as part of a one-time exercise. The command posts remained in operation, however, long after the estimate was published and the exercise was completed.

In reviewing both estimates, the Board was struck by how categorical and unqualified were the judgments made about the likelihood of the war scare, particularly given the extremely important consequences of those assessments. In fact, the NIO for Warning in 1984 made the same point in his commentary on the draft

~~TOP SECRET~~ UMBRA GAMMA
WNINTEL NOFORN NOCONTRACT ORCON

August estimate. Although unable procedurally to comment in the estimate itself, he sent a memorandum to the NIE drafter arguing:

This episode highlights a latent conflict between Soviet analysts and warning specialists. Most intelligence officers involved in the warning process are not necessarily trained Soviet experts; indeed, the staff tends to come from a military pool for a two-year rotational assignment. Within the intelligence community, an assignment to the Warning Staff has not always been viewed as career-enhancing. Disputes with geographic or other "substantive" analysts are often not resolved in favor of the warning officers. We have been told by senior intelligence officials that the problem of establishing credibility for warning experts, particularly in the Soviet affairs arena, is one that is recognized but not solved easily.[10] Conversely, Sovietologists are not often likely to have a deep grounding in warning issues.

NEW INFORMATION

The Board found that after the 1984 assessments were issued, the intelligence community did not again address the war scare until after the defection to Great Britain of KGB Colonel Oleg Gordiyevskiy in July, 1985. Gordiyevskiy had achieved the rank of Acting Resident in the United Kingdom, but he fell under suspicion as a Western agent. Recalled to the Soviet Union, he was placed under house arrest and intensely interrogated. Able to flee his watchers, Gordiyevskiy was exfiltrated from Moscow by the British Secret Intelligence Service.

During lengthy debriefing sessions that followed, Gordiyevskiy supplied a fuller report on the Soviet war hysteria. This report, complete with documentation from KGB Headquarters and entitled "KGB Response to Soviet Leadership Concern over US Nuclear Attack," was first disseminated in a restricted manner within the US intelligence community in October, 1985. Gordiyevskiy described the extraordinary KGB collection plan, initiated in 1981, to look for signs that the US would conduct a surprise nuclear attack on the Soviet Union. He identified and reviewed the factors driving leadership fears. Based on the perception that the US was achieving a strategic advantage, those in the Kremlin were said to believe that the US was likely to resort to nuclear weapons much earlier in a crisis than previously expected. They also were concerned that the US might seek to exploit its first-strike capability outside the

[10]We note that the National Warning Staff does tend to view events with a long-range perspective. Clearly, we believe this to be an asset in evaluating the Soviet war scare.

context of a crisis, probably during a military exercise. He described the leadership's worries of a "decapitating" strike from the Pershing II's, and its belief that the US could mobilize for a surprise attack in a mere seven to ten days. He explained how the London Residency responded to the requirements, and the effects that reporting had back at Moscow Center in reinforcing Soviet fears. He described conversations he had held with colleagues from Center and from the GRU. The next month, President Reagan held his first summit with Mikhail Gorbachev and relations began to thaw.

PERCEPTIONS EVOLVE

Some in the intelligence community have argued that the war scare was a massive Soviet propaganda and deception campaign that not only included attempts to manipulate public opinions but intelligence community perceptions as well. Central to this theory is that the Soviets intended for secret intelligence directives -- like the taskings sent from Moscow Center to London Residency -- to become known to the US. In July 1985, a National Intelligence Estimate entitled "Denial and Deception in Soviet Strategic Military Programs: Implications for US Security" (NIE 11-11-85), however, dashed cold water on this assumption. Analysts judged: "We strongly doubt that the Soviets intended for official documents to reach intelligence sources." Further, Soviet reliance on verbal disclosures of secret communications was also judged unlikely: "The uncertainty of the potential for such disclosures . . . combined with the lack of control over timing and content probably would have led the Soviets to conclude that such a device represents an unreliable means of communicating with the West." The estimate concluded that, "The intelligence directives probably represent efforts by the Soviet intelligence services to respond to concerns of Soviet leaders that since at least 1980 worsening relations with the United States increased the danger of war."

Although Gordiyevskiy's reporting remained closely held, by June 1986, assessments giving more credence to the legitimacy of the war scare began to surface in intelligence products.[11] By August, the Washington Post broke Gordiyevskiy's story to the American public.[12] The article quoted informed sources as saying that many high-level officials with extensive experience in East-West relations were still unaware of Gordiyevskiy's information. It maintained that many Western specialists, some with access to the Gordiyevskiy material, attributed Soviet anxieties in the early 1980's to genuine apprehension about Reagan Administration policies and to a tactical decision to exploit that concern through propaganda channels. The CIA then downgraded and re-released the Gordiyevskiy material. Despite the public disclosure and the broader circulation of Gordiyevskiy's material within government channels, the issue remained strangely dormant as a national intelligence topic.

Other [3.3(b)(1)] sources supported Gordiyevskiy's reporting. Perhaps the most important [3.3(b)(1)] [3.3(b)(1)] information on the war scare became available in the spring of 1987. [3.3(b)(1)] a KGB computer model called VRYAN (meaning Sudden Nuclear Missile Attack), and how it was used as a tool to predict US strategic intentions in the early 1980's. At the same time, [3.3(b)(1)] the accompanying Pact-wide emphasis on collecting strategic intelligence against the US, including efforts to enhance illegal agent operations to detect US plans for a surprise nuclear attack. [3.3(b)(1)] the seemingly improbable, but apparently widespread, Soviet belief that the US leadership would attack first to a deeply-seated Soviet fear of foreign invasion.

---

[11] Warsaw Pact Military Perceptions of NATO Nuclear Initiation, CIA Intelligence Assessment.

[12] Defector told of Soviet Alert, Aug 6, by Murrey Marder.

1.3(b)(1) CIA's <u>Science and Weapons Daily Review</u> in which analysts declared: "We believe that the existence of the VRYAN model is likely and that it may have contributed to a 'war scare' in the Soviet Government from 1981 until about 1985."

<u>BUT DOUBTS REMAIN . . .</u>

Conflicting opinions on the validity of the war scare continued to rage within the intelligence community. Analysts stated in the NIE entitled "Soviet Forces and Capabilities for Strategic Nuclear Conflict Through the Late 1990's" (11/3-8) issued in December, 1987: "Taking all the evidence into consideration, we judge that some leaders may have become more concerned in the early 1980's that the United States had lowered the threshold somewhat for nuclear escalation, but that <u>the top leaders on the whole did not believe a surprise nuclear attack on the West in peacetime had become a serious prospect</u>." The authors made clear their views of the war scare: ". . . the attempted manipulation . . . is highly disturbing as an indication of the potential for irresponsible behavior by some prominent Soviet leaders in dealing with the grave issue of nuclear war." (Underlining added.) Moreover, the authors repeated phrases from their earlier estimates, including one in 1984. They said that the Soviets were confident that the open nature of US society made "unlikely" a successful US surprise strike. Analysts' assessments then of Soviet leaders belief on the survivability of their strategic forces differs markedly from recent analysis of the same period (see Part Two, page 46). In fact, analysts at the time assessed that the Soviets had confidence that their forces would be capable of mounting massive retaliatory strikes after a US surprise attack -- an interpretation now viewed to have been probably erroneous.

~~TOP SECRET~~ UMBRA GAMMA
WNINTEL NOFORN NOCONTRACT ORCON

THE LAST WORD

By 1988, the intelligence community had received reporting -- in some detail -- on Soviet fears of a surprise US strike during the early 1980's from [3.3(b)(1)] [3.3(b)(1)] A new assessment was evident in a NIE (Soviet Intelligence Capabilities [NIE 11-21-88]) that clearly accepted the validity of the reporting on VRYAN. While acknowledging that available information was incomplete, the community said, "We consider the information we have to be reliable" and "consistent." In providing a comprehensive analysis of the VYRAN program, the estimate made explicit its view of leadership involvement in the war scare and of the Kremlin-KGB relationship: "It is essential to note . . . that the VRYAN collection requirement resulted from high-level political concern, and was not solely an intelligence initiative."

As for the VRYAN computer model, the authors said: "KGB analysts working on VRYAN operated under the premise that the United States, when it had decisive overall superiority, might be inclined to launch an attack on the Soviet Union. In light of this assumption and because the program was supposed to determine, in a quantifiable way, when such a situation might be approaching, they believed it could provide strategic warning when the USSR was in a critically weak position relative to the United States, and conditions therefore were potentially conducive to a US attack. These views reflected a widespread Soviet belief that definitive US superiority over the Soviet Union was inherently unstable." The authors also believed that ". . . it is possible that the results of this analysis [from the VRYAN computer model] themselves were a factor in the air of immediacy surrounding KGB Headquarters' concern over the possibility of a US surprise nuclear strike."

However, this estimate received extremely limited dissemina-

WNINTEL NOFORN NOCONTRACT ORCON
~~TOP SECRET~~ UMBRA GAMMA

tion. Access to the publication was strictly need to know: this was the first estimate of its kind, and US assessments of Soviet intelligence capabilities would be of keen interest to the KGB. Moreover, the discussion of the VRYAN program was contained in an annex that was even more tightly controlled than the estimate itself.

The more widely disseminated and most recent edition of NIE 11/3-8 ("Soviet Forces and Capabilities for Strategic Nuclear Conflict Through the Late 1990's," issued in December of 1988) failed to reflect the presumably changed community position. While this edition acknowledged that Soviet intelligence services had been tasked to look for indications of US preparations for a surprise nuclear attack, it nonetheless echoed doubts expressed in earlier publications: "Soviet leaders failed in any event to take certain precautionary measures that would appear to have been an appropriate response to such a situation." It did note, however, under the section entitled "Soviet Concern Over a US Surprise Attack From a Peacetime Posture," that "in a mid-1980's Soviet classified military discussion," Soviet expectations of a crisis stage were "described as potentially being as short as a few hours." This marked a change in normal expectation stages from several days to months.

THE RECORD MUDDIED

The last, most definitive intelligence community word on the Soviet war scare seemed destined to languish in an annex to a National Intelligence Estimate on Soviet intelligence capabilities that was unintended for policymakers' eyes. However, in January 1989, former DIA Director, Lieutenant General Leonard Perroots, sent -- as his parting shot before retirement -- a letter outlining his disquiet over the inadequate treatment of the Soviet war scare to, among others, the DCI and this Board. General Perroots personally experienced the war scare as Assistant Chief of Staff for Intelligence, US Air Forces Europe, during the 1983 Able Archer exercise. Following the detection of the Soviet Air Forces' increased alert status, it was his recommendation, made in ignorance, not to raise US readiness in response -- a fortuitous, if ill-informed, decision given the changed political environment at the time.

The Board was puzzled by the intelligence community's response to the Perroots letter. In March, 1989, the National Intelligence Council (NIC) sent a memorandum to the DCI that seemed to reflect unresolved opinions. In the covering note, the Chairman of the NIC acknowledged that the 1984 SNIE on the war scare concluded "while Moscow was very unhappy with Ronald Reagan's policies, it was not gearing up for a military confrontation." Expressing his personal view, he said: "the failing here was not grave." However, the "thoroughly researched" commentary that followed portrayed the judgments of the May and August 1984 SNIE's -- which downplayed the war scare -- as synonymous ("reached the same broad conclusions") with the judgment of the 1988 National Intelligence Estimate (Soviet Intelligence Capabilities) that said the war scare was real. In fact, it was noted that the 1984 estimates "judged that the Soviets displayed a heightened sense of concern . . . because . . . of the leadership instability in the USSR from the successive deaths of three general secretaries between 1981 and 1985" -- an impossibility since Chernenko did not die until seven months after the last 1984 SNIE was issued. It was noted that the Perroots letter "neither raises new issues nor contains new data that change the strategic judgments already written." But in a reversal from previous, coordinated judgments written about the significance of USSR military developments during the war scare, and in refutation of the covering NIC note itself, the commentary included: "The Soviets had concern that the West might decide to attack the USSR without warning during a time of vulnerability -- such as when military transport was used to support the harvest -

- thus compelling the Soviets to consider a preemptive strike at the first sign of US preparations for a nuclear strike." Moreover, it noted: "From Brezhnev's death in 1982 through late 1984, the Soviets ordered a number of unusual [military and civil defense] measures not previously detected except during periods of crisis with the West . . .", and "The cumulative effect of these . . . was to reduce the Soviet and Warsaw Pact vulnerability to a surprise attack."

CONCLUSIONS: THE ESTIMATIVE PROCESS

In (ironically) December 1983, the DCI's Senior Review Panel (SRP) issued a prescient study of intelligence judgments preceding significant historical estimative failures. We believe key parts of that report merit reiteration:

> In the estimates that failed, there were a number of recurrent common factors which, in retrospect, seem critical to the quality of the analysis . . . each involved historical discontinuity and, in the early stages, apparently unlikely outcomes.

The Board is deeply disturbed by the US handling of the war scare, both at the time and since. In the early stages of the war scare period, when evidence was thin, little effort was made to examine the various possible Soviet motivations behind some very anomalous events. Later, when enough intelligence existed on the abnormal Soviet behavior to create conflicting views within the community, no national intelligence assessments were prepared until after tensions began to subside. When written, the 1984 SNIE's were overconfident, particularly in the judgments pertaining to Soviet leadership intentions -- since little intelligence, human or technical, existed to support them. In its review of previous estimates, the SRP was equally troubled by this very same "process" shortcoming:

> The basic problem in each was to recognize qualitative change and to deal with situations in which trend continuity and precedent were of marginal, if not counterproductive value. Analysts . . . clearly lacked a doctrine or a model for coping with improbable outcomes . . . and [were] unchallenged by a requirement to analyze or clarify subordinate and lesser probabilities. Too many of the analyses were incident-oriented and episodic; too few addressed the processes that produced the incidents or speculated about underlying forces and trends . . . addiction to single-outcome forecasting defied both estimative odds and much recorded history. It reinforced some of the worst analytical hazards -- status quo bias and a prejudice towards continuity of previous trends, 'playing it safe,' mirror-imaging, and predispositions towards consensus intelligence.

Reasonable people can disagree about the conclusions of the 1984 SNIE's. The PFIAB does disagree with many of them. More worrisome to us, however, is the process by which the estimates were made and subsequently reassessed. Although both estimates were reportedly reviewed by outside readers -- and both, but particularly the first, contained alternative scenarios -- strongly worded interpretations were defended by explaining away facts inconsistent with them. Consequently, both estimates contained, in essence, single outcome forecasting based in large part on near-term anomalous behavior. Moreover, neither alerted the reader to the risks of erroneously rejecting the correct scenario.

Archivist's Note: This page is not present in the LP-GB original. It was added by ISCAP during their review.

We understand that analysts will always have legitimate disagreements over the meaning of inevitably incomplete and uncertain events. This is as it should be. But we believe that when analysts attempt to arrive at a single strong conclusion, they not only run the risk of being wrong, they run two additional and perhaps more worrisome risks. They are likely to underestimate the possibility of change (the safest prediction is always that tomorrow will be like today) and they are likely to rely on mirror-imaging (our adversaries think the way we do). In this era of increasing instability in the USSR, we cannot know who may long retain or quickly assume the mantle of Soviet leadership. Will he understand that US leaders are not going to start World War III and behave as if he understands? Again, from the SRP report:

> The world will stay a chancy and changeable place and the only rule is perhaps that there is an inevitability of uncertainty which we ignore at our peril. Information at best will always be in some part fragmentary, obsolete, and ambiguous.

The Board believes that in cases of grave importance to US survival, intelligence estimates must be cast in terms of alternative scenarios that are in turn subjected to comparative risk assessments. This is the most critical flaw in the war scare episode. By "alternative scenarios," we mean a full statement of each major possible interpretation of a set of intelligence indicators. In this case, these scenarios might have included (but not limited to) the following:

1. Soviet leaders had not changed their strategic thinking but were attempting by means of propaganda and deception to slow the US military build-up, prevent the deployment of new weapons, and isolate the US from its allies.

2. Soviet leaders may or may not have changed their strategic thinking, but a power struggle among Kremlin factions and the need to deflect blame for poor economic conditions made it useful to exaggerate the military intentions and capabilities of the US.

3. Soviet leaders had changed their strategic thinking and in fact believed that the US was attempting to gain decisive strategic superiority in order, possibly, to launch a nuclear first strike.

By "comparative risk assessment," we mean assigning two kinds of weights to each scenario: one that estimates (in rough approximation, like "slightly better than even" or "two to one") the probability that the scenario is correct; and a second that assesses the risk to the United States if we wrongly reject the correct scenario. While any of the three scenarios, or a portion thereof, could have been true to some degree, a risk assessment could have helped focus subsequent US actions. If Soviet leaders did not believe a US attack was possible, and we erroneously imputed that view to them, then it is unlikely we would have taken actions that would have increased the risk of war. If Soviet leaders did have that belief, and we wrongly denied that they had it, then we could have materially but inadvertently increased the risk of war by (for example) conducting provocative military exercises or redeploying forces in ways that would trigger the Soviet indications and warning system.

We emphasize that we are not arguing for "competitive analysis," greater use of dissenting opinions, or policy guidance from the intelligence community. Rather, in special cases like the Soviet "war scare," it is less important to arrive at a single consensus than it is to identify a small number of possibilities associated with rough probabilities that allows policymakers to understand the risks and opportunities.

We also want to emphasize that by comparative risk analysis, we do not wish to encourage the formulation of watered-down, bland assessments whereby the reader is unable to determine what conclusions the authors have drawn. Instead we urge that when information is inadequate to allow reasonable people to draw conclusions relating to our adversary's intentions, analysts should withstand the pressure to arrive at a single judgment and thereby avoid turning an acknowledged collection deficiency into an analytic problem.

The SRP report recommended that estimates incorporate what we view as an extremely vital "road-map" perspective for policymakers:

> A list of future indicators should invariably be included. Its aim should be to underline those contingent developments, decision points, and future policy crossroads which could affect the durability of the analysis, alter its major judgments, or influence the odds on outcomes.

Other than vague references to a full-force mobilization and more strident [3.3(b)(3); (b)(3)] the SNIE analyses of the war scare, unfortunately, did not offer such signposts. Moreover, the Soviet response to Able Archer 83 was dismissed as an exercise, despite an acknowledged inability to conduct a thorough examination of the events. Again, the SRP report:

> It [the problem] was compounded by what the British call 'perseveration' (a tendency for judgments made in the early stages of a developing situation to be allowed to affect later appraisals and an unreadiness to alter earlier views even when evidence requiring them to be revised becomes available) which

narrowed collection requirements and froze their priorities to overtaken analytical frameworks. The practice invited failure.

After 1984, and as new evidence started emerging that began clarifying anomalous Soviet behavior, succeeding intelligence analyses seesawed between giving credence to the war scare and completely dismissing it. Despite the conflicting views, no comprehensive intelligence collection requirements were levied that might have revealed even more information.

When the intelligence community did offer a revised community position in 1988, it was buried in an annex of a tightly-held assessment not authored for policymakers. Narrow in scope, it did not include a comprehensive review of the political, military, and economic factors impacting the Soviet Union at the time, nor did it attempt to match US activities with anomalous Soviet behavior. Thus it is incomplete. Despite laudable individual efforts to address VRYAN -- and the importance of a "real" war scare to our understanding of the Soviet Union today -- it has never become the subject of a national intelligence assessment since the earlier 1984 judgments.[13]

A recent piece of reporting on dangerous Soviet thinking during the Andropov period maintains that many Soviet officials were discussing the possibility of a USSR preemptive, desperation strike to "level the playing field." The Chairman of the National Intelligence Council was right to point out to us that "the leak of this material would occasion politically very unfortunate charges that the Administration is either fabricating or concealing frightening perceptions of the USSR." We understand the political sensitivities associated with this study. At the same time, we

[13]See Special Program Intelligence Exploitation Study "Sudden Nuclear Missile Attack" authored by (b)(3)

believe the implications of the war scare period -- chiefly that Soviet leaders, despite our open society, might be capable of a fundamental misunderstanding of US strategic motives and increase the likelihood of nuclear war -- need to be brought to the attention of senior US policymakers. Honest intellectual discourse must take place, using all available data, about the pivotal and dangerous period of US-USSR relations in the early to mid-1980's. Lessons learned from these events cannot be truly understood nor course corrections made until such analysis takes place, including a possible dialogue with the Soviets.

AND UNFINISHED BUSINESS . . .

During the course of our study, we identified a number of related intelligence issues that, in our judgment, could withstand closer scrutiny. 3.3(b)(3); (b)(3) Had we not obtained this piece of intelligence, the Able Archer exercise likely would have been viewed in even more benign ways than it was. We believe this calls into question the kinds of signals we are likely to get from national technical means when, in times of internal Soviet crisis, the USSR military behaves in a defensive, reactive manner, particularly to US or NATO maneuvers.

We noticed a tendency for most to describe the annual Able Archer exercise simply as "a command and control" exercise, and thus, clearly nonthreatening to the Warsaw Pact. Not only was Able Archer 83 unique in some significant ways from earlier ones, it also incorporated live mobilization exercises from some US military forces in Europe. For example, we are told that some US aircraft practiced the nuclear warhead handling procedures, including taxiing out of hangars carrying realistic-looking dummy warheads.

We are concerned about the human intelligence collection effort regarding the Soviet war scare, particularly the lack of coordinated intelligence community strategy in the exploitation of double agents. For example, we found evidence that while the Warsaw Pact intelligence services changed their targeting and collection in significant ways in response to Soviet leadership fears, this information derived from double agent operations was not linked to the national warning system's key indicators list. Moreover, the FBI noted: "In some double agent operations, US-controlling agencies have supplied materials that bear on current or proposed military programs or strategies that could be interpreted to imply US capabilities and intentions to initiate a preemptive attack."

We now know that KGB Headquarters tasked the Residency in the US with extensive requirements to find evidence of an imminent US attack, which in turn necessitated the creation of a large VRYAN unit within the Residency. While the FBI did not detect the establishment of the new unit, it did note an increase in Soviet targeting and collection of US military plans beginning in 1982. Domestically, it also was aware of a marked and aggressive increase in Czechoslovak intelligence efforts to obtain indications and warning data, particularly during 1983 and 1984. However, this information did not find its way into community analysis.

Similarly, many US officials have described an inability to equate US secret or "blue force" activity with Soviet activity that might be in response. United States military commanders had a great deal of autonomy to exercise their forces in ways they saw best -- some more aggressively than others, we are told. The Board did not specifically match "blue force/red force" activity or probe US strategic deception programs underway at the time. We did, however, learn enough about them to realize such a review would be highly helpful to the study of the Soviet war scare.

~~TOP SECRET~~ UMBRA GAMMA
WNINTEL NOFORN NOCONTRACT ORCON

PART II: THE SOVIET "WAR SCARE"

INTRODUCTION

Over the last year, as PFIAB endeavored to come to a better understanding of events surrounding the war scare episode, it examined intelligence available at the time as well as considerable subsequent reporting of direct relevance. While some of the anomalous Soviet behavior that remains unclarified by subsequent reporting can be explained in singularly unthreatening ways, we chose not to assume them as individual events. Rather, we see these "anomalies" as a pattern, which, taken in totality, strongly indicates that the war scare was real, at least in the minds of some Soviet leaders.

The following discussion, therefore, is what we view as a plausible interpretation of events based upon a sizable, but incomplete, body of evidence. It tries to put into context and draw parallels among developments inside the Soviet political hierarchy, the intelligence apparatus, and the military establishment that, to us, strongly point to genuine Soviet concern and preparations for hostile US action. We also try to show that Soviet media pronouncements of the danger of war with the US -- dismissed by US analysts at the time as "propaganda" -- probably did, in fact, mirror private and secret communications by senior Soviet officials.

The Board does not intend this discussion to constitute the "final word" on the war scare. Instead, we hope it prompts renewed interest, vigorous dialogue, and rigorous reanalysis of the events.

WNINTEL NOFORN NOCONTRACT ORCON
~~TOP SECRET~~ UMBRA GAMMA

ORIGINS OF THE SCARE

Vulnerability of Soviet Nuclear Forces to a US Surprise Attack

Although the Soviet strategic nuclear force in the late 1970's was powerful and versatile (over 7,000 strategic nuclear weapons), it was nonetheless highly vulnerable to a US surprise attack -- a so-called bolt from the blue. Deficiencies in the early warning network, an inadequate, highly centralized command and control system, and a strategic force that was never at full readiness left sizable chinks in the USSR's strategic armor. Until the latter half of the 1970's, the Soviets did not appear to be overly concerned about this shortfall, probably in part because they did not see a US surprise attack as a likely scenario for the outbreak of hostilities.

The USSR may have felt confident that the open nature of US society and Soviet intelligence capabilities made any prospect of the US achieving complete surprise quite remote. Whatever the underlying reasons, Soviet military doctrine at the time generally posited that a strategic nuclear war would probably occur in escalating stages: from a major political crisis, to conventional conflict, to theater nuclear war, to intercontinental exchange. The Soviets' early warning system, command and control network, and strategic forces were geared accordingly: complete wartime readiness could be achieved only after several days of preparation. Nevertheless, as prudent planners, they hedged; part of their strategic forces, particularly silo-based ICBM's, were always held at a high-level of readiness.[14]

[14] For a complete listing of reference documents, see originator.

Strategic Warning System

Before the early 1980's, the Soviet early warning system probably could not provide its leaders with much advance warning of a surprise US nuclear attack outside the context of a political crisis. Ballistic missile early warning (BMEW) radars, located along the periphery of the Soviet Union, were probably able to give about 13 minutes of warning against US ICBM's and about 5 to 15 minutes against SLBM's.

The Soviets apparently came to recognize that they would need much more time to initiate a response. They began several improvement programs in the late 1970's, including the addition of several new BMEW radars -- to extend coverage to nearly all threat corridors -- as well as the development of two over-the-horizon (OTH) radars and launch-detection satellites.

The completion of the OTH radars in 1981 and the comprehensive coverage of US ICBM fields by launch-detection satellites in 1983 significantly increased warning time -- about 30 minutes for US ICBM's and a little over 15 minutes for SLBM's attacking Moscow. However, the introduction by NATO of Pershing II missiles into Europe in late 1983 by Soviet calculations probably reduced their warning of a US first strike on Moscow to about 8 minutes -- less time than they had before their improvement program began.[15]

---

[15]The Pershing II missile 1800 km range would not have reached Moscow from planned deployment sites in West Germany. Warsaw Pact sources, however, attributed to this system a range of 2500 km, an accuracy of 30 meters, and an earth-penetrating warhead. With a range of 2500 km the Soviets feared it would have been able to strike command and control targets in the Moscow area with little or no warning.

~~TOP SECRET~~ UMBRA GAMMA
WNINTEL NOFORN NOCONTRACT ORCON

Command and Control

Once warning of an intercontinental nuclear strike is received, Moscow's ability to initiate a response depends on how quickly the leadership can authorize a retaliation and communicate the orders. [3.3(b)(1)] the Soviet nuclear release process, [3.3(b)(1)] it hinges directly on the survival and, indeed, performance of the top leadership. Probably no more than three political leaders can authorize the use of nuclear weapons. Under severe time constraints -- such as a short-warning preemptive strike or a "launch on tactical warning" -- that authority probably resides with only the General Secretary and the Minister of Defense. When response time is extremely limited, the General Secretary alone may order a launch. There is no evidence that nuclear release authority has devolved to the General Staff or the nuclear force commanders. This strict centralization (along with a nuclear warfighting strategy) undoubtedly was a prime reason for the elaborate measures the Soviets have taken over the last 30 years to ensure leadership survival -- particularly the construction of numerous hardened underground command posts in and around Moscow.

In responding to a surprise US attack, the Soviet decision-making process would be extremely compressed. After confirmation of an incoming attack, the Soviet leadership in most circumstances may have no more than ten minutes to decide on the appropriate response. In that time, they would need to confer, come to an agreement, and issue commands to the General Staff. While this process was under way, if near the Kremlin, they would probably be moving to one of the nearby underground command posts.

If the leadership failed to initiate the appropriate authorization procedures, the USSR's strategic arsenal would probably sit by, helpless. With regard to strategic missiles,

WNINTEL NOFORN NOCONTRACT ORCON
~~TOP SECRET~~ UMBRA GAMMA

only the top leadership can release special "unlocking" codes that permit launch. Similar procedures are in place for the other Soviet strategic nuclear forces.

Once a decision to launch is made, however, orders to the operating forces would be transmitted quickly and accurately. The Soviets introduced several automated communication networks to ensure rapid and reliable command dissemination at the same time they were upgrading their early warning system. All nuclear-capable elements of the Soviet armed forces would receive launching orders: land-based missiles under the control of the Strategic Rocket Forces (SRF); ballistic and cruise missile submarines in the Navy; and bombers of the Strategic Air Force (SAF). Theater nuclear forces would also receive strike commands to counter the anticipated NATO offensive in Europe.

We believe the evidence, therefore, strongly indicates that Soviet nuclear release authority during the war scare period (1980-1984) was held captive to the tumultuous series of leadership successions at the very top. The post of party General Secretary changed hands three times in three years.[16] The only "constant" in the line of authority was Defense Minister Ustinov, who also died in late 1984.

Some high-ranking Soviet military leaders at the time apparently doubted whether the political leadership was up to the task. Marshal Ogarkov, chief of the General Staff in the early 1980,s, seemed to question whether the aged and ill Soviet leadership would be willing or able to meet its strategic decisionmaking responsibilities in times of crisis. He surfaced this issue publicly on three occasions: during the waning months of Brezhnev's rule; during Andropov's short tenure; and following

[16]Brezhnev died 10 November, 1982; Andropov died 9 February 1984; Chernenko died 10 March 1985.

Chernenko's accession. Through these conspicuous articles, Ogarkov may have been arguing in a veiled way for some pre-delegation of nuclear release authority to the general staff.

Force Readiness

During the late 1970's and early 1980's, Soviet forces best able to respond to a surprise attack were the silo-based ICBM's. The US estimates that 95 percent of this force (approximately 4,500 weapons then) was ready to launch within several minutes' notice. In strategic war exercises during this time, some Soviet silo-based missiles were launched within three minutes of receipt of the order. In most simulations of a US first strike, without surprise, the force was usually able to leave its silos before notional US warheads struck. These quick reaction times, however, occurred during exercises when missile crews anticipated orders. They could be much slower in a real-life situation wherein a US surprise missile strike was already inbound.

We believe the high readiness of the silo-based missiles was compensation for the high vulnerability of the other parts of the Soviet strategic arsenal:

o Soviet long-range bombers were extremely vulnerable to a US surprise attack. They were (and are still) kept at a low state of readiness -- none were on strip alert. Many hours, perhaps days, probably would have been needed to prepare a large number of bombers for a wartime footing. The Soviets may well have assumed that their entire force would be destroyed in a surprise strike.

o The Soviets probably believed that their ballistic submarines would not fare much better. Normally most of the force were in port; only about 15-18 percent were on combat patrol or in transit to operating areas. During this period, several days may have been required to bring the in-port force to full readiness. Moreover, the Soviets probably had grave concerns about the survivability of their submarines on patrol -- they were able to learn much about US successes at tracking their submarine movements through the Walker-Whitworth espionage ring.

o The Soviet theater nuclear forces were similarly vulnerable. Dispersing missile and artillery units from garrison and supplying them with nuclear weapons would have entailed considerable logistic support. For example, [3.3(b)(1)] [3.3(b)(1)] it would have taken six hours to deploy all of the missiles and warheads stored at a tactical missile base.

Soviet Analysis of the US-USSR Strategic Balance

A major factor influencing Soviet leaders' perceptions about a US surprise attack probably was their reliance on one peculiar mode of intelligence analysis. [3.3(b)(1)] [3.3(b)(1)] during the war scare they were highly dependent on a computer model. [3.3(b)(1)] the KGB developed the model in the mid-1970's to measure perceived changes in the "correlation of forces." Put on-line in 1979, the model's foremost function was identifying inherently unstable political situations in which a deterioration of Soviet power might tempt a US first strike.

[3.3(b)(1)] the model became for the KGB an increasingly important analytic tool. Western scientific and technological advances, as well as the growing complexity of US-USSR relations, were evidently making accurate assessments of the US-USSR strategic balance increasingly more difficult. The KGB reportedly advised the Politburo in the late 1970's that without such a model it would be unable to provide such evaluations. The

Politburo subsequently approved the computer concept.

The computer model program was called VRYAN, an acronym for "Surprise Nuclear Missile Attack." KGB analysts responsible for assessing American strategic intentions operated under the premise that if the US ever obtained decisive, overall superiority, it might be inclined to launch a surprise attack on the Soviet Union. Because the program was supposed to determine quantitatively when such a situation might be approaching, analysts believed it would accurately provide strategic warning.

The KGB computer model was reportedly developed by military and economic specialists. Consisting of a data base of 40,000 weighted elements, its core was a complex software program that processed and continually reevaluated the data. Although we are not privy to the individual data elements, they reportedly were based on those military, political, and economic factors that the Soviets assessed as decisive during World War II.

VRYAN clearly had a high priority far beyond the corridors of the KGB. A special component of the KGB, consisting of about 200 employees, was responsible for inserting fresh data. Prominent economists and military experts from other elements of the Soviet government assisted. In addition, the State Planning Committee submitted classified data on the Soviet economy, such as details on the state budget, the labor pool, Soviet natural resources, and currency reserves. The cost of building and maintaining such a computer was presumably very high, particularly given the state of Soviet computer technology in those years.

The model reportedly assigned a fixed value of 100 to the combined economic-military-political power of the United States. On this scale, the program experts believed that the USSR would be safe against a US first strike at a value of 60 (i.e., 60 percent of overall US power), though they felt that a level of 70 would provide a desirable margin. The data base was constantly updated, and force correlations could be assessed at any time. Reports derived from VRYAN reportedly were sent to the Politburo once a month.

Before long, VRYAN began spewing very unwelcome news -- which brought dire predictions. Initially, there was some optimism within the KGB that, with technological progress, the Soviet Union would gradually improve its position vis-a-vis the US. However, by 1984 VRYAN calculated that Soviet power had actually declined to 45 percent of that of the United States. Forty percent was viewed as a critical threshold. Below this level, the Soviet Union would be considered dangerously inferior to the United States. [3.3(b)(1)] if the Soviet rating fell below 40 percent, the KGB and the military leadership would inform the political leadership that the security of the USSR could not be guaranteed. [3.3(b)(1)] [3.3(b)(1)] the USSR would launch a preemptive attack within a few weeks of falling below the 40-percent mark.

The extent to which VRYAN was driving Politburo thinking is not clear. The computer model apparently was not tied to any military operational plans, nor is there evidence that the Politburo ever established any contingency plans based on its assessments. Nevertheless, [3.3(b)(1)] Politburo deliberations on security issues during this time involved only a few members. [3.3(b)(1)] [3.3(b)(1)]

We believe that if VRYAN accurately depicted the strategic balance of the time, it would have shown the USSR highly vulnerable to a US surprise attack. Recent US intelligence computer simulations approximating the VRYAN model suggest that the Soviets would have expected only a fraction of their strategic nuclear forces to survive a coordinated US attack. Figure 1, for example, shows how Soviet military planners may have viewed the status of their forces if caught by surprise and forced to ride out a massive attack. We believe the VRYAN model would have shown that after such an attack, Soviet strategic forces could have delivered only about a quarter of the 6,100 warheads necessary to achieve wartime military objectives.

Although it may seem absurd to some that the Soviets would put much stock in a computer model to assess something as complex as the strategic balance, we suspect this approach may have been especially appealing to top Soviet leaders at the time. Almost all were formally trained as engineers. A computer model which purported to be scientifically based and capable of quantifying the seemingly confusing strategic balance may therefore have had a high degree of credibility, particularly during a period in which the Soviet leadership seemed genuinely and increasingly wary of a US surprise attack.

We believe Soviet strategic doctrine also played a key role in how the leadership reacted to VRYAN assessments. Soviet military writings consistently assert that overwhelming advantage lies with the side that launches massed nuclear strikes first. In their exercises and classified writings, the Soviets regularly depict the transition from conventional to nuclear war in Europe occurring when Soviet forces preempt an imminent NATO large-scale nuclear strike. The inherent danger of this doctrine of preemption is that in a period like the war scare, strong misperceptions could easily precipitate a strong, ill-founded reaction.

<u>"THE WAR SCARE"</u>

<u>Late 1970's: Changing Soviet Perceptions of US Intentions</u>

~~SECRET NOFORN~~

Figure 1

Soviet Strategic Retaliatory Capabilities Given a US "Bolt from the Blue"

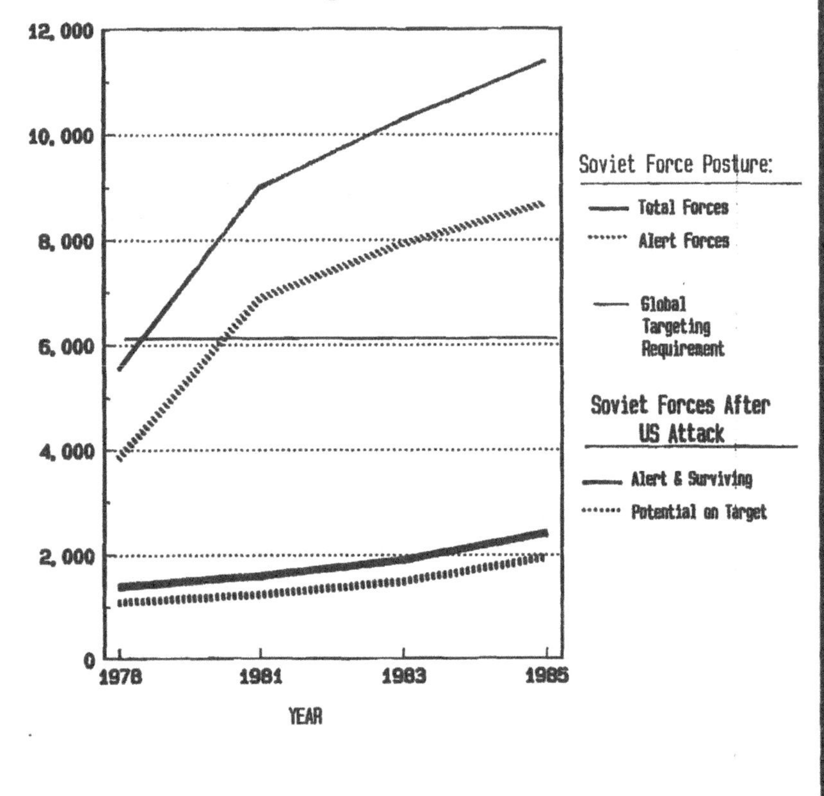

~~SECRET~~ NOFORN

Although Soviet leadership anxieties about US military intentions reached a crescendo in 1983-1984, concern may have been manifest by the late 1970's, when detente began to unravel. Long before the invasion of Afghanistan, Soviet political leaders publicly charged that US policy seemed aimed at "applying the brakes" to detente and increasing the level of competition with the Soviet Union. This shift, they argued, began during the mid-1970's and intensified during the last few years of the decade.

The Soviets' public response to US punitive measures following the Afghanistan invasion seemed to highlight a growing concern and confusion about the direction of US-Soviet relations.[17] [3.3(b)(1)] reports indicate that they were genuinely surprised at the intensity of the US reaction to Afghanistan -- they apparently thought that Washington would recognize their security concerns as legitimate. [3.3(b)(1)] reporting also suggests that the Soviet leadership was becoming seriously perplexed by the perceived shift in US policy: was it a continuation of the tougher tactics they had been witnessing for some time, or did it reflect a calculated turn away from detente and toward increased confrontation?

United States nuclear force modernization plans may have been particularly vexing to Moscow. In the late 1970's, the US made public its plans to field new generations of ICBM's (MX), SLBM's (D-5), and intercontinental bombers (stealth). The Soviets apparently viewed these new systems as highly lethal against their silos and most other hardened targets, providing the US with more strategic nuclear power than was necessary for its long-held strategy of mutually assured destruction. Evidence from sensitive reporting suggests Soviet analysts calculated that the US intended

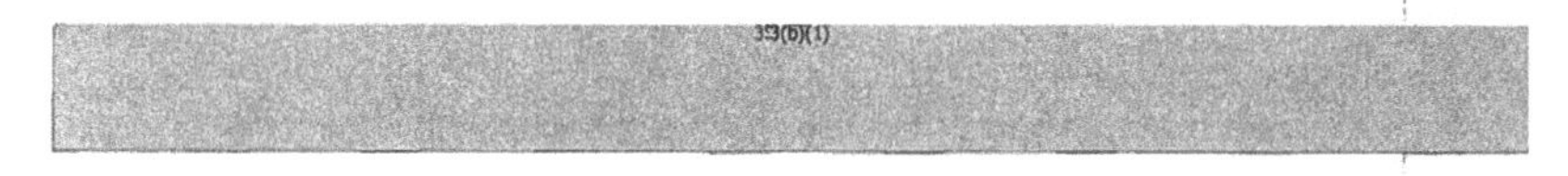

them as a means for developing a first-strike force. In addition, the Soviets perhaps calculated that NATO's decision to field 600 Pershing II's and cruise missiles was not to counter their SS-20 force, but yet another step toward a first-strike capability.

Party Secretary Suslov and Defense Minister Ustinov, the senior guardians of Soviet ideology and national security, were among the first to express these apparent misgivings. In an address before the Polish party congress in February 1980, Suslov asserted that there was a "profound interconnection" to recent US-inspired actions: the "aggression" by China against Vietnam, the NATO decisions "aimed at a new arms race," the deployment of "enormous numbers" of US armed forces around Iran, and the "training and sending of armed terrorist groups" into Afghanistan. Several days later, Ustinov condemned alleged US and Chinese interference in Afghanistan, US delay in ratification of the SALT II treaty, the NATO theater nuclear force decision, and the buildup of US naval forces in the Persian Gulf as "interconnected elements of an aggressive US policy."

Not long after, Premier Kosygin, a more moderate member of the top leadership, echoed the same misgivings. He charged that US policy had become a "fully defined political policy calculated to undermine detente and provoke conflict situations. We cannot but draw the necessary conclusions from this for our practical activities." As a CIA analyst has pointed out, Kosygin's remarks may have mirrored the uncertainty underlying many Politburo members' perceptions of US intentions and behavior in the post-Afghanistan period. On the one hand, he seemed to be joining Suslov in suggesting that "reactionary forces" had gained the upper hand in US policymaking and were determined to force a confrontation. On the other hand, he seemed to be fervently reassuring domestic and East European audiences that this was not necessarily the case and that US policy could moderate:

> It must be said that realistic representatives of the ruling circles in the West, not to mention broad sections of the population, are concerned with the consequences of the present course of the US Administration . . . . Clearly it would be wrong to assume that in the United States there are no soberminded politicians who are aware of the significance of detente.[18]

1980: Heightened Concern

By the summer of 1980, Soviet public pronouncements on the future of US-USSR relations had soured markedly. A 23 June Central Committee resolution referred to "adventuristic actions of the United States," which it asserted led to a "heightening of the danger of war." Claiming the United States was undermining detente, attempting to form an anti-Soviet alliance with China, and refusing to acknowledge legitimate Soviet security interests, the resolution called for "constant vigilance and all-round strengthening of defense."

Public and private statements by top Soviet leaders suggested that many did not expect any near-term improvements in US-Soviet relations. In June, Politburo member Andrei Kirilenko alluded to the need for "augmenting the country's economic and defense potential," because "imperialist circles, primarily those in the United States, are causing considerable complications in the international situation." In a private meeting with visiting Indian communists in July, Kirilenko and other officials reportedly described the world situation as "grim," and accused the US

3.3(b)(1)

~~TOP SECRET~~ UMBRA GAMMA
WNINTEL NOFORN NOCONTRACT ORCON

Administration of creating a "war psychosis" by trying to "isolate" and "encircle" the Soviet Union. In a June address to the heads of government of the Council of Mutual Economic Assistance, Kosygin seemed to be preparing his audience for the possibility that NATO-Warsaw Pact tensions might require greater Bloc expenditures for military programs. He charged that the United States has already embarked on "a course hostile to the cause of detente, a course of cranking up the arms race, leading to the intensification of the war danger in the world." Brezhnev seemed to be alone in expressing limited optimism. In August, for example, he noted that "sooner or later" the US would conclude that "sabre rattling" would fail.

After the US Presidential election, the Soviet leadership sent out feelers to determine if the tough speeches delivered during the campaign indeed indicated the future course of Reagan Administration foreign policy. In a 17 November, 1980, speech, Brezhnev said that he would not dwell on statements made by the President-elect during "the heat of the election struggle" and would welcome any "constructive steps" on ways to improve US-Soviet relations. This opening was repeated privately by Soviet diplomats, officials, and foreign policy analysts, who stressed to their US contacts that Moscow was interested in bilateral exchanges and a good start in "businesslike" relations. United States-Soviet relations were dealt a blow in December, however, with the death of the usually moderate Premier Kosygin.[19]

* * *

Behind the scenes, the Soviet intelligence services were giving equally dour assessments on the future of US-Soviet relations. A secret Soviet intelligence document prepared in

3.3(b)(1)

WNINTEL NOFORN NOCONTRACT ORCON
~~TOP SECRET~~ UMBRA GAMMA

October for General Ivashutin, Chief of Soviet military intelligence, the GRU, stated that the US and NATO, rather than "maintaining the approximate parity" that had developed, were trying to tip the strategic balance of forces in their favor. The document also assessed a US Presidential directive (PD-59) signed by President Carter as a "new nuclear strategy" intended to enhance "the readiness of US strategic nuclear forces to deliver a sudden preemptive strike against . . . the Soviet Union and Warsaw Pact." Vladimir Kryuchkov, then head of the KGB's foreign intelligence directorate, evidently shared this evaluation. In a secret speech in late 1980, he reportedly declared that "US imperialism is again becoming aggressive and is striving to change the strategic balance." He also revealed that the party had admonished its intelligence organs not to "overlook the possibility of a US missile attack on our country."

* * *

Meanwhile, the Soviet Navy began to implement steps to reduce the missile launch readiness of "duty status" submarines. Prior to 1980, submarines were required to be able to launch their missiles within 4 hours after receiving orders. In the summer of 1980, a much reduced launch readiness, perhaps as low as 30 minutes, was being considered by Northern Fleet commanders. By October 1980, they had achieved a readiness of 3 hours, and sometime between 1982 and 1985, duty status submarines were able to launch within 20 minutes.

1981: Reducing Vulnerabilities

By early March 1981, the Soviet leadership may well have concluded that a period of US-Soviet confrontation had arrived. Moscow's trial balloon suggesting an early summit never got off the ground. The US declared that Brezhnev's proposals on arms control did not provide a basis for serious negotiations and insisted that future talks would be contingent upon Soviet behavior in Poland, Afghanistan, Central America, and other trouble spots.

Moscow's response was hard line. The first salvo appeared in Pravda on March 25 in an article by "I. Aleksandrov" -- a pseudonym signifying leadership endorsement. It attacked US foreign policy on a broad front -- the first such barrage since the Reagan Administration had entered office. Increasingly strident attacks followed in April and May. Brezhnev took the US to task in major speeches on 7 and 27 April, as did his protege, Chernenko, at a Lenin Day address on 22 April. Brezhnev's delivery commemorating Soviet VE day charged that the Reagan Administration no longer belonged to the "sober-minded" forces in the West and that Washington had made military superiority its "main political credo" -- while relegating arms control to the bottom of the priority list. [3.3(b)(1)] senior Soviet officials with high-level contacts said that during this time Soviet leaders formally cautioned the bureaucracy that the new US Administration was considering the possibility of starting nuclear war, and that the prospect of a surprise nuclear strike against the Soviet Union had to be taken seriously.

In August 1981, Brezhnev met secretly in the Crimea with each of the Warsaw Pact leaders to obtain signatures on a strategic war planning document that streamlined the decisionmaking process to go to war. This top secret accord in essence codified the Soviet Union's authority to order Warsaw Pact forces to war without prior Pact consultations. It included a discussion of likely Soviet responses to possible changes in the correlation of forces. Soviet preemption of an attempted US surprise attack was one of the scenarios depicted. [3.3(b)(1)] the Soviets had become concerned that there might be little time to react in a fast-moving political crisis and that the upper hand could be lost militarily if Pact consultations were required before committing forces.

~~TOP SECRET~~ UMBRA GAMMA
WNINTEL NOFORN NOCONTRACT ORCON

* * *

Probably reflecting the rising concern among the political leaders, the Soviet intelligence services clearly began girding its officers for difficult times ahead. In a secret February speech, Vladimir Kryuchkov -- on this occasion to a group of mid-level KGB officers -- stressed that ". . . the political situation world-wide is going from bad to worse and there is no end in sight . . . China continues to be a threat . . . the general situation in East Europe, both politically and economically, is not good . . . the Soviet economy is currently in a poor position resulting from poor harvests, bad planning and a general lack of discipline." He also exhorted all KGB Residencies to work to "prevent the US and its allies from deciding to make a first strike attack on the Soviet Union and the KGB."

By the spring, unease at the top of the political hierarchy evidently had become so pronounced that it called for extraordinary efforts from its foreign intelligence apparatus. In late May, then KGB chief and Politburo member Yuriy Andropov declared to a major KGB conference that the new US Administration was actively preparing for war and that a nuclear first strike was possible. Andropov disclosed that, in response, the KGB was placing strategic military intelligence at the top of its collection priorities list. The KGB had always been tasked to report on US political intentions, but this was the first time it had been ordered to obtain such strategic military information. Thus, VRYAN took on a new dimension, and now both the KGB and the GRU had as their foremost mission the collection of intelligence to protect the USSR from strategic nuclear attack. [3.3(b)(1)] Kryuchkov and several of his key officers in the First Chief Directorate -- including the Chief of the "US Department" -- increasingly became strong VRYAN proponents.

~~TOP SECRET~~ UMBRA GAMMA
WNINTEL NOFORN NOCONTRACT ORCON

The rank and file began to respond. While many senior KGB specialists in US and military affairs apparently had serious reservations about some of Andropov's views on this matter, there reportedly was general accord on two important points. First, KGB officers in the Center agreed that the United States might initiate a nuclear strike if it achieved a level of overall strength markedly greater than that of the Soviet Union. And many apparently were convinced that events were leading in that direction. A group of technocrats advising Andropov reportedly persuaded him that the USSR would continue to fall behind the US in economic power and scientific expertise. Second, there was common concern that the Soviet domestic situation, as well as Moscow's hold on Eastern Europe, was deteriorating, further weakening Soviet capacity to compete strategically with the US.[20]

Andropov hastily ordered a special "institute" within the KGB to implement the new strategic military intelligence program. The institute was told -- despite protestations for more time -- to quickly define the task, develop a plan, and be ready to levy the initial collection and reporting requirements to KGB Residencies by November 1981. Some KGB officers in the field reportedly felt that the short, arbitrary deadlines for developing VRYAN requirements resulted in poorly conceived requirements.[21]

As the KGB mobilized, it also began pressuring its East European allies for strong support. Both Andropov and Kryuchkov actively lobbied the Czechoslovak intelligence service on this score. Andropov approached Czechoslovak Interior Minister Obzina early in 1981 regarding the VRYAN collection effort, presenting it as an unprecedented KGB collection effort that demanded the "best intelligence techniques." He followed up with a private visit to

3.3(b)(1)

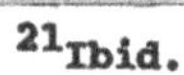

[21] Ibid.

WNINTEL NOFORN NOCONTRACT ORCON
~~TOP SECRET~~ UMBRA GAMMA

Prague, where he expressed strong disappointment with the Czechoslovak response and solicited the direct intervention of senior intelligence officials.

Andropov's efforts at personalizing the issue evidently paid off. Obzina subsequently gave an emotional presentation to the Czechoslovak Politburo describing the immediacy of the threat from the US, which he said sooner or later would result in a surprise nuclear attack. Reflecting Moscow's urgency, Obzina described the requirement as the biggest and most important strategic task the Czechoslovak service had ever undertaken. Not long after, Prague issued to its field offices a "Minister's Directive of Top Priority" to collect VRYAN-related data on five substantive areas -- political, economic, military, science and technology, and civil defense.

* * *

Developments within the Soviet military, meanwhile, also strongly suggested a growing apprehension about a possible US strategic first-strike. Military leaders began to improve the readiness of nuclear forces most vulnerable to surprise attack. 3.3(b)(1) in May, 1981, for example, Soviet Navy officials initiated a program to shorten launch times for ballistic missile submarines in port. Submarines undergoing repairs were ordered to be ready to launch within 48 hours notice (as opposed to 8 days), and boats awaiting redeployment were told to be ready to launch within 3 to 4 hours. Lower-level Navy officials reportedly viewed these new readiness times as unrealistic because they would strain maintenance capabilities and be difficult to sustain indefinitely. In addition, the Navy began experimenting with missile launches from submarines pierside, reportedly achieving a notice-to-launch time of one hour.

Furthermore, the Soviet military took several steps during

this time to improve their theater nuclear forces. All-weather capable SU-24 bombers were deployed in East Germany, Poland, and Hungary, greatly enhancing the availability of nuclear strike forces in the forward area. The Soviets for the first time also deployed nuclear-capable artillery to the front-line ground forces opposite NATO.[22]

1982: Strategic Preparations

Signs of disquiet within the Soviet military hierarchy over national strategic vulnerabilities became more openly pronounced in 1982. Marshal Ogarkov, in particular, publicly expressed his concern over the readiness of Soviet society to respond to US challenges. Notably, he called for moving Soviet economic priorities from business-as-usual to a prewar footing. In his book History Teaches Vigilance, he sternly admonished his countrymen:

> The element of surprise already played a certain role in World War II. Today it is becoming a factor of the greatest strategic importance. The question of prompt and expeditious shifting of the Armed Forces and the entire national economy to a war footing and their mobilization deployment in a short period of time is much more critical today . . . coordination between the Armed Forces and the national economy as a whole is required today as never before, especially in . . . ensuring the stability and survivability of the nation's entire vast economic mechanism. Essential in this connection is a constant search for improving the system of co-production among enterprises producing the

[22] Warning of War in Europe, NIE 4-1-4.

> principal types of weapons . . . to establish a reserve supply of equipment and materials in case of war.

The view of impending nuclear war with the United States was apparently seeping into the mid-level officer corps. A Soviet emigre who attended a 1982 training course at the Moscow Civil Defense Headquarters quoted one instructor -- a lieutenant colonel -- as saying that the Soviet Union intended to deliver a preemptive strike against the United States, using 50 percent of its warheads.

The Soviet leadership convened a conference in late October, perhaps in part to reassure the military. Top political deputies, ministry officials, marshals, service commanders, regional military commanders and commanders of Soviet forces abroad were in attendance. Defense Minister Ustinov, in his introduction of General Secretary Brezhnev, declared that "the acute intensification of the aggressive nature of imperialism threatens to incite the world into flames of a nuclear war." In his address to the conference, Brezhnev promised the Soviet armed forces that the Central Committee would take measures "to meet all your needs."[23]

* * *

Meanwhile, KGB Headquarters had issued formal instructions to KGB Residencies abroad to strengthen significantly their work on strategic warning. [3.3(b)(1)] these instructions were sent first to KGB elements in the US, and within a month, an abridged version was sent to Residencies in Western Europe. Reflecting the same concerns expressed by Andropov at the March 1981 KGB conference, the tasking from Moscow primarily focused on detecting US plans to launch a surprise attack:

---

[23]FBIS TV Report, 28 October 1982.

> The current international situation, which is characterized by a considerable strengthening of the adversary's military preparations as well as by a growing threat of war, requires that active and effective steps be taken to strengthen intelligence work dealing with military-strategic problems. It is of special importance to discover the adversary's concrete plans and measures linked with his preparation for a surprise nuclear missile attack on the USSR and other socialist countries.

The cable went on to specify information to be collected in direct support of the VRYAN requirement, including NATO war plans; preparations for launching a nuclear missile attack against the USSR; and political decisionmaking leading to the initiation of war (see Figure 2 for VRYAN requirements).[24]

Indeed, KGB bosses seemed already convinced that US war plans were real. A former KGB officer said that while attending a senior officer course, he read an order to all departments of the KGB's foreign intelligence arm -- but especially those targeting the US and NATO -- to increase their collection efforts because there was information indicating NATO was preparing for a "third world war."

The reactions of Soviet intelligence to the death of General Secretary Brezhnev on November 10 suggests to us that there was serious concern that the USSR was militarily in jeopardy and that the US might take advantage of the confusion concomitant with a leadership change. [3.3(b)(1)] KGB and GRU Residencies in at least two Soviet missions abroad were placed on

~~TOP SECRET~~ UMBRA GAMMA
WNINTEL NOFORN NOCONTRACT ORCON

Figure 2. VRYAN Collection Requirements

Throughout the early 1980's, VRYAN requirements were the number one (and urgent) collection priority for Soviet intelligence and, subsequently, some East European services as well. They were tasked to collect:

- Plans and measures of the United States, other NATO countries, Japan, and China directed at the preparation for and unleashing of war against the "socialist" countries, as well as the preparation for and unleashing of armed conflicts in various other regions of the world.
- Plans for hostile operational deployments and mobilizations.
- Plans for hostile operations in the initial stage of war; primarily operations to deliver nuclear strikes and for assessments of aftereffects.
- Plans indicating the preparation for and adoption and implementation of decisions by the NATO political and military leadership dealing with the unleashing of a nuclear war and other armed conflicts.

Some specific tasking concerning the United States included:

- Any information on President Reagan's "flying headquarters," including individual airfields and logistic data.
- Succession and matters of state leadership, to include attention to the Federal Emergency Management Agency.
- Information from the level of Deputy Assistant Secretary on up at the Department of State, as it was believed that these officials might talk.
- Monitoring of activities of the National Security Council and the Vice President's crisis staff.
- Monitoring of the flow of money and gold on Wall Street as well as the movement of high-grade jewelry, collections of rare paintings, and similar items. (This was regarded as useful geostrategic information.)

WNINTEL NOFORN NOCONTRACT ORCON
~~TOP SECRET~~ UMBRA GAMMA

alert. Intelligence officers were tasked with monitoring US installations, both military and civilian, for indications of US military mobilization or other actions which might portend a move against the USSR, and to report frequently to Moscow. This alert, [3.3(b)(1)] continued until Brezhnev was buried on November 15. [3.3(b)(1)] [3.3(b)(1)] considerable anxiety within the Soviet military during this time over who had nuclear release authority in case of a feared US surprise attack.

* * *

As Yuriy Andropov settled into the General Secretaryship, Soviet strategic forces continued to improve their readiness posture. In December, for example, the Strategic Air Force Commander-in-Chief authorized a plan for the improvement of the combat readiness of Arctic air bases. [3.3(b)(1)] [3.3(b)(1)] this initiative provided greater flexibility in dispersing the Soviet bomber force and reducing the flight time for attacks on the US.[25] Moreover, beginning at about this time and continuing through 1985, Soviet bomber training was devoted largely to the problem of enemy surprise nuclear strikes. One solution that evolved was launching aircraft on tactical warning.

1983: Nearing the Precipice

Growing Pessimism, Additional Precautions

The new Soviet leadership's public reaction to two major US Presidential speeches early in 1983 seems to indicate that its concern about American strategic intentions was mounting markedly. In response to the President's so-called "evil empire" speech on

---

[25] Soviet Forces and Capabilities for Strategic Nuclear Conflict Through the Late 1990's, NIE 11-3/8, December, 1987.

March 8, the Soviet press charged that Reagan "can think only in terms of confrontation and bellicose, lunatic anti-communism." Later that month, Andropov responded in Pravda to the President's Strategic Defense Initiative speech:

> On the face of it, layman may even find it attractive, since the President speaks about what seem to be defensive measures . . . . In fact, the strategic offensive forces of the United States will continue to be developed and upgraded at full tilt and along quite a definitive line at that, namely that of acquiring a nuclear first-strike capability.

In the early 1980's, many "civilian" Soviet foreign affairs experts apparently looked upon US actions as aggressive and diplomatically hostile, but not necessarily as precursors to strategic war. By early 1983, however, these specialists, probably realizing they were out of step with Soviet officialdom, also seemed to take a bleaker view of the US-USSR relationship. In January, the Soviet Institute of the US and Canada (IUSAC) held a conference on "strategic stability," and the overall mood was characterized 3.3(b)(1) as "pessimistic." The group appeared particularly disturbed by the planned Pershing II deployments and underlying US motivations: "The Pershing II, with a flight of 5-6 minutes, represents surprise, and cruise missiles in great numbers also are first-strike weapons." But some optimism prevailed. Evidently expressing the views of many of his colleagues, one participant reportedly commented, "Strategic stability is being disturbed in the 1980's, but is not broken."

Also early in the year, Marshal Ogarkov began to earn a reputation: his pessimism toward relations with the US was almost unequalled among senior Soviet officials. Ogarkov's strident advocacy for increased military expenditures to counter the US military buildup led one [3.3(b)(1)] to call him a "dangerous man." In a February press article, he cited the US "Defense Directive of Fiscal 1984-1985" as proof of "how far the 'hawks' have gone," and implied that procuring new, sophisticated military hardware had to proceed apace in the USSR. Sometime thereafter, in a meeting with a Deputy Minister of Defense Industry, he urged that Soviet industry begin preparing for war, [3.3(b)(1)] In a speech in March, Ogarkov revealed that his pressure on the political leadership seemed to be having an effect:

> The CPSU Central Committee and the Soviet Government are implementing important measures to further increase the defense potential and the mobilization readiness of industry, agriculture, transport, and other sectors of the national economy, and to ensure their timely preparation for the transfer to a war footing . . . .

By late summer, General Secretary Andropov's own attitudes seemed to be increasingly accentuated by the same foreboding, judging from the signals he apparently was sending Washington. In August, he told a delegation of six US Democratic Senators that "the tension which is at this time characteristic of practically all areas of our relationship is not our choice. The United States' rationale in this is possibly clearer to you." Moreover, in a comment to the Senators but probably directed at President Reagan, Andropov warned:

> There may be someone in Washington who believes that in circumstances of tension, in a 'game without rules,' it will be easier to achieve one's objectives. I do not think so. In the grand scheme of things it is not so at

> all. It will not work for one side to be the dominant one. Would the United States permit someone to achieve superiority over them? I doubt it. And this is why we would not tolerate it either.[26]

* * *

And there apparently was little doubt at the top of the Soviet intelligence services about where US policy was heading. In February, KGB headquarters issued a new, compelling operational directive to the KGB Residence in London, as well as to other Residences in NATO countries. The "Permanent Operational Assignment to uncover NATO Preparations for a Nuclear Attack on the Soviet Union" reaffirmed the Residency's task of "discovering promptly any preparations by the adversary for a nuclear attack (RYAN) on the USSR." It also included an assessment of the Pershing II missile that concluded that the weapon's short flight time would present an especially acute warning problem. Moscow emphasized that insight on NATO's war planning had thus become even more critical:

> Immediate preparation for a nuclear attack begins at the moment when the other side's political leadership reaches the conclusion that it is expedient to use military force as the international situation becomes progressively more acute and makes a preliminary decision to launch an attack on the Soviet Union . . . the so-called nuclear consultations in NATO are probably one of the states of

---

[26] Dangerous Stalemate: Superpower Relations in Autumn 1983, a Report of a Delegation of Eight Senators to the Soviet Union, September, 1983.

immediate preparation by the adversary for VRYAN.

The time between NATO's preliminary decision to launch a surprise attack and when the strike would occur was assessed to be 7-10 days. Residents were also requested to submit reports concerning this requirement every two weeks -- regardless of whether there was any new information. This marked the first time that KGB Residencies were required to submit "negative" collection reports.

The immediacy of the threat also permeated GRU reporting requirements. Directives from Soviet military intelligence headquarters stated that war could break out at any moment. Residencies were constantly reminded that they must prepare for war and be able to recycle their operations to a war footing in a moment's notice.

About the same time, the GRU also took direct steps to ensure that intelligence reporting would continue after the outbreak of war. It created a new directorate to oversee illegal agents (assets operating in a foreign country without diplomatic or other official status). This unit, [3.3(b)(1)] was tasked to move quickly to form agent networks that could communicate independently with headquarters in Moscow. [3.3(b)(1)] [3.3(b)(1)] "The idea of creating such illegal nets was not new, but the urgency was." [3.3(b)(1)] the urgency reflected Soviet perceptions of an increased "threat of war . . . ."

Throughout the summer of 1983, Moscow pressed KGB and GRU Residencies hard to collect on the VRYAN requirement. A June dispatch from KGB Center in Moscow to the Resident in London, for example, declared that, "the US Administration is continuing its preparations for nuclear war and is augmenting its nuclear potential." [3.3(b)(1)] KGB and GRU Residents world-wide were also instructed to increase operational coordination with each other and "define" their relationship with ambassadors and chiefs of mission. [3.3(b)(1)] that this was designed to improve the overall effectiveness of the intelligence effort. In August, the Center dispatched additional VRYAN requirements, some quite specific. It alerted Residencies to increased NATO intelligence activities, submarine operations, and counterintelligence efforts.

But not everyone was on board. [3.3(b)(1)] [3.3(b)(1)] some KGB officers overseas during this time became increasingly skeptical of the VRYAN requirement. Its obsessive nature seemed to indicate to some in the London KGB Residency, for example, that something was askew in Moscow. None of the political reporting officers who concentrated on VYRAN believed in the immediacy of the threat, especially a US surprise attack. In fact, two officers complained to the Resident that Moscow was mistaken in believing the United States was preparing for a unilateral war. They felt that the Residency itself might be partly to blame -- it had, willy-nilly, submitted alarmist reports on the West's military preparations, intensified ideological struggle, and similar themes to try to satiate Moscow's demands for VRYAN reporting.

* * *

Inside the Soviet armed forces, commanders evidently had sufficiently voiced alarm regarding their forces' state of preparedness against a surprise attack. In January 1983, Moscow issued a new key element to its military readiness system: a condition called "Surprise Enemy Attack Using Weapons of Mass Destruction in Progress." It augmented the four existing levels of readiness: (1) Constant Combat Readiness, (2) Increased Combat Readiness, (3) Threat of War, and (4) Full Combat Readiness. This fifth condition could be declared regardless of the readiness stage in effect at the time. It involved a wide variety of immediate defensive and offensive measures -- such as dispersing forces, taking shelter, and preparing to launch forces.

Probably in response to new US and NATO strategies and equipment upgrades, the Soviet military forces also initiated a number of steps to reduce vulnerabilities to attack:

o A crash program to build additional ammunition storage bunkers at Bulgarian airfields. This would improve capabilities to preposition air ammunition for Soviet aircraft deployed to support the air defense force against an improved NATO air threat on the Southern Front.

o The institution of a new regulation to bring tactical missile brigades from peacetime conditions to full readiness within eight hours. (In the late 1970's, a day or more was needed.) Moreover, improvements were introduced at nuclear warhead storage facilities that halved the time needed to remove warheads.

o Creation of a unique Soviet naval infantry brigade on the Kola peninsula to repel amphibious landings -- probably a direct response to the US Navy's new forward maritime strategy.

o For the first time, a test of combat and airborne command post aircraft in a simulated electromagnetic pulse (EMP) environment. Soviet planners evidently had come to recognize the serious EMP threat to their command and control systems posed by a US nuclear strike.

Reflecting the heightened emphasis on defense preparedness, Moscow increased procurement of military equipment in 1983 by 5 to 10 percent, apparently by reducing production of civilian goods. Commercial aircraft production, for example, was reduced by about 14 percent in favor of military transports. To overcome this particular shortfall, the Soviets reportedly bought back airframes from East European airlines. They also converted some vehicle plants from tractor to tank production. One such plant -- at Chelyabinsk -- had not produced tank chassis since World War II.

Mounting Tensions

By September 1983, in a sign probably reflecting perceptions at the top that the USSR was increasingly in peril, military officers began assuming more of a role as official spokesmen. Marshal Ogarkov, for example, was the Soviet official who offered explanations for shooting down KAL-007. In the past, high-ranking officers rarely commented in public on major defense issues. The increased public role of the military, particularly by Ogarkov, coincided with the deterioration of Yuriy Andropov's health. The General Secretary was suffering from long-standing hypertension and diabetes, complicated by kidney disease. Kidney failure in late September led to a long period of illness, which ended in his death in February 1984.

Typical of the Soviet military attacks against US policy during this period, Marshal Kulikov, Commander of the Warsaw Pact, warned in Pravda that the deployment of US Pershing II and cruise missiles "could give rise to an irresistible temptation in Washington to use it against the socialist community countries." An Ogarkov Tass article on 22 September, in which he warned that a sudden strike against the USSR would not go unpunished, was particularly vitriolic:

> The USA is stepping up the buildup of strategic nuclear forces . . . to deal a 'disarming' nuclear blow to the USSR. This is a reckless step. Given the present development and spread of nuclear weapons in the world, the defending side will always be left with a quantity of nuclear means capable of responding to the aggressor with a retaliatory

strike causing an 'unacceptable damage'.

He further warned that "only suicides can stake on dealing a first nuclear strike in the present-day conditions . . . and . . . new 'Pershings' and cruise missiles in Western Europe are a means for a first strike." Perhaps most ominous, however, was the comparisons Ogarkov made between the US and prewar Nazi Germany.

The conspicuous public appearance of Soviet military leaders and their relentless, often crude attacks on US policy seemed to spread the fear of war among the population. In Moscow, programs highlighting the seriousness of the international situation and the possibility of a US attack were broadcast on radio and television several times a day. At least some Westerners living in Moscow, [3.3(b)(1)] have said that these programs appeared not for external consumption, but to prepare Soviet citizens for the inevitability of nuclear war with the US. The propaganda campaign seemed to work. Conversations by Westerners with Soviet citizens at the time revealed that the "war danger" line was widely accepted.[27]

From September onward, the Kremlin offered up increasingly bitter public diatribes against the US. Its language suggested that there was almost no hope for repairing relations. Soviet spokesmen accused President Reagan and his advisors of "madness," "extremism," and "criminality." By this time, Moscow evidently recognized that its massive propaganda campaign to derail the Pershing II and cruise missile deployments had failed. According to press reports, Soviet officials had concluded that the Reagan Administration deliberately engineered the KAL incident to poison the international atmosphere and thereby ensure the missiles would be deployed -- i.e., a demonstration of resolve. Yuriy Andropov,

[27] Soviet Thinking on the Possibility of Armed Confrontation with the United States, CIA, 22 December 1983.

commenting in late September on the KAL-007 shootdown, wrote in Pravda: "Even if someone had illusions as to the possible evolution for the better in the policy of the present Administration, the latest developments have finally dispelled them."

By late summer, the leadership appeared to be bracing the population for the worst. [3.3(b)(1)] [3.3(b)(1)] the population was being prepared for a possible war. [3.3(b)(1)] [3.3(b)(1)] signs were being posted everywhere showing the location of air raid shelters. Factories reportedly were required to include air raid drills in their normal work plans. Moreover, a Western visitor to Moscow reported that Andropov sent a letter to all party organizations declaring that the motherland was truly in danger and there was no chance for an improvement in relations with the United States. This letter was reportedly read at closed party meetings throughout the country. In October, Marshal Kulikov announced that preparations for deploying new nuclear missiles to Czechoslovakia and East Germany had begun. The US invasion of Grenada brought a renewed shrillness to the Soviets' public attacks on the US. The Kremlin said it held the President personally responsible for what it described as a "bandit attack" and a "crime against peace and humanity."

* * *

Also toward the end of the year, clear evidence of the Soviet military's preoccupation with readiness again surfaced. The 4th Air Army in Poland received orders to reduce arming times for aircraft with nuclear missions. This apparently stemmed from a new readiness directive issued in October, which ordered several procedural reviews, including: the time needed to prepare nuclear weapons for transport; the time needed to transport nuclear weapons from storage sites to the aircraft; and the time needed to hand over nuclear weapons to aircraft crews. The instructions also included maximum allowable times for loading nuclear weapons onto aircraft -- 25 minutes for one weapon, 40 minutes for two. In October, the 4th Air Army apparently exercised these new procedures during an inspection by Marshal Ogarkov.

* * *

Within the Soviet leadership, another crisis of transition was in the offing. Andropov apparently became gravely ill and, sometime during October, may have had one of his kidneys removed. His failing health very likely caused the cancellation of a state trip to Bulgaria -- even though the official reason given was the intense international climate. The seriousness of Andropov's condition was apparent when he failed to appear in Kremlin celebrations on November 7 commemorating the 1917 Bolshevik Revolution. 3.3(b)(1)

This event, code-named "Able Archer," occurred at a time when some Soviet leaders seemed almost frantic over the threat of war. According to press accounts, Politburo member Gregory Romanov grimly stated in a speech at the Kremlin on the same day that Able Archer commenced: "The international situation at present is white hot, thoroughly white hot."

Able Archer 83

From 7-11 November, NATO conducted its annual command post exercise to practice nuclear release procedures. This is a recurring event that includes NATO forces from Turkey to England,

and is routinely monitored by Soviet intelligence. Typical Soviet responses in the past have included increased intelligence collection and increased readiness levels at select military garrisons.

The 1983 version of Able Archer, however, had some special wrinkles, which we believe probably fueled Soviet anxieties. NATO tested new procedures for releasing nuclear weaponry that emphasized command communications from headquarters to subordinate units. In addition, unlike previous scenarios wherein NATO forces remained at General Alert throughout, the 1983 plan featured pre-exercise communications that notionally moved forces from normal readiness, through various alert phases, to a General Alert.

Soviet intelligence clearly had tip-offs to the exercise, and HUMINT elements underwent a major mobilization to collect against it. On 8 or 9 November, Moscow sent a circular telegram to KGB Residencies in Western Europe ordering them to report on the increased alert status of US military bases in Europe. Residencies were also instructed to check for indications of an impending nuclear attack against the Soviet Union; the London KGB Residency interpreted this as a sign of Moscow's VRYAN concern. Similar messages to search for US military activity were received by GRU Residencies.[28]

Other Warsaw Pact intelligence services reacted strongly as well. [3.3(b)(1)] intelligence officer intimated that during the Able Archer time frame he had been, "particularly occupied trying to obtain information on a major NATO exercise . . . ." The officer said that his efforts were in response to a year-old, high-priority requirement from Moscow "to look for any indication that the United States was about

[3.3(b)(1)]

~~TOP SECRET~~ UMBRA GAMMA
WNINTEL NOFORN NOCONTRACT ORCON

to launch a preemptive nuclear strike against the countries of the Warsaw Pact."

The Pact also launched an unprecedented technical collection foray against Able Archer 83. [3.3(b)(3); (b)(3)] [3.3(b)(3); (b)(3)] The Soviets also conducted over 36 intelligence flights, significantly more than in previous Able Archers. These included Soviet strategic and naval aviation missions over the Norwegian, North, Baltic, and Barents Seas -- probably to determine whether US naval forces were deploying forward in support of Able Archer.

Warsaw Pact military reactions to this particular exercise were also unparalleled in scale. This fact, together with the timing of their response, strongly suggests to us that Soviet military leaders may have been seriously concerned that the US would use Able Archer 83 as a cover for launching a real attack.

The Soviets evidently believed the exercise would take place sometime between 3 and 11 November, but they initiated significant military preparations well in advance. Beginning October 20, for example, [3.3(b)(3); (b)(3)]

These [3.3(b)(3); (b)(3)] were highly unusual. Most notably, they probably involved 3.3(b)(3); (b)(3) activity seen only during crisis periods in the past. Moreover, 3.3(b)(3); (b)(3)

o Transporting nuclear weapons from storage sites to delivery units by helicopter.

o A "standdown," or suspension of all flight operations, from 4 to 10 November -- with the exception of intelligence collection flights -- probably to have available as many aircraft as possible for combat.

o Invoking a 30-minute, around-the-clock readiness time and assigning priority targets 3.3(b)(3); (b)(3) 3.3(b)(3); (b)(3)

Similar measures were taken by about a third of the Soviet Air Force units 3.3(b)(3); (b)(3)

~~TOP SECRET~~ UMBRA GAMMA
WNINTEL NOFORN NOCONTRACT ORCON

3.3(b)(3); (b)(3)

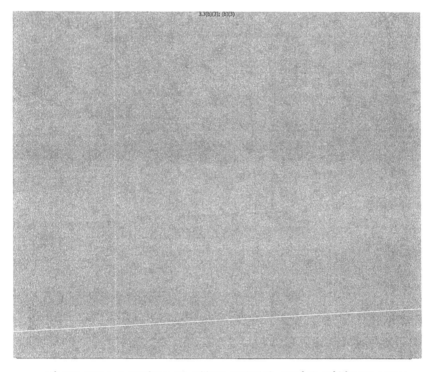

There were a number of other unusual Soviet military moves that, taken in the aggregate, also strongly suggest heightened concern:

3.3(b)(3); (b)(3)

~~TOP SECRET~~ UMBRA GAMMA
WNINTEL NOFORN NOCONTRACT ORCON

By November 11, the Soviet alert evidently was withdrawn. Flight training by Soviet Air Force units in East Germany returned to normal on the 11th [3.3(b)(3); (b)(3)]

On the same day that Soviet forces returned to normal status, Marshal Ustinov delivered a speech in Moscow to a group of high-ranking military officers that, in our view, offers a plausible explanation for the unusual Soviet reactions to Able Archer 83. Calling the US "reckless" and "adventurist," and charging it was pushing the world toward "nuclear catastrophe," Ustinov implied that the Kremlin saw US military actions as sufficiently real to order an increase in Soviet combat readiness. Finally, possibly referring to the use of an exercise to launch a surprise attack, he warned that "no enemy intrigues will catch us unawares."

Ustinov also voiced his apparent conviction that the threat

~~TOP SECRET~~ UMBRA GAMMA
WNINTEL NOFORN NOCONTRACT ORCON

of war loomed heavy. Exhorting his forces, he declared that the international situation -- "the increased danger of an outbreak of a new world war" -- called for extraordinary measures:

> We must actively and persistently foster high vigilance and mobilize all servicemen both to increase combat readiness . . . and to strengthen military discipline.

There is little doubt in our minds that the Soviets were genuinely worried by Able Archer; however, the depth of that concern is difficult to gauge. On one hand, it appears that at least some Soviet forces were preparing to preempt or counterattack a NATO strike launched under cover of Able Archer. Such apprehensions stemmed, in our view, from several factors:

o US-Soviet relations at the time were probably at their lowest ebb in 20 years. Indeed, the threat of war with the US was an ever-present media theme throughout the USSR, especially the armed forces.

o Yuriy Andropov, probably the only man in the Soviet Union who could authorize the use of nuclear weapons at a moment's notice, was seriously ill [3.3(b)(1)] [3.3(b)(1)]

[3.3(b)(1)] [3.3(b)(1)] Pact exercises to counter a NATO surprise attack always portrayed NATO "jumping off" from a large training maneuver before reaching full combat readiness. Soviet doctrine and war plans have long posited such a scenario for a Warsaw Pact preemptive attack on NATO.

On the other hand, the US intelligence community detected no evidence of large-scale Warsaw Pact preparations. Conventional

WNINTEL NOFORN NOCONTRACT ORCON
~~TOP SECRET~~ UMBRA GAMMA

thinking assumes that the Soviets would probably undertake such a mobilization and force buildup prior to a massive attack on NATO. The Board questions, however, whether we would indeed detect as many "indicators" as we might expect, [3.3(b)(3); (b)(3)] [3.3(b)(3); (b)(3)]

The "mixed" Soviet reaction may, in fact, directly reflect the degree of uncertainty within the Soviet military and the Kremlin over US intentions. Although the Soviets usually have been able to make correct evaluations of US alerts, their increased number of intelligence reconnaissance flights and special telegrams to intelligence Residencies regarding possible US force mobilization, for example, suggests to us serious doubts about the true intent of Able Archer. To us, Soviet actions preceding and during the exercise appear to have been the logical steps to be taken in a period when suspicions were running high. Moreover, many of these steps were ordered to be made secretly to avoid detection by US intelligence. This suggests that Soviet forces were either preparing to launch a surprise preemptive attack (which never occurred) or making preparations that would allow them a minimum capability to retaliate, but at the same time not provoke the attack they apparently feared. This situation could have been extremely dangerous if during the exercise -- perhaps through a series of ill-timed coincidences or because of faulty intelligence -- the Soviets had misperceived US actions as preparations for a real attack.

<u>Winter, 1983-84: Winter of Crisis</u>

[3.3(b)(1)] by December 1983, rumors of imminent war were circulating at all levels of Soviet society. For example, at the Warsaw Pact Defense Ministers' Conference in Sofia, Pact Commander Kulikov characterized the international situation as "prewar." He called for more active reserve training, as well as stockpiling of ammunition, food, and fuel in case of an "emergency." In Moscow, a respected US expert on the USSR, after extensive conversations with Soviet government officials, came away convinced that there was an obsessive fear of war, an emotionalism, and a paranoia among his contacts.

Nevertheless, the General Secretary continued to participate actively in foreign policy matters. In late November, he sent a toughly worded letter to Margaret Thatcher, calling the cruise missiles slated for Greenham Common a "threat" to the Soviet Union that had to be removed. This letter, undoubtedly a last ditch effort to prevent cruise missile deployments in England, was characterized [3.3(b)(1)] as "resentful to the point of anger, and even threatening." When the first Pershing II's arrived in West Germany in December, Andropov reportedly ordered his negotiators to leave the Geneva strategic arms talks and not return until the missiles were removed.

Andropov's lengthy infirmity very possibly left the USSR with a feckless leader for several months thereafter, a situation that could have exacerbated any uneasiness among his colleagues over international tensions. [3.3(b)(1)]

[3.3(b)(1)]

~~TOP SECRET~~ UMBRA GAMMA
WNINTEL NOFORN NOCONTRACT ORCON

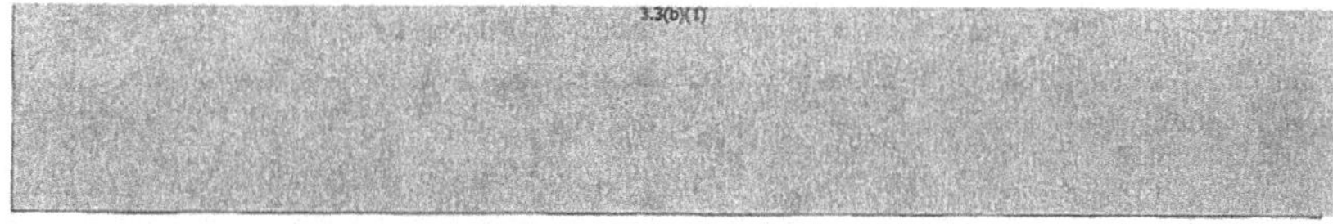

He died on 9 February.

Konstantine Chernenko's ascent to power left the reins of the USSR in the hands of another seriously ill man. Chernenko had long suffered from emphysema, complicated by pulmonary cardiac insufficiency, as well as from chronic hepatitis. His weak condition was clearly visible during his televised acceptance speech.

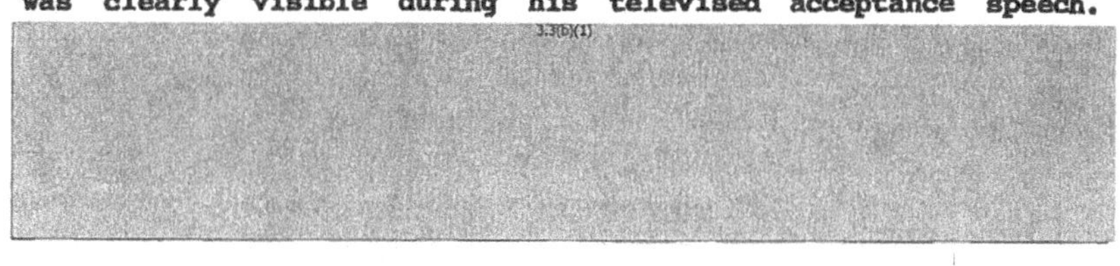

* * *

The change at the top had no outward effect on the leadership's apparent preoccupation with the danger of war. The media campaign, intelligence collection efforts, and military preparations, in fact, appeared to accelerate in Chernenko's first months in office.

Speeches by Soviet military leaders in February continued to warn that US policies were flirting with war. The major themes gave notice to Washington that a surprise attack would not succeed, and exhorted the Soviet population to steel itself for a possible confrontation. Marshal Kulikov warned in a 24 February Red Star article that,

WNINTEL NOFORN NOCONTRACT ORCON
~~TOP SECRET~~ UMBRA GAMMA

> When the United States and NATO play with fire, as they are now doing, theirs is not simply an irresponsible activity, but . . . an extremely dangerous one . . . the US-NATO military and political leadership must realize that whatever they create and whatever means they elaborate for unleashing an aggressive war and conducting combat operations, the Soviet Union and its Warsaw Pact allies will be capable of a fitting response . . . .

Two days later, in a statement commemorating the Soviet armed forces, Marshal Ustinov made public, in vague but pointed language, efforts underway to bolster the national defense:

> The CPSU Central Committee and the Soviet government have adopted the necessary measures to strengthen the country's defense, enhance the armed forces' combat readiness, and do all they can to prevent the forces of aggression from wrecking the military equilibrium which has been achieved.

He also quoted General Secretary Chernenko as justifying these measures "to cool the hot heads of the bellicose adventurists."

Judging from his exhortations to the Soviet bureaucracy, we conclude that Chernenko probably shared his predecessor's apparent concerns. In early March, for example, a circular telegram to Soviet diplomats abroad continued to emphasize the same war scare themes. Chernenko was quoted as declaring, "The present tension in the world is caused by the sharply stepped-up policies of the more aggressive forces of American imperialism, a policy of outright militarism, of claims to world supremacy." He reiterated earlier charges that the US deployment of nuclear missiles in

Europe had "seriously increased the threat of war."

* * *

Intelligence collection on VRYAN also continued apace during this period. [3.3(b)(1)] 50 KGB officers were assembled into a new "strategic section," expressly to process VRYAN information. At a special KGB conference in January, the VRYAN requirement received special emphasis. In his speech to the conference, General Kryuchkov told KGB officers that the threat of nuclear war had reached "dangerous proportions."

> The White House is advancing on its propaganda the adventurist and extremely dangerous notion of 'survival' in the fire of a thermonuclear catastrophe. This is nothing else but psychological preparation of the population for nuclear war. . . .

Urging the KGB officers to increase their efforts, he added:

> Everything indicates that the threshold for using nuclear weapons is being lowered and the significance of the surprise factor has sharply increased. For the intelligence service this means that it must concentrate its efforts to the maximum extent on the principal task to be pursued -- it must not fail to perceive direct preparation by the adversary for a nuclear missile attack against the USSR nor overlook the real danger of war breaking out.

The fear that seemed to grip the KGB leadership evidently had a hold on many lower-level officials as well. [3.3(b)(1)]

3.3(b)(1) a KGB official 3.3(b)(1) told him in April 1984, that the US and USSR were on the brink of war. This same official also confided that it was very important that the Soviet Union guard against surprise nuclear attack. Moscow Center generated even more, often curiously esoteric, VRYAN tasking to the field. The Residency in London received instructions to watch for government efforts to build up anti-Soviet feelings among the public; monitor activities at Greenham Common; and conduct surveillance of military and civilian groups, as well as banks, slaughterhouses and post offices.

There was also a clear signal of VRYAN's significance among the high echelons of Soviet government. Moscow dispatched a circular telegram to all ambassadors and chiefs of mission instructing them not to interfere in or obstruct the work of KGB or GRU personnel. 3.3(b)(1) this cable, signed by Foreign Minister Gromyko, was unprecedented.

Indeed, a self-reinforcing cycle seemed to have taken life, wherein leadership concern was provoking more VRYAN reporting, and increased VRYAN data, in turn, was adding fuel to leadership anxieties. Because Moscow continued to demand every tidbit of information that might bear on NATO war preparations, many of the London KGB Residency's reports, 3.3(b)(1) contained information that had, at best, only tenuous connections to real military activities. Ambiguous information went to Moscow without clarification and, as is customary in KGB field reporting, without specific sourcing. In March, for example, the KGB Resident in London instructed the officer in charge of VRYAN data to forward a report on a cruise missile exercise at Greenham Common. Although the Residency had gleaned the story from a British newspaper, the report arrived in Moscow as a top-priority cable, marked "of strategic importance" -- the first use of this format by the Residency in over three years. That same month London Residency sent a second "flash" message to Moscow, this time on the initiative of a junior officer who had been listening to a BBC report on cruise missiles.

Because VRYAN reports were very selective, and usually not put into context, they tended to corroborate Headquarters' fears, further building the "case" of NATO war preparations. Even innocuous information from overt sources found their way into the data base. [3.3(b)(1)] one such story about a local campaign for blood donors met a VRYAN requirement to report evidence of blood drives; and the information was duly submitted.

And Moscow kept stoking the fire. In praising the London Residency for its VRYAN reporting in March 1984, Headquarters cited the "blood donor" report as especially interesting. Even though by this time most Residency officers had grown increasingly skeptical of the VRYAN effort, they nonetheless adopted a "can do" approach, forwarding any "evidence" they could find. Still, London Residency often failed to submit its mandatory bi-weekly reports, and Moscow repeatedly had to issue reminders.

The Center sometimes tried to spur on London Residency by sharing information from other sources. On one occasion, it offered an assessment of a NATO document that called for improvements in crisis-related communications links. According to the Center, this was yet another "significant sign of preparations for a sudden nuclear missile attack against the Soviet Union and socialist countries."

Moscow also heaped praise on its allies' efforts. [3.3(b)(1)] [3.3(b)(1)] the head of the KGB's VRYAN program singled out Czechoslovak reporting on the US Federal Emergency Management Agency as "priceless." The same official also lauded Prague for its collection of military intelligence, which, he said, helped make its civilian service second only to the KGB in fulfilling the

VRYAN requirement. The East Germans reportedly placed third.

In addition, GRU Residencies geared up. In fact, there were some indications that Residencies were about to be placed on wartime readiness. [3.3(b)(3); (b)(3)] As a result, Residencies put as many agents as possible in direct radio contact with Moscow. This measure was intended to ensure that Headquarters could handle the agents directly should a rupture in diplomatic relations occur and an embassy had to be abandoned. To timely monitor military developments abroad, the GRU implemented a special 24-hour watch staff at Headquarters. These tasks, according to GRU training, were to be implemented during time of war.

Moscow's emphasis on wartime preparedness was reflected in training exercises throughout 1984. For the first time that year, the Soviet strategic forces training program concentrated on surviving and responding to a surprise enemy strike. This seeming obsession with wartime preparedness really came to the fore in March and April: the Soviet armed forces conducted the most comprehensive rehearsal for nuclear war ever detected [3.3(b)(1); 3.3(b)(3); (b)(3)] Indeed, several of the component events were, by themselves, the largest, or most extensive of their type ever observed. This activity included [3.3(b)(3); (b)(3)]

The naval exercise involved over 148 surface ships and probably close to 50 submarines. At one stage, approximately 23 ballistic missile submarines were activated, making it the most extensive dispersal of its kind ever detected. The Northern and

Baltic Fleets were especially active, conducting dispersals, defensive maneuvers, anti-submarine operations, simulated reactions to nuclear attack, and offensive nuclear strikes.

The naval exercises ended just as the Strategic Aviation and Strategic Rocket Force maneuvers jumped off. Here, too, the level of effort was impressive:

o The Strategic Rocket Force exercise and associated naval activity involved 33 missile launches, including SLBM's, MRBM's, and ICBM's. 3.3(b)(3); (b)(3)

o The Soviet Strategic Aviation exercise involved at least 17 bombers deployed to various staging bases. On one day alone, over 80 bombers conducted a large-scale strike exercise.

Summer, 1984: Preparations for War

In mid-May Ustinov, in response to a series of questions published by Tass, continued the media attack against the US by accusing Washington of trying to "achieve military superiority" to blackmail the Soviet Union. He warned that "any attempts at resolving the historical dispute with socialism by means of military force are doomed to inevitable, utter failure." In addition, he reemphasized the military's readiness theme by quoting Chernenko: "No military adventure of imperialism will take us by surprise, any aggressor will immediately get his deserts." And he called upon the Soviet people to work even more "perseveringly" and "purposefully" to strengthen the economy. Finally, Ustinov revealed that "the Army and Navy are in permanent readiness for resolutely repelling any aggressor."

About this time, Chernenko's leadership position may well have been significantly impacted by his declining health. 3.3(b)(1)

3.3(b)(1) Chernenko's physical deterioration and lack of stamina could well have accelerated the accumulation of power by younger Politburo members, namely Mikhail Gorbachev. 3.3(b)(1) Moreover, according to a public statement by the then Deputy Director of IUSAC, Gorbachev, during this period assumed the responsibility for "strategy formulation" on defense matters.

We do not know how strongly Gorbachev subscribed to the same view on the threat of a surprise attack apparently held by many of his Politburo colleagues. There are some very slim pieces of evidence suggesting the opposite. 3.3(b)(1) 3.3(b)(1) some officials in Soviet intelligence believed he was less bellicose toward the US, and might even "surrender" if conditions in the USSR continued to deteriorate. 3.3(b)(1) 3.3(b)(1) by "surrender," 3.3(b)(1) meant retreat or withdrawal from an expanding Soviet empire, not military submission.

Gorbachev's speech to the people of Smolensk in late June betrayed no obvious obsession with the war scare. He was there to award the city the Order of Lenin for its citizens' bravery during the Second World War -- presumably a good setting in which to attack the US publicly. The speech, however, focused primarily on improving the economy and the standard of living. Rather than exhorting the people to increase military readiness, he called for the mobilization of "creative potentialities of each person; the further strengthening of discipline and the increase of responsibility at work; and the implementation of school reform and an integrated solution to the contemporary problems of education."

Nevertheless, the fear of a US attack apparently persisted among some Soviet leaders into the fall. [3.3(b)(1)] [3.3(b)(1)] the Politburo secretly forbade the Minister of Defense, the Chief of the General Staff, and other responsible military and KGB leaders from being absent from their offices for any length of time. [3.3(b)(1)] General Akhromeyev, then First Deputy Minister of Defense, was quoted during this period as saying that war was "imminent." Akhromeyev reportedly compared the situation in Europe to the weeks preceding the Nazi attack on the Soviet Union in 1941. He asked GRU Chief Ivashutin whether, in case of war, there were sufficient agents in place in NATO's rear areas. He also asked whether the GRU had agents in NATO General Staffs who could give twenty days warning of hostile action.

* * *

In fact, Soviet military actions into the early fall suggested continued deep concern about Western hostility. Presumably at the behest of the Soviet military leadership, Warsaw Pact security services increased harassment of Western attaches and imposed greater restrictions on their travel. [3.3(b)(3); (b)(3)]

~~TOP SECRET~~ UMBRA GAMMA
WNINTEL NOFORN NOCONTRACT ORCON

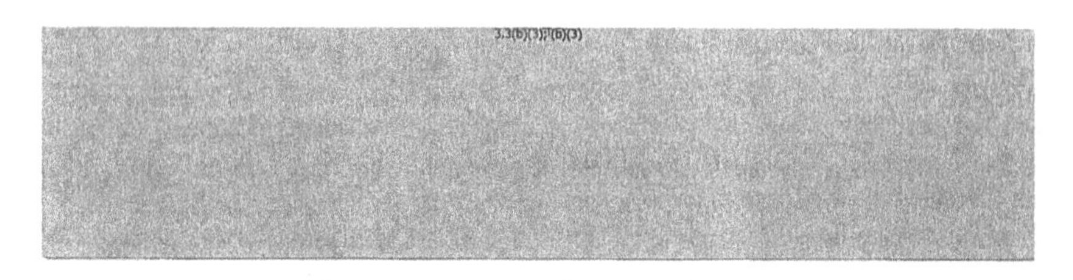

Through early summer, Moscow's emphasis on preparedness evidently led to a number of military developments aimed at increasing the Warsaw Pact's ability to go to war:

o In March, to avoid reducing readiness among combat troops, the Politburo decided for the first time since the 1968 invasion of Czechoslovakia not to use military trucks and personnel to support the harvest.

o In April, the East German ammunition plant in Luebben increased to 24-hour production and more than doubled its output.

o In May, Polish women in several cities were called up for a short military exercise. In some families with young children, both husband and wife were called. Reservists were told that readiness alerts would be expanded and occur more frequently in factories and relief organizations.

o In Hungary, a recall of an undetermined number of reservists was conducted in May.

o In June, [3.3(b)(1)] [3.3(b)(1)] during the previous 6-12 months additional SPETSNAZ troops had arrived in Hungary. [3.3(b)(1)] an increase of SPETSNAZ forces in Hungary and Czechoslovakia, as well as an ongoing "aggressive indoctrination" of Warsaw Pact forces.

o Also in June, the Soviets conducted their largest ever

unilateral combat exercise in Eastern Europe. At least 60,000 Soviet troops in Hungary and Czechoslovakia were involved.

o A mobilization exercise in June in Czechoslovakia involved the armed forces, territorial forces, and civil defense elements.

o During the spring, according to Western press reports, Soviet civil defense associations were activated. Volunteers were knocking on apartment doors explaining what to do when sirens go off.

o For the first time in 30 years, Soviet railroad troops in the Transcaucasus conducted an exercise to test their ability to move supplies to the forward area while under air attack.

o [3.3(b)(1)] the Soviets abolished draft deferments, even at defense plants.

o Both the Soviets and Czechs separately practiced modifying mobilization procedures in exercises to facilitate call-up of civilian reservists earlier in the force readiness sequence.

o In Poland, the length of required military service for new reserve officers was increased from 12 to 18 months.

o In an effort to limit contact with foreigners, the Supreme Soviet decreed, effective 1 July, that Soviet citizens who provided foreigners with housing, transportation, or other services would be fined.

o [3.3(b)(1)] since 1983 men up to 35 years old had been drafted without consideration of family difficulties or their profession.

* * *

Inside the intelligence bureaucracy, however, there were signs by midyear that attention was shifting away from "surprise nuclear attack." [3.3(b)(1)] Moscow Headquarters continued to press for VRYAN reporting, but the previous sense of urgency had dissipated. Both in London and at Moscow Center KGB officers were beginning to sense that official guidance on VRYAN was becoming ritualistic, reflecting less concern. KGB officers returning from Moscow to London had the clear impression that the primary strategic concern was focused on the possibility of a US technological breakthrough. This was expressed in tasking to both the KGB and GRU. Information on US scientific-technical developments that could lead to a weapons technology breakthrough began to assume a high priority.[30]

Autumn, 1984: Reason Restored

By late summer, there were public hints of possible differences inside the Kremlin over how to deal with Washington on strategic matters. In an interview on September 2, Chernenko omitted any reference to the removal of US Pershing II or cruise missiles as a condition for resuming strategic arms talks. Gromyko, however, reiterated this condition in a tough speech to the UN on 27 September. On 6 October, Gromyko gave a characteristically harsh speech to the United Nations in which he attacked the Reagan Administration's "reckless designs" and "obsession" with achieving military superiority. Chernenko's interview with the Washington Post on 17 October was lighter in tone.

By that time, a number of factors may have prompted some serious reflecting within the Politburo. Probably most important, the imminent US nuclear attack -- expected for more than two years

[30]Ibid.

~~TOP SECRET~~ UMBRA GAMMA
WNINTEL NOFORN NOCONTRACT ORCON

-- did not materialize. Likewise, the massive VRYAN collection effort, we presume, ultimately did not yield the kind of concrete indicators of US war preparations for which the Soviet leadership was searching. Other events that also may have prompted some policy reexamination included:

-- The ineffectiveness of "countermeasures" in slowing US INF deployments or significantly stimulating the West European "peace" movement.

-- Moscow's inability to match the US military buildup -- because of severe economic problems.

-- Growing concern for possible US technological break-throughs in space weaponry.

-- Soviet perceptions of the increasing likelihood of President Reagan's reelection.

In addition, several leadership personalities perhaps most suspicious of US intentions departed the scene. Notably, Chief of the General Staff Ogarkov, whose public statements on US-USSR relations were particularly onerous, was sacked and reassigned. Although we do not know for certain, Ogarkov may have been the casualty of a changing Politburo, which seemed to want improved relations with the US and greater control over the military. 3.3(b)(1) the impetus for improved US-USSR relations was coming from the "younger" generation -- specifically Gorbachev, Romanov, and Aliev -- whose views had prevailed over those of Gromyko and Ustinov. 3.3(b)(1) 3.3(b)(1) Ogarkov was replaced with Akhromeyev to make the Soviet military more flexible on arms control issues.

WNINTEL NOFORN NOCONTRACT ORCON
~~TOP SECRET~~ UMBRA GAMMA

Not long after Ogarkov was dismissed, Dimitry Ustinov -- another key believer in the US surprise attack -- became seriously ill with pneumonia. His condition worsened in the late fall, and he died on December 20. Ustinov's demise was paralleled by a softening in the Kremlin's arms control policy. In late November, Chernenko abandoned Andropov's vow not to return to the Geneva talks as long as US INF missiles remained in Europe and agreed to resume talks in January 1985.

* * *

Attitudes were also changing inside Soviet intelligence. By late 1984, a new KGB collection requirement (levied during the summer) for scientific-technical intelligence had acquired equal standing with VRYAN. By early 1985, [3.3(b)(1)] [3.3(b)(1)] the threat of surprise nuclear attack was not being taken seriously at all in the KGB, even within the First Chief Directorate. On a visit to Moscow in January 1985, the Acting Resident from London reportedly attempted to discuss the VRYAN requirement with a senior First Chief Directorate friend, but was put off by "a strong Russian expletive." Officers at the London Residency reportedly welcomed the decline of VRYAN because it would diminish the possibility of misperceptions about US preparations for nuclear attack.[31]

By early 1985, Soviet leadership fears of a US surprise attack seemed to evaporate steadily. Chernenko's health eroded throughout the early months of 1985 and he died on March 10. Within hours, Gorbachev became General Secretary.

* * *

For some time after Gorbachev assumed power, tensions remained

[31]Ibid.

high between Washington and Moscow. However, Soviet public expressions of fear that the US was plotting a sudden nuclear attack eventually subsided. A new, more upbeat mood among the leadership began to emerge. In July 1985, Gorbachev delivered a speech to a group of military officers in Minsk in which, according to a Western reporter, he distanced himself from the policies of his immediate predecessors and placed a high priority on achieving arms agreements -- to facilitate a reduction in arms spending and help bail out the disastrous economy.

In the military arena, however, the vestiges of the war scare seemed to have a lasting effect. The Soviets continued until 1987 the forward deployment of their ballistic missile submarines. In late 1984, they also began conducting strategic bomber "combat" patrols over the Arctic as part of their "analogous" response to US INF deployments. And they continued to reduce their vulnerabilities to a surprise nuclear attack -- in 1985, for example, by moving the SRF alternate command post at Smolensk eastward to Orenburg and out of Pershing II range.

<u>The Legacy</u>

Indeed, the Soviet military's experience during this period may well have had at least some influence in subsequent policy decisions regarding strategic force modernization and training. Soviet strategic military developments and exercises since then have particularly emphasized improving capabilities to survive and retaliate against a surprise nuclear attack. Such efforts have included:

o The orchestration of five SRF exercises in 1986 and 1987 to test the ability of mobile missile units to respond to a US surprise attack.

o Beginning in March 1986, a change in strategic aviation

exercises that featured "takeoff on strategic warning," i.e., aircraft were sent aloft during the onset of heightened international tensions.

o Impressive improvements in the survivability of their strategic arsenal. By the late 1990's, 75 percent of the force will be highly survivable mobile platforms -- compared to 25 percent in 1979. Although much of this change reflects the introduction of land-based systems, the sea-based and bomber forces have also greatly enhanced their ability to survive a sudden first strike.

The legacy of the war scare, however, has perhaps been most obvious within the Soviet intelligence establishment. [3.3(b)(1)] [3.3(b)(1)] while the VRYAN collection requirement is no longer at the top of the KGB's priority list, it nonetheless ranks third -- behind only (1) US/NATO strategic and political-economic issues, and (2) significant international political changes. These updated priorities were stipulated in a paper jointly issued last summer by the new chief of the First Chief Directorate (FCD) and the new KGB party secretary. Moreover, the FCD evidently continues to process VRYAN reporting through a "situation room" at its headquarters, and still requires the larger Residencies abroad -- such as Washington -- to man VRYAN "sections." The same source says that the KGB's "illegals" and counterintelligence components have become major contributors of VRYAN reporting. Inside the GRU, warning of imminent nuclear attack remains the (traditionally) top collection objective, but [3.3(b)(1)] a headquarters directive late last year reemphasized its importance.

IMPLICATIONS FOR TODAY

Recent events in Europe reinforce the Board's deep concern that US intelligence must be better able to assess likely Soviet attitudes and intentions. Today, the dark clouds of political instability inside the Kremlin loom far heavier than even during those evidently precarious days of leadership transition in the early 1980's. Popular political expectations -- more often, demands -- throughout the Bloc have almost certainly outdistanced even Mikhail Gorbachev's reform-minded vision. As the Soviet empire in Eastern Europe crumbles, prospects are very good that strongly anti-communist governments will eventually emerge, making very likely a total realignment of the European political landscape. Domestically, ethnic strife threatens to rip the very fabric of the Soviets' socialist "Union." The economy continues to slide, while the leadership invokes so-called reforms that, at best, are only half-measures. All the while, Gorbachev is trying to project an image of control, but is probably barely able to hang on to the reins. And his political opposition may be preparing to pounce at the earliest, most opportune moment.

It's no news to our policymakers that this turmoil in the USSR makes for very unsettled and virtually unpredictable governmental relationships -- a conundrum that will probably last for some time. In such a charged atmosphere, particularly if events degenerate into a Kremlin power struggle that favors the "conservatives," misperceptions on either side could lead willy-nilly to unwarranted reactions -- and counterreactions.

It is clear to this Board that the US intelligence community, therefore, has a compelling obligation to make a determined effort to minimize the chances that future Soviet actions will be misinterpreted in Washington.

Document 2: CIA *Studies in Intelligence* Article by Benjamin Fischer, "The 1983 War Scare in U.S.-Soviet Relations," Undated (Circa 1996), Secret

Source: Central Intelligence Agency Freedom of Information Act release

"The 1983 War Scare in U.S.-Soviet Relations," by Ben B. Fischer, then a fellow at the CIA's Center for the Study of Intelligence, was written for the CIA's classified in-house journal, *Studies in Intelligence.*

The classified article—which appears to have been written without access to the information within the PFIAB report—concludes that Soviet fears of a preemptive U.S. nuclear strike, "while exaggerated, were scarcely insane." Fischer's account starkly claims that American dismissal of legitimate Soviet fears, including fears of a "decapitating" nuclear strike, left the United States vulnerable to the possibility that they could lead to very real dangers, including a preemptive Soviet nuclear strike based purely on misinformation.

After President Reagan's March 1983 assertion that the USSR had violated a self-imposed moratorium on deploying intermediate range SS-20 missiles facing Western Europe, General Secretary Andropov declared that Reagan was "insane and a liar," repeatedly compared him to Hitler, and espoused rhetoric that made it seem war was imminent. Fischer writes that U.S. officials gave little credence to Soviet concerns—or dismissed them as propaganda—and argues that their fears were more nuanced than mere political pandering, as evidenced by Operation RYaN.

According to Fischer's account, based largely on the MI6 and KGB double agent Oleg Gordievsky, in 1981 the Soviet Union launched Operation RYaN, a combined intelligence effort between the KGB and their GRU (military intelligence) counterparts, to monitor indications and warnings of U.S. war-planning, and by 1983 RYaN had acquired "an especial degree of urgency." RYaN was, according to Fischer, "for real," and was likely in part a byproduct of American PSYOPs tactics conducted throughout the previous two years.

The report discloses that a Czechoslovakian intelligence officer corroborated Gordievsky's reporting to the CIA. According to the source, the Soviets were obsesses with Hitler's 1941 invasion. He reported that this feeling was almost visceral, not intellectual, and deeply affected Soviet thinking."

This CIA history also reveals that the U.S. military had been probing Soviet airspace to pinpoint vulnerabilities since the beginning of the Reagan administration, and that in 1981 the U.S. Navy led an armada of eighty-three ships through Soviet waters, effectively eluding "the USSR's massive ocean reconnaissance system and early-warning systems." In addition to the PSYOPs exercises, the U.S. Navy flew aircraft twenty miles inside Soviet airspace, prompting Andropov to issue orders that "any aircraft discovered in Soviet airspace be shot down. Air-defense commanders were warned that if they refused to execute Andropov's order, they would be dismissed."

Tensions, and Moscow's suspicions of a possible U.S. attack, were high. These events rattled Soviet leaders, already aware that their technological capabilities were lagging behind those of the United States, and they ramped up Operation RYaN efforts.

Fischer writes that as the Soviets were conducting Operation RYaN, the United States began Able Archer 83, an annual NATO command post exercise that the Soviets were familiar with. However, Gordievsky told MI6 that during Able Archer 83, Moscow incorrectly informed its KGB and GRU stations that U.S. forces were mobilizing in Europe. Air bases in East Germany and Poland were put on alert "for the first and last time during the Cold War."

Threat Perception, Scare Tactic, or False Alarm?

The 1983 War Scare in US-Soviet Relations

Ben B. Fischer

> **"Reagan was repeatedly compared to Hitler and accused of "fanning the flames of war"—a more sinister image than Andropov as a Red Darth Vader."**

Ben B. Fischer is in CIA's Center for the Study of Intelligence.

Never, perhaps, in the postwar decades was the situation in the world as explosive, and hence, more difficult and unfavorable, as in the first half of the 1980s.

Mikhail Gorbachev, February 1986

US-Soviet relations had come full circle in 1983. Europeans were declaring the outbreak of a Cold War II, and President Mitterrand compared the situation to the 1962 Cuban crisis and the 1948 Berlin blockade. Such fears were exaggerated. Nowhere in the world were the superpowers squared off in a conflict likely to erupt into war. But a modern-day Rip Van Winkle waking up that year would not have noticed much change in the international political landscape or realized that a substantial period of détente had come and gone while he slept.

The second Cold War was mainly a war of words. In March, President Reagan referred to the Soviet Union as the "focus of evil in the world," as an "evil empire." General Secretary Andropov suggested Reagan was insane and a liar. Then things got nasty. Following Andropov's lead and no doubt his direction, the Soviet media launched a verbal offensive of a kind not seen since Stalin that far surpassed Reagan's broadsides. Reagan was repeatedly compared to Hitler and accused of "fanning the flames of war"—a more sinister image than Andropov as a Red Darth Vader.

The Soviet War Scare

Such rhetoric was the consequence rather than the cause of tension, but frightening words masked real fears. The Hitler analogy was more than an insult and may have been a Freudian slip, because war was on the minds of Soviet leaders. Moscow was in the midst of a "war scare" that had two distinct phases and two different dimensions—one concealed in the world of clandestine intelligence operations since 1981, and the other revealed in the Soviet media two years later.

C05661070

Secret
War Scare

The KGB assessment was more of a storm warning than a hurricane alert. But Politburo forecasters reached a stark political judgment: the chances of a nuclear war, including a US surprise nuclear attack, were higher than at any time during the entire Cold War. In May 1981, General Secretary Brezhnev and then KGB chief Andropov briefed the Politburo assessment to a closed KGB conference. Then Andropov took the podium to tell the assembled intelligence managers and officers that the KGB and the GRU were being placed on a permanent intelligence watch to monitor indications and warning of US war-planning and preparations. Codenamed RYAN, this alert was the largest Soviet peacetime intelligence effort.

During 1982, KGB Center assigned RYAN a high, but not overriding, priority. Then, on 17 February 1983, KGB residents already on alert received "eyes only" cables telling them that it had "acquired an especial degree of urgency" and was "now of particularly grave importance." They were ordered to organize a permanent watch using their entire operational staff, recruit new agents, and redirect existing ones to RYAN requirements. A circular message from the Moscow Center to all KGB residencies put on alert status stated:

> *Therefore one of the chief directions for the activity of the KGB's foreign service is to organize detection and assessment of signs of preparation for RYAN in all possible areas, i.e., political, economic, and military sectors, civil defense and the activity of special services. Our military neighbors [the GRU] are actively engaged in similar work in relation to the activity of the adversary's armed forces.*

"And, for the first time since 1953, a Soviet leader was telling the Soviet people that the world was on the verge of a nuclear holocaust."

Moscow's urgency was linked to the impending US deployment of Pershing II intermediate-range missiles in West Germany. Very accurate and with a flight time under 10 minutes, these missiles could destroy hard targets, including Soviet command and control bunkers and missile silos, with little or no warning. Guidance cables referred to RYAN's critical importance to Soviet military strategy and the need for advance warning "to take retaliatory measures." But Soviet leaders were less interested in retaliation than in preemption and needed RYAN data as strategic warning to launch an attack on the new US missile sites.

The overt war scare erupted two years later. On 23 March 1983, President Reagan announced a program to develop a ground- and space-based, laser-armed, anti-ballistic-missile shield designated Strategic Defense Initiative (SDI) but quickly dubbed "Star Wars" by the media. Four days later—and in direct response—Andropov lashed out. He accused the United States of preparing a first-strike attack on the USSR and asserted that Reagan was "inventing new plans on how to unleash a nuclear war in the best way, with the hope of winning it." The war scare had joined the intelligence alert.

Andropov's remarks were unprecedented. He violated a longstanding taboo by describing US nuclear weapons' numbers and capabilities in the mass media. He referred to Soviet weapons and capabilities—also highly unusual—and said explicitly that the USSR had, at best, only parity with the United States in strategic weaponry. And, for the first time since 1953, a Soviet leader was telling the Soviet people that the world was on the verge of a nuclear holocaust. If candor is a sign of sincerity, Moscow was worried.

The War Scare as an Intelligence Issue

The Soviet war scare posed two questions for the Intelligence Community: was it genuine, that is, did the Soviet leadership actually believe that the United States might attack? If so, why had the Kremlin reached that conclusion? If the alarm was not genuine, then what purpose did it serve?

By and large, the Community played down both the intelligence alert and the war-scare propaganda as evidence of an authentic threat perception. It did so in part because the information reaching it about the alert came primarily from British intelligence and was fragmentary, incomplete, and ambiguous. Moreover, the British protected the identity of the source—KGB Col. Oleg Gordievsky, number two in the London residency— and his bona fides could not be independently established. US intelligence did have partially corroborating information from a Czechoslovak intelligence officer, but apparently it was not detailed enough or considered reliable enough to confirm what was coming from Gordievsky.

C05661070

Secret
War Scare

"Searching for an explanation of the war scare, intelligence analysts and other interested observers offered three answers: propaganda, paranoia, and politics."

The Intelligence Community continued to scoff at the war scare even after Gordievsky defected—actually, after MI6 exfiltrated him from the USSR—and was made available for debriefing.[2] But intelligence analysts were not alone in their skepticism. For example, one critic who attributes many of the problems in US-Soviet relations to the Reagan administration concluded *10 years later* and with the benefit of hindsight: "Above all, the idea that the new American administration might actually attack the Soviet Union seems too far out of touch with reality to have been given credence."[3] A Soviet émigré scholar who wrote the most perceptive article on Soviet war-scare propaganda found the analytic task so daunting that he refused to speculate on *why* the Kremlin had adopted this line or *to whom* the message was directed—West European governments, the US electorate, or the Soviet people.

Searching for an explanation of the war scare, intelligence analysts and other interested observers offered three answers: propaganda, paranoia, and politics.

The consensus view regarded RYAN and the war scare as grist for the KGB disinformation mill—a sophisticated political-psychological scare tactic operation. Who was the KGB trying to scare? Answers differed. Most agreed that the Soviets wanted to frighten the West Europeans and above all the nervous West Germans into backing out of an agreement to deploy US intermediate-range Pershing II and cruise missiles on their territory. Besides, Moscow was engaged in an all-out, go-for-broke propaganda and covert action program that was flagging and needed a boost.

Some observers, however, believed that the campaign was inwardly, not outwardly, directed toward the Soviet people. There was evidence to support this interpretation. Andropov had launched an anticorruption and discipline campaign to get the long-suffering proletariat to work harder, drink less, and sacrifice more while cutting down on the theft of state property. War scares had been used in the past to prepare people for bad times, and, with ideology dead and consumer goods in short supply, the Kremlin was trotting out a tried and true mobilization gimmick.

A second explanation argued that the war scare was clearly bogus but potentially dangerous because it was rooted in Soviet leadership paranoia. Paranoia is a catchall explanation for Russian/Soviet external behavior that goes back to early tsarist times. But it was given credence. This was how Gordievsky explained the war scare, and the advanced age and poor health of Andropov and the rest of the gerontocracy suggested that the leadership's debilitation might be mental as well as physical.

The third explanation held that the war scare was rooted in internal bureaucratic or succession politics. The military and intelligence services might be using it as a form of bureaucratic turfbuilder to make their budgets and missions grow at a time when the competition for resources was fierce. Or the war scare might have been connected in some way—a debate over foreign and defense policy?—to a succession struggle that was continuing despite, or because of, Andropov's poor health. Explanations were plentiful, but evidence was scarce.

Although quite different, these explanations had much in common. Each started from the premise, whether articulated or not, that there was no objective threat of a US surprise attack on the USSR; therefore, the war scare was all smoke and mirrors, a false alarm being used for some other purpose. In most instances, outside observers did not give the war scare credence, refusing to imagine that the Soviet leadership could view the United States as the potential aggressor in an unprovoked nuclear war, because they themselves could not imagine the United States in that role. This idea was "too far out of touch with reality." Reagan was not Hitler, and America does not do Pearl Harbors.

US perceptions of the US-Soviet balance of strategic power also weighed against the idea that the war scare could indicate genuine, even if greatly exaggerated, concern on Moscow's part. The United States was in the midst of the largest military buildup in its history whose aim was to close a perceived "window of vulnerability" in the mid-1980s created by US loss of superiority in delivery vehicles and then counterforce capabilities. The buildup had begun during the previous administration, but was greatly accelerated during Reagan's first term in the belief that the USSR might exploit a temporary advantage—appropriately called a

C05661070

Secret
War Scare

window of opportunity—to engage in adventuresome behavior, use nuclear blackmail, or even perhaps attack the United States. Moreover, Soviet claims about the "irreversibility" of changes in the "correlation of forces" in the 1970s—a reference to both Soviet gains in the Third World and achievement of "robust parity" in strategic power with the US—did little to allay US concerns.

US observers were half right in dismissing the war scare as groundless, but also half wrong in viewing it as artificially contrived. Moscow apparently was worried about something.

Evidence From the Soviet Union and Eastern Europe

For a long time, Gordievsky was the only publicly acknowledged source of information on RYAN.

Meanwhile, former Soviet Ambassador to the United States Anatoly Dobryinin and ex-KGB officers Oleg Kalugin and Yuriy Shvets have published memoirs that dovetail with Gordievsky's account. We know a lot more than we did about the war scare, even though a complete understanding is still elusive.

Gordievsky, the original source, is also the most prolific. Almost a decade after he arrived in London, he and British coauthor Christopher Andrew published a sheaf of KGB cables that describe the alert and collection requirements. No one in the US, British, or Soviet/Russian intelligence communities has questioned these documents, so silence is tantamount to authentication.

C05661070

War Scare

Spooking the Russians

During the first Reagan administration, US policy toward the Soviet Union was conducted on two tracks. The first encompassed normal diplomatic relations and arms control negotiations. The second was a covert political-psychological effort to attack Soviet vulnerabilities and undermine the system. According to a recent account based on interviews with Reagan-era policymakers, it was a "secret offensive on economic, geostrategic, and psychological fronts designed to roll back and weaken Soviet power."[5] For most of 1981-83, there were more trains running on the second track than on the first.

RYAN may have been a response to the first in a series of US military probes along Soviet borders initiated in the Reagan administration's first months. These probes—called psychological warfare operations, or PSYOP, in Pentagon jargon—aimed at exploiting Soviet psychological vulnerabilities and deterring Soviet actions. The administration's "silent campaign" was also practically invisible, except to a small circle of White House and Pentagon aides—and, of course, the Kremlin. "It was very sensitive," recalls former Undersecretary of Defense Fred Ikle. "Nothing was written down about [redacted]e would be no paper trail."[6]

The PSYOP was calculated to play on what the White House perceived as a Soviet image of the President as a "cowboy" and reckless practitioner of nuclear politics. US purpose was not to signal intentions so much as keep the Soviets guessing what might happen next:

> *"Sometimes we would send bombers over the North Pole, and their radars would click on," recalls Gen. Jack Chain the former Strategic Air Command commander. "Other times fighter-bombers would probe their Asian or European periphery." During peak times, the operation would include several maneuvers a week. They would come at irregular intervals to make the effect all the more unsettling. Then, as quickly as the unannounced flights began, they would stop, only to begin a few weeks later.*

Another participant echoes this assessment:

> *"It really got to them," recalls Dr. William Schneider, Undersecretary of State for Military Assistance and Technology, who saw classified "after-action reports" that indicated US flight activity. "They didn't know what it all meant. A squadron would fly straight at Soviet airspace, and other radars would*

C05661070

Secret
War Scare

light up and units would go on alert. Then, at the last minute, the squadron would peel off and return home."[8]

The Navy played an even bigger role than SAC after President Reagan authorized it in March 1981 to operate and exercise in areas where the US fleet had rarely—or never—gone before. Major exercises in 1981 and 1983 in the Soviet far northern and far eastern maritime approaches demonstrated US ability to deploy aircraft carrier battle groups close to sensitive military and industrial areas without being detected or challenged.[9] Using sophisticated and carefully rehearsed deception and denial techniques, the Navy eluded the USSR's massive ocean reconnaissance system and early-warning systems.[10] Some naval exercises included "classified" operations in which carrier-launched aircraft managed to penetrate Soviet shore-based radar and air-defense systems and simulate "attacks" on Soviet targets. Summing up a 1983 Pacific Fleet exercise, the US chief of naval operations noted that the Soviets "are as naked as jaybird there [on the Kamchatka Peninsula], and they know it." [11] His remark applied equally to the Kola Peninsula in the far north.

Was there a connection between PSYOP and RYAN? There clearly was a temporal correlation. The first US missions began in mid-February 1981; Andropov briefed RYAN to the KGB the following May. Moreover, when top officials first learned of RYAN, they reportedly connected it to the Soviet border probes, noting that the Soviets were "increasingly frightened by the Reagan administration."

> **"Andropov's advisers urged him not to overreact, but overreact he did, accusing the President of "deliberately lying" about Soviet military power to justify SDI."**

The Intelligence Community, not clued in to the PSYOP program, could be forgiven for not understanding the cause-and-effect relationship. This is a reminder of a perennial problem in preparing estimates that assess another country's behavior in terms of its interaction with the United States and in response to US actions. The impact of the action-reaction-interaction dynamic is often overlooked or neglected, not because of analytic failure or conceptual inadequacy, but for the simple reason that the intelligence left hand does not always know what the policy right hand is doing.

There may have been another problem in perception that affected policymakers as well as intelligence analysts. While the US probes caught the Kremlin by surprise, they were not unprecedented. There was a Cold War antecedent that Soviet leaders may have found troubling. From 1950 to 1969, the Strategic Air Command conducted similar operations, both intelligence-gathering and "ferret" missions aimed at detecting the location, reaction, and gaps in radar and air-defense installations along the USSR's Eurasian periphery in preparation for nuclear war.[13] It is possible, though not provable, that the Soviets remembered something the American side had already forgotten.

1983 Through the War-Scare Prism

Despite their private assessment, Soviet leaders maintained a public posture of relative calm during 1981-82. Even Reagan's erstwhile Secretary of State Alexander Haig gave them credit, saying "[t]he Soviets stayed very, very moderate, very, very responsible during the first three years of this administration. I was mind-boggled with their patience." But that patience wore thin as 1983 wore on. In September, Andropov would officially close off an internal debate over the causes and consequences of the collapse of détente in an unusual foreign policy "declaration." In it, he limned the outline of the war scare:

> *The Soviet leadership deems it necessary to inform the Soviet people, other peoples, and all who are responsible for determining the policy of states, of its assessment of the course pursued in international affairs by the current United States administration. In brief, it is a militarist course that represents a serious threat to peace.... If anyone had any illusions about the possibility of an evolution for the better in the policy of the present American administration, recent events have dispelled them once and for all.* [emphasis added]

What were those "recent events"?

SDI. The SDI announcement came out of the blue for the Kremlin—and most of the Cabinet. Andropov's advisers urged him not to overreact, but overreact he did, accusing the President of "deliberately lying" about Soviet military power to justify SDI. He denounced it as a "bid to disarm the Soviet Union in the face

of the US nuclear threat." Space-based defense, he added,

> *... would open the floodgates of a runaway race of all types of strategic arms, both offensive and defensive. Such is the real significance, the seamy side of, so to say, of Washington's 'defensive conception'.... The Soviet Union will never be caught defenseless by any threat.... Engaging in this is not just irresponsible, it is insane.... Washington's actions are putting the entire world in jeopardy.*

SDI had obviously touched a sensitive nerve. The Soviets seemed to treat it more seriously than many US scientists and even some White House aides did at the time. There were two reasons. First, the Soviets, despite their boasting in the 1970s, had practically unlimited faith in US technical capability. Second, SDI had a profound psychological impact that reinforced the trend predicted by the computer-based "correlation of forces" model. In a remarkable tête-à-tête with a US journalist and former arms control official, Marshal Nikolai Ogarkov, first deputy defense minister and chief of the general staff, assessed the symbolic significance of SDI:

> *... We cannot equal the quality of United States arms for a generation or two. Modern military power is based on technology, and technology is based on computers.*
>
> *In the United States, small children...play with computers.... Here, we don't even have computers in every office of the Defense Ministry. And, for reasons you know well, we cannot make computers widely available in our society.*
>
> *...We will never be able to catch up with you in modern arms until we have an economic revolution. And the question is whether we can have an economic revolution without a political revolution.*

Ogarkov's private rumination is all the more remarkable because in his public statements he was a hawk's hawk, frequently comparing the United States to Nazi Germany and warning of the advent of new weapon systems based on entirely "new physical principles." The duality, even dichotomy, between Ogarkov's public stance calling for continuation of the Cold War and his private acknowledgment that the USSR could not compete may have been typical of other Soviet leaders and contributed to their frustration and anxiety.

KAL 007. At 3:26 a.m. Tokyo time on 1 September 1983, a Soviet Su-15 interceptor fired two air-to-air missiles at a Korean Boeing 747 airliner, destroying the aircraft and killing all 269 crew and passengers. Soviet air-defense units had been tracking KAL Flight 007 for more than an hour as it first entered and then left Soviet airspace over the Kamchatka Peninsula. The order to destroy the aircraft was given as the airliner was about to leave Soviet airspace for the second time after overflying Sakhalin Island. The ill-fated Boeing 747 was probably downed in international airspace.

the White House learned about the shootdown within a few hours of the event and, with Secretary of State Shultz taking the lead, denounced the Soviet act as one of deliberate mass murder of innocent civilians. President Reagan called it "an act of barbarism, born of a society which wantonly disregards individual rights and the value of human life and seeks constantly to expand and dominate other nations."

Air Force intelligence dissented at the time of the incident, and eventually US intelligence reached a consensus view that the Soviets probably did not know they were destroying a civilian airliner. The charge should have been criminally negligent manslaughter, not premeditated murder. But the official US position never deviated from the initial assessment. The incident was used to keep up a noisy campaign in the UN and to spur worldwide efforts to punish the USSR with commercial boycotts, law suits, and denial of landing rights for Aeroflot airliners. These various efforts focused on indicting the Soviet system itself and the top leadership as being ultimately responsible.

Moscow's public response to the incident came more than a week later on 9 September in the form of an unprecedented two-hour live press conference conducted by Marshal Nikolai Ogarkov with support from Deputy Foreign Minister Georgi Kornienko and Leonid Zamyatin, chief of the Central Committee's International Information Department. The five-star spin-doctor's goal was to prove—despite 269 bodies to the contrary—that the Soviet Union had behaved rationally in deciding to destroy Flight 007. At first, Ustinov said the regional Soviet air defense unit had identified the aircraft as a US intelligence platform, an RC-135 of the type that routinely performed intelligence collection operations along a similar flightpath. In any event, Ogarkov asserted, whether an RC-135 or a 747, the plane was unquestionably on a US or joint US-Japanese intelligence mission, and the local Soviet commander had carried out the correct order. The real blame for the tragedy, he argued, lay with the United States, not the USSR.

Remarkably, a classified memorandum coordinated by the Ministry of Defense and the KGB shows that privately the Soviet leadership took pretty much the same view as their public pronouncement on KAL 007. Released in 1992, the secret memorandum was sent to Andropov by Ustinov and KGB Chairman Chebrikov. It claimed that:

> ... *We are dealing with a major, dual-purpose political provocation carefully organized by the US special [intelligence] services. The first purpose was to use the incursion of the intruder aircraft into Soviet airspace to create a favorable situation for the gathering of defense data on our air-defense system in the Far East, involving the most diverse systems, including the Ferret reconnaissance satellite. Second, they envisaged, if this flight were terminated by us, using that fact to mount a global anti-Soviet campaign to discredit the Soviet Union*

Soviet angst was reflected in the rapid and harsh propaganda reaction, with Andropov once again taking the lead rather than remaining silent. He moved quickly to exploit KAL 007, like SDI before it, for US-baiting propaganda. Asserting that an "outrageous military psychosis" had overtaken the United States, he declared that:

> *The Reagan administration, in its imperial ambitions, goes so far that one begins to doubt whether Washington has any brakes at all preventing it from crossing the point at which any sober-minded person must stop.* [emphasis added]

the Soviet air-defense commander made an honest, though serious, error because the entire air-defense system was on high alert and in a state of anxiety. He claims this was a result of incursions by US aircraft from the Pacific Fleet in recent months during a joint fleet exercise with the Japanese. He could not provide details, but he did know that there was concern about both military and military reconnaissance aircraft.

The specific incident to which he almost certainly was referring occurred on or about 4 April, when at least six US Navy planes from the carriers Midway and Enterprise flew simulated bombing runs over a heavily fortified Soviet island in the Kuril chain called Zeleny. The two carriers were part of a 40-ship armada that was patrolling in the largest-ever exercise in the north Pacific. According to the Soviet démarche protesting the incursion, the Navy aircraft flew 20 miles inside Soviet airspace and remained there for up to 20 minutes each time.[14] As a result, the Soviet air-defense organization was put on alert for the rest of the spring and summer—and perhaps longer—and some senior officers were transferred, reprimanded, or dismissed.

Andropov himself issued a "draconian" order that readiness be increased and that any aircraft discovered in Soviet airspace be shot down. Air-defense commanders were warned that if they refused to execute Andropov's order, they would be dismissed. There is corroborating information for this from a curious source—an apparent KGB disinformation project executed in Japan and then fed back into the USSR. A *Novosti* news agency pamphlet entitled *President's Crime: Who Ordered the Espionage Flight of KAL 007?* revealed that two important changes—one in Article 53 of the Soviet Air Code on 24 November 1982 and the other in Article 36 of the Soviet Law on State Borders on 11 May 1993—in effect had closed Soviet borders to all intruders and made Andropov's shoot-to-kill order a matter of law, changing the Soviet (and internationally recognized) rules of engagement.[1]

This incident raised Soviet fears of a possible US attack and made Moscow more suspicious that US military exercises might conceal preparations for an actual attack. Within weeks, Soviet intelligence would react in exactly that way to a US-NATO exercise in Western Europe—with potentially dangerous consequences.

Able Archer 83. The second significant incident of 1983 occurred during an annual NATO command post exercise codenamed Able Archer 83.

The Soviets were familiar with Able Archer from previous years, but the 1983 version included several changes. First, in the original scenario that was later changed, the exercise was to involve high-level officials, including the Secretary of Defense and the Chairman of the Joint Chiefs of Staff in major roles with cameo appearances by the President and Vice President. Second, the exercise included a practice drill that took NATO forces from the use of conventional forces through a full-scale mock release of nuclear weapons.

The story of Able Archer has been told many times, growing and changing with each retelling. The original version came from Gordievsky, who claims that on the night of 8 or 9 November—he cannot remember which—Moscow sent a flash cable from the Center advising, incorrectly, that US forces in Europe had been put on alert and that troops at some US bases were being mobilized. The cable reportedly said that the alert may have been in response to the recent bombing attack on a US Marine barracks in Beirut, Lebanon, or related to impending US Army maneuvers, or the US may have begun the countdown to a surprise nuclear war. Recipients were asked to evaluate these hypotheses. At two airbases in East Germany and Poland, Soviet fighters were put on alert—for the first and last time during the Cold War. As Gordievsky described it:

> *In the tense atmosphere generated by the crises and rhetoric of the past few months, the KGB concluded that American forces had been placed on alert—and might even have begun the countdown to war.... The world did not quite reach the edge of the nuclear abyss during Operation RYAN. But during Able Archer 83 it had, without realizing it, come frighteningly close—certainly closer than at any time since the Cuban missile crisis of 1962.* [emphasis added]

British and US journalists with inside access to Whitehall and the White House have repeated the same story.[16] Three themes run through it. The United States and USSR came close to war as a result of Kremlin overreaction; only Gordievsky's timely warning to Washington via MI6 kept things from going too far; and Gordievsky's information was an epiphany for President Reagan, who was shaken by the idea that the Soviet Union was fearful of a US surprise attack. According to US journalist Don Oberdorfer:

> *Within a few weeks after...Able Archer 83, the London CIA station reported, presumably on the basis of information obtained by the British from Gordievsky, that the Soviets had been alarmed about the real possibility that the United States was preparing a nuclear attack against them. A similar report came from a well-connected American who had heard it from senior officials in an East European country closely allied to Moscow. McFarlane, who received the reports at the White House, initially discounted them as Soviet scare tactics rather than evidence of real concern about American intentions, and told Reagan of his view in presenting them to the President. But a more extensive survey of Soviet attitudes sent to the White House early in 1984 by CIA Director William Casey, based in part on reports from the double agent Gordievsky, had a more sobering effect. Reagan seemed uncharacteristically grave after reading the report and asked McFarlane, "Do you suppose they really believe that?"... I don't see how they could believe that—but it's something to think about," Reagan replied. In a meeting that same day, Reagan spoke about the biblical prophecy of Armageddon, a final world-ending battle between good and evil, a topic that fascinated the President. McFarlane though it was not accidental that Armageddon was on Reagan's mind.*[17]

For all its drama, however, Able Archer seems to have made more of an impression on the White House than on the Kremlin. A senior Soviet affairs expert who queried Soviet political and military leaders reported that none had heard of Able Archer, and all denied that it had reached the Politburo or even the upper levels of the defense ministry.[18] The GRU officer cited above said that watch officers were concerned over the exercise. Tensions were high as a result of the KAL 007 incident, and Soviet intelligence always worried that US military movements might indicate war, especially when conducted during major holidays.[19] Other than that, he saw nothing unusual about Able Archer.

The Iron Lady and the Great Communicator

Did Gordievsky's reporting, especially his account of the KGB Center's reaction to Able Archer,

influence US attitudes toward the Soviet Union? Gordievsky and coauthor Andrew believe so and have repeated the story dozens of times in books, articles, and interviews. The British agent's information, Andrew noted, "was of enormous importance in providing warning of the almost paranoid fear within some sections of the Reagan leadership that President Reagan was planning a nuclear first strike against the Soviet Union."[20]

But did the British go further and put their own spin on the reporting in an effort to influence Reagan? Analysts who worked with the Gordievsky file during the war scare think so, and their suspicions are supported, if not confirmed, in British accounts. Prime Minister Thatcher was engaged in an effort to moderate US policy toward the USSR, convinced that the US hard line had become counterproductive, even risky, and was threatening to undermine the NATO consensus on INF deployments. She also was mindful of the growing strength of the peace movement in Britain and especially in West Germany.

Thatcher launched her campaign to modify US policy, appropriately enough, in Washington at the annual dinner of the Churchill Foundation Award on 29 September, where her remarks were certain to reach the White House and attract US media coverage. Her theme—"we live on the same planet and must go on sharing it"—was a plea for a more accommodating alliance policy that she repeated in subsequent addressees. As her biographer notes, Thatcher did not make an urgent plea or sudden flight to Washington to press her views, rather:

"Stalin's heirs decided that it is better to look through a glass darkly than through rose-colored glasses."

> *... the essence of the [Thatcher-Reagan] partnership at this stage was that the two governments were basing their decisions on much the same evidence and on shared assessments at professional [sic] level. In particular, both governments would have had the same intelligence. A critical contribution in this field was made over a period of years by Oleg Gordievski [sic]....*[21]

British intelligence sources confided to a US journalist that London used the Gordievsky material to influence Reagan, because his hardline policy was strengthening Soviet hawks:

> *Since KGB reporting is thought to be aimed at confirming views already held in Moscow—to bolster the current line—the British worried that the impact on Moscow of the bluster in Washington would be enlarged by the KGB itself. They had cause to worry.*[22]

The question is: how much spin did MI6 use? Unfortunately, Gordievsky did not include the KGB Center's flash message on Able Archer in his otherwise comprehensive collection of cables published in 1992. Gordievsky's claim to fame for influencing White House perceptions of Soviet "paranoia" is probably justified, but his assertion that a paranoid Kremlin almost went to war by overreacting to Able Archer is questionable.

RYAN and the Soviet Pearl Harbor

A Czechoslovak intelligence officer who worked closely with the KGB on RYAN noted that his counterparts were obsessed with the historical parallel between 1941 and 1983. He believed this feeling was almost visceral, not intellectual, and deeply affected Soviet thinking.

The German invasion was the Soviet Union's greatest military disaster, similar to—but much more traumatic than—Pearl Harbor. It began with a surprise attack that could have been anticipated and countered, but was not because of an intelligence failure. The connection between surprise attack and inadequate warning was never forgotten.

The historical example of Operation Barbarossa may account for the urgency, even alarm, that field intelligence officers like Gordievsky and Shvets attributed to Kremlin paranoia. This gap in perceptions may have reflected a generation gap. The Brezhnev-Andropov generation had experienced the war firsthand as the formative experience of their political lives; for younger Soviets, it was history rather than living memory.

The intelligence "failure" of 1941 was a failure of analysis, not collection.[23] Stalin received multiple detailed and timely warnings of the impending attack from a variety of open and clandestine sources. But he gave the data a best case or not-so-bad case interpretation, assuming—incorrectly—that Hitler would not attack without issuing an ultimatum or fight a two-front war while still engaged in the West. Stalin erred in part because he deceived himself and in part because German counterintelligence also deceived him. Stalin's heirs decided

C05661070

that it is better to look through a glass darkly than through rose-colored glasses. This was probably one reason why RYAN employed an explicit worst case methodology.

RYAN appears to have incorporated—or misappropriated—another lesson from 1941. Despite the prowess of his intelligence services, the ever-suspicious Stalin ironically distrusted clandestinely acquired intelligence, including agent reporting and even communications and signals intercepts. He did so because he believed that all sources could be controlled by the enemy and corrupted by disinformation, leading him to reject both accurate and inaccurate information. As a corrective, he insisted that Soviet intelligence select indirect indicators of war planning that could not be concealed or manipulated. His chief of military intelligence had the idea of surveying mutton prices in Nazi-occupied Europe, arguing that the Germans would need sheepskin coats for winter campaigning in Russia, and, by buying up available livestock supplies for skins, they would flood the market with cheap mutton.[24] This deceptively simple indicator turned out to be simply deceptive. Hitler believed he could defeat the Red Army by fall and did not prepare for wintertime operations.

RYAN requirements reveal the same kind of unorthodox thinking. For example, the KGB residency in London was instructed to monitor prices paid for blood at urban donor banks. The Center assumed that prices would increase on the eve of war as the banks scurried to stockpile supplies. But there was a problem: British donor banks do not pay donors, all of whom are volunteers. Another example: the London

"What the Soviets feared most was that they were losing the Cold War and the technological arms race with the US."

residency was told to visit meat-packing plants, looking for signs of "mass slaughter of cattle and putting of meat into long cold storage" in preparation for RYAN. The parallel with 1941 is so close as to suggest that some of the RYAN requirements were dug out of the NKVD and GRU files.

Finally, there is another plausible, but unprovable, lesson learned from 1941. The prewar intelligence failure was Stalin's, but he blamed the intelligence services. This left an indelible stain on Soviet intelligence that Andropov, as KGB chief and later party chief, may have been determined not to let happen again. Soviet intelligence certainly had a vested interest in promoting a dire threat assessment of US intentions, but bureaucratic self-interest may not have been as important as professional, not to say hurt, pride.

Conclusion

RYAN was for real. Skeptics should consider Dobrynin's response to a doubting Thomas TV interviewer: "Make your conclusions from what he [Andropov] said in telegrams to his residents." The KGB-GRU—or more appropriately the joint Warsaw Pact—alert was a crash effort to build a strategic warning system by substituting manpower for technology, HUMINT for satellites and sensors. Soviet actions were panicky, but not paranoid or unprecedented.

As one historian noted, even under the tsars Russian strategists were often quite fearful when confronted by superior Western military technology, but their fears, while exaggerated, were scarcely insane.[25] Dobrynin claims that Andropov worried because President Reagan was "unpredictable." But this places too much weight on a single personality. What the Soviets feared most was what their "correlation of forces" calculations told them—that they were losing the Cold War and the technological arms race with the US.

The real war scare almost certainly was not the one the Kremlin envisioned. The presumed threat of a US surprise nuclear attack was nonexistent. The possibility of Soviet preemptive strike may have been more likely. Well-informed observers like Gyula Horn, the last Communist foreign minister and current Prime Minister of Hungary, revealed in his memoirs that Soviet marshals, fortified with a little vodka, openly advocated an attack on the West "before the imperialists gain superiority in every sphere." The information is anecdotal, but there is a certain grim logic to it.

The war scare was the last paroxysm of the Cold War. It was a fitting end.

NOTES

1. This was a reference to the 1973 overthrow of Marxist President Salvador Allende.

2. According to interviews conducted by Murray Marder, "[m]any senior administration officials scoff now, as they did then, at the suggestion that the Soviet Union was genuinely alarmed by US military moves or

public statements, or that Moscow had any justification for feeling vulnerable. The "war scare" in the Soviet Union in 1982-83 was deliberately engineered for propaganda purposes, these officials maintain—a pretext to create a siege mentality in the Soviet Union and to frighten the outside world about US intentions. ("Defector Told of Soviet Alert; KGB Station Reportedly Warned US Would Attack," *Washington Post*, 8 August 1986, p. A1.)

3. Raymond L. Garthoff, *The Great Transition: American-Soviet Relations and the End of the Cold War* (Washington, DC: The Brookings Institution, 1994), p. 60. Garthoff carefully considers all the details surrounding Gordievsky's recruitment and espionage for British intelligence, his bona fides, and his defection, but still questions whether the Soviets could have really believed in the war-scare scenario. Garthoff states, wrongly, that Gordievsky's information on RYAN was given to US intelligence only after his defection in May 1985. The British shared the information—in sanitized form to conceal the source—contemporaneously with the United States. Garthoff speculates that the British had some doubts about Gordievsky's reporting and did not want to offend the Reagan administration with intelligence that might suggest that its hardline policies were raising Soviet anxiety to an unusually high level. In fact, one reason the British pressed Gordievsky's information on US intelligence was precisely to influence Reagan's views on the USSR.

4. Vladimir Shlapentokh, "Moscow's War Propaganda and Soviet Public Opinion," *Problems of Communism*, Vol. 33 (September-October 1983), p. 88.

5. Peter Schweizer, *Victory: The Reagan Administration's Secret Strategy That Hastened the Collapse of the Soviet Union* (New York: The Atlantic Monthly Press, 1994), p. xvi.

6. *Ibid.*

7. *Ibid.*

8. *Ibid.*

9. See Gregory L. Vistica, *Fall from Glory: The Men Who Sank the U.S. Navy* (New York: Simon & Schuster, 1996), pp. 105-108, 116-118, and 129-135, *passim*.

10. Equally important, the Navy was able to offset the Soviets' ability to track the fleet by reading naval communications, which the KGB had been able to decrypt since the late 1960s, thanks to ex-sailor John Walker and his spy ring. The FBI arrested Walker in 1985.

11. As cited in Seymour Hersh, *"The Target is Destroyed": What Really Happened to Flight 007 and What Americans Really Knew About It* (New York: Random House, 1986), p. 18.

12. Schweizer, *Victory*, p. 190.

13. In 1970, the United States abandoned the risky practice of flying into Soviet, Chinese, and North Korean airspace to provoke reactions by radar and air-defense installations. For recently declassified information on the US overflight program, see "Secrets of the Cold War," *U.S. News & World Report*, Vol. 114, No. 10 (15 March 1993), pp. 30-50.

14. This incident is recounted in Seymour Hersh, *"The Target is Destroyed"*, chapter 2, *passim*. The Soviets saw both political and military machinations in the overflight, because Zeleny is one of several islands that comprise the so-called northern territories that have been in dispute between Moscow and Tokyo since the Soviets seized them in 1945. The United States does not recognize the Soviet claim to the islands and supports Japan. The Soviets viewed the overflight as provocative and a challenge to their sovereignty over the islands. Hersh notes on p. 18 that the "Navy never publicly acknowledged either the overflight or its error; it also chose to say nothing further inside the government."

15. This strange pamphlet was issued by a one-room Japanese "publishing" firm in editions of 1,000 each in English and Japanese. However, *Novosti* "reprinted" 100,000 copies in Russian. This suggests two things: the pamphlet was intended primarily for the internal Soviet audience, and the Soviet people did not believe their government's explanation of the KAL 007 tragedy. See Murray Sayle, "Closing the File on Flight 007," *The New Yorker*, Vol. LXIX, No. 42 (13 December 1993), pp. 90-101, especially 94-95.

16. The two British accounts of Gordievsky's role and how British intelligence used him to influence President Reagan's thinking on Soviet policy are: Gordon Brook-Shepherd, *The Storm Birds: The Dramatic Stories of the Top Soviet Spies Who Have Defected Since World War II* (New York: Weidenfeld & Nicolson, 1989), chapter 18, *passim*; and Geoffrey Smith, *Reagan and Thatcher* (New York: W.W. Norton & Company, 1991), pp. 122-23. See also Nicholas Bethell, *Spies and Other Secrets: Memoirs from the Second Cold War* (New York: Viking, 1994), p. 191. Brooke-Shepard received assistance from British and US intelligence. Smith's book is an "authorized" inside account of its subject. Bethell is a Tory MP and friend and fan of Gordievsky's. The US version, which is identical in many respects, is Don Oberdorfer, *The Turn: From Cold War to a New Era* (New York: Poseidon Press, 1991), p. 67.

17. Oberdorfer, *The Turn*, p. 67.

18. Garthoff, *The Great Transition*, p. 139, n. 160.

19. Able Archer coincided with October Revolution Day, the USSR's national holiday. Holidays turned into national drinking binges that incapacitated practically the entire country. This is an interesting bit of mirror-imaging, because NATO military planners almost certainly did not factor the holiday into Allied war plans.

20. Christopher Andrew, "We Will Always Need Spies," *The London Times*, 3 March 1994, Features, p. 1

21. Smith, *Thatcher and Reagan*, p. 122.

22. John Newhouse, *War and Peace in the Nuclear Age* (New York: Alfred A. Knopf, 1989), p. 338.

23. For a discussion of the wealth of accurate information that was available to Stalin, see John Costello and Oleg Tsarev, *Deadly Illusions: The KGB Dossier Reveals Stalin's Master Spy* (New York: Crown Publishers, 1993), pp. 85-90. This analysis is based on declassified Soviet intelligence reports from the KGB archive. See also Barton Whaley, *Codeword BARBAROSSA* (Cambridge, MA.: MIT Press, 1973), which details more than 80 indications and warnings received by Soviet intelligence.

24. Viktor Suvorov, *Icebreaker: Who Started World War II?* (London: Hamish Hamilton, 1990), pp. 320-321.

25. William J. Fuller, Jr., *Strategy and Power in Russia 1600-1914* (New York: The Free Press, 1992), p. 12.

Document 3: KGB Chairman Yuri Andropov to General Secretary Leonid Brezhnev, "Report on the Work of the KGB in 1981," May 10, 1982

Source: Dmitri Antonovich Volkogonov Papers. Available at the National Security Archive

Yuri Andropov's "Report on the Work of the KGB in 1981," provided to Leonid Brezhnev in May of 1982, did not use the specific term "Operation RYaN," but it did state that the KGB had "implemented measures to strengthen intelligence work in order to prevent a possible sudden outbreak of war by the enemy." To do this, the KGB "actively obtained information on military and strategic issues, and the aggressive military and political plans of imperialism [the United States] and its accomplices," and "enhanced the relevance and effectiveness of its active intelligence abilities."

A year later, the 1982 "Report on the Work of the KGB"—this time sent to General Secretary Andropov from KGB Chairman Victor Chebrikov—confirmed genuine Soviet fears of encirclement. It noted the challenges of counting on "U.S. and NATO aspirations to change the existing military-strategic balance," and, given that, "primary attention was paid to military and strategic issues related to the danger of the enemy's thermonuclear attack."

The two KGB reports* square with Gordievsky's account or the establishment of RYaN.

* The full Russian versions of these documents can be found at nsarchive.gwu.edu/nukevault/ablearcher.

79

Особой важности
ОСОБАЯ ПАПКА

КОМИТЕТ
ГОСУДАРСТВЕННОЙ БЕЗОПАСНОСТИ СССР

[illegible] № [illegible]

Москва

Товарищу Л.И.Брежневу

Отчет о работе Комитета государственной безопасности СССР за 1981 год

Деятельность Комитета государственной безопасности была полностью подчинена задачам неуклонного претворения в жизнь решений XXVI съезда КПСС, осуществлялась в строгом соответствии с Конституцией СССР и советскими законами.

Огромное мобилизующее значение для всей практической работы чекистов имеют высокая оценка их труда XXVI съездом КПСС, положения и выводы, содержащиеся в докладах, выступлениях товарища Л.И.Брежнева, указания и советы, данные им на Всесоюзном совещании руководящего состава органов и войск КГБ в мае 1981 года.

Комитетом выработаны и реализуются на практике организационные решения и тактические установки по дальнейшему повышению в условиях острой классовой борьбы на международной арене боеспособности чекистских аппаратов, эффективности их разведывательной и контрразведывательной деятельности.

Последовательно утверждались ленинские принципы работы с кадрами. Совершенствовалась система их подбора, расстановки и воспитания. Чекистские органы ныне укомплектованы преданными партии кадрами, способными успешно выполнять ее указания в любых сложных условиях.

2556

80

2

Большая работа проведена по обеспечению безопасности в период подготовки и работы XXVI съезда КПСС. Сорваны многие замышлявшиеся противником подрывные акции, имевшие своей целью принизить значение высшего форума КПСС, нанести политический ущерб нашей стране. Осуществлен комплекс мер политического, оперативного характера за рубежом, среди членов дипломатического корпуса, журналистов, некоторых других категорий иностранцев, находившихся в Советском Союзе; предотвращены провокационные акции, готовившиеся враждебными элементами внутри страны.

В отчетном году улучшена на ряде ключевых направлений работа разведки Комитета государственной безопасности.

Первостепенное внимание уделялось разведывательной подготовке и обеспечению встреч и переговоров товарища Л.И.Брежнева с зарубежными государственными и политическими деятелями.

Осуществлены меры по усилению разведывательной работы в целях предупреждения возможного внезапного развязывания противником войны. Активнее добывалась информация по военно-стратегической проблематике, об агрессивных военно-политических планах империализма и его пособников. Полнее освещались внешняя политика ведущих капиталистических стран, крупные международные экономические проблемы, положение в странах и районах мира, где складывалась кризисная обстановка, процессы в области внутренней и внешней политики Китая.

Успешнее вскрывалась враждебная деятельность против СССР спецслужб США, других капиталистических государств и Китая, центров идеологической диверсии противника, зарубежных антисоветских националистических и эмигрантских формирований, террористических организаций и групп.

2556

Document 4: Central Intelligence Agency Biographical Profile of Yuriy Vladimirovich Andropov, January 11, 1983, Classification Redacted

Source: Central Intelligence Agency Freedom of Information Act release

The CIA's biographical profile of Andropov describes him as "clearly in charge" but "perhaps the most complicated and puzzling of all the current Soviet leaders."

"A sophisticated man," Andropov the former KGB chief "is probably better informed on foreign affairs, and on at least some domestic matters, than any other Soviet party chief since Lenin."

The CIA analysis reported that Andropov "has warned that a nuclear war would have catastrophic consequences and has spoken out in favor of East-West détente."

The agency missed the mark somewhat in their assessment of his health, stating that Andropov "had a heart attack several years ago but appears to be in fairly good health at present," making no mention of his kidney ailments.

3.5(c)

16 FEB 1983

Yuriy Vladimirovich ANDROPOV **USSR**
(Phonetic: ahnDRAWpuf)

General Secretary and Member, Politburo, Central Committee, Communist Party of the Soviet Union

Addressed as:
Mr. Secretary

Yuriy Andropov succeeded Leonid Brezhnev as General Secretary of the CPSU on 12 November 1982, the day after Brezhnev's death was announced. A member of the ruling Politburo since 1973, Andropov is one of only three people who have dual status as full members and Central Committee secretaries. When he took his new job, he indicated that collective leadership would continue to be the rule in the Soviet Union. At present, however, he appears to be clearly in charge, even though the extent of his power has not yet been defined. As the Soviet leader, Andropov faces formidable domestic challenges, including an entrenched and aging bureaucratic structure, a Communist Party riddled with cynicism and corruption, and an economy whose performance is in serious decline. We believe that he has the resourcefulness, astuteness, and political skills needed to take on these problems. 3.5(c)

Andropov is perhaps the most complicated and puzzling of all the current Soviet leaders. A sophisticated man, he is probably better informed on foreign affairs, and on at least some domestic matters, than any other Soviet party chief since Lenin. Throughout his entire career, Andropov has shown a single-minded devotion to the Communist cause. He appears to have a capacity for ruthlessness, but it is possible that what seems ruthless to a non-Soviet observer is, to Andropov, merely an action to support or further the cause of Communism and the supremacy of the Soviet state. 3.5(c)

Andropov does not fit the stereotype of the dull, gray bureaucrat. He is reserved and unassuming; his quiet approach is unusual among Soviet leaders. Serious minded and pragmatic, he exudes self-confidence. He is suave and gentlemanly—even when dealing with his victims. He listens to new ideas, gathers information carefully, relies on exhaustive staff work, evaluates consequences and possible actions cautiously, and acts resolutely. His approach is to try to win through stratagem and maneuver but to resort to force when all else fails and he deems the risks acceptable 3.5(c)

Among his closest personal and professional friends, Andropov counts Defense Minister Dmitriy Ustinov, Foreign Minister Andrey Gromyko, and, paradoxically, former CPSU Secretary Andrey Kirilenko—one of those he edged out in the competition for leadership. He appears to have been close to the late party ideologue Mikhail Suslov, the patron of Soviet conservatives, whose views are still shared by many in the leadership. Andropov was close to Brezhnev professionally for years, and the late General Secretary clearly regarded him as an astute adviser. 3.5(c)

At the same time, one of the most striking features of Andropov's background is his independence. He is a political loner. Unlike many of his colleagues, he did not fawn upon Brezhnev but treated him in a straightforward manner. Andropov is not regarded as the protege of any senior Soviet leader past or present. By the same token, unusual for the Soviet system, only a few men can be characterized as his own proteges. Even though he has long functioned within a framework of collective decisionmaking, he is, by all accounts, his own man. 3.5(c)

(cont.)
CR M 83-10298 3.5(c)

 3.5(c)

Views on Major Issues

Andropov's views on major issues are known primarily from his public statements. He has emphasized the need for a strong Soviet defense capability, but he has also said that military strength alone will not maintain peace. He has warned that a nuclear war would have catastrophic consequences and has spoken out in favor of East-West detente, arms control, and the reduction of international tensions. Like other Soviet leaders, Andropov has blamed Washington for the deterioration of East-West relations since the late 1970s while professing optimism about the long-range prospects for detente. His remarks have been distinguished by a sensitvity to the diversity of opinion among Western leaders. 3.5(c)

When Andropov was chairman of the KGB during 1967-82, he spoke at greater length than most Soviet leaders about external and internal threats to the Soviet system. He maintained that human rights pledges signed by Moscow at the 1975 Helsinki Conference on Security and Cooperation in Europe did not restrict Soviet actions against dissidents. He has stressed the need for constant vigilance against the threat of Western-inspired subversion. Andropov has consistently maintained that Moscow has a duty to assist "national liberation" struggles in the Third World, particularly when they are opposed by Western nations. His comments on China over the years have followed the dominant leadership line of the moment. 3.5(c)

Career and Personal Data

During his career Andropov has alternated between party and government posts. After holding positions in the Komsomol (Young Communists League) and party in the Karelo-Finnish republic, he worked in the central party apparatus in Moscow before being appointed Ambassador to Hungary in 1954. In that capacity, he was an intermediary between the Soviet and Hungarian Governments at the time of the 1956 Hungarian revolt. During 1957-67 he was in charge of party relations with Bloc Communist parties in the CPSU Secretariat, and he was a party secretary from 1962 until 1967. Andropov spent the next 15 years in the government as chairman of the KGB. He left that post in May 1982, when he was again elected a Central Committee secretary. 3.5(c)

Despite press reports that the KGB became less repressive under Andropov's chairmanship, the trend away from mass terror and toward lawful procedures had actually begun earlier. Compared to the operations of the secret police during the Stalin years, KGB operations under Andropov appeared restrained, tolerant, and restricted by the letter of Soviet law—even though by Western standards, those operations were seen as repressive, coercive, and sometimes brutal 3.5(c)

It is in the crippling of the Soviet dissident movement that Andropov's sophistication and cleverness seem most apparent. Through a mixture of tactics from leniency to brutality, the KGB largely eradicated the "dissident" movement in the USSR, doing so without derailing the Soviet policy of detente. There were some arrests, trials, and harsh sentences; but there were also cases in which mild sentences were imposed or the subject of the proceeding was allowed to emigrate or was expelled. Dissent seems to have been handled on a case-by-case basis, with the emphasis on defusing each problem as it arose 3.5(c)

Andropov is an art collector and enjoys music and literature. He speaks English and Hungarian. He had a heart attack several years ago but appears to be in fairly good health at present. A recent press report states that Andropov, 68, is a widower. He has a grown son and daughter. 3.5(c)

3.5(c)

Document 5: Memorandum of Conversation Between General Secretary Yuri Andropov and Averell Harriman, CPSU Central Committee Headquarters, Moscow, 3:00 p.m. June 2, 1983

Source: W. Averell Harriman Papers, Library of Congress, Manuscript Division, Box 655

The notes of the former U.S. ambassador to Moscow Averell Harriman describe his eighty-minute meeting with General Secretary Andropov on June 2, 1983. Harriman told Andropov he was traveling as a private citizen, but he was accompanied by a translator provided by the Department of State. Harriman's notes show that he believed that Andropov's fear of war through miscalculation was genuine.

Andropov opened the conversation by stating: "Let me say that there are indeed grounds for alarm." He bemoaned the harsh anti-Soviet tone of President Reagan and warned that "the previous experience of relations between the Soviet Union and the United States cautions beyond all doubt that such a policy can merely lead to aggravation, complexity and danger." Andropov alluded to nuclear war four times during his short statement; most ominously, he morosely observed that "awareness of this danger should be precisely the common denominator with which statesmen of both countries would exercise restraint and seek mutual understanding to strengthen confidence, to avoid the irreparable. However, I must say that I do not see it on the part of the current administration and they may be moving toward the dangerous 'red line.'"

Harriman concluded: "the principal point which the General Secretary appeared to be trying to get . . . was a genuine concern over the state of U.S.-Soviet relations and his desire to see them at least 'normalized,' if not improved. He seemed to have a real worry that we could come into conflict through miscalculation."

FINAL-DEPARTMENT

MEMORANDUM OF CONVERSATION
MEETING WITH CPSU GENERAL SECRETARY ANDROPOV
3:00 p.m., Thursday, June 2, 1983
CPSU CENTRAL COMMITTEE HEADQUARTERS, THE OLD SQUARE, MOSCOW

General Secretary Andropov welcomed me back to the Soviet Union, saying that he would not ask me how I felt being back, since I was an old Muscovite. I responded that I was struck by all the beautiful buildings that had gone up in recent years. It was not so when I first came here nearly sixty years ago.

I then said to the General Secretary that I would like to give him a remembrance of the man who first brought about relations between the United States and the Soviet Union. I noted that it was now the fiftieth anniversary of the institution of U.S.-Soviet relations, and we really should have a celebration, but I could only leave the General Secretary an autographed picture of President Roosevelt.

I also said that I wished to give him a copy of my memoirs of our relations during the war with Stalin. The General Secretary thanked me warmly for these two gifts and went immediately into reading a prepared statement. The statement was as follows:

-2-

"Mr. Harriman, Mrs. Harriman, we would like to say that we value that both of you considered it necessary to come to Moscow at this time. We know you are active champions of improved U.S.-Soviet relations and know you are guided by concern where relations are going at this time."

I interjected that the General Secretary was absolutely correct in that perception.

The General Secretary continued:

"Let me say that there are indeed grounds for alarm. The situation, such as it is, is no fault of ours and unless reasonable measures are taken the relations could become still worse. At this time they are developing quite unfavorably and this does not suit us at all. We hope that you can influence those who think along the same lines.

"Forty years ago, Mr. Harriman, you came as Ambassador of the United States to the Soviet Union. We were then allies. We succeeded in rising above the differences in our social systems and united in the face of the fascists and defended peace in the world. We saw your own personal contribution at that time, and we do not forget it.

"Today the Soviet people and the American people have a common foe -- the threat of a war incomparable with the horrors we went through previously. This war may perhaps not occur

-3-

through evil intent, but could happen through miscalculation. Then nothing could save mankind.

"It would seem that awareness of this danger should be precisely the common denominator with which statesmen of both countries would exercise restraint and seek mutual understanding to strengthen confidence, to avoid the irreparable. However, I must say that I do not see it on the part of the current Administration and they may be moving toward the dangerous 'red line'.

"I shall not pass judgment on the peculiarities of the American political system. Nevertheless, why is it that every election campaign, especially the Presidential campaigns, must be accompanied by anti-Soviet statements? Why must there be a hullabaloo about a lag in armaments or windows of vulnerability?

"It is probably far easier to appeal to chauvinism and to other such sentiments than to tell the truth. The elections pass, but they leave their aftermath. Mistrust and emnity have heated up, and there is a sharpening of the arms race and new arms programs.

"But we would prefer to think that the policy of a country such as the United States should be built not on a momentary but on a realistic, stable basis. For instance, what is the

-4-

line of the present Administration in respect to the Soviet Union? It appears oriented on speaking ill, military preponderance and economic and other kinds of harm. I venture to say to you, quite frankly, that such a line in the first instance shows a lack of understanding of the role and potential of my country and of the United States, and you know better than us the impact it has in relations between the United States and its allies. It is exceptionally damaging for international relations as a whole.

"The previous experience of relations between the Soviet Union and the United States cautions beyond all doubt that such a policy can merely lead to aggravation, complexity and danger. No results can be expected from it; both sides lose -- not ours alone. And the engendering of new types of arms complicates our task.

"Nothing is left to the imagination in what Washington throws down as threats, damnations and outright abuse, but they are mistaken. We are not that kind of people nor that kind of politicians. Nothing can come of it.

"We are convinced that in present international conditions, taking into account the military situation and the growing number of explosive problems, we cannot afford the luxury of destructive rivalry in interaction between the United States and the Soviet Union.

-5-

"We treat our relations with the United States seriously, fully understanding their significance for peace and the need to avoid nuclear war. We would prefer peaceful coexistence, mutually-beneficial or, even better, good relations as our policy.

"However, I will make no secret of the fact that beyond all doubt there is one victim of the evil which may come from the attitude taken by the White House. That is confidence, the confidence which began in the last decade and was valued throughout the world. These are not just swear words that are being put out but an attempt to undermine all the things created bilaterally and on a broader plane in that period.

"In these conditions, we can simply have no confidence in the present Administration and certain people should really give that a lot of thought.

"Nor are we in the habit of interfering in election campaigns. We conduct our affairs with the United States and those leaders elected by the people. We make no linkages for understandings between the United States Government to how they would reflect on chances of this or that party or this or that candidate for President. We do not evade contact with the Republican or Democratic Parties. Our conversation today is a graphic example. We want to normalize our relations on an equitable basis to benefit all Americans, regardless of their party.

-6-

"Finally, I would like to say that we pay tribute to the personal dedication of Mrs. Harriman and the Governor to strengthen mutual understanding for better relations, for building on our common interest in peace and good relations. I also note that we follow with interest the efforts by your family that the United States have solid and thoughtful experts on the Soviet Union. We welcome that through your lucky hand it would appear that scholars, diplomats and others can develop an objective understanding of the Soviet Union.

We know that the Harriman family is actively participating in the political life of the United States. We would appreciate your setting out a few views on the prospects in your country and for relations with the Soviet Union."

When the General Secretary finished this statement, I responded that I wished to address first his last remarks. I said that I was grateful that he understood the attitudes of my wife and myself which we hoped could be to the benefit not only to the people of our country, but of his. I continued that he had asked for my comments. I would be glad to make some.

I wished to say that his remarks appeared directed both against the United States and against the current Administration. It was not clear to me which of his remarks were general and which were directed against the Administration. The General

-7-

Secretary responded that all of what he had said that was critical was related to the current Administration, but he should not be taken as criticizing when he said that it is a fact of life that in an American election campaign a wave of anti-Sovietism is raised. He was, however, not faulting the people or the United States as a nation.

I responded that it would not be appropriate for me as a private citizen to make comments regarding an American administration. If I were to do so, the place would be in the United States and not in the General Secretary's office. The General Secretary immediately responded that that would go without saying, and it was certainly not something which they expected of me.

I continued that regarding his suggestion that in an election campaign adverse comments were always being made about the Soviets, many people speak during these campaigns and many say some difficult things. I said that I did not know the source of his information, but in my view they were not the rule but the exception. I also continued that it was our general policy to develop sound relations with the Soviet Union, to develop trade, and to take actions which would be beneficial not only to the people of the United States but to the people of the Soviet Union.

-8-

I could say that as far as I am concerned, and my wife, our attitude would be as we have said, and one beneficial to the improvement of relations.

I added that I wished to recall that I had been in Moscow under more agreeable circumstances, when we negotiated the Limited Test Ban Treaty, still one of the most successful agreements between the United States and the Soviet Union. Its twentieth anniversary would be next month. I said that I believed we could return to those days, if we could cooperate, if we could work together to improve relations. I was dedicated to that goal and so was my wife, and I felt that our visit would help in that respect.

I also noted that I fully agreed with the General Secretary that it was not his affair to become involved in American politics, but I felt it was possible for the Soviet Union to take steps which could help to improve relations. I also had to note that other actions were sometimes taken which made it more difficult to do so. I said it would be helpful if the General Secretary could give me a significant message to take back or if he could make some statement beneficial, to and which would improve relations.

I noted that I was not here to speak of things which could make our relations more difficult; the General Secretary knows them already. I repeated that I hoped the General

-9-

Secretary could make statements on improving relations which would encourage American opinion towards their improvement. I said that I felt there was more goodwill in the United States than perhaps apparent at this time. That goodwill was latent, but ready to express itself.

I then noted that my wife would like to say something at this time. Mrs. Harriman then expressed her gratitude to be included in the conversation and reaffirmed that she shared her husband's views. She said that she knew there were many things which we cannot do, but she said that we should talk about those things which could work to our common good.

My wife asked whether it might be a good idea if more Members of Congress should ask to visit the Soviet Union this summer. Mrs. Harriman noted that House Majority Whip Tom Foley was already heading a delegation arriving July 1. She said she would like to know whether they would be well received. Mrs. Harriman emphasized her belief that it was better to meet and to talk directly rather than through written communications.

The General Secretary responded that in principle the Soviets were in favor of meetings of that sort. Each visit would, of course, be weighed on its merits, but it was important that people meet with each other. The meetings did not necessarily have to be with the General Secretary himself, but they certainly could be with his colleagues. In short, his answer was yes.

-10-

I then continued that I appreciated his recalling our wartime relations. I had come at that period with the British and other Americans to find out what was needed. We were able to send supplies to enable the Red Army to resist so gallantly as it did, so effectively, and eventually to drive the enemy out. I said that not just myself but others would be ready to support the improvement of relations again if the Soviets could take appropriate actions.

The General Secretary responded that in making my observations I had mentioned that there were some Americans who wanted good relations between the United States and the Soviet Union. He also took note of my comment that the critical remarks were incidental, since as he had said the Soviets were prepared to work with any Administration in our common interest. He said that he would like my leaving him with that impression.

The General Secretary said he still had one more point to raise. He added that in regard to my comment that the Soviets take at times certain actions which complicate the situation, he wanted to note that we stand on different positions. What the Soviets believe are the right steps, the Administration thinks are wrong, and vice versa. He wanted to know how to do this, by what mutual steps. He said, however, it could not be by the one step which it appears President Reagan wants -- a Soviet unilateral laying-down of its arms. That could not be.

-11-

I said that I agreed on the need for reciprocity. I emphasized again that I was not here to discuss difficulties -- that is, to review the steps that the Soviets have taken or what they say the U.S. has taken. Nevertheless, our discussion should be in general terms how to work on or to get around our difficulties.

I said we must continue, however, to be able to tell the Soviets frankly what we are against. I said I wished to emphasize that whoever is saying the American people are not for peace, as are the Soviets, was informing the General Secretary incorrectly. Americans are just as anxious as the Soviets to develop and improve relations.

I reiterated my view that we should first deal with those matters which stand the best chance of success. There are those which are more difficult and it is not useful in the first instance to go into those with which we are at variance. We should go into those on which we can have agreement. I repeated my belief that the General Secretary knew the areas in which the United States is opposed to what the Soviets have done. I felt then we could discuss how to overcome them if the General Secretary indicated how important it is to have good relations.

Frankness remains all-important, and from what the General Secretary had told me, I said that I believed that it was his point of view. The General Secretary interjected that that was certainly his point of view.

-12-

I then asked whether the General Secretary could tell me of anything he could do to make the situation easier for those who wanted to improve relations -- what messages he might have or what actions he might take on his own toward progress as a whole. The General Secretary responded that he would think it over.

I reiterated my hope that he would do something, and my wife supported me. The General Secretary then responded somewhat heatedly, asking whether what the Soviets were supposed to do was to make unilateral concessions. He said that he felt the Reagan Administration was demanding one-sided actions by the Soviets and refusing to act reciprocally. He maintained that the Soviets' suggestion of the freeze would not work against the interests of either side. He also said that in his view, of late the United States Administration was not even answering the Soviet approaches.

I then asked if I could talk to Ambassador Dobrynin whenever I met him, which was regularly, of possibilities, and the General Secretary responded that I was always welcome to talk. I said that I was glad to hear the General Secretary was ready to think over ways of moving relations forward. I noted that I would be seeing the press this afternoon -- my usual practice when I am in Moscow. I asked whether there was anything that I could say to them to encourage their reports along this line.

-13-

The General Secretary asked me to tell the media that it was the most sincere and fervent desire of the Soviet government to have normal relations with the United States and to develop them in the best traditions of those relations. He emphasized that there were good traditions in Soviet-American relations and that the Soviets do not forget them.

When I noted that the press at the conference would not be just Americans but from other countries and Soviets as well, the General Secretary asked me to say in addition that he was ready and interested in developing Soviet-American relations, to search for joint initiatives, proposals which might make the present situation easier. He added that he would in that instance be awaiting the U.S. response.

I then thanked him for his courtesy in receiving me. I wished him well in his important leadership of his great country. I hoped that he would remain in good health and achieve what he desired, with the objective we had discussed in mind. I noted that I had one last statement.

I was now 91 years old, and I did not know how many more times I could come to the Soviet Union. I wished to let the General Secretary know, however, that I was someone in the United States with whom I hoped he would speak, just as I would be talking to his Ambassador, on matters important to our relations. He thanked me and said that he would certainly do so.

-14-

I then noted that I should not take any more of his time and hoped that the meeting had been as useful to him as it had been to me. He noted that he was very happy with the meeting (Arbatov later informed me that Andropov had passed the word that he felt the meeting was a success).

COMMENT:

The principal point which the General Secretary appeared to be trying to get across to Mrs. Harriman and me was a genuine concern over the state of U.S.-Soviet relations and his desire to see them at least "normalized", if not improved. He seemed to have a real worry that we could come into conflict through miscalculation. He was critical of the current state of relations, but was careful to stress -- several times -- that efforts for improvement had to be mutual. This point about the need for Soviet, as well as U.S. steps was included in the Pravda and Tass summaries of our talk.

I felt Andropov was making a major effort to be non-polemical in our conversation.

I am not in a position to make a real judgment on Andropov's health, although we noted occasional tremors of his hands, but not when they were in repose, and a rather rigid walk. He was in full command of himself and his part of the meeting: read his statement without effort, and responded or made points during the exchange quickly and without reference to Aleksandrov.

-15-

Also present, besides Mrs. Harriman, the General Secretary and myself, were the General Secretary's Assistant, Andrey M. Aleksandrov-Agentov, and the interpreter, Viktor Sukhodrev, both of whom had been at all my previous meetings with Brezhnev, as well as Peter Swiers, who was able to accompany me again on a trip to the Soviet Union through the courtesy of the Department of State.

Document 6: U.S. Army Intelligence and Security Command Daily INTSUM, November 10, 1983, Secret

Source: Defense Intelligence Agency FOIA release

The first known intelligence about Able Archer 83 inaccurately reported that nothing was amiss. The Army's raw intelligence summary was based on information from a German "military staff agency which consistently provides reliable assessment information, detailed intelligence studies, and current intelligence." The INTSUM reported "continued [Soviet] sigint missions to monitor NATO" exercise Able Archer 83. This included monitoring by the Soviet and East German fleets and flight operations by Soviet and Warsaw Pact air forces at low level.

INSCOM's initial intelligence incorrectly reported that "the continued low level of [Warsaw Pact] ground, air, and naval forces overall renders no intelligence indicating any change in the substance of the threat." But the U.S. military initially missed many signals. According to the subsequent President's Foreign Intelligence Advisory Board review, it was not until two weeks after the completion of Able Archer 83 that analysts noticed and reported fully armed MiG-23 aircraft on air defense alert in East Germany.

~~SECRET~~
DEPARTMENT OF DEFENSE
JCS MESSAGE CENTER

IMMEDIATE ZYUW RUFHODA4411 3141600
O 101545Z NOV 83
FM DCSI ULO BONN GE//
TO DIA WASH DC// (b)(3) per DIA
DIA WASH DC//DIAMI-ISH// HQ ESC KELLY AFB TX//IN//
CINCUSAREUR HEIDELBERG GE//AEAGB-C(RE)//
CINCUSAREUR HEIDELBERG GE//AEAGB-PD-CUR//
CDR 66TH MI GP MUNICH GE//IAGPE-OO-ICC//
DCSI USCOB BERLIN GE//
CINCEUCOM J-2 VAIHINGEN GE//ECJ2//
CINCUSNAVEUR LONDON UK//N2//
CDR V CORPS FRANKFURT GE//AETVGB//
CDR VII CORPS MOEHRINGEN GE//AETSGB//
CDR USAITAC AHS VA//IAX-TA-N// CIA WASH DC//OSR/TF//
HQ USAFE RAMSTEIN AB GE//INOIR/INRMM//
ZEN/OCA AMEMBASSY BONN GE//MR b6 //
ZEN/OCA AMEMBASSY BONN GE//MR b6 //
ZEN/DATT AMEMBASSY BONN GE//COL b6 //

(b)(3) 10 USC 424 Per DIA

~~S-E-C-R-E-T~~ NOFORN
SERIAL: (U) IR 2 196 0592 83
PASS: (U) DIA FOR COL b6
COUNTRY: (U) USSR (UR); EAST GERMANY (GC); CZECHOSLOVAKIA (CZ); POLAND (PL); ROMANIA (RO); BULGARIA (BU); HUNGARY (HU).
SUBJ. (U) IIR 2 196 0592 83/DAILY INTSUM
WARNING: (U) THIS IS AN INFO REPORT, NOT FINALLY EVALUATED INTEL.
DOI: (U) 831110
REQS. (U) (b)(7)(E)
SOURCE: (U) 2210-0009, A GE MILITARY STAFF AGENCY WHICH CONSISTENTLY PROVIDES RELIABLE ASSESSMENT INFORMATION, DETAILED INTELLIGENCE STUDIES AND CURRENT INTELLIGENCE.

SUMMARY: (U) ~~(S/NOFORN)~~ REPORT IS ADVANCE BI-LATERAL RELEASE TO U.S. OF SOURCE'S CURRENT INTELLIGENCE ASSESSMENT ON DAILY BASIS WHICH COVERS WARSAW PACT FORWARD AREA, CRISES AREAS, AND SPECIAL SIGNIFICANT DEVELOPMENTS.

TEXT: (U) ~~(S)~~
1. ~~(S)~~ HIGHLIGHTS
- CONTINUED WP SIGINT MISSIONS TO MONITOR NATO EX (CF. PARA 2.A.)
- USSR IS DEVELOPING NEW LONG-RANGE VERSION OF THE IL-86 CAMBER (CF PARA 3.).
2. (U) ~~(S/ENTIRE PARA)~~ WP MILITARY ACTIVITIES IN THE USSR AND IN THE FORWARD AREA
A. ARMED SERVICES
BORDER-CROSSING AND OVERLAPPING ACTIVITIES
NO CHANGE IN MISSIONS BY SIGINT ELMS TO THE GSFG AND CGF AS WELL AS THE GDR ARMED FORCES ALONG THE INNER GERMAN BORDER. ELMS OF THE CSSR ARMED FORCES WERE ONLY OBSERVED ON 08 NOV.
A/C OF THE SAF IN THE GDR AND THE SOVIET BALTIC FLEET WERE ADDITIONALLY EMPLOYED OVER THE GDR AS WELL AS THE BALTIC.
IT IS FURTHERMORE POSSIBLE THAT THE EMPLOYMENT OF SIGINT SHIPS IN THE BALTIC SERVED TO GATHER ADDITIONAL INTELLIGENCE.
ALL OF THESE ACTIVITIES MAY HAVE BEEN TARGETTED AGAINST THE NATO CPX "ABLE ARCHER 83".
B. GROUND FORCES
GDR
THE COMMAND ACTIVITIES WHICH HAVE BEEN OBSERVED IN THE GSFG, ITS SUBORDINATE ARMIES AND IN SOME INSTANCES ALSO IN THE SUBORDINATE DIVS SINCE 02 NOV WHILE CENTERING ON THE 2(UR)GA, THE 3(UR)SA AND 8(UR)GA WERE STILL IN PROGRESS ON 09 NOV.
THESE ACTIVITIES ARE PROBABLY LINKED TO THE TRG/PRACTICE OF NEWLY ROTATED COMMAND TROOPS PERSONNEL.
CSSR
THE COMMAND ACTIVITIES WHICH ELMS OF THE CGF HAVE REPORTEDLY BEEN STAGING IN NORTHWESTERN BOHEMIA SINCE 01 NOV CONTINUED ON 09 NOV.
POLAND
COMMAND ACTIVITIES IN NGF ELMS THAT HAVE BEEN OBSERVED SINCE 02 NOV STILL CONTINUED.
C. AIR FORCES
SUMMARY
THE AIR FORCES IN THE FORWARD AREA CONDUCTED FLIGHT TRG ACTIVITIES AT LOW LEVEL. THIS WAS ON THE ONE HAND DUE TO THE FACT THAT FLIGHT ACTIVITIES HAVE NOT YET BEEN RESUMED AT FULL LEVELS FOLLOWING CELEBRATIONS ON THE 66TH ANNIVERSARY OF THE OCTOBER REVOLUTION AND ON THE OTHER CAUSED BY HEAVY FOG WHICH IMPEDED FLIGHT ACTIVITIES.
D. NAVAL FORCES IN THE BALTIC
- NORMAL SURVEILLANCE OF THE BALTIC APPROACHES. ADDITIONAL RECCE ACTIVITIES CONDUCTED BY ONE SIGINT SHIP IN THE CENTRAL BALTIC AND PRESUMABLY ANOTHER ONE IN THE WATERS OFF THE SKAW.
- FOUR MEDIUM-SIZED FROSCH-CLASS LANDING SHIPS AND THREE AUXILIARIES OF THE GDR NAVAL FORCES WERE OBSERVED AT TRG ACTIVITIES EAST OF RUEGEN.
- THE EMPLOYMENT OF AMPHIBIOUS ELMS AND GUNNERY EX ACTIVITIES IN THE POMERANIAN BAY WERE OBSERVED IN THE POLISH NAVY. ASW AND SWEEPEX WERE ADDITIONALLY OBSERVED IN THE GULF OF GDANSK.
F. FINAL ASSESSMENT
THE CONTINUED LOW LEVEL OF EX AND TRG ACTIVITIES IN THE WP GROUND, AIR AND NAVAL FORCES OVERALL RENDERS NO INTELLIGENCE INDICATING ANY CHANGE IN THE SUBSTANCE OF THE THREAT.
3. ~~(C)~~ LOGISITCS, TRANSPORTATION SYSTEM
USSR
DURING A MEETING OF REPRESENTATIVES OF COMECON AIRLINE COMPANIES IN THE CONTEXT OF THE 50TH ANNIVERSARY OF THE ILYUSHIN ENGINEERING AGENCY, THAT AGENCY S CHIEF DESIGNER G. NOVOZHILOV ANNOUNCED THAT A LONG-RANGE VERSION OF THE CAMBER IL-86 IS BEING DEVELOPED.
HE DISCLOSED THE FOLLOWING DATA:
RANGE: UP TO 8 000 KM
TAKEOFF WEIGHT: 230 TONS (APPROX 30 TONS ABOVE THAT OF THE IL-86 PROTOTYPE)
WINGSPAN: 58 M (AN INCREASE OF 10 M IN COMPARISON TO THE BASIC VERSION)
PASSENGER CAPACITY: 300
COMMENT
THIS AIRCRAFT IS PROBABLY THE IL-96 WHICH HAS REPEATEDLY BEEN ALLUDED TO FOR SOME TIME ALREADY.
A NEW ENGINE DEVELOPMENT IS ALSO TO BE EXPECTED SINCE THE PROGRAM CANNOT BE REALIZED WITHOUT MORE POWERFUL DUCTED-FAN TURBINE ENGINES. THE USE OF FOREIGN DUCTED-FAN TURBINE ENGINES IN THE IL-86 ALREADY FAILED AND IS HARDLY LIKELY TO BE ENVISAGED SINCE IT WOULD NOT BE IN THE INTEREST OF THE USSR.
THE STEADY DELIVERY OF CAMBER AND THE PLANNED LONG-RANGE VERSION WILL RESULT IN NOT ONLY THE REPEATEDLY CALLED FOR STRUCTURAL IMPROVEMENTS OF SOVIET AIR TRAFFIC THAT ARE OF ECONOMIC RELEVANCE BUT ALSO IN AN ENHANCED CAPABILITY TO EFFECTIVELY EMPLOY THE NATIONAL AIR TRAFFIC POTENTIAL IN THE CONTEXT OF MILITARY STRATEGIC OBJECTIVES.
THE PRESENTLY AVAILABLE 30 CAMBER TYPE A/C ALREADY HAVE ENOUGH LIFT CAPACITY FOR TRANSPORTING MORE THAN 7 000 TROOPS INCLUDING BAGGAGE AND SMALL ARMS IN ONE WAVE OVER A MAXIMUM DISTANCE OF 7 000 KM, ASSUMING THAT 70 PERCENT OF THE A/C ARE READY FOR TAKEOFF.
COMMENTS: (U) ~~(C)~~ ONLY IDENTIFICATION OF SOURCE AND FACT OF BI-LATERAL ADVANCE RELEASE TO U.S. REQUIRE NOFORN CAVEAT. SOURCE RELEASES THIS INFORMATION TO NATO AS NATO ~~SECRET~~.
PROJ: (U) 911500
COLL: (U) NONE
INSTR: (U) US. NO
PREP: (U) (b)(6) & (b)(7)(E)
APPR: (U) b6 GN-14, ULO BONN
EVAL: (U) NO, REL TO: NONE
ENCL: (U) NONE
DISSEM: (U) N/A
WARNING: (U) NOT RELEASABLE TO FOREIGN NATIONALS.
DECL: OADR BT

ACTION DC-4(1) (U,P,T,F)
INFO SIDS(1) J3:NMCC(1) J5(2) SECDEF:(1) SECDEF(9)
USDP(15) ASD:PA&E(1) DI-1(1) AMIC(1) RTS-2B(1)
OS-1B(1) OS-1(1) NWS(1) JSI(1) JSI-5B(1) DC-1/CCF(1)
AT-2(1) AT-4(1) AIS(1) DIO(1) DE-1(1) DB-1B(1) (b)(3) per DIA
DB-1B(1) DB-1D(1) DB-1F(1) DB-1G(1) DB-3B(2)
DB-5B(1) DB-1E(1) DT-2(1) DIA(1) DT-5(1)
+CNO WASHINGTON DC
+CSAF WASHINGTON DC
+SECSTATE WASHINGTON DC
+CMC CC WASHINGTON DC
+DIRNSA FT GEORGE G MEADE MD
+CMC WASHINGTON DC
+SAFE

(b)(3) 10 USC 424 Per DIA

57 7676 DIA 9 NOV 1983

MCN=83314/04262 TOR=83314/1656Z TAD=83314/1657Z CDSN=MIA175
PAGE 1 OF 1
101545Z NOV 83
~~SECRET~~

AD

1

Document 7: Air Force Seventh Air Division, Ramstein Air Base, "Exercise Able Archer 83, SAC ADVON, After Action Report," December 1, 1983, Secret NOFORN

Source: U.S. Air Force Freedom of Information Act release

A declassified seventeen-page after-action report prepared by the Seventh Air Division provides the most thorough summary of the "on the ground action" as reported by aircrews during Able Archer 83. The report describes three days of "low spectrum" conventional play followed by two days of "high spectrum" nuclear warfare. "Due to the low spectrum lead-in for [Able Archer 83], SAC was invited to provide liaison officers/advisors to observe and comment on the operation of B-52 and KC-135 assets in accordance with SACEUR OPLANs 10604, FANCY GIRL and 10605, GOLDEN EAGLE." The details for these war plans remain unknown, but they were the Air Force plans for operations in a Europe-wide hostile environment.

According to the after-action report, "Orange [the Warsaw Pact] conducted chemical attacks throughout the exercise." Because of this, war gamers "were directed to go to the Alternate War HQ (CREST-HIGH)" at Heinrich-Hertz Kaserne in Birkenfeld, Germany. There, "helmets, gas masks and chemical suits" were worn by actors. On November 11, eight KC-135 Stratotankers in the United Kingdom were "launched for survival," likely in response to a simulated Orange nuclear attack. The SHAPE summary states that Blue conducted a simulated nuclear attack that same day.

There was "a SACEUR decision" before the beginning of the exercise "to reduce the level of nuclear exchange between Blue and Orange." The after-action report does not disclose the reason why SACEUR decided to reduce the nuclear exchange element of the exercise; the SHAPE summary states that "because the exercise scenario began at a low crisis level, there was actually less nuclear play than in previous years."

Finally, the after-action report includes one startling observation: "The presence of the SAC ADVON [an advance echelon vanguard], especially in large numbers for an exercise of this nature, raises a sensitive, political issue concerning the role of the B-52. One may see an implication or make the inference that if B-52 aircraft are present in a nuclear scenario exercise, are they being used to perform strike missions? Numerous times during the exercise the word 'strike' was used in reference to B-52 sorties. While this is an obvious slip of the tongue and was quickly corrected, in most cases, it does serve to fuel any inference should a remark be made in a non-secure environment."

~~SECRET~~

~~NOFORN~~

SEVENTH AIR DIVISION

EXERCISE ABLE ARCHER 83

SAC ADVON

AFTER ACTION REPORT (U)

HEADQUARTERS

7th AIR DIVISION (SAC)

RAMSTEIN AB, GERMANY

~~SECRET~~

~~NOFORN~~

Ex 28'

~~SECRET~~

SACEUR Exercise ABLE ARCHER 83 (U)

After Action Report (U)

I. (U) General.

A. ~~(S)~~ ABLE ARCHER (AA) is an annual SACEUR-sponsored Allied Command Europe CPX to practice command and control procedures with particular emphasis on the transition from purely conventional operations to chemical, nuclear and conventional operations. It is the culmination of SACEUR's annual AUTUMN FORGE exercise series.

B. ~~(S)~~ ABLE ARCHER 83 was conducted 7-11 Nov 83 with three days of "low spectrum" conventional play followed by two days of "high spectrum" nuclear warfare. Due to the low spectrum lead-in for AA 83, SAC was invited to provide liaison officers/advisors to observe and comment on operation of B-52 and KC-135 assets in accordance with SACEUR OPLANs 10604, FANCY GIRL and 10605, GOLDEN EAGLE.

C. (U) SAC Participation (Background)

1. ~~(S)~~ SAC participated in a previous AA with two observers. Due to the nature of the exercise and the possible political implications or inferences of B-52 involvement, future SAC participation was discouraged.

2. ~~(S)~~ SHAPE announced that AA 83 scenario had been changed to include three days of low spectrum activity and requested that SAC take an active part in the exercise. SAC proposed sending a team of two observers to each MSC, SHAPE and UK RAOC. SHAPE accepted this proposal, with the understanding that personnel were to act as observers/advisors to the staff at each level. A description of ADVON activities at these locations is contained in Section II.

D. (U) SAC objectives for ABLE ARCHER 83 were to:

1. ~~(S)~~ Observe NATO play of B-52 and KC-135 employment in accordance with SACEUR OPLANs.

2. (U) Determine if future participation is warranted, and if so, to what extent.

3. (U) Interface with SACEUR and MSC War Headquarters' staffs for mutual education.

4. (U) Update location guides.

E. (U) SAC ADVON composition for ABLE ARCHER 83 was as follows:

1. (U) AFNORTH:
Maj Paul J. Erbacher, 7AD/DOO, Bomber Planner
Maj Arunas Siulte, 7AD/DO8, Tanker Planner

~~SECRET~~

Ex 287

SECRET

2. (U) AFCENT:
Lt Col Arthur J. Lindemer, HQ SAC/DOO, Bomber Planner
Maj Ronald J. Valentine, HQ SAC/XOO, Tanker Planner

3. (U) AFSOUTH:
Lt Col Michael J. DePaul, 8AF/DOX, Bomber Planner
Lt Col John P. Bateman, 8AF/DOX, Tanker Planner

4. (U) SHAPE:
Lt Col William N. Maxwell, 7AD/DOX, Bomber Planner
Maj Peter W. Hardin, 8AF/DOO, Tanker Planner

5. (U) UK RAOC:
Maj Geoffrey C. Wenke, 15AF/DOXX, Tanker Planner

SECRET

Ex 287

~~SECRET~~

II. (U) ADVON OBSERVATIONS

A. (U) SHAPE

1. (S) GENERAL. ABLE ARCHER is too short for ADVON training or participation. The level of play PSC to MSC only dilutes the B-52 targeting process and the allocation of support packages. The level of SAC procedures training is almost nonexistent. Since ABLE ARCHER is primarily a nuclear procedures exercise, the viability of SAC play also comes into question. The AA Ops Order excepted SAC as players and stated they would act as observers (TAB C to APP III to Annex C). SAC observers at SHAPE were forced into playing SAC ADVON roles because there was no coordinated starting position for SAC assets. Each PSC was directed by SHAPE Op Order to develop unique Air Directives prior to SAC observer arrival. SHAPE started with full SAC force of bombers and tankers. Since the PSCs had developed their Air Directives for the first exercise day and published day two Air Directive at exercise initiation there were no requirements for B-52 allocation requests for days one and two. The underlying reason for the delay was a SACEUR B-52 allocation message for real-world tasking that had exercise information as the last paragraph. The last para (in summary) stated "Allocation from SACEUR was good for 48 hours." Thus, there were no requests from the PSCs for 7 and 8 Nov. However, CS SHAPE (Gen Dalton) wanted B-52 play. So the observers became ADVON players by default.

2. (S) ADVON OBSERVATIONS. Because of the level of play and the individual PSC scenarios only the bomber monitor had activity. The tanker planner at SHAPE had almost no activity due to use of SACEUR OPLAN, GOLDEN EAGLE, preallocations and no SACEUR direction to reallocate. The bomber observer acted as an advisor to the Air Operations Officer. Slides reflecting bomber beddown were initiated and updated with aircraft available daily. Since the USAFE OSC was not playing and units were not playing, a "Best Estimate" on bomber availability was made daily by the bomber observer. Attrition was neither planned for nor expected to be played, however, Southern Region reported one loss. During nuclear strikes SACEUR would only deconflict B-52s and strike assets plus or minus two hours of the TOT. The bomber planner also had to review B-52 targets for deconfliction with strike targets. SHAPE is the only place this can be done totally. PSCs can deconflict targets in their regions but a bomber strike near the border between two regions cannot be deconflicted at the PSC level. SACEUR bomber allocation messages were drafted and finalized for the Air Ops Officer. One mining request was received from AFNORTH but time lines would have made the mission occur after ENDEX. The request was denied because the TOT requested was far ahead of mine availability. An AFCENT request to disperse KC-135s to other UK bases was not acted upon due to SHAPE scenario inputs for chemical attacks and airfield attacks on the requested bases.

3. (S) FUTURE PARTICIPATION. SAC ADVON participation is not recommended for future AA exercises because the duration of play is too short for training; the exercise is primarily designed to exercise nuclear release procedures; the level of play does not allow the full target request allocation process to be exercised; the OSC does not play for logistics support; response cell and unit reports are not available and each region designs its own scenario.

~~SECRET~~

Ex 287

~~SECRET~~

4. ~~(S)~~ OTHER COMMENTS. An interesting sidelight was a request by SACEUR's Action Cell to provide a real-world type answer to a scenario situation. The problem was to relieve pressure on northern Norway. B-52 capabilities and F-111 capabilities were briefed to the team for their knowledge and consideration. The area to be targeted would have been the Kola Peninsula. Based on the scenario, the massed troops and mobile defenses coupled with static defenses made high altitude attacks highly questionable and low altitude better. However, the F-111 with 24 bombs and hard TFR would be the optimum air delivery vehicle. (My opinion).

4

~~SECRET~~

Ex 287

~~SECRET~~

B. (U) AFCENT.

1. (S) GENERAL. NATO was heavily engaged in conventional warfare at STARTEX. In the Central Region (CR), ORANGE (OR) forces were attacking along the entire German border with air attacks against BLUE (BL) airfields in Germany. OR attacks on UK airfields disrupted B-52 and KC-135 operations as well as destroying some aircraft. OR conducted chemical attacks throughout the exercise. (b)(5)
(b)(5)

2. (U) ADVON ACTIVITY. ADVON observer activities during AA 83 included:

(a) (U) Inputing correct data into the CCIS data base.

(b) (U) Observe the exercise and provide assistance. ERWIN desired 24-hour bomber and tanker coverage but it was impossible with two players. The 0600 to 1800L time frame was covered. We performed ADVON functions of drafting bomber request/allocation messages, tanker FCE allocation requests and coordinated on Air Directive inputs.

(c) (S) On E+1, we were directed to go to the Alternate War HQ (CREST-HIGH) which was located, for this exercise, at Heinrich Hertz Kaserne in Birkenfeld. The alternate staff desired SAC force expertise while they were in charge of OR operations which lasted all day E+1.

(d) (U) Helmets, gas masks and chemical suits were required. Gas masks were used by players at CREST HIGH for several hours after an OR chemical attack.

(e) (U) ERWIN was sealed for several hours during the evening of E+2.

3. (U) OPERATIONS.

(a) (S) Bomber Operations. SHAPE MSG 040900Z Nov established the initial CR bomber allocation at nine sorties per day along with tactical control for use against mobile targets. Nine sorties were also allocated for 8-10 Nov. The 11-12 Nov allocation was 18 sorties. B-52s were allocated to 2ATAF and 4ATAF to apply almost exclusively against mobile troop concentrations by using the target change tactic. There was incomplete information at AAFCE to determine the exact targets or the results of the attacks.

(1) (U) The B-52s were not included in the initial AAFCE data base and were added 7 Nov.

(2) (S) AAFCE did not receive any bomber request messages from 2 and 4ATAF even though they were requested several times. The ATAFs were addressed on the SHAPE message providing the initial allocation and new

~~SECRET~~

Ex 287

~~SECRET~~

procedures. As a result, the AAFCE players examined the battle situation and made the bomber request to SACEUR as well as the subsequent suballocation to 2/4ATAF. The ADVON observer assisted with the process. Bombers were included in the Air Directive.

(3) ~~(S)~~ It is extremely difficult for the ATAFs to identify a mobile target in the detail requested by SHAPE for them to base the B-52 allocation. This may be the reason the ATAFs did not submit request messages.

(4) ~~(S)~~ A major BL counterattack was planned and conducted by 2ATAF. They requested 30 B-52s to provide support of their objectives. SACEUR denied the request because of heavy commitment of B-52s to the Northern Region. Nine sorties previously allocated were employed in the counterattack.

(b) ~~(S)~~ Tanker Operations. In the STARTEX AAFCE Air Directive the KC-135 force was suballocated to 2ATAF and 4ATAF by base. The status of the allocated force, with pre-exercise scenario attrition, was as follows:

BEDFORD	13	2ATAF
GREENHAM COMMON	26	2ATAF
BRIZE NORTON	12	4ATAF
FAIRFORD	17	4ATAF
TOTAL	68	AAFCE

Tankers were employed at an average sortie rate of 1.0 due to sortie generation degrade at all tanker bases IAW exercise scenario, high daily first-wave sortie requirements, and DISTAFF OPSTAT inputs. On E+2 AAFCE planners realized that the remaining allocated tankers would not meet their planned air refueling requirements on E+3 and 4. The refueling requirements increased due to increased effort given to air defense and OCA. AAFCE requested from SACEUR allocation of FCE assets from Mildenhall to provide 20 additional sorties for the next two days. SACEUR allocated 15 aircraft from Mildenhall to satisfy this urgent requirement. On E+3 AAFCE sent request to SACEUR/USCINCEUR/USAFE/3AF for authorization to use civilian UK airports Gatwick and Stanstead for gas and go operations. This request was prompted to increase survivability and sortie offload capability. By ENDEX this proposal was not approved.

4. (U) FUTURE PARTICIPATION. Future CR SAC ADVON participation in ABLE ARCHER is recommended only with the following stipulations:

(a) (U) Scenario must include at least three days of conventional activity.

(b) (U) Two bomber and two tanker planners participate at ERWIN/2ATAF/4ATAF (six personnel) for 24-hour coverage.

(c) (U) No B-52 fragging of sorties.

~~SECRET~~

Ex 287

~~SECRET~~

(d) (U) Two DISTAFF representatives (24-hour coverage) are provided to input unit reports.

(e) (U) SAC ADVON bags are complete and available at 7 AD so minimum preparation is required.

(f) (U) ADVON players must be experienced.

(g) (U) ADVON support is strongly desired by COMAAFCE/SACEUR.

5. (U) OTHER COMMENTS. This exercise again reinforced the need to improve the SAC ADVON capability to conduct wartime operations. Emphasis must be placed on completing the following:

-- CINCSAC OPLAN 4102

-- SAC ADVON bags built/maintained and in readiness for real-world crisis situations.

-- SACR 55-7 Vol VII/VIII (staff conventional directive)

-- Integration of B-52/KC-135 reporting procedures into the NATO system.

~~SECRET~~

Ex 287

~~SECRET~~

C. (U) AFNORTH

1. (U) GENERAL.

(a) (U) The AFNORTH staff received the SAC ADVON with great enthusiasm but were somewhat disappointed when we were unable to provide 24-hour coverage. It was finally agreed that we would cover the day shift, since it would provide the majority of our activity.

(b) (U) The tanker representative took up a position in the RAOC (Regional Air Operations Center). The bomber representative was asked to divide his presence between the Targets Division and the RAOC, since his expertise and coordination would be required in both areas.

(c) ~~(S)~~ The target staff at AFNORTH appeared to be perfectly willing to manage the bomber allocation, select targets, and make request to SHAPE, in accordance with SHAPE message. They were relieved to have the SAC ADVON, since they were unsure of the mechanics to make such a request. Had the SAC Reporting Guide been available to them, they could have accomplished necessary messages.

2. (U) ADVON ACTIVITIES.

(a) ~~(S)~~ The bomber representative was involved in the Target Action Group Meeting, as an observer, since this dealt primarily with the deconfliction of NATO nuclear strikes and B-52/other aircraft conventional attacks. Both representatives attended Shift Changeover/Update Briefing, and Air Resources meeting. Level of questions for ADVON could have easily been answered by AFNORTH target staff.

(b) ~~(S)~~ With PSCs at COMNON, COMSONOR, and COMBALTAP at minimal manning levels, requests from AFNORTH staff for B-52 target nominations went unanswered. COMBALTAP did make one request for attacks and implementation of "EBB HORN" mining in COMLAND ZEELAND area.

(c) (U) Overall activity for the ADVON in the exercise was extremely limited.

3. (U) OPERATIONS.

(a) (U) BOMBER

(b)(5)

~~SECRET~~

Ex 287

~~SECRET~~

and execution time, and lack of escort on a heavily defended target, support could not be provided.

(b) (U) TANKER

(1) ~~(S)~~ AFNORTH was allocated 20 tankers to support operations in the Northern European Command (NEC). These were all used at a sortie rate of 1.5 each day. On 8 Nov AFNORTH requested that five KC-135s be positioned at Sola Airfield in Norway. These were used to provide more responsive refueling to marine and air defense aircraft in region. They also became an integral part of massed raid to extend range of F-111, F-4 and F-16 aircraft involved.

4. (U) FUTURE PARTICIPATION.

(a) ~~(S)~~ With PSCs at COMNON, COMSONOR, and COMBALTAP operating at minimum manning levels, requests from AFNORTH for target nominations for all aircraft went, for the most part, unanswered. What did filter up was oriented to the nuclear/chemical aspect of the exercise. The low play level at these locations did not allow for the feedback that should be available. Without increased NATO and US manning at all levels, we cannot justify expanded SAC ADVON participation.

(b) ~~(S)~~ As cited in paragraph 1c, the AFNORTH staff was willing to try operating without the SAC ADVON. Since in an actual conflict, the SAC ADVON may be delayed in arrival at locations, ABLE ARCHER would give NATO staffs an opportunity to at least become familiar with operations without SAC ADVON assistance. A small ADVON DISTAFF Cell at SHAPE could monitor inputs and act on them accordingly.

(c) ~~(S)~~ The presence of the SAC ADVON, especially in large numbers for an exercise of this nature, raises a sensitive, political issue concerning the role of the B-52. One may see an implication or make the inference that if B-52 aircraft are present in a nuclear scenario exercise, are they being used to perform strike missions? Numerous times during the exercise, the word "strike" was used in reference to B-52 sorties. While this is an obvious slip of the tongue and was quickly corrected, in most cases, it does serve to fuel any inference should a remark be made in a nonsecure environment. A large, if not fully manned, ADVON team which would be required to properly support ABLE ARCHER, being deployed to the many locations would only again give rise to speculation about the B-52 role.

~~SECRET~~

Ex 287

~~SECRET~~

D. (U) AFSOUTH

1. (U) GENERAL.

(a) (U) MG Brown (AIRSOUTH C/S) (USAF) was briefed on the capabilities and tactics for the B-52 and KC-135. The briefing was based on the WINTEX 83 briefing in the "RED BOOK" updated for B-52G only operations. The briefing was then given to LG Brown (COMAIRSOUTH) (USAF) who later offered the briefing to Admiral Small (AFSOUTH) (USN) and his C/S LG Blont (USA).

(b) ~~(S)~~ Due to the numerous new personnel in AIRSOUTH, the published timelines were modified to gain maximum training to all personnel involved in B-52 operations. MG Brown was particularly helpful in guiding the AIRSOUTH planners to select targets that not only provided optimum utilization of the B-52, but also had significant impact on the overall war plan.

(c) ~~(S)~~ We worked with AIRSOUTH personnel to encourage composite attack profiles for maximum disruption of enemy air and mutual support for Allied aircraft. A coordinated attack against Verna and Burgas Harbors (B-52s), airfields in the harbor areas (fighters) and F-111 airfield attacks on the Crimean Peninsula were planned providing maximum mutual defense. Support packages utilizing F-4Gs, EA-6Bs and fighter cap were included in the attack. NOTE: The harbor attacks were planned three days earlier. Unconventional warfare personnel were inserted into the area two days prior to pass the updated DMPI to the planners for maximum effectiveness of the sortie. Beacon bombing was also discussed, but not used.

(d) ~~(S)~~ The level of play required us to be more than advisors and observers. To provide the coordination required we split into two shifts shortly after arrival. We had to press people to get the required data. This was an artificialty created since the ATAFs did not have SAC ADVON representation. AFSOUTH is extremely interested in B-52 operations and the added capability it presents. Personnel participating in Dense Crop need to aggressively justify B-52 allocation requests to insure AFSOUTH has proper representation during the allocation cycle.

(e) ~~(S)~~ AFSOUTH needs data to update DIRE JUMBO. Recommend aircraft location and timelines be sent from HQ SAC to Maj Richard M. Meeboer, AIRSOUTH Plans and Policy (AIRSOUTH/PPPL). Also need a remark about E-3A refueling support, i.e., SHAPE will allocate E-3s and direct PSC/MSC to support.

(f) ~~(S)~~ Recommend "Red Book" be sent to US plans shops, PSCs and MSCs. The "Red Book" needs to be releasable to NATO (Print on cover). Also NATO Reporting Guide needs to be sent to PSCs and MSCs.

(g) ~~(S)~~ There is no set procedure for the AIRSOUTH/AFSOUTH staffs (OPS, IN, TGTS, ADVON) to get together to review the ATAF bomber requests, to have a coordinated, prioritized listing to send to SHAPE NLT 1100Z. There is little collective memory in the AIRSOUTH staff, even from the last WINTEX, hence it's been an education process to attempt to try to get the staffs together. The appearance is that the ATAFs sent their priority

~~SECRET~~

Ex 287

~~SECRET~~

lists to AFSOUTH, who passes it to AIRSOUTH and it comes down to the AIRSOUTH Intel, Ops and SAC ADVON to select the targets. The targets are then selected by the Ops Chief who was at the AFSOUTH briefing (in most cases the targeting philosophy is different). As a result target nomination lists are late or not sent and the only request sent is the BOMREQ, which does not provide SACEUR with the required data to make proper allocations.

(h) ~~(S)~~ A complete review of COMAIRSOUTH OPLAN 45604, "DIRE JUMBO" was completed. The COMM, Restricted areas, ECM, safe passage, emergency fields, procedures, etc. should be reviewed for possible inclusion in SAC 4102 or a SACR. This also applies to review of all MSC/PSC/SACEUR plans impacting SAC 4102. 45604 also requires backup targets from the ATAFs. It was explained that this should be removed from their plan.

(i) ~~(S)~~ We received only one written answer to the BOMREQ during the exercise. This mission was coordinated requiring all aircraft in the same time block. As it turned out half of the aircraft were in a different time block, and during daylight hours (SHAPE MSG 081315Z Nov for 10 Nov allocation). For staff training, to keep from destroying the combined, coordinated attack on Vara and Burgan we flew as planned.

(j) ~~(S)~~ No message allocation for 11 Nov was received. Telecon received on morning of 10th from Col Brown (SHAPE) cut the precoordinated number with LTC Hass from 15 to 9.

(k) ~~(S)~~ E-3A refueling were coordinated at the AFSOUTH level. I feel the refueling should be handled at the ATAF level to afford the tanker scheduler the opportunity to manage his scarce refueling assets. Each E-3 is using one and one half tankers (three sorties) each per day. We consistently had one in FIVE ATAF and one in SIX ATAF. At one point we had one in each ATAF, which would be a heavy load on the AFSOUTH tankers.

2. (U) ADVON ACTIVITY.

(a) (U) Attend TGT selection meeting (held one in AIRSOUTH last day).

(b) (U) Prepare slides for AIRSOUTH update briefing 1900L/0900L.

(1) (U) BDA (yesterday's missions).

(2) (U) Bomber activity (Today--actually next morning).

(3) (U) Bomber activity (Tomorrow--actually two days away).

(4) (U) Tanker activity.

(c) (U) Prepare TGTs message.

(d) (U) Prepare BOMREQ.

(e) (U) Prepare SUBALL.

~~SECRET~~

Ex 287

SECRET

(f) (U) Prepare TFG tasking to ATAFs (artificial due to exercise).

(g) (U) Tanker messages to support E-3 (artificial due to exercise).

(h) (U) Input to COMAIRSOUTH ASSESSREP due by 1700L.

3. (U) OPERATIONS.

(a) (S) Bomber. A total of 71 sorties were requested, 59 scheduled (based on final allocation) 50 of the 59 were flown by ENDEX. A total of four aircraft were lost due to ground and shipborne SAMs. Targets attacked included massed troops, soft armor, choke points and supply routes. One three-ship sortie was against a helicopter landing area prior to ADVON arrival (a total of on three helos were destroyed on that mission).

(b) (S) Tanker. The only tanker involvement was with E-3A refueling. We received sporadic tanker inputs from ATAFs due to no SAC participation at that level.

4. (S) FUTURE PARTICIPATION. With only a few locations with a SAC ADVON, too many simulations are required. It is confusing to the MSCs because they expect it to work like WINTEX. Recommend SHAPE allocate the B-52s and KC-135s to the MSCs at start of exercise and the MSCs work the exercise without the SAC ADVON.

Ex 287

SECRET

E. (U) UK RAOC

1. (S) GENERAL. I was in place at exercise location at STARTEX. I visited 3 AF Liaison Cell, DISTAFF, and RAF tanker personnel to determine level of exercise play. Although the Master Scenario Events List indicated a significant requirement for KC-135 air refueling support of UK Air Defense operations and multiple vertical dispersals, UK AIR staff personnel viewed ABLE ARCHER as a "nuclear procedures" exercise and chose not to play actively from the ADOC and SOCS during the conventional phase (7-9 Nov). The first KC-135 air refueling missions took place at 0600Z on 9 Nov. Since the ADOC and SOCS are the prime employers of air refueling and direct vertical dispersals their lack of participation left little requirement for SAC participation in this exercise.

(U) I spent the majority of my time learning how to use the Air Staff Management Aid (ASMA) computer system, becoming familiar with the RAOC layout and what each cell does, and discussing present and future concepts with RAF and 3 AF liaision personnel.

2. (U) ADVON ACTIVITY. The following represents Tanker ADVON duties based on my WINTEX 83 participation at UK RAOC:

(a) (U) Coordinate KC-135 allocation to the SOCS with the ADOC.

(b) (S) Prepare ATOs for TPW. (NOTE: This is only done for planned missions such as E-3A support or fighter deployments. OPCON of UK tanker assets supporting Air Defense rests with the SOCS and they launch the tankers unless sufficient warning is available, then the tanker cell will direct the launch by telecon. In lieu of an ATO for Air Defense we pass an alert response condition (60 min, 30 min, or 15 min) for the required number of KC-135s for a time block and the controlling SOCs.

(c) (S) Coordinate dispersal bases for all U.K. based airborne KC-135s and vertically dispersed KC-135s with 3 AF Liaison Cell, Ground Defense Cell, Contingency Plans Cell, and the Operations Support Cell when under air attack.

(d) (S) Coordinate air refueling requirements with the Tactical Air Support for Maritime Operations (TASMO) Cell.

(e) (S) Provide backup to 3 AF Liaison Cell in notifying TPW response cells of airborne dispersal when directed by ADOC.

(f) (U) Provide 3 AF Liaison Cell with a daily operations summary for CINCUKAIR's daily briefing.

As noted in para 1f only a limited amount of item 1 was played during ABLE ARCHER 83 due to reduced play by UKRAOC cells.

3. (U) OPERATIONS.

(S) KC-135 Activity

DAY	NO. OF SORTIES	TOTAL FLY TIME	NO. RCVRs	TOTAL OFFLOAD
7 Nov	0	0	0	0

SECRET

Ex 28'1

SECRET

DAY	NO. OF SORTIES	TOTAL FLY TIME	NO. RCVRs	TOTAL OFFLOAD
8 Nov	0	0	0	0
9 Nov	8	24.0	32 F-4	192.0M
10 Nov	11*	39.0	12 F-4	72.0M
11 Nov	0	0	0	0
TOTAL	19	63.0	44	264.0M

*Eight KC-135s launched for survival.

4. (S) FUTURE PARTICIPATION. The CINCUKAIR Staff's decisions not to man all RAOC cells or actively respond to exercise events during ABLE ARCHER 83 made it non cost effective for SAC ADVON participation. CINCUKAIR personnel view this exercise as strictly a nuclear procedures CPX. A SACEUR decision (sometime between EXORD development and STARTEX) to reduce the level of nuclear exchange between Blue and Orange cancelled most of the British interest in ABLE ARCHER. The British also view that if Blue is resorting to the use of nuclear weapons to stop the Orange advance, then most of their Air Defense assets have been lost (fighter and tanker) and there is no requirement for air refueling. Also, the lack of unit response cell play (BOTH US TPWs, and RAF SOCS and tanker bases) makes SAC ADVON play unrealistic. The tanker advisor is reduced to simulating all coordination required between TPWs, SOCs and the UKRAOC cells on ATOs, airborne dispersal, and daily Ops summaries. This is not a good exercise for SAC ADVON training if procedural play by participants does not change for future exercises.

(U) SAC ADVON participation at UKRAOC for future ABLE ARCHERs should be eliminated unless the following conditions can be met:

(a) (S) Full manning and active participation by UKRAOC cells in ADOC, Ground Defense, Tanker, USAFE, and contingency plans.

(b) (U) Active response cell play from the SOCs and a TPW for UKAIR allocated KC-135s.

(c) (U) 7 AD, 306 SW or 11 SG provide the tanker advisor to reduce the cost of sending CONUS-based ADVON personnel and provide flexibility if UKAIR reduces its enthusiasm during future exercises.

5. (U) OTHER

(a) (U) Tanker beddown in UK.

(1) (S) Discussion: I was briefed we would use the CRESTED EAGLE 84 tanker beddown for ABLE ARCHER. The MSEL called for a beddown based on the ENDEX position for WINTEX 83 which was based on FY 82 UK beddown. This caused concern among several strike command personnel over (1) the use of Scampton by both RAF Victors and US KC-135s (they claim Scampton can't

SECRET

Ex 287

~~SECRET~~

support both); (2) The ability of Cottesmore to support KC-135s presently (they are delighted that UKAIR-allocated KC-135s are not collocated with other MSCs' assets) and (3) that the 84 position was not officially sanctioned or approved. I had a long discussion with SQ LDR John Ward, CINCUKAIR/ Contingency Plans about future initiatives for US COBs in UK. Basically they are as follows: (1) Replace Scampton with Elvington, (2) move US A-7s from Finningly to Manston opening up Finningly for KC-135s, (3) reduce the base loading at Fairford, Greenham Common, and Mildenhall by using other UK airfields not specifically identified for KC-135. NOTE: SQ LDR Ward's views, however, may only be Strike Command's position and not that of MODUKAIR or USAFE.

(2) ~~(S)~~ Recommendations: (1) More preexercise coordination between SAC and 7 AD and UKAIR ADVON players on tanker beddown to be used. It would also be helpful if RAOC ADVON players were given as much background information as possible on the actual tanker beddown status of negotiations to preclude future embarrassment. (2) None. SQ LDR Ward's comments are provided for your information.

(b) (U) Status of CINCUKAIR Air Refueling Plan.

(1) ~~(S)~~ Discussion: The CINCUKAIR Air Refueling Plan is still in the conceptual stage. SQD LDR Graham Lanchbury has been the only tanker planner assigned to Strike Command/Plans since March 1983. His daily involvement with the Ascension Island to Falkland Islands refueling missions has precluded any work on the MSC plan. FLT LT Paul McKernan has recently been assigned to Strike/Plans on a temporary basis until a permanent second position is filled (in about three months). He has been given the MSC refueling plan as his top priority. I spent an entire day with him over GOLDEN EAGLE, COTTON CURE and AFNORTH's BENT BOOM (Draft), providing recommendation on plan format and content, and providing points of contact at 11 SG and 7 AD to get assistance in plan development. I recommended he use BENT BOOM as a model since operations to be conducted in AFNORTH are the most similar to UKAIR. The unique procedures used by UKAIR in Command control, airborne dispersal/survival scramble, enroute communications, and air refueling during hostilities required they be formulated into a written plan for use by our TPWs and all MSC tasking UK-based KC-135s as soon as possible.

(2) (U) Recommendation: That 7 AD actively monitor the progress of CINCUKAIR's air refueling plan and provide any expertise in tanker operations/command control required by Strike Command to expedite plan completion.

~~SECRET~~

Ex 287

~~SECRET~~

III. FUTURE PARTICIPATION

A. ~~(S)~~ The preceding section contained the critiques written by the ADVON representatives. Due to travel restrictions, only an informal meeting was held at 7 AD, which not all members were able to attend. The comments and observations are printed virtually verbatim--only editorial changes made--from the reports received. The critiques were prepared in isolation, yet the same themes occur in all. These themes are: short duration of exercise does not allow for real allocation cycle to be played; time lines are unrealistically reduced; short duration demands experienced personnel since there is no time for training; low level of play at most headquarters does not allow for realistic play or appraisal; and the sensitive issue of B-52 operations being conducted in conjunction with an exercise primarily designed to test nuclear release procedures.

B. (U) Based on above comments and our participation in ABLE ARCHER 83, 7AD recommends no further SAC ADVON participation in the ABLE ARCHER series of exercises.

Gary G. Durkee

GARY G. DURKEE, Colonel, USAF
Director of Operations

16

SECRET

Ex 287

UNCLASSIFIED

DISTRIBUTION

APO NEW YORK 09012..5
7AD DOO-1
HO-5

BARKSDALE AFB, LA 71110..................................2
8AF DOX-2

MARCH AFB, CA 92508......................................1
15AF DOX-1

OFFUTT AFB, NE 68113.....................................2
HQ SAC DOO-2

TOTAL 10

UNCLASSIFIED

Document 8: Memorandum for National Security Advisor Robert McFarlane from Soviet Expert Jack Matlock, "Subject: American Academic on Soviet Policy," December 13, 1983, Confidential with Attached EXDIS Cable from the American Embassy in Moscow

Source: Ronald Reagan Presidential Library, Matlock Files, Chron December 1983 [1 of 2], Box 2, 90888

In December 1983 Reagan's Soviet expert Jack Matlock sent National Security Advisor Robert McFarlane a memo warning that in the Soviet Union since mid-1983, a "fear of war seemed to affect the elite as well as the man on the street." The cable described information from "an American academic with excellent entrée to the Soviet political elite." The academic warned of "growing paranoia among Soviet officials and sees them literally obsessed by fear of war," while sensing a mounting "emotionality and even irrationality" in their worldview. The attached EXDIS cable goes further, recounting "a high degree of paranoia among Soviet officials . . . not unlike the atmosphere of thirty years ago."

9039

MEMORANDUM

NATIONAL SECURITY COUNCIL

~~CONFIDENTIAL~~ December 13, 1983

INFORMATION

MEMORANDUM FOR ROBERT C. McFARLANE

FROM: JACK MATLOCK

SUBJECT: American Academic on Soviet Policy

The telegram from Moscow I mentioned this morning is attached at Tab I. It reports on the observations of an experienced American academic who spent about ten days in discussions with senior Soviet officials, including Boris Ponomarev, candidate member of the Politburo and head of the Central Committee's International Department, and several other Party and Institute officials not often seen by Americans.

Among the source's conclusions were:

--Fear of war seemed to affect the elite as well as the man on the street.

--A degree of paranoia seemed rampant among high officials, and the danger of irrational elements in Soviet decision making seems higher.

--The election next year seems to have become a key determinant in Soviet foreign policy making, with the aim not to permit the President to assume the role of peacemaker.

--There seems to be a growing climate of neo-Stalinism and outright chauvinism on the lower levels of the bureaucracy.

The scholar also was told that Andropov had directed a more activist role in the Middle East, and that Andropov is increasingly seeking to take control over foreign policy and to undermine Gromyko.

Paragraphs 2-11 are the most relevant ones in the long cable.

Attachment:

Tab I Moscow telegram 15409 of December 10, 1983.

~~CONFIDENTIAL~~
Declassify on: OADR

CONFIDENTIAL

NATIONAL SECURITY COUNCIL
MESSAGE CENTER

PAGE 01 OF 02 MOSCOW 5409 DTG: 101007Z DEC 83 PSN: 074922
E08974 ANCC0253 TOR: 344/2110Z CSN: HCE355

DISTRIBUTION: FORT-01 DOBR-01 LEVN-01 LILA-01 MART-01 ROBN-01
LENC-01 MAT-01 /008 A1

WHTS ASSIGNED DISTRIBUTION:
SIT: PUBS SIT
EOB:

PRIORITY
STU4585
DE RUEHMO #5409/01 3441015
P 101007Z DEC 83
FM AMEMBASSY MOSCOW

TO SECSTATE WASHDC PRIORITY 3385

C O N F I D E N T I A L SECTION 01 OF 04 MOSCOW 15409

EXDIS
E.O. 12356: DECL: OADR
TAGS: PGOV, PREL, ECON, PINR, UR
SUBJECT: AMERICAN ACADEMIC ON SOVIET FOREIGN AND
-- DOMESTIC POLICY

1. (C - ENTIRE TEXT)

2. SUMMARY: AN AMERICAN ACADEMIC WITH EXCELLENT ENTREE TO THE SOVIET POLITICAL ELITE BRIEFED EMBASSY ON HIS DISCUSSIONS HERE NOVEMBER 28-DECEMBER 8. HE BELIEVES, BASED ON THESE DISCUSSIONS, THAT A SIGNIFICANT SHIFT HAS TAKEN PLACE IN SOVIET THINKING AND ATTITUDES, ESPECIALLY TOWARDS THE U.S., OVER THE PAST SIX MONTHS. WHERE EARLIER SOVIET DECISION-MAKING WAS FOUNDED ALMOST EXCLUSIVELY ON PRAGMATISM AND REASONED CALCULATION OF SOVIET INTERESTS, EMOTIONALISM AND EVEN IRRATIONALITY ARE NOW ENTERING INTO PLAY. THE ACADEMIC PERCEIVES A GROWING PARANOIA AMONG SOVIET OFFICIALS, AND SEES THEM LITERALLY OBSESSED BY FEAR OF WAR. HE BELIEVES THAT THE U.S. PRESIDENTIAL ELECTIONS HAVE BECOME THE CENTRAL DETERMINING FACTOR IN SOVIET FOREIGN POLICY.

3. THE ACADEMIC HAS NOTED, FURTHER, A CERTAIN SENSE OF LEADERLESSNESS AND A LACK OF AN INTEGRATED FOREIGN POLICY, WHICH HE ATTRIBUTES TO ANDROPOV'S LENGTHY ABSENCE FROM THE SCENE AND THE UNCERTAINTY THIS HAS GENERATED. HE FEELS THAT THERE ARE SIGNIFICANT DIFFERENCES WITHIN THE LEADERSHIP--PARTICULARLY ON DOMESTIC POLICY--AND PINPOINTS THE LOWER PARTY ORGANS (AT THE DISTRICT LEVEL) AND THE ECONOMIC BUREAUCRACIES AS THE MAJOR SOURCES OF OPPOSITION TO ANDROPOV'S DOMESTIC PROGRAMS, AND ANTICIPATES THAT ANDROPOV WILL SHORTLY ATTEMPT TO OVERCOME THIS OPPOSITION THROUGH WIDESPREAD PERSONNEL CHANGES IN THE ECONOMIC MINISTRIES AND AT LOWER PARTY LEVELS. ALTHOUGH THE ACADEMIC SENSED THE SAME WIDESPREAD RECOGNITION AMONG HIS INTERLOCUTORS AS HE HAD DURING A PREVIOUS VISIT IN MAY OF THE NECESSITY FOR ECONOMIC CHANGE, HE DETECTED MUCH LESS OPTIMISM THAT THE KIND OF CHANGES REQUIRED TO BREAK OUT OF THE CURRENT IMPASSE COULD BE REALIZED. HIS OWN BELIEF IS THAT THE LEADERSHIP IS EITHER UNWILLING OR UNABLE TO PURSUE OTHER THAN A GRADUAL, INCREMENTAL APPROACH TO ECONOMIC CHANGE, AND THAT EACH SMALL STEP WILL BE ABSORBED BY THE SYSTEM RATHER THAN REFORM IT.

CONFIDENTIAL

CONFIDENTIAL

NATIONAL SECURITY COUNCIL
MESSAGE CENTER

PAGE 02 OF 02 MOSCOW 5409 DTG: 101007Z DEC 83 PSN: 074922

4. THE ACADEMIC'S INTERLOCUTORS ACKNOWLEDGED THAT ANDROPOV HAD UNDERGONE AN OPERATION BUT CLAIMED THAT HE WAS NOW BACK AT WORK ALBEIT ON A SOMEWHAT LIMITED SCHEDULE. THE ACADEMIC GAINED THE IMPRESSION THAT USTINOV HAD STOOD IN FOR THE GENERAL SECRETARY DURING THE LATTER'S ABSENCE: CHERNENKO HAD BEEN COMPLETELY BYPASSED. END SUMMARY.

5. THE ACADEMIC IDENTIFIED THREE MAJOR CURRENTS IN SOVIET THINKING THAT HAD EMERGED SINCE HIS VISIT HERE IN MAY:

-- A GENUINE SENSE OF CONCERN OVER TRENDS ON THE INTERNATIONAL STAGE AND A FEAR OF WAR THAT SEEMED TO BE SHARED BY SOVIET CITIZENS GENERALLY. THE OFFICIAL LINE ON FOREIGN AFFARIS IS GENERALLLY BELIEVED BY THE POPULACE.

-- A GROWING CLIMATE OF NEO-STALINISM, PARTICULARLY EVIDENT AT THE RAION (DISTRICT) LEVEL AND AMONGST THE YOUNGER GENERATION. FED BY STRONG FEELINGS OF PATRIOTISM AND EVEN CHAUVINISM. THERE IS A GROWING SENSE THAT THE SOVIET UNION IS BEING PUSHED AROUND BY THE U.S., AND THAT RESOURCES MUST BE MOBILIZED TO COUNTERACT THIS THREAT, UTILIZING THE ADVANTAGES WHICH A CENTRALIZED ECONOMY POSSESSES IN THIS REGARD. THE COROLLARY TO THIS IS THAT DOMESTIC ECONOMIC CHANGES CANNOT BE AFFORDED AT THIS TIME.

-- A HIGH DEGREE OF PARANOIA AMONG HIGH OFFICIALS WITH WHOM THE ACADEMIC SPOKE, NOT UNLIKE THE ATMOSPHERE OF THIRTY YEARS AGO. SINCE HIS MAY VISIT, THE ACADEMIC HAS NOTICED THAT ATTITUDES HAVE BECOME MORE PERSONAL AND EMOTIONAL, ESPECIALLY WITH RESPECT TO THE U.S., AND HE DID NOT DISCOUNT THE POSSIBILITY OF IRRATIONAL ELEMENTS IN SOVIET DECISION-MAKING. HE CITED THE STRAIGHTFACED CLAIM MADE TO HIM BY ONE OFFICIAL THAT THE KAL FLIGHT HAD BEEN DELIBERATELY STAGED BY THE U.S.--NOT AS AN INTELLIGENCE FLIGHT--BUT TO PROVOKE THE USSR AND ANTI-SOVIET FEELINGS IN THE WORLD.

6. THE ACADEMIC DECLARED THAT THE STATEMENT RECENTLY MADE BY BRZEZINSKI THAT THE SOVIETS "WOULD CRAWL BACK TO THE NEGOTIATING TABLE" WAS COMPLETELY INCONSISTENT
BT

EXDIS EXDIS EXDIS EXDIS

CONFIDENTIAL

CONFIDENTIAL

NATIONAL SECURITY COUNCIL
MESSAGE CENTER

PAGE 01 OF 02 MOSCOW 5409 DTG: 101007Z DEC 83 PSN: 074924
EOB976 AN000252 TOR: 344/2112Z CSN: HCE356

DISTRIBUTION: FORT-01 DOBR-01 LEVN-01 LILA-01 MART-01 RCBN-01
LENC-01 MAT-01 /008 A1

WHTS ASSIGNED DISTRIBUTION:
SIT:
EOB:

PRIORITY
STU4586
DE RUEHMO #5409/02 3441016
P 101007Z DEC 83
FM AMEMBASSY MOSCOW

TO SECSTATE WASHDC PRIORITY 3386

C O N F I D E N T I A L SECTION 02 OF 04 MOSCOW 15409

EXDIS
E.O. 12356: DECL: OADR
TAGS: PGOV, PREL, ECON, PINR, UR
SUBJECT: AMERICAN ACADEMIC ON SOVIET FOREIGN AND
-- DOMESTIC POLICY
WITH THE POSITIONS TAKEN BY HIS SOVIET CONTACTS HERE. ALL OF HIS SOVIET INTERLOCUTORS HAD UNEQUIVOCALLY STATED THAT THE SOVIETS WOULD NOT RETURN TO SEPARATE INF TALKS. MOREOVER, ALL HAD EXPECTED THAT THE SOVIET UNION WOULD NOT CONTINUE WITH START NEGOTIATIONS EITHER, BUT THIS HAD BEEN EXPRESSED AS PERSONAL OPINION RATHER THAN AS A CATEGORICAL STATEMENT.

7. THE ACADEMIC FELT THAT THE U.S. PRESIDENTIAL ELECTIONS HAVE BECOME THE KEY DETERMINANT OF SOVIET FOREIGN POLICY MAKING. IN THEIR EFFORTS TO PREVENT THE PRESIDENT'S RE-ELECTION, THE SOVIETS ARE DETERMINED NOT TO ALLOW HIM TO ASSUME THE MANTLE OF PEACEMAKER. SOVIET INTERLOCUTORS CLAIMED THAT THE SOVIET SIDE HAD CONSISTENTLY SHOWED RESTRAINT VIS-A-VIS THE U.S. BUT HAD MET WITH NO RESPONSE FROM PRESIDENT REAGAN. THEY CLAIMED TO SEE NO INCENTIVE WHATEVER FOR A POLICY OF RESTRAINT IN THE FUTURE. (IN RESPONSE TO A QUESTION FROM THE AMBASSADOR, THE ACADEMIC ACKNOWLEDGED THAT NONE OF HIS SOVIET CONTACTS HAD CITED ANY SPECIFIC EXAMPLES OF PAST SOVIET RESTRAINT.)

8. ON THE SOVIET SIDE, HE FELT THAT THE PARAMETERS OF ASSESSING RISK HAD SHIFTED AWAY FROM THE BASICALLY PRAGMATIC APPROACH WHICH HAD IN THE PAST CHARACTERIZED SOVIET BEHAVIOR ABROAD. THE ACADEMIC SENSED, MOREOVER, THAT THE SOVIETS DO NOT, AT THIS TIME, HAVE AN INTEGRATED FOREIGN POLICY. THIS WAS PARTIALLY A FUNCTION OF THE SERIOUSNESS AND COMPLEXITY OF THE PROBLEMS FACING THEM. A MORE IMPORTANT FACTOR, HE FELT, WAS THE UNSETTLED STATE OF THE LEADERSHIP.

THE MIDDLE EAST

9. THE ACADEMIC CITED THE MIDDLE EAST AS AN EXAMPLE OF AN AREA WHERE THE LACK OF A COHERENT SOVIET POLICY IS EVIDENT. WHILE SOVIET OFFICIALS HAD WARNED THAT "YOU CAN BE SURE WE WILL REACT" TO ANY U.S. ACTION AGAINST SYRIA, THE SCHOLAR FELT THAT IN FACT HIS INTERLOCUTORS HAD NO CLEAR IDEA WHAT FORM THIS REACTION WOULD

CONFIDENTIAL

CONFIDENTIAL

NATIONAL SECURITY COUNCIL
MESSAGE CENTER

PAGE 02 OF 02 MOSCOW 5409 DTG: 101007Z DEC 83 PSN: 074924

TAKE. THERE SEEMED, MOREOVER, TO BE CERTAIN BASIC CONTRADICTIONS IN SOVIET ASSESSMENTS OF THE CURRENT SITUATION IN LEBANON. ON THE ONE HAND, THE ACADEMIC HEARD REPEATED EXPRESSIONS OF CONCERN OVER THE POSSIBILITY OF A U.S.-SOVIET CLASH OVER LEBANON; ON THE OTHER, THE SOVIETS SEEMED TO DERIVE "SATISFACTION" FROM THE PRESENCE OF U.S. MARINE "HOSTAGES" IN LEBANON, WHICH WAS PERCEIVED AS GENERATING ARAB ENMITY WITH THE U.S. AND, ULTIMATELY, CREATING DOMESTIC POLITICAL PROBLEMS FOR THE PRESIDENT.

EXDIS

10. THE SCHOLAR WAS TOLD THAT ANDROPOV HAD RECENTLY WRITTEN A MEMORANDUM ADDRESSED TO THE CENTRAL COMMITTEE INTERNATIONAL DEPARTMENT IN WHICH HE REPORTEDLY ASSERTED THAT SOVIET POLICY IN THE MIDDLE EAST WAS TOO PASSIVE AND REACTIVE AND DIRECTED THAT THE SOVIET UNION TAKE THE INITIATIVE. WHETHER ANDROPOV HAD IN MIND DIPLOMATIC OR MILITARY ACTIONS WAS UNCLEAR. THE SCHOLAR MAINTAINED THAT, ON A MORE GENERAL PLANE, THE GENERAL SECRETARY WAS INCREASINGLY SEEKING TO TAKE CONTROL OVER FOREIGN POLICY AND TO UNDERMINE GROMYKO.

EXDIS

11. THE AMBASSADOR SUGGESTED THREE FACTORS WHICH HE THOUGHT COULD ACCOUNT FOR THE CHANGE IN THE ATMOSPHERE AND ATTITUDES WHICH THE ACADEMIC HAD ENCOUNTERED HERE: THE TURN FOR THE WORSE IN ANDROPOV'S HEALTH, THE KAL INCIDENT, AND THE REALITY OF THE INF DEPLOYMENTS. THE ACADEMIC AGREED WITH THIS ASSESSMENT, LAYING PARTICULAR STRESS ON THE FIRST FACTOR. THERE HAD BEEN A GREAT SENSE OF CONFIDENCE AMONGST HIS INTERLOCUTORS HALF A YEAR AGO, HE SAID. A SENSE OF THE POSSIBILITY OF POSITIVE CHANGE BECAUSE OF THE UNITY FORGED BY A STRONG LEADER. ANDROPOV'S ABSENCE FROM THE SCENE FOR THE

EXDIS

LAST FEW MONTHS HAD PERMITTED DIFFERENCES TO EMERGE AND HAD GENERATED A SENSE OF LEADERLESSNESS. WHETHER ANDROPOV COULD AGAIN ASSERT HIMSELF AS THE STRONG LEADER WHOM ALL BELIEVED WAS NECESSARY AND BEHIND WHOM ALL COULD UNITE WAS FOR THE MOMENT PROBLEMATICAL.

ANDROPOV'S HEALTH

EXDIS

12. THE SCHOLAR'S CONTACTS INDICATED THAT THE GENERAL SECRETARY HAD UNDERGONE AN OPERATION (THE DATE AND NATURE OF WHICH WERE NOT SPECIFIED) AND HAD BEEN
BT

CONFIDENTIAL

~~CONFIDENTIAL~~

NATIONAL SECURITY COUNCIL
MESSAGE CENTER

PAGE 01 OF 02 MOSCOW 5409 DTG: 101007Z DEC 83 PSN: 074926
EOB977 AN020251 TOR: 344/2114Z CSN: HCE357

DISTRIBUTION: FORT-01 DOBR-01 LEVN-01 LILA-01 MART-01 ROBN-01
LENC-01 MAT-01 /008 A1

WHTS ASSIGNED DISTRIBUTION:
SIT:
EOB:

PRIORITY
STU4587
DE RUEHMO #5409/03 3441017
P 101007Z DEC 83
FM AMEMBASSY MOSCOW

TO SECSTATE WASHDC PRIORITY 3387

~~C O N F I D E N T I A L~~ SECTION 03 OF 04 MOSCOW 15409

EXDIS
E. O. 12356: DECL: OADR
TAGS: PGOV, PREL, ECON, PINR, UR
SUBJECT: AMERICAN ACADEMIC ON SOVIET FOREIGN AND
-- DOMESTIC POLICY
ORDERED TO REST FOR AT LEAST FOUR OR FIVE WEEKS. WHILE RECUPERATING AT HIS DACHA, HOWEVER, MAJOR DECISIONS HAD BEEN SUBMITTED TO HIM AND RESOLUTIONS HAD BEEN WRITTEN UNDER HIS DIRECTION. DURING THIS RECUPERATIVE PERIOD, USTINOV HAD SERVED AS ANDROPOV'S STAND-IN; CHERNENKO HAD BEEN COMPLETELY BYPASSED. ANDROPOV HAD CONTINUED TO MEET WITH SENIOR FIGURES INDIVIDUALLY WHEN HE HAD BEEN UNABLE TO ATTEND POLITBURO MEETINGS. (THE PERIOD OF TIME DURING WHICH ANDROPOV HAD NOT ATTENDED THESE MEETINGS WAS UNCLEAR.)

13. AT ANY RATE, ACCORDING TO THE ACADEMIC, ANDROPOV WAS NOW BACK AT WORK ALTHOUGH UNDER STRICT ORDERS TO LIMIT HIS SCHEDULE. THE SCHOLAR HAD BEEN TOLD THAT THE GENERAL SECRETARY WORKS CURRENTLY EIGHT HOURS A DAY WITH A BREAK FOR A MID-DAY REST. (COMMENT: THIS SCHEDULE WOULD ACCORD WITH THE PATTERN OF ANDROPOV'S MOTORCADE MOVEMENTS.) WEEKENDS WERE TO BE RESERVED FOR REST.

OPPOSITION TO ANDROPOV
----

14. THE SCHOLAR IS CONVINCED THAT THERE ARE SIGNIFICANT DIFFERENCES WITHIN THE LEADERSHIP (HE DID NOT PROVIDE ANY ELABORATION) AND THAT OPPOSITION TO ANDROPOV'S EFFORTS AT ECONOMIC REVIVAL IS CENTERED IN THE ECONOMIC BUREAUCRACY AND IN MID-LEVEL PARTY ORGANS AT THE RAION (DISTRICT) LEVEL. THE SCHOLAR CHARACTERIZED THE RAIKOM SECRETARIES, TYPICALLY MEN IN THEIR 30'S AND 40'S, AS INTENSE PATRIOTS--EVEN CHAUVINISTS--WHO BELIEVED THAT THE COUNTRY SHOULD BE MOBILIZED TO MEET THE CHALLENGE FROM THE U.S. THEY WERE NOT ACTIVE SUPPORTERS OF ECONOMIC CHANGE. "IT WAS ANYBODY'S GUESS" WHETHER ANDROPOV'S RETURN TO A MORE ACTIVE ROLE WOULD RESULT IN THE ELIMINATION OR ISOLATION OF THIS OPPOSITION TO CHANGE, BUT THE SCHOLAR FELT SURE THAT ONE OF HIS GENERAL SECRETARY'S GOALS WILL BE TO UNDERTAKE A "CLEANING-OUT." HE BELIEVED THAT THERE WOULD SOON BE MAJOR PERSONNEL CHANGES IN THE MINISTRIES AND AT LOWER PARTY LEVELS, AND SAID THAT PROMOTIONS INTO THE POLITBURO MIGHT BE ANNOUNCED AT THE UPCOMING PLENUM. (COMMENT: PRESS COVERAGE OF THE ONGOING PARTY-ELECTION CAMPAIGN

~~CONFIDENTIAL~~

CONFIDENTIAL

NATIONAL SECURITY COUNCIL
MESSAGE CENTER

PAGE 02 OF 02 MOSCOW 5409 DTG: 101007Z DEC 83 PSN: 074926

HAS INDEED BEEN SHARPLY CRITICAL OF THE PERFORMANCE OF NUMEROUS DISTRICT LEVEL ORGANIZATIONS. WHILE THE CAMPAIGN HAS NOW REACHED THE OBLAST LEVEL, DISTRICT LEVEL OFFICIALS ARE STILL BEING SINGLED OUT FOR SHORTCOMINGS.)

15. THE SCHOLAR SAID THAT HE HAD HEARD FROM TWO SOURCES THAT ANDROPOV HAD SENT A HARD-HITTING LETTER TO ALL PARTY ORGANIZATIONS IN OCTOBER THAT DECLARED IN NO UNCERTAIN TERMS THAT THE FATHERLAND WAS IN DANGER AND UNDERSCORED THE NECESSITY OF REVIVING AND REINVIGORATING THE SOVIET ECONOMY. REPORTEDLY ANDROPOV STRESSED THAT HE WAS NOT EXAGGERATING THE EXTERNAL DANGER TO THE NATION, AND HE WARNED THAT THE TIME HAD PASSED WHEN A "FORMALISTIC" APPROACH TOWARD CHANGES MANDATED BY THE CENTER WOULD BE TOLERATED AND THAT THOSE WHO DID NOT SUPPORT THESE CHANGES ASSIDUOUSLY WOULD BE DEALT WITH RUTHLESSLY. (COMMENT: WE HAVE RECENTLY HEARD A SIMILAR REPORT FROM A CHINESE DIPLOMAT, WHO SPECULATED THAT THE INTENT OF THE LETTER HAD BEEN TO PREPARE THE COUNTRY FOR AN INCREASED DEFENSE BURDEN.)

ECONOMIC REFORM
----

16. WHILE SOVIET CONTACTS EVINCED A CONTINUED RECOGNITION THAT MAJOR ECONOMIC CHANGES WERE ESSENTIAL, THE SCHOLAR DETECTED A MARKEDLY DECREASED CONVICTION THAT SUCH CHANGES COULD BE SUCCESSFULLY IMPLEMENTED. THE SCHOLAR HIMSELF WAS PESSIMISTIC THAT CURRENT EFFORTS WOULD MAKE AN APPRECIABLE DENT IN A SYSTEM STILL GOVERNED BY AN UNREAL PRICING MECHANISM AND A LACK OF MEANINGFUL MATERIAL INCENTIVES. THERE SEEMED TO BE NO WAY, HE ASSERTED, OF BREAKING THE VICIOUS PRODUCTIVITY/INCENTIVES CIRCLE. WHILE THE SOON-TO-BE INTRODUCED EXPERIMENT IN INCREASED ENTERPRISE AUTONOMY DID INDEED REPRESENT THE MOST MEANINGFUL STEP TAKEN IN THE SPHERE OF ECONOMIC CHANGE SINCE THE LATE 60'S, IT WAS ULTIMATELY DOOMED TO FAILURE. IT WAS TYPICAL OF PREVIOUS EFFORTS AT ECONOMIC CHANGE IN THAT IT WAS LIMITED IN APPLICATION AND INCREMENTAL IN APPROACH. AS IT STOOD, IT WAS LIKELY TO BE ABSORBED AND THUS SMOTHERED WITHIN THE SYSTEM EVEN IF THE EXPERIMENT PRODUCED POSITIVE RESULTS WITHIN THE FIVE MINISTRIES WHERE IT IS TO GET UNDERWAY NEXT JANUARY. THE SCHOLAR
BT

EXDIS EXDIS EXDIS

CONFIDENTIAL

NATIONAL SECURITY COUNCIL
MESSAGE CENTER

PAGE 01 OF 03 MOSCOW 5409 DTG: 101007Z DEC 83 PSN: 074929
E09978 AN000250 TOR: 344/2115Z CSN: HCE359

DISTRIBUTION: FORT-01 DOBR-01 LEVN-01 LILA-01 MART-01 ROBN-01
ENC-01 MAT-01 /008 A1

WHTS ASSIGNED DISTRIBUTION:
SIT:
EOB

PRIORITY
STU4588
DE RUEHMO #5409/04 3441018
P 101007Z DEC 83
FM AMEMBASSY MOSCOW

TO SECSTATE WASHDC PRIORITY 3388

C O N F I D E N T I A L SECTION 04 OF 04 MOSCOW 15409

EXDIS
E.O. 12356: DECL: OADR
TAGS: PGOV, PREL, ECON, PINR, UR
SUBJECT: AMERICAN ACADEMIC ON SOVIET FOREIGN AND
-- DOMESTIC POLICY
CITED ONE ECONOMIC OFFICIAL WHO CONCURRED WITH HIS OWN PESSIMISTIC ASSESSMENT OF THE EXPERIMENT'S LIKELIHOOD OF HAVING A MEASURABLE IMPACT ON THE ECONOMY AS A WHOLE.

17. THE ACADEMIC COMMENTED THAT THE MILITARY APPEARS TO HAVE SOMETHING OF AN AMBIVALENT ATTITUDE TOWARDS ECONOMIC CHANGE. ON THE ONE HAND, THEY ARE WORRIED ABOUT THE WEAKNESS OF THE CIVILIAN ECONOMY AND ARE ESPECIALLY CONCERNED ABOUT SCIENTIFIC AND TECHNOLOGICAL PROGRESS. THIS IMPELS THEM TO SUPPORT CHANGE ON A FAIRLY MAJOR SCALE. ON THE OTHER HAND, THE MILITARY RECOGNIZE THAT THE PROCESS OF CHANGE WILL YIELD LITTLE IMMEDIATE BENEFITS FOR THEM AND MAY EVEN CONSTRICT THEIR SHARE OF THE RESOURCES PIE. ONE THING IS CERTAIN-- THE MILITARY STRONGLY BACK THE ANDROPOV DRIVE FOR GREATER WORK DISCIPLINE.

18. IN RESPONSE TO A QUERY ON RYZHKOV (WHOM THE SCHOLAR DID NOT SEE ON THIS TRIP), THE SCHOLAR SAID THAT HE REMAINED ACTIVE AS HEAD OF THE CC'S ECONOMICS DEPARTMENT, WHICH WAS CONCENTRATING ON THE STRATEGIC ECONOMIC ISSUES AS DISTINCT FROM DAY-TO-DAY OPERATIONAL ISSUES. THE ACADEMIC REFERRED TO HIS EARLIER UNDERSTANDING THAT THIS NEW DEPARTMENT WOULD SUPERSEDE THE OTHER CC ECONOMIC DEPARTMENTS (REF MOSCOW 5473) AS NO LONGER CURRENT. WHILE THERE WOULD BE NO ACROSS-THE-BOARD ABOLITION OF THE OTHER ECONOMIC DEPARTMENTS OF THE CC AS HE REPORTED IN MAY, SEVERAL OF THEM MAY BE FUSED. IN ANY EVENT, THE ECONOMICS DEPARTMENT HEADED BY RYZHKOV IS CLEARLY IN CHARGE OF LONG-TERM STRATEGIC THINKING ON THE ECONOMY.

19. THE SCHOLAR HAD HEARD LAST MAY THAT A NEW STAFF WOULD BE CREATED FOR THE DEFENSE COUNCIL - IT WOULD BE PART OF AN NSC STAFF COMPOSED OF MILITARY OFFICERS IN MUFTI AND CIVILIANS. THE IDEA WOULD BE TO GIVE ANDROPOV A STRONGER STAFF. ON THIS TRIP THE ACADEMIC HAS HEARD THAT THIS STAFF EXISTS BUT IS NOT PLAYING A MAJOR ROLE - PERHAPS ANOTHER CASUALTY OF ANDROPOV'S ILLNESS. THE SCHOLAR EXPECTS ITS ROLE TO INCREASE, HOWEVER.

CONFIDENTIAL

CONFIDENTIAL

NATIONAL SECURITY COUNCIL
MESSAGE CENTER

PAGE 02 OF 02 MOSCOW 5409 DTG: 121007Z DEC 83 PSN: 074929

20. THE ACADEMIC'S INTERLOCUTORS HAVE INCLUDED POLITBURO
CANDIDATE MEMBER PONOMAREV, CC INTERNATIONAL DEPARTMENT
DEPUTY CHIEF ZAGLADIN, IMEMO DIRECTOR YAKOVLEV, IUSAC
DIRECTOR ARBATOV, IEWSS DIRECTOR BOGOMOLOV AND OTHER
OFFICIALS IN ECONOMIC ORGANS AND INSTITUTES.
HARTMAN
BT

SIXDIS

CONFIDENTIAL

Document 9: UK Ministry of Defence, "Soviet Union Concern About a Surprise Nuclear Attack," May 9, 1983

Source: British Ministry of Defence Freedom of Information Act release to the Nuclear Information Service

This MOD paper represents a culmination of high-level UK discussions about the Soviet reaction to Able Archer 83 and what to do about it. According to other documents released under UK FOIA, the Joint Intelligence Committee drafted a paper on March 23, 1984, also entitled "Soviet Union: Concern About a Surprise NATO Attack," which remains secret despite attempts by the National Security Archive to win its declassification.* The information in this March 1983 report was subsequently discussed by Prime Minister Margaret Thatcher, senior cabinet members, and intelligence heads on April 10, 1984. According to notes of the meeting, Thatcher instructed the government to "consider what could be done to remove the danger that, by mis-calculating Western intentions, the Soviet Union would over-react," she also noted the need to "urgently consider how to approach the Americans on the question of possible Soviet misapprehensions about a surprise NATO attack."

This May paper memorializes the points presented at the prime minister's meeting, including the "unprecedented" Soviet reaction to Able Archer 83. The paper concluded that improved notification of command post exercises could prevent future crises, and continued work with the Americans to avoid nuclear war with the Soviets through miscalculation—UK officials had warned U.S. officials of the Soviet reaction to Able Archer 83 in March of 1984—"should be acted upon as soon as possible."

* Despite its historical importance, Great Britain has released only the cover page of this key comprehensive report about the danger of Able Archer 83. For more information about this report and Great Britain's reasons for its continued withholding, see Nate Jones, "Why the Key Able Archer 83 Report Should Be Released Under UK FOIA," November 18, 2015, https://nsarchive.wordpress.com/2015/11/18/why-the-key-able-archer-83-report-should-be-released-under-uk-foia/ and Richard Norton-Taylor, "Security Chiefs Block Release of Report on 1983 Soviet Nuclear Scare," *The Guardian*, December 7, 2015.

184

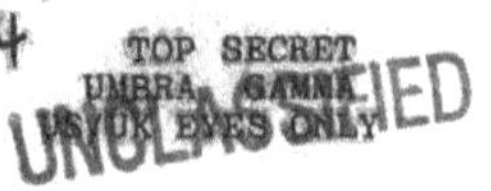

TOP SECRET
UMBRA, GAMMA
US/UK EYES ONLY

UNCLASSIFIED

Page No 1 of 6
Copy No 5 of 9

SOVIET UNION: CONCERN ABOUT A SURPRISE NATO ATTACK

I INTRODUCTION

1. This paper considers whether specific options exist for minimising the risk of Soviet misinterpretation of NATO Command Post Exercises (CPXs), particularly nuclear ones. Although it has been prepared in the context of an unprecedented Soviet reaction to Able Archer 83 and other reports of alleged concern about a surprise NATO attack (JIC(84)(N)45), the paper examines the inherent advantages and disadvantages of prior notification of nuclear CPXs as an overall Confidence Building Measure (CBM).

2.

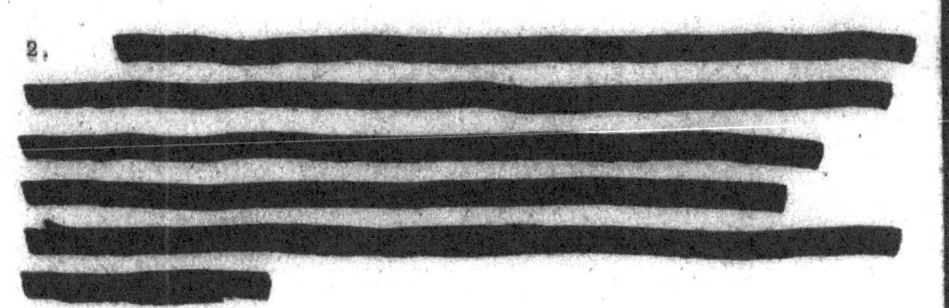

3. Although the JIC reached no firm conclusion, we cannot discount the possibility that at least some Soviet officials/officers may have misinterpreted Able Archer 83 and possibly other nuclear CPXs as posing a real threat. Quite apart from their reaction to Able Archer and

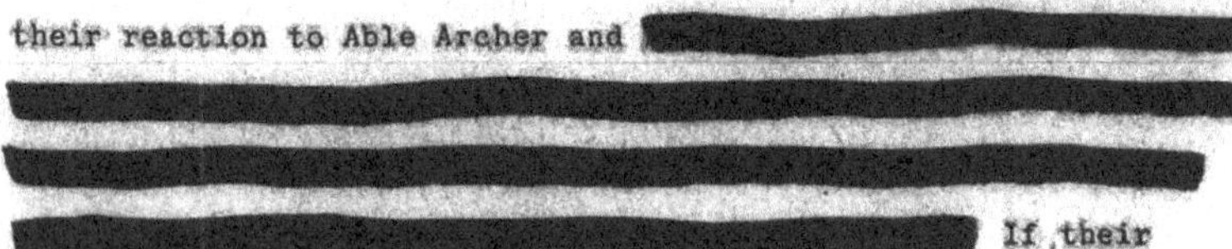

If their response involves the taking of actual precautions against what

UNCLASSIFIED

/they

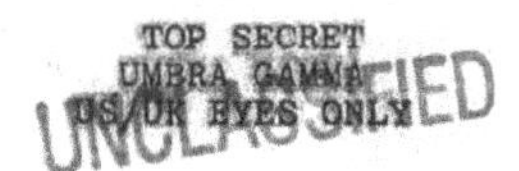

they judge to be threatening and ambiguous warning indicators, should we seek to establish a system which makes the holding of high level nuclear CPXs subject to an obligation to notify in advance? Should the practice of promoting military transparency through Confidence Building Measures be extended from field exercises and the movement of actual forces to CPXs themselves? Provided a proposal can be assembled which does not constrain nuclear CPX activity, (which is militarily vital for the training of commanders and their staffs in extremely complicated procedures), could there be advantage in exploring this with the Russians?

II SUBJECTS FOR NEGOTIATION

4. While an element of uncertainty is implicit in the concept of deterrence, it is assumed that there is mutual benefit in ensuring that each side does not misconstrue the other's CPXs as posing a real threat. Since certain notification measures relating to test ICBM launches already exist for reducing the possibility of misinterpretation (SALT II, Chapter XVI) there seems no inherent reason why similar procedures could not be devised which extended to certain nuclear CPXs as well. Prior warning of field exercises has become an accepted feature of the conventional arms control process, and as such, could be capable

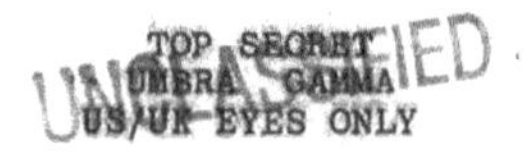

Page No 3 of 6
Copy No of

of expansion, although not perhaps within existing fora (see paragraph 7 below). It is for discussion whether notification of nuclear CPXs would have to be balanced (the reciprocal nature of conventional notification is an important factor which needs to be taken into account) or whether notification might be asymmetric or even unilateral.

5. It is also for discussion what CPXs might be notified and the extent of information which might be provided. It may for example be asked whether awareness of the existence of a nuclear CPX would of itself generate confidence. In our view simple notification could indeed be effective in reassuring the other side if it was given sufficiently far in advance to make it clear that such exercises formed a normal pattern of activity and took place in relative isolation from the changing temperature of political relationships between the major powers. It might prove possible to construct notification in such a way as to avoid giving details of particular scenarios or inhibit in any way US or NATO exercises.

6. Although the Russians appear to have reacted in an unprecedented way to the NATO exercise Able Archer 83, [redacted] This, coupled with the fact that the Soviet Union is the only nuclear power in the Warsaw Pact, indicates that super-power nuclear CPXs should form the centrepiece of any notification procedure, supplemented perhaps on the West's side with notification of NATO-wide exercises involving a substantial American nuclear role. We do not consider that every exercise

UNCLASSIFIED
TOP SECRET
UMBRA GAMMA

/involving

involving simulated nuclear release would require notification [redacted] In the immediate future it might be enough to attempt early discussions with the Russians, [redacted]

III FRAMEWORK FOR DISCUSSION

7. [redacted] There may be a requirement for speed [redacted] This effectively rules out most of the existing arms control negotiations as suitable fora since discussion of CBMs in any of these is likely to be unduly prolonged (MBFR), complicated by an involvement of extraneous participants (CDE, CSCE) or indefinitely delayed (START). A number of existing bilateral US/USSR agreements theoretically provide a framework ('hotline' agreements 1963/71, Article XVI of SALT II or Prevention of Nuclear War Agreement 1973), but none of them seem easily adaptable to current requirements.

8. An *ad hoc* forum may therefore be required. A special contact between the US and the USSR seems the most practical

/option

TOP SECRET
UMBRA GAMMA
US/UK EYES ONLY

Page No 5 of 6
Copy No of

option in terms of speed, simplicity and security. Although it was a NATO CPX about which the Soviets appear to have been concerned, prior consultation within a NATO forum, [redacted]. Although we could fully justify attempts to increase confidence about nuclear matters and anticipate considerable support for such efforts, on balance the search for CBMs is likely to be more effectively pursued [redacted] However recent experience suggests that a bilateral discussion involving possible notification of NATO and US national nuclear CPXs is unlikely to cause problems within the Alliance [redacted] strengthen the case for discussion of CBMs relating to Command Post Exercises, specifically nuclear ones, to be conducted bilaterally between the United States and the Soviet Union. [redacted]

9. The President's Commission on Strategic Forces (the Scowcroft Report, 21 March 1984) proposes a bilateral exchange

/of

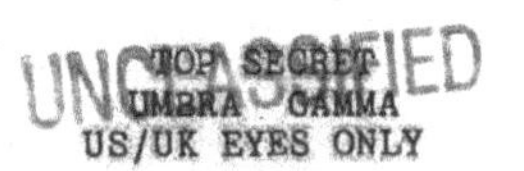

TOP SECRET
UMBRA GAMMA
US/UK EYES ONLY

TOP SECRET
UMBRA GAMMA
US/UK EYES ONLY

UNCLASSIFIED

Page No 6 of 6
Copy No of

information between US and Soviet Defence officials about steps which could be misconstrued as indications of an attack. The Report proposes that a variety of measures should be constructed to improve communication and predictability which would 'contribute to stability by improving mutual understanding and reducing surprise and misinterpretation'. It is our view that [redacted] should be acted upon as soon as possible.

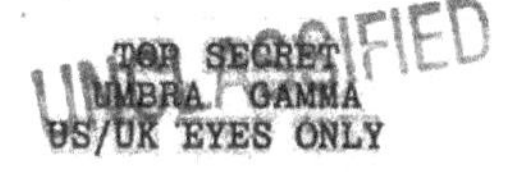

TOP SECRET
UMBRA GAMMA
US/UK EYES ONLY

UNCLASSIFIED

Document 10: Central Intelligence Agency, Special National Intelligence Estimate, "Implications of Recent Soviet Military-Political Activities," May 18, 1984, Top Secret

Source: Central Intelligence Agency Freedom of Information Act release

SNIE 11-10-84/JX, authored primarily by the CIA's national intelligence officer for the Soviet Union, Fritz Ermarth, was the first officially declassified document on Able Archer 83 and the War Scare, though some key portions remain redacted. The SNIE concludes by saying that the authors "believe strongly that Soviet actions are not inspired by, and Soviet leaders do not perceive, a genuine danger of imminent conflict or confrontation with the United States," but it acknowledges that "since November 1983 there has been a high level of Soviet military activity, with new deployments of weapons and strike forces."

The CIA's estimate reports that these deployments were at least partially in response to Able Archer 83 (it does not mention the nineteen thousand troops transported to Europe during Reforger 83 and Autumn Forge 83). The estimate stated that Able Archer 83 "was larger than previous 'Able Archer' exercises and included new command, control, and communications procedures for authorizing use of nuclear weapons." The "elaborate" Soviet reaction to this exercise included "increased intelligence collection flights, and the placing of Soviet air units in East Germany and Poland on heightened readiness in what was declared to be a threat of possible aggression against the USSR and Warsaw Pact countries." Two other Soviet reactions to Able Archer 83 remain redacted in the estimate.

The final page of the SNIE acknowledged that the CIA had "inadequate information about . . . the Soviet reading of our own military operations [and] current reconnaissance and exercises," but that notwithstanding these uncertainties the Soviets did not fear "an imminent military clash."

Director of Central Intelligence

Top Secret

Special National Intelligence Estimate

Implications of Recent Soviet Military-Political Activities

Top Secret

SNIE 11-10-84/JX

~~TCS 4347/84~~

18 May 1984

Copy 31

Warning Notice
Sensitive Intelligence Sources and Methods Involved
(WNINTEL)

NATIONAL SECURITY INFORMATION
Unauthorized Disclosure Subject to Criminal Sanctions

Top Secret

SNIE 11-10-84

IMPLICATIONS OF RECENT SOVIET MILITARY-POLITICAL ACTIVITIES

~~TCS 6347-84~~

Top Secret

THIS ESTIMATE IS ISSUED BY THE DIRECTOR OF CENTRAL INTELLIGENCE.

THE NATIONAL FOREIGN INTELLIGENCE BOARD CONCURS, EXCEPT AS NOTED IN THE TEXT.

The following intelligence organizations participated in the preparation of the Estimate:

The Central Intelligence Agency, the Defense Intelligence Agency, the National Security Agency, and the intelligence organization of the Department of State.

Also Participating:

The Assistant Chief of Staff for Intelligence, Department of the Army

The Director of Naval Intelligence, Department of the Navy

The Assistant Chief of Staff, Intelligence, Department of the Air Force

The Director of Intelligence, Headquarters, Marine Corps

KEY JUDGMENTS

During the past several months, a number of coincident Soviet activities have created concern that they reflect abnormal Soviet fear of conflict with the United States, belligerent intent that might risk conflict, or some other underlying Soviet purpose. These activities have included large-scale military exercises (among them a major naval exercise in the Norwegian Sea, unprecedented SS-20 launch activity, and large-scale SSBN dispersal); preparations for air operations against Afghanistan; attempts to change the air corridor regime in Berlin; new military measures termed responsive to NATO INF deployments; and shrill propaganda attributing a heightened danger of war to US behavior.

Examining these developments in terms of several hypotheses, we reach the following conclusions:

— We believe strongly that Soviet actions are not inspired by, and Soviet leaders do not perceive, a genuine danger of imminent conflict or confrontation with the United States. This judgment is based on the absence of forcewide combat readiness or other war preparation moves in the USSR, and the absence of a tone of fear or belligerence in Soviet diplomatic communications, although the latter remain uncompromising on many issues. There have also been instances where the Soviets appear to have avoided belligerent propaganda or actions. Recent Soviet "war scare" propaganda, of declining intensity over the period examined, is aimed primarily at discrediting US policies and mobilizing "peace" pressures among various audiences abroad. This war scare propaganda has reverberated in Soviet security bureaucracies and emanated through other channels such as human sources. We do not believe it reflects authentic leadership fears of imminent conflict.

— We do not believe that Soviet war talk and other actions "mask" Soviet preparations for an imminent move toward confrontation on the part of the USSR, although they have an incentive to take initiatives that discredit US policies even at some risk. Were the Soviets preparing an initiative they believed carried a real risk of military confrontation with the United States, we would see preparatory signs which the Soviets could not mask.

— The Soviet actions examined are influenced to some extent by Soviet perceptions of a mounting challenge from US foreign and defense policy. However, these activities do not all fit into an integrated pattern of current Soviet foreign policy tactics.

— Each Soviet action has its own military or political purpose sufficient to explain it. Soviet military exercises are designed to meet long-term requirements for force development and training which have become ever more complex with the growth of Soviet military capabilities.

— In specific cases, Soviet military exercises are probably intended to have the ancillary effect of signaling Soviet power and resolve to some audience. For instance, maneuvers in the Tonkin Gulf were aimed at backing Vietnam against China; Soviet airpower use in Afghanistan could have been partly aimed at intimidating Pakistan; and Soviet action on Berlin has the effect of reminding the West of its vulnerable access, but very low-key Soviet handling has muted this effect.

Taken in their totality, Soviet talk about the increased likelihood of nuclear war and Soviet military actions do suggest a political intention of speaking with a louder voice and showing firmness through a controlled display of military muscle. The apprehensive outlook we believe the Soviet leadership has toward the longer term US arms buildup could in the future increase its willingness to consider actions—even at some heightened risk—that recapture the initiative and neutralize the challenge posed by the United States.

These judgments are tempered by some uncertainty as to current Soviet leadership perceptions of the United States, by continued uncertainty about Politburo decisionmaking processes, and by our inability at this point to conduct a detailed examination of how the Soviets might have assessed recent US/NATO military exercises and reconnaissance operations. Notwithstanding these uncertainties, however, we are confident that, as of now, the Soviets see not an imminent military clash but a costly and—to some extent—more perilous strategic and political struggle over the rest of the decade.

DISCUSSION

Introduction

1. There has been much Soviet talk about the increased danger of nuclear war. This theme has appeared in public pronouncements by Soviet political and military leaders, in statements by high officials targeted at both domestic and foreign audiences, in internal communications, and in other channels. Soviet authorities have declared that Washington is preparing for war, and have issued dire warnings that the USSR will not give in to nuclear blackmail or other military pressure. The articulation of this theme has paralleled the Soviet campaign to derail US INF deployment. It continues to this day, although at a somewhat lower intensity in recent months than in late 1983.

2. Since November 1983 there has been a high level of Soviet military activity, with new deployments of weapons and strike forces, large-scale military exercises, and several other noteworthy events:

— *INF response:* Start of construction of additional SS-20 bases following Andropov's announcement on 24 November 1983 of termination of the 20-month moratorium on SS-20 deployments opposite NATO; initiation in late December of patrols by E-II nuclear-powered cruise missile submarines off the US coast; first-ever forward deployment in mid-January 1984 of long-range missile-carrying D-class SSBNs; and the start of deployment also in mid-January of 925-km range SS-12/22 missiles in East Germany and Czechoslovakia, and continued propaganda and active measures against INF deployment.

— *Response to NATO exercise:* Assumption by Soviet air units in Germany and Poland from November 1983 of high alert status with readying of nuclear strike forces as NATO conducted "Able Archer-83," a nuclear release command post exercise.

— *Soviet exercises:* Large-scale exercise activity during spring 1984 which has stressed integrated strategic strike operations, featuring the multiple launches of SS-20s and SLBMs; survivability training including the dispersal of operational Northern Fleet SSBNs supported by a large number of ships; and the use of survivable command, control, and communications platforms, possibly in a transattack scenario

— *Berlin air corridors:* Periodic Soviet imposition beginning 20 February 1984 of minimum flight altitudes for the entire length of one or more of the Berlin air corridors—a unilateral change in the rules governing air access to Berlin.

— *Afghanistan:* Deployment in mid-April of several airborne units to Afghanistan, launching of a major spring offensive into the Panjsher Valley, and initiation on 21 April for the first time of high-intensity bombing of Afghanistan by over 105 TU-16 and SU-24 bombers based in the USSR.

— *East Asia:* Deployment in mid-November 1983 of naval TU-16 strike aircraft to Vietnam for the first time; positioning of both Soviet operational aircraft carriers for the first time simultaneously in Asian waters in March 1984; and the first joint Soviet/Vietnamese amphibious assault exercises on the coast of Vietnam in April.

— *Caribbean:* A small combined Soviet/Cuban naval exercise in the Gulf of Mexico, with the first-ever visit of a Soviet helicopter carrier in April/May, and Soviet/Cuban antisubmarine drills.

— *Troop rotation:* Initiation of the airlift portion of Soviet troop rotation in Eastern Europe 10 days later in April than this has occurred for the past five years.

This Estimate explores whether the Soviet talk about the increasing likelihood of nuclear war and the Soviet military activities listed above constitute a pattern of behavior intended either to alarm or intimidate the United States and its allies or to achieve other goals.

Possible Explanations

3. Specifically, in examining the facts we address five explanatory hypotheses:

a. Both the Soviet talk about war and the military activities have been consciously orchestrated across the board to achieve political effects through posturing and propaganda. The object has been to discredit US defense and foreign policies; to put Washington on notice that the USSR will pursue a hard—perhaps even dangerous—line, unless US concessions are forthcoming; to maintain an atmosphere of tension conducive to pressure by "peace" groups on Western governments; and, if possible, to undercut President Reagan's reelection prospects.

b. Soviet behavior is a response to Washington's rhetoric, US military procurement and R&D goals, and US military exercises and reconnaissance activities near Soviet territory—which have excited Soviet concerns and caused Moscow to flex its own military responsiveness, signaling to Washington that it is prepared for any eventuality.

c. Moscow itself is preparing for threatening military action in the future requiring a degree of surprise. The real aim behind its recent actions is not to alarm, but to desensitize the United States to higher levels of Soviet military activity—thus masking intended future moves and reducing US warning time.

d. A weak General Secretary and political jockeying in the Soviet leadership have lessened policy control at the top and permitted a hardline faction, under abnormally high military influence, to pursue its own agenda, which—intentionally or not—looks more confrontational to the observer.

e. The Soviet military actions at issue are not linked with the talk about war and are basically unrelated events, each with its own rationale.

Soviet Talk About Nuclear War

4. Our assessment of the meaning of alarmist statements and propaganda about the danger of nuclear war provides a starting point for evaluating recent Soviet military activities.

5. Soviet talk about the war danger is unquestionably highly orchestrated. It has obvious external aims:

— To create a tense international climate that fosters "peace" activism in the West and public pressure on Western governments to backtrack on INF deployment, reduce commitments to NATO, and distance themselves from US foreign policy objectives.

— To elicit concessions in arms control negotiations by manipulating the anxieties of Western political leaders about Soviet thinking.

— To strengthen cohesion within the Warsaw Pact and reinforce Soviet pressure for higher military outlays by non-Soviet member states.

The overall propaganda campaign against the United States has recently been supplemented with the boycott of the Olympic Games.

6. The talk about the danger of nuclear war also has a clear domestic propaganda function: to rationalize demands on the Soviet labor force, continued consumer deprivation, and ideological vigilance in the society. This message is also being disseminated within the Soviet and East European bureaucracies,

7. The central question remains: what are the real perceptions at top decisionmaking levels of the regime? Our information about such leadership perceptions is largely inferential. Nevertheless, we have confidence in several broad conclusions.

8. First, we believe that there *is* a serious concern with US defense and foreign policy trends. There is a large measure of agreement among both political and military leaders that the United States has undertaken a global offensive against Soviet interests. Central to this perception is the overall scope and momentum of the US military buildup. Fundamentally, the Soviets are concerned that US programs will undercut overall Soviet military strategy and force posture. Seen in this context, Moscow condemns INF deployment as a telling—but subordinate—element in a more far-reaching and comprehensive US effort aimed at "regaining military superiority." *The threat here is not immediate, but longer term.* However, the ability of the United States to carry out its longer term plans is questioned by Soviet leaders not only to reassure domestic audiences but also because they genuinely see some uncertainty in the ability of the United States to sustain its military effort.

9. Secondly, in our judgment *the nature of the concern is as much political as it is military.* There is a healthy respect for US technological prowess and anxiety that this could in due course be used against the USSR. The Soviets are thus concerned that the United States might pursue an arms competition that could over time strain the Soviet economy and disrupt the regime's ability to manage competing military and

civilian requirements. More immediately, the Soviets are concerned that the United States could achieve a shift in the overall balance of military power which, through more interventionist foreign policies, could effectively thwart the extension of Soviet influence in world affairs and even roll back past Soviet gains. From this perspective, the United States' actions in Central America, Lebanon, Grenada, and southern Africa are seen as a token of what could be expected on a broader scale in the future.

10. Third, and most important for this assessment, we do not believe the Soviet leadership sees an imminent threat of war with the United States. It is conceivable that the stridency of Soviet "war scare" propaganda reflects a genuine Soviet worry about a near-future attack on them. This concern could be inspired by Soviet views about the depth of anti-Soviet intentions in Washington combined with elements of their own military doctrine projected onto the United States, such as the virtues of surprise, striking first, and masking hostile initiatives in exercises. Some political and military leaders have stressed the danger of war more forcefully than others, suggesting that there may have been differences on this score—or at least how to talk about the issue—over the past half year.

11. However, on the basis of what we believe to be very strong evidence, we judge that the Soviet leadership does not perceive an imminent danger of war. Our reasons are the following:

— The Soviets have not initiated the military readiness moves they would have made if they believed a US attack were imminent.

— In private US diplomatic exchanges with Moscow over the past six months the Soviets have neither made any direct threats connected with regional or other issues nor betrayed any fear of a US attack.

— Obligatory public assertions of the viability of the Soviet nuclear deterrent have been paralleled by private assertions within regime circles by Soviet experts that there is currently a stable nuclear balance in which the United States does not have sufficient strength for a first strike.

— In recent months top leaders, including the Minister of Defense and Politburo member Dmitriy Ustinov, have somewhat downplayed the nuclear war danger, noting that it should not be "overdramatized" (although Ustinov's recent Victory Day speech returned to a somewhat shriller tone). At the same time, high foreign affairs officials have challenged the thesis that the United States can unleash nuclear war and have emphasized constraints on such a course of action.

Moreover, the Soviets know that the United States is at present far from having accomplished all of its force buildup objectives.

Recent Soviet Military Activities

12. ***Intimidation?*** It is possible that some of the Soviet military activities listed above were intended, as ancillary to their military objectives, to intimidate selected audiences:

— The East Asian naval maneuvers, deployment of strike aircraft to Vietnam, and amphibious exercises have displayed military muscle to China.

— The bombing campaign in Afghanistan could be seen not only as an operation against the insurgency but also as an implicit threat to neighboring countries—Pakistan and perhaps Iran.

— In mounting large-scale and visible exercises (such as the March-April Northern and Baltic Fleet exercise in the Norwegian Sea) Moscow would understand that they could be perceived as threatening by NATO audiences.

13. Soviet INF-related military activities have also been designed to convey an impression to the West that the world *is* a more dangerous place following US INF deployment and that the USSR is making good on its predeployment threats to counter with deployments of its own.

14. There is uncertainty within the Intelligence Community on the origins of Soviet behavior with respect to the Berlin air corridors. It is possible that Soviet action was a deliberate reminder of Western vulnerability. Alternatively, airspace requirements for exercises may have motivated this move. The low-key manner in which the Soviets have handled the issue does not suggest that they have been interested in squeezing access to Berlin for intimidation purposes. Nevertheless, the Soviets have been in the process of unilaterally changing the corridor flight rules and thereby reminding the West of their ultimate power to control access to Berlin. After a short hiatus in late April and early May, the Soviets declared new air corridor restrictions, indicating that this effort contin-

ues. In a possibly related, very recent development, the Soviets declared tight new restrictions on travel in East Germany by allied missions located in Potsdam. (s)

15. In a number of instances we have observed the Soviets avoiding threatening behavior or propaganda when they might have acted otherwise, perhaps in some cases to avoid embarrassment or overcommitment. For example, they:

— Never publicly acknowledged the incident in November 1983 in which a Soviet attack submarine was disabled off the US coast as it attempted to evade a US ASW ship, and moved the sub quickly out of Cuba where it had come for emergency repairs.

— Warned Soviet ships in late January to stay away from US ships in the eastern Mediterranean.

— Took no tangible action in March when one of their merchant tankers hit a mine off Nicaragua.

— Notified Washington of multiple missile launches in early April as a gesture of "good will."

16. ***Reaction to US actions?*** The new Soviet deployments of nuclear-armed submarines off US coasts and the forward deployment of SS-12/22 missiles in Eastern Europe are a Soviet reaction to NATO INF deployment, which the Soviets claim is very threatening to them—although the threat perceived here by Moscow is certainly not one of imminent nuclear attack.

17. Soviet military exercises themselves sometimes embody a "reactive" element. They frequently incorporate Western operational concepts and weapon systems into exercise scenarios, including projected US/NATO weapons and systems well before these systems are actually deployed. On occasion there is real- or near-real-time counterexercising, in which US/NATO exercise activity is incorporated into "Red" scenarios, thereby sensitizing Soviet forces to the US/NATO opponent. A key issue is whether this counterexercising takes on the character of actual preparation for response to a perceived threat of possible US attack.

18. A case in point is the Soviet reaction to "Able Archer-83." This was a NATO command post exercise held in November 1983 that was larger than previous "Able Archer" exercises and included new command, control, and communications procedures for authorizing use of nuclear weapons. The elaborate Soviet reaction to this recent exercise included

increased intelligence collection flights, and the placing of Soviet air units in East Germany and Poland in heightened readiness in what was declared to be a threat of possible aggression against the USSR and Warsaw Pact countries. Alert measures included increasing the number of fighter-interceptors on strip alert,

Although the Soviet reaction was somewhat greater than usual, by confining heightened readiness to selected air units Moscow clearly revealed that it did not in fact think there was a possibility at this time of a NATO attack.

19. How the Soviets choose to respond to ongoing US military activities, such as exercises and reconnaissance operations, depends on how they assess their scope, the trends they may display, and above all the hostile intent that might be read into them. We are at present uncertain as to what novelty or possible military objectives the Soviets may have read into recent US and NATO exercises and reconnaissance operations because a detailed comparison of simultaneous "Red" and "Blue" actions has not been accomplished. The Soviets have, as in the past, ascribed the same threatening character to these activities as to US military buildup plans, that is, calling them preparations for war. But they have not charged a US intent to prepare for imminent war.

20. ***Preparation for surprise military action?*** There is one case in our set of military activities that might conceivably be ascribed to the "masking" of threatening Soviet initiatives. For the first time in five years, the airlift portion of the troop rotation in Eastern Europe began on 25 April rather than 15 April. This may have reflected a change in training and manning practices or the introduction of new airlift procedures. The change of timing of the airlift portion of the annual troop rotation could also be a step toward blurring a warning indicator—a comprehensive delay of annual Soviet troop rotations which would prevent degradation of the forces by withdrawing trained men. But the rail portion of the rotation began ahead of schedule and, in any event, the pattern of rotation was within broad historical norms.

21. In early April, when the Soviets began to assemble a bomber strike force in the Turkestan Military

District, there was some concern that it might represent masking of preparations for operations against Pakistan, or even Iran, rather than against the most obvious target, Afghanistan. At this point the force is clearly occupied against Afghanistan. It was never suitably deployed for use against Iran. We believe that, although the force could be used against Pakistan, a major air offensive against Pakistan without forewarning or precursor political pressure would serve no Soviet purpose and is extremely unlikely.

22. Soviet military exercises display and contribute to steadily growing Soviet force capabilities. These exercises have become increasingly complex as Moscow has deployed more capable and sophisticated weapons and command and control systems. The exercises have stressed the ability to assume a wartime posture rapidly and respond flexibly to a variety of contingencies. We know that this activity

is planned and scheduled months or years in advance. Typically, these plans have not been significantly affected by concurrent US or NATO exercise activity. We see no evidence that this program is now being driven by some sort of target date or deadline. Rather, it appears to respond—in annual and five-year plan increments—to new problems and operational considerations that constantly arise with ongoing force modernization. Thus, we interpret the accelerated tempo of Soviet live exercise activity as a reflection of the learning curve inherent in the exercise process itself and of long-term Soviet military objectives, rather than of preparations for, or masking of, surprise Soviet military actions.

23. ***Policy impact of leadership weakness or factionalism?*** The Soviet Union has had three General Secretaries in as many years and, given the age and frail health of Chernenko, yet another change can be expected in a few years. This uncertain political environment could be conducive to increased maneuvering within the leadership and magnification of policy disagreements. Some have argued that either the Soviet military or a hardline foreign policy faction led by Gromyko and Ustinov exerts more influence than it could were Chernenko a stronger figure. Although individual Soviet military leaders enjoy great authority in the regime and military priorities remain high for the whole leadership, we do not believe that the Soviet military, as an institution, is exerting unusually heavy influence on Soviet policy. Nor do we believe that any faction is exerting influence other than through Politburo consensus. Consequently we reject the hypothesis that weak central leadership accounts for the Soviet actions examined here.

24. ***A comprehensive pattern?*** In our view, the military activities under examination here do tend to have their own military rationales and the exercises are integrated by long-term Soviet force development plans. However, these activities do not all fit into an integrated pattern of current Soviet foreign policy tactics. The different leadtimes involved in initiating various activities argue against orchestration for a political purpose. A number of the activities represent routine training or simply refine previous exercises. In other cases, the activities respond to circumstances that could not have been predicted ahead of time.

Conclusions

25. Taken in their totality, Soviet talk about the increased likelihood of nuclear war and Soviet military actions do suggest a political intention of speaking with a louder voice and showing firmness through a controlled display of military muscle. At the same time, Moscow has given little sign of desiring to escalate tensions sharply or to provoke possible armed confrontation with the United States.

26. Soviet talk of nuclear war has been deliberately manipulated to rationalize military efforts with domestic audiences and to influence Western electorates and political elites. Some Soviet military activities have also been designed to have an alarming or intimidating effect on various audiences (notably INF "counterdeployments," the naval exercise in the Norwegian Sea, and naval and air activities in Asia).

27. Our assessment of both Soviet talk about nuclear war and Soviet military activities indicates a very low probability that the top Soviet leadership is seriously worried about the imminent outbreak of nuclear war, although it is quite possible that official propaganda and vigilance campaigning have generated an atmosphere of anxiety throughout the military and security apparatus. The available evidence suggests that none of the military activities discussed in this Estimate have been generated by a real fear of imminent US attack.

28. Although recent Soviet military exercises combine with other ongoing Soviet programs to heighten overall military capabilities, we believe it unlikely that they are intended to mask current or near-future preparations by the USSR for some directly hostile military initiative. Moreover, we are confident that the activities we have examined in this Estimate would

not successfully mask all the extensive logistic and other military preparations the Soviets would have to commence well before a realistic offensive initiative against any major regional security target.

29. Both the talk of nuclear war and the military activities address the concerns of a longer time horizon. Moscow's inability to elicit major concessions in the arms talks, successful US INF deployment, and—most important by far—the long-term prospect of a buildup of US strategic and conventional military forces, have created serious concern in the Kremlin. We judge that the Soviet leadership does indeed believe that the United States is attempting to restore a military posture that severely undercuts the Soviet power position in the world.

30. The apprehensive outlook we believe the Soviet leadership has toward the longer term Western arms buildup could in the future increase its willingness to consider actions—even at some heightened risk—that recapture the initiative and neutralize the military challenge posed by the United States. Warning of such actions could be ambiguous.

31. Our judgments in this Estimate are subject to three main sources of uncertainty. We have inadequate information about:

a. The current mind-set of the Soviet political leadership, which has seen some of its optimistic international expectations from the Brezhnev era disappointed.

b. The ways in which military operations and foreign policy tactics may be influenced by political differences and the policy process in the Kremlin.

c. The Soviet reading of our own military operations, that is, current reconnaissance and exercises.

Notwithstanding these uncertainties, however, we are confident that, as of now, the Soviets see not an imminent military clash but a costly and—to some extent—more perilous strategic and political struggle over the rest of the decade.

Document 11: Central Intelligence Agency Memorandum for the President, Vice President, Secretary of State, Secretary of Defense, Assistant to the President for National Security Affairs, and Chairman of the Joint Chiefs of Staff, from CIA Director William Casey, "U.S./Soviet Tension," June 19, 1984, Secret

Source: Central Intelligence Agency Mandatory Declassification Review release

Six months after Able Archer 83, the director of the CIA wrote to the highest levels of government, including the president, warning of "a rather stunning array of indicators [primarily drawn from SNIE 11-10-1984] of an increasing aggressiveness in Soviet policy and activities." These indicators included large increases in troop numbers, ramped up production of materiel, and the fact that "for the first time during peace time" the Soviets may have kept nuclear forces in East Germany and Czechoslovakia on "quick-alert status."

Casey concluded: "The behavior of the armed forces is perhaps the most disturbing. From the operational deployment of submarines to the termination of harvest support to the delayed troop rotation there is a central theme of not being strategically vulnerable, even if it means taking some risks. It is important to distinguish in this category those acts which are political blustering and those which may be, but also carry large costs. The point of blustering is to do something that makes the opponent pay high costs while the blusterer pays none or little. The military behaviors we have observed involve high military costs . . . adding thereby a dimension of genuineness to the Soviet expressions of concern that is often not reflected in intelligence issuances."

SECRET

The Director of Central Intelligence

Washington, D.C. 20505

ER 84-2648

CR - NIC U3508-84

memo chrono

EO 13526 3.3(b)(1)>25Yrs

19 June 1984

MEMORANDUM FOR: The President
The Vice President
Secretary of State
Secretary of Defense
Assistant to the President for
National Security Affairs
Chairman, Joint Chiefs of Staff

SUBJECT: US/Soviet Tension

1. I attach here a rather stunning array of indicators of an increasing aggressiveness in Soviet policy and activities. These include developments in the media, civil defense sector, security operations, political harassment, logistical steps, the economy, intelligence preparations and political activity.

2. The depth and breadth of these activities demand increased and continual review to assess whether they are in preparation for a crisis or merely to embarrass or politically influence events in the United States.

3. In the light of the increasing number and accelerating tempo of developments of this type, we will shortly begin to produce a biweekly strategic warning report which will monitor and assess the implications of these incidents which we report on as they occur, but have not, thus far, pulled together in any systematic way.

/S/

William J. Casey

Distribution by ER/19 Jun 84 w/Atch

EO 13526 3.5(c)

Orig - Each Addressee
1 - DCI
1 - DDCI
1 - EXDIR
1 - C/NIC
1 - VC/NIC
1 - NIO/Warning
1 - ER File

SECRET

DCI EXEC REG

U.S./Soviet Tension

The recent SNIE-11-10-84 JX examined a range of Soviet political and military activities that are influenced by Soviet perceptions or a mounting challenge from U.S. foreign and defense policy. Each Soviet action could be sufficiently explained by its own military or political purpose consistent with developing military readiness or a "get-tough" policy to counter the current U.S. stance.

This summary will consider some longer term events that may cause some reflections about the kinds of actions the Soviets could orchestrate that would create a political embarrassment for the U.S. in the wake of deployment of INF in Europe. We believe the Soviets have concluded that the danger of war is greater than it was before the INF decision, that Soviet vulnerability is greater and will grow with additional INF emplacements and that the reduced warning time inherent in Pershing II has lowered Soviet confidence in their ability to warn of sudden attack. These perceptions, perhaps driven by a building U.S. defense budget, new initiatives in continental defense, improvements in force readiness, and a potentially massive space defense program may be propelling the USSR to take national readiness measures at a deliberate pace. There is a certain consistency and coherence in the symptoms of measures being taken that suggests central decisionmaking. Some of "civilian to wartime-type" of activity suggest a broad-based plan. These activities may all be prudent precautions in a period of anxiety and uncertainty on the part of the Soviets. Some of the measures we perceive follow.

A. Media

Soviet media have portrayed the environment as dangerous to the domestic populace. The risks involved have been recognized in that in December 1983, the Soviets carefully modulated the tone to allay what appeared to be brewing hysteria. A message has been that the present state of U.S.-Soviet relations is comparable to those between Nazi Germany and the USSR prior to WWII and that the Soviets will not be surprised again.

B. Civil Defense

It is difficult to document an increase in attention to this area, but the civil defense exercise at Omsk in March in which 800 persons walked 50 km was without precedent in our knowledge. Civil defense remains an area of perennially high interest in the Soviet domestic media.

C. Security Procedures

--Leningrad has become a closed city to Western attaches. U.S., UK, French and Canadian attaches in Moscow have been denied travel to Leningrad on numerous occasions in 1984. The Soviets prevented attache travel by international visas from Helsinki to Leningrad to Helsinki in May 1984. Their willingness to ignore the international portion of that trip to prevent attache travel indicates high-interest activity in the Leningrad area and/or a critical time-frame.

--In May 1984, valid visas for 58 Americans planning tour travel of USSR were cancelled. Apparently, the decision was made by the Soviet Ministry of Foreign Affairs in Moscow. The trip included a flight from Naples to Leningrad and it appears that those with defense security clearances were denied visas.

--According to the DAO Moscow, there has been an important change in the "political atmospherics" surrounding attache operations. [ ] in particular, has become intense. The publication of an article in Red Star, 25 May 1984, against U.S. Naval Attaches suggests the Soviet campaign will be generalized and expanded. 3.3(b)(1)

-[ ] a Hungarian Ambassador at a non-European Embassy has forbidden all of his staff to have contact with Western officials. 3.3(b)(1)

--The Czechoslovak Ministry of Foreign Affairs reportedly issued a directive in late 1983 that officials abroad should terminate contact with U.S. British and West German officials.

--The changes in Permanent Restricted Areas (PRA) in East Germany impose significant restraints on operations of the Allied MLM. Most of the training areas, major unit facilities (air and ground) and their observation vantage points are now in the PRA. The new boundaries effectively restrict the missions to autobahns when traveling any distance in East Germany. [ ] [ ] restrictions severely hamper the right to free and unimpeded transit guaranteed under the Huebner-Malinin agreements and similar agreements. 3.3(b)(1) 3.3(b)(1)

--In June 1984, for the first time since 1972 a portion of the City of Potsdam was included in a TRA.

SECRET

3.5(c)

--The Soviets continue to declare multiple TRA's in addition to the PRAs.

--There have also been other travel restrictions. In Poland, there has been a perceptible increase in surveillance of attaches in the southwest corner of the country (Wroclaw, Zegnia, Swietoszow, Zagan), but not elsewhere. There has also been an increase in instances of surveillance since late 1983.

--Three recent incidents occurred in Poland where army and security personnel detained NATO attaches and then forced them to drive through a military restricted area for posed photography. In each case, the attaches were detained on public roads in an apparently well-planned effort at intimidation.

--In the Soviet Union, Pravda articles in June called for greater vigilance of Westerners and Soviet dissenters. Other reporting indicates that harrassment of Western reporters has increased. Soviet border guards are conducting more intensive searches of Western visitors.

[redacted] there has been a steady increase in civilian companies apparently enforcing discipline and improving "piece rates." The greater presence of guards and security people at defense-related production plants is also reported.

3.3(b)(1)

D. Political Harrassment

--On 20 February 1984, the Soviets imposed new restrictions on Allied flights in the three corridors linking Berling to West Germany. Basically, altitude restrictions apply to the entire length of the corridors, rather than the central portions as had been the practice. New traffic-identification demands have also been made and met by the Allies.

--On 22 March 1984, an East German military vehicle rammed a French MLM vehicle killing the driver and injuring two others.

--On 18 April 1984, the Soviets briefly detained an eight-vehicle French Army convoy at an Autobahn Checkpoint.

--On 2 May 1984, a U.S. military train bound for Berlin was delayed by East German railroad officials.

--On 16 May, East Germans refused to pull a French military train to Berlin until the French protested to the Soviet Embassy.

SECRET

3.5(c)

SECRET

3.5(c)

-- East Germany party official, the Soviet leadership wants to remind the West of the fragility of free air access to Berlin. East Germans look to take advantage of the Soviet behavior.

3.3(b)(1)

--On 8 June, the U.S. Consul General in Leningrad was called to a Soviet review of the assault on Ronald Harms on 17 April accusing the press coverage of being an exaggerated claim in a U.S. Government anti-Soviet campaign.

E. Logistics

The 1983 study of Soviet railroads concluded that the industry must improve its performance. The need for attention to the railroads is beyond question, but the new campaign which features early completion of the BALCOM line adds a sense of urgency to transportation improvements.

F. The Economy

--There has been a significant reduction in production of commercial aircraft in favor of military transport production since about June 1982. DIA studies show commercial aircraft production down 14 percent in 1983. Not only are traditional Soviet aircraft customers not adding new aircraft of Soviet make to their fleets, but the Soviets are buying back civil aircraft from Eastern European airlines. The increased allocation of resources for military aircraft production is supported by DIA production data.

--Other changes under way in selected segments of the economy point toward shifts to military needs. The termination of military support to the harvest, by directive of March 1984, may say that the success of the harvest is less important than the maintenance of military capabilities at high readiness. Such a decision is consistent with a leadership perception that danger is present, but inconsistent with the alleged priority of the food program and stated Soviet concerns about internal security problems owing to shortages and consumer dissatisfaction.

--In December 1983, production of tank chassis at the Chelyabinsk tractor plant for the first time since World War II. A second plant has also converted from tractors to tanks. Since July 1983, the first new nuclear weapons storage facility in a decade is under construction at Komsomolsk. Throughout the USSR, floorspace for ammunition

3.3(b)(1)

4

SECRET

3.5(c)

and explosives plants has been expanding since about 1980 after a decline of several years' duration. In April, the East German ammunition plant at Luebben increased to full three-shift 24-hour production and has more than doubled its output. These developments cross several sectors of national economic life and indicate that decisions are being made consistently across economic sectors.

--The increases in production are complemented by developments in the factors of production, especially labor and management. These have been subjected to one of the most strenuous and long-lasting campaigns to improve performance and expand output ever undertaken by Soviet authorities.

--At the same time, there has been a cutback in Soviet support for the East European economies, Soviet demands for better quality products from them, and higher prices for Soviet exports. These trends became evident in the fall of 1980 during the Polish crisis and have persisted. Although there are many sound reasons for the trends, they complement those already mentioned.

--Rationing of key products may be affecting commercial interests. State-owned trucking companies in Czechoslovakia are reported operating far below capacity due to insufficient fuel rations allotted as of 1 January 1984.

--In Poland, Jaruzelski apparently has formally agreed with the USSR to give up civilian production capacity to supply the Soviets with more military hardware.

--In a Magdeburg, East Germany metal processing cooperative, there are resource allocation shortages and increased target plans for 1984. While the imbalance could be blamed on poor management, the situation was exacerbated by a new bank law that prevents using state financial reserves since 1 January 1984.

G. Military Activity

--In June, DAO Moscow reported that rail movement in support of Soviet troop rotation, although with a slightly reduced volume, was continuing. (This extension also occurred during the last two rotation periods.) Extending the rotation seems to conflict with other Soviet efforts to minimize the impact of rotation, and the flow of personnel over three months would seem to disrupt programmed training.

SECRET 3.5(c)

--Other irregularities have occurred in the troop rotation. Past railroad rotation activity was marked by a regularity of arrival and departure times. This rotation has been scheduled inconsistently. Additionally, there have been a number of anomalies. Railroad cars have arrived at Weimar, East Germany with approximately 75 troops but departed with only 35. 3.3(b)(1)

--The Soviets may, for the first time during peacetime, be keeping a portion of their nuclear forces in Eastern Europe on quick-alert status, using sites for their SS-22 brigades in East Germany and Czechoslovakia.

--On 23, 24, 25 and 26 March 1984, approximately 3,650 Soviet troops arrived in Hungary.

--In June 1984, 3.3(b)(1) that during the past 6-12 months additional 3.3(b)(1) SPETNAZ troops have arrived in Hungary. 3.3(b)(1) an increase of SPETNAZ forces in Hungary and Czechoslovakia 3.3(b)(1) as well as an ongoing "aggressive indoctrination" of Warsaw Pact forces.

-- 3.3(b)(1) he is concerned about stockpiling of material and an increase in Soviet troop strength in Hungary.

--In Hungary, a recall of an undetermined number of reservists was under way in May 1984.

--In the fall of 1983, the length of service for Czechoslovakian Army draftees with missile/rocket specialities was reportedly extended from two to three years. The length of service for air defense draftees with missile training was similarly extended.

--In Poland, the length of required military service for new reserve officers was to be increased from 12 to 18 months effective in 1984.

-- , a mobilization exercise 3.3(b)(1) involving armed forces and territorial forces as well as civil defense elements is to occur in June in Czechoslovakia.

SECRET 3.5(c

-[redacted] since 1983, men up to 35 years old have been drafted without consideration of family difficulties or their profession. 3.3(b)(1)

--The Soviets have pressed for stationing additional troops in Poland. [redacted] additional Soviet air elements are already sanctioned by the Poles. 3.3(b)(1)

H. Intelligence Activity

A spate of clandestine source reports have related the extraordinary intelligence directives that have been issued. The thrust of these directives is to increase the authority of the intelligence agencies at the expense of career diplomats and to focus intelligence collection on survivability of networks and on warning. [redacted] 3.3(b)(1)

I. Political Activity

--In external relations, Soviet activity has been intense. A series of relatively low-level harrassments concerning Berlin air corridors and ground access to Berlin fall into this category and have the potential to become more escalatory. The Soviets have recently cancelled a long-standing commercial accord with the U.S. The level of official harrassment of Western attaches is high throughout the Warsaw Pact, even including a shooting incident in Bulgaria. New travel restrictions have been placed on Western diplomats in the USSR.

--A message of dissatisfaction in U.S.-Soviet relations is clear, but more than the message the Soviets may actually be paying costs--surrendering commercial contacts and their own freedom of access. Activity resembles a calculated and careful withdrawal on multiple fronts; a limitation of exposure and vulnerability.

J. Military Behavior

The behavior of the armed forces is perhaps the most disturbing. From the operational deployment of submarines to the termination of harvest support to the delayed troop rotation there is a central theme of not being strategically vulnerable, even if it means taking some risks. It is important to distinguish in this category those acts which are political blustering and those which may be, but also carry large costs. The point of blustering is to do something that makes the opponent pay

SECRET
3.5(c)

high costs while the blusterer pays none or little. The military behaviors we have observed involve high military costs in terms of vulnerability of resources for the sake of improved national military power, or enhanced readiness at the price of consumer discontent, or enhanced readiness at the price of troop dissatisfaction. None of these are trivial costs, adding thereby a dimension of genuineness to the Soviet expressions of concern that is often not reflected in intelligence issuances.

SECRET
3.5(

Document 12: Small Group Meeting of November 19, 1983, 7:30 a.m., The Secretary's Dining Room, Department of State, Secret/Sensitive

Source: Ronald Reagan Presidential Library, Matlock Files, Saturday Group–Notes (Nov–Dec 1983) Box 34, OA 92219

Seven days after the conclusion of Able Archer 83, President Reagan wrote in his diary, "George Shultz & I had a talk mainly about setting up a little in house group of experts on the Soviet U. to help us in setting up some channels. I feel the Soviets are so defense minded, so paranoid about being attacked that without being soft on them we ought to tell them no one here has any intention of doing anything like that."

The next morning, November 19, 1983, the group held its first meeting. The Small Group consisted of Vice President George Bush, Secretary of State George Shultz, and National Security Advisor Robert McFarlane. Additionally, Jack Matlock, Edwin Meese, and Donald Fortier represented the National Security Council; Kenneth Dam, Lawrence Eagleburger, Richard Burt, and Jeremy Azrael represented the Department of State; Paul Thayer represented the Department of Defense; and Robert Gates represented the CIA. It was established to be secretive, members were told not to mention it to others, and Matlock would keep the sole copy of meeting notes.

The group reviewed past meetings with the Soviets and noted a series of limited mutual success, including the emigration of Soviet Pentacostals to the United States and a U.S.-Soviet grain pact. However, the KAL shootdown had "derailed" plans for further initiatives.

Vice President Bush argued that the public was "uneasy" with the perception that the United States was not communicating with the Soviet Union and stated that there was a need to show the public that communication was in fact occurring. Eagleburger concurred, stating that U.S.-Soviet dialogue was "like ships passing in the night." Meese stated that through the view of U.S. politics, many were criticizing the president for "excessive rhetoric and for not being serious about negotiation" while others further to the right felt "he has not taken enough punitive action" against the Soviets.

The principals agreed that to allay these concerns, "we need to articulate our policy more clearly and develop a unique Reagan Administration view." Schultz agreed that the administration needed "an authoritative statement" and stated that work had begun on a policy speech; this draft would eventually become President Reagan's pivotal January 16, 1984, address.

Almost as an afterthought, Eagleburger "pointed out that the Soviets could be dangerous when they are in trouble and there is uncertainty in their leadership. We must keep that in mind and take steps to reduce the potential for miscalculation."

SMALL GROUP

Meeting of November 19, 1983
7:30 A.M., Secretary's Dining Room, Department of State

Present: The Vice President, The Secretary of State, Mr. Meese, Mr. McFarlane, and the following representatives of agencies: NSC: Matlock, Fortier; State: Dam, Eagleburger, Burt, Azrael; DOD: Thayer; CIA: Gates. (Gen. Scowcroft and Amb. Hartman were not in Washington.)

Two preliminary papers, "U.S.-Soviet Relations: The Next Twelve Months," and "Suggested Policy Framework" were distributed before and during breakfast.

Secretary Shultz opened the meeting by going over the following topics:

Ground Rules: During a meeting with Shultz and McFarlane November 16, the President had directed that a small group be formed to work in complete confidentiality to review the state of our relations with the Soviet Union and to consider appropriate policy. Members had been chosen either because of their overall responsibility for developing U.S. policy, or their expertise and positions enabling them to request studies and information from their organizational units in the normal course of their duties. The group should not be mentioned to persons not members, although discussion among members is encouraged. Matlock would serve as executive secretary and would keep the sole copy of any papers developed by the group.

Related Study: Secretary Shultz had earlier requested Eagleburger and Bosworth to do a special study relevant to the group's interests. It seemed in pretty good shape and would be distributed to members soon for their consideration.

Pattern of Relations with Soviets: In the spring we initiated a pattern of meetings: Shultz with Dobrynin and Hartman with Gromyko, and the President had met with Dobrynin once for two hours. He stressed his interest in the Pentacostalists at that time, and their subsequent release was probably a result, although we are careful not to claim credit publicly. We went on to negotiate a grain agreement (which the Soviets are unlikely to give us credit for since they understand the domestic pressures here) and to start negotiations on bilateral matters such as consulates and an exchanges agreement. We had intended that the Shultz-Gromyko meeting in Madrid would be the first in a series, with Gromyko coming here for meetings in New York and perhaps with the President in Washington, followed perhaps by a Shultz visit to Moscow. KAL had derailed these plans, and furthermore

- 2 -

the Soviets seemed to have welched on a deal we thought we had for Shcharansky's release.

Recent meetings with Dobrynin: Shultz resumed meeting Dobrynin a couple of weeks ago, but the latter seemed uninstructed on any subject except INF. Two recent meetings by Hartman and Gromyko also seemed unproductive. At the meeting with Dobrynin yesterday (Nov. 18), attended by Eagleburger, Dobrynin seemed totally uninstructed.

At that meeting, Shultz had told Dobrynin that we were willing to have a totally private dialogue. He mentioned our dismay in our experience with the Shcharansky deal and also with the Soviet misrepresentation of our INF position to our allies. He asked if the Soviets were interested in discussing START conceptually, and stressed the explosiveness of the situation in the Middle East and the dangers of their involvement with the Syrians. Overall, his presentation was an attempt to stick to our agenda, by making it clear that arms control cannot be dealt with in isolation.

Mr. McFarlane pointed out that we can proceed on the foundation of three years of work by the Administration, during which we have been able to mend the disrepair in our defenses, get our economy moving again, and shore up the Alliance. Now we are in a position of strength in dealing with the Soviets.

Regarding the items on the agenda for the meeting, Matlock observed (1) that we probably cannot expect major adjustments in Soviet policy over the next 12 months because of the leadership situation in the Soviet Union and other factors such as INF deployments and the U.S. Presidential election; (2) that it is nevertheless important to convey, both publicly and privately, a clear message to the Soviets, since this could be a factor in the leadership struggle and could prepare for significant changes in 1985; and (3) that we must have a credible and consistent negotiating stance to ensure the sustainability of our policies with our public and with our allies. He noted the paper headed "Suggested Policy Framework" as an initial attempt to articulate our policy.

The Vice President observed that there is a public perception that we are not communicating with the Soviets, and this makes the public uneasy. There is a need to convince the public that we are in fact in communication.

Eagleburger observed that our dialogue is like ships passing in the night. We must get into more discussion of fundamental questions. We should structure the discussions so that we are conveying to them clearly our views on various important issues such as the Middle East and Cuba in some detail. He recalled that studies had been done sometime back of the view from Moscow and the view from Washington, in order to get a feel for the

- 3 -

difference in perspectives, and wondered whether it might not be useful to commission updated studies on these topics at this time.

Secretary Shultz agreed on the need for discussing regional issues with the Soviets and noted that this does not mean formal negotiations or formal consultation.

McFarlane observed that the Soviets are facing an abrupt change in their expectations. Their expectation of a decline in the West has been dashed. They have not decided how to react to this and are uncertain regarding our global intentions.

Burt noted that the past year has been a difficult one for the Soviets. The INF deployments will put great strain on the relationship, but further out there may be opportunities. The Soviets have painted themselves in a corner to a degree that it may be impossible for them to do business for a while.

Secretary Shultz observed that we should turn around the Soviet charge that they cannot do business with the Reagan Administration, by pointing out that in fact we cannot do business with them.

Burt suggested that we (a) state a willingness to engage in a dialogue on the issues; (b) point out to them that START has the greatest potential if the Soviets are willing to bite; (c) consider discussions of regional issues as a form of pre-crisis management; and (d) examine the possibilities of trade-offs, since the Soviets have more interest in some issues and we in others.

Dam agreed that we should look for tradeoffs in the bilateral area.

Matlock pointed out that we need to make a basic decision whether to continue the suspension of negotiations on bilateral issues because of KAL or whether to proceed at some point, and under what conditions.

Secretary Shultz noted that he had suggested to Dobrynin yesterday that, even if the Soviets were unwilling to pay compensation, they could easily cooperate in providing navigation assistance to planes flying the route in order to avert tragedies in the future.

Gates observed that the prospects for an improvement in US-Soviet relations are dismal over the next 12 months. The Soviets must turn inward and look at their succession problem. It will be hard for them to react to new initiatives. Furthermore, any initiatives from us will be seen in the context of election-year politics. The question is really how to use the next year to put down building blocks for the second term. Indeed, the

- 4 -

election of the President to a second term will convey an important message, that the U.S. has recovered from the vacillations of the recent past and is on a steady course. Thus, we need to convey our views for the role they can plan in the Soviet succession and in order to establish a basis for 1985.

Meese pointed out some of the political factors involved: many are criticizing the President for excessive rhetoric and for not being serious about negotiation, while the right feels he has not taken enough punitive action, and indeed would like a policy based on the "missing elements" in the paper suggesting a policy framework. We thus need to articulate our policy more clearly and develop a unique Reagan Administration view.

Azrael observed (1) that there were some areas where we might desire to "push" the Soviets, and that this could cause complications in relations, and (2) that at some point we must come to grips with the fact that some proposals are non-negotiable from the Soviet point of view.

Burt predicted that the Soviets would not come back to the INF talks as such. A continuation will have to take another form. We must consider what sort of forum we should seek.

Secretary Shultz noted that we need an authoritative statement, and that work had been done on a speech. It could be by the President, or he could make it. But we need a clear public statement of our policy to build on.

Eagleburger pointed out that the Soviets could be dangerous when they are in trouble and there is uncertainty in their leadership. We must keep that in mind and take steps to reduce the potential for miscalculation.

The meeting ended at approximately 9:30.

Document 13: Reagan's Handwritten Addition of Ivan and Anya to His January 16, 1984, Speech on United States–Soviet Relations

Source: Ronald Reagan Presidential Library, Matlock Files, Chron January 1984, Box 3

The first draft of this speech was initially completed by Jack Matlock in mid-December 1983. According to Matlock, it was delayed until mid-January "on the advice of Mrs. Reagan's astrologer friend in California," a delay that he believes "did no harm." Only Reagan's State of the Union speech drafts received more attention than this speech. Delivered at 10 a.m. in the East Room of the White House, it was written to address four audiences: the American public, Western Europeans, Soviet leaders, and the Soviet people. According to Matlock, there was a message in the speech for each: "for the American public, that we were not risking war and were strong enough to negotiate effectively; for Europe, that the United States had a coherent strategy for dealing with the USSR; for the Soviet leaders, that we were willing to deal with them in a cooperative spirit; for the Soviet people, that we were not threatening them and wished them well."

This version of the speech includes Reagan's own handwritten edits, including his now-famous addition of a folksy meeting of Ivan and Anya and Jim and Sally—two couples, one Soviet, one American. "Suppose," Reagan wrote, that "there was no language barrier"; after speaking of their jobs, their children, and their hopes, Ivan, Anya, Jim, and Sally would soon prove "that people want to raise their children in a world without fear and without war."*

The president's last handwritten line concluded: "If the Soviet government wants peace, then there will be peace. Together we can strengthen peace, reduce the level of arms and know in doing so we have helped fulfill the hopes and dreams of those we represent and, indeed, of people everywhere. Let us begin now."

---

* Matlock had to edit the president's version "to make it seem less sexist." Reagan's original version had the men speaking about their work and the women about their children and recipes. Though Reagan's Ivan and Anya parable was the only section of this pivotal speech that is still remembered today, one White House staffer, confused by the handwritten addition to the text, allegedly asked, a bit too loudly, "Who wrote this shit?" See Jack Matlock Jr., *Reagan and Gorbachev: How the Cold War Ended* (New York: Random House, 2004), 80–83 and John Lewis Gaddis, *The Cold War: A New History* (New York: Penguin, 2005), 228.

KR's changes al

(NSC/Myer/BE/RR)
January 6, 1984
2:00 p.m.

PRESIDENTIAL ADDRESS: U.S.-SOVIET RELATIONS
NATIONAL PRESS CLUB

Thank you very much for inviting me back to visit your distinguished group. I'm grateful for this opportunity during these first days of 1984, to speak through you to the people of the world on a subject of great importance to the cause of peace -- relations between the United States and the Soviet Union.

In just a few days, the United States will join the Soviet Union and the other nations of Europe at an international security conference in Stockholm. We intend to uphold our responsibility as a major power in easing potential sources of conflict. The conference will search for practical and meaningful ways to increase European security and preserve peace. We will go to Stockholm bearing the heartfelt wishes of our people for genuine progress.

We live in a time of challenges to peace, but also of opportunities for peace. Through decades of difficulty and frustration, America's highest aspiration has never wavered: We have and will continue to struggle for a lasting peace that enhances dignity for men and women everywhere. I believe 1984 finds the United States in its strongest position in years to establish a constructive and realistic working relationship with the Soviet Union.

Some fundamental changes have taken place since the decade of the seventies -- years when the United States questioned its

Page 2

role in the world and neglected its defenses, while the Soviet Union increased its military might and sought to expand its influence through threats and use of force.

Three years ago we embraced a mandate from the American people to change course, and we have. Today America can once again demonstrate, with equal conviction, our commitment to stay secure and to find peaceful solutions to problems through negotiations. January 1984 is a time of opportunities for peace.

History teaches that wars begin when governments believe the price of aggression is cheap. To keep the peace, we and our allies must remain strong enough to convince any potential aggressor that war could bring no benefit, only disaster. In other words, our goal is deterrence, plain and simple.

With the support of the American people and the Congress, we halted America's decline. Our economy is in the midst of the best recovery since the sixties. Our defenses are being rebuilt. Our alliances are solid and our commitment to defend our values has never been more clear. There is credibility and consistency.

America's recovery may have taken Soviet leaders by surprise. They may have counted on us to keep weakening ourselves. They have been saying for years that our demise was inevitable. They said it so often they probably started believing it. ~~But~~ I think they can see now they were wrong.

Neither we nor the Soviet Union can wish away the differences between our two societies. But we should always remember that we do have common interests. And the foremost among them is to avoid war and reduce the level of arms. There

Page 3

is no rational alternative but to steer a course which I would call credible deterrence and peaceful competition; and if we do so, we might find areas in which we could engage in constructive cooperation.

Recently we've been hearing some very strident rhetoric from the Kremlin. These harsh words have led some to speak of heightened uncertainty and an increased danger of conflict. This is understandable, but profoundly mistaken. Look beyond the words, and one fact stands out plainly: Deterrence is being restored and it is making the world a safer place; safer because there is less danger that the Soviet leadership will underestimate our strength or resolve.

We do not threaten the Soviet Union. Freedom poses no threat, it is the language of progress. We proved this 35 years ago when we had a monopoly of nuclear weapons, and could have dominated the world. But we didn't. Instead we used our power to write a new chapter in the history of mankind. We helped rebuild the war-ravaged economies of East and West, including those nations who had been our enemies. Indeed, those former enemies are now numbered among our staunchest friends.

America's character has not changed. Our strength and vision of progress provide the basis for stability and meaningful negotiations. Soviet leaders know it makes sense to compromise only if they can get something in return. America's economic and military strength permit us to offer something in return. Yes, today is a time of opportunities for peace.

Page 4

But to say that the world is safer is not to say that it is safe enough. We are witnessing tragic conflicts in many parts of the world. Nuclear arsenals are far too high. And our working relationship with the Soviet Union is not what it must be. These are conditions which must be addressed and improved.

Deterrence is essential to preserve peace and protect our way of life, but deterrence is not the beginning and end of our policy toward the Soviet Union. We must and will engage the Soviets in a dialogue as cordial and cooperative as possible, a dialogue that will serve to promote peace in the troubled regions of the world, reduce the level of arms, and build a constructive working relationship.

First, we must find ways to eliminate the use and threat of force in solving international disputes.

The world has witnessed more than 150 conflicts since the end of World War II alone. Armed conflicts are raging in the Middle East, Afghanistan, Southeast Asia, Central America, and Africa. In other regions, independent nations are confronted by heavily armed neighbors seeking to dominate by threatening attack or subversion.

Most of these conflicts have their roots in local problems, but many have been fanned and exploited by the Soviet Union and its surrogates -- and, of course, Afghanistan has suffered an outright Soviet invasion. Fueling regional conflicts and exporting revolution only exacerbates local conflicts, increases suffering, and makes solutions to real social and economic problems more difficult.

Page 5

Would it not be better and safer to assist the peoples and governments in areas of conflict in negotiating peaceful solutions? Today, I am asking the Soviet leaders to join with us in cooperative efforts to move the world in this safer direction.

Second, our aim is to find ways to reduce the vast stockpiles of armaments in the world, particularly nuclear weapons.

It is tragic to see the world's developing nations spending more than $150 billion a year on arms -- almost 20 percent of their national budgets. We must find ways to reverse the vicious cycle of threat and response which drives arms races everywhere it occurs.

While modernizing our defenses, we have done only what is needed to establish a stable military balance. The simple truth is, America's total nuclear stockpile has declined. We have fewer warheads today than we had 28 years ago. And our nuclear stockpile is at the lowest level in 25 years in terms of its total destructive power.

Just 2 months ago, we and our allies agreed to withdraw an additional 1,400 nuclear warheads from Western Europe. This comes after the removal of a thousand nuclear warheads from Europe over the last 3 years. Even if all our planned intermediate-range missiles have to be deployed in Europe over the next 5 years -- and we hope this will not be necessary -- we will have eliminated five existing warheads for each new warhead deployed.

Page 6

But this is not enough. We must accelerate our efforts to reach agreements to reduce greatly the numbers of nuclear weapons. It was with this goal in mind that I first proposed here, in November 1981, the "zero option" for intermediate-range missiles. Our aim was then and is now to eliminate in one fell swoop an entire class of nuclear arms. Although NATO's initial deployment of INF missiles was an important achievement, I would still prefer that there be no INF missile deployments on either side. Indeed, I support a zero option for all nuclear arms. As I have said before, my dream is to see the day when nuclear weapons will be banished from the face of the Earth.

Last month, the Soviet Defense Minister stated that his country shares the vision of a world free of nuclear weapons. These are encouraging words. Well, now is a time to move from words to deeds.

Our third aim is to work with the Soviet Union to establish a better working relationship with greater cooperation and understanding.

Cooperation and understanding are built on deeds, not words. Complying with agreements helps; violating them hurts. Respecting the rights of individual citizens bolsters the relationship; denying these rights harms it. Expanding contacts across borders and permitting a free interchange of information and ideas increase confidence; sealing off one's people from the rest of the world reduces it. Peaceful trade helps, while organized theft of industrial secrets certainly hurts.

Page 7

These examples illustrate clearly why our relationship with the Soviet Union is not what it should be. We have a long way to go, but we are determined to try and try again.

In working toward these goals, our approach is based on three guiding principles: realism, strength, and dialogue.

Realism means we start by understanding the world we live in. We must recognize that we are in a long-term competition with a government that does not share our notions of individual liberties at home and peaceful change abroad. We must be frank in acknowledging our differences and unafraid to promote our values.

Strength means we know we cannot negotiate successfully or protect our interests if we are weak. Our strength is necessary not only to deter war, but to facilitate negotiation and compromise.

Strength is more than military power. Economic strength is crucial and America's economy is leading the world into recovery. Equally important is unity among our people at home and with our allies abroad. We are stronger in all these areas than (WE WERE) 3 years ago.

Dialogue means we are determined to deal with our differences peacefully, through negotiation. We are prepared to discuss all the problems that divide us, and to work for practical, fair solutions on the basis of mutual compromise. We will never retreat from negotiations.

I have openly expressed my view of the Soviet system. I don't know why this should come as a surprise to Soviet leaders

Page 8

who have never shied away from expressing their view of our system. But this does not mean we can't deal with each other. We do not refuse to talk when the Soviets call us "imperialist aggressors," or because they cling to the fantasy of a communist triumph over democracy. The fact that neither of us likes the other's system is no reason to refuse to talk. Living in this nuclear age makes it imperative that we talk.

Our commitment to dialogue is firm and unshakeable. But we do insist that our negotiations deal with real problems, not atmospherics.

In our approach to negotiations, reducing the risk of war -- and especially nuclear war -- is priority number one. A nuclear confrontation could well be mankind's last. The comprehensive set of initiatives that we have proposed would reduce substantially the size of nuclear arsenals. And again, I would hope that in the years ahead we could go much further toward the ultimate goal of ridding our planet of the nuclear threat altogether.

The world regrets that the Soviet Union broke off negotiations on intermediate-range nuclear forces, and has refused to set a date for further talks on strategic arms. Our negotiators are ready to return to the negotiating table, and to conclude agreements in INF and START. We will negotiate in good faith. Whenever the Soviet Union is ready to do likewise, we will meet them half way.

We seek not only to reduce the numbers of nuclear weapons, but also to reduce the chances for dangerous misunderstanding and

Page 9

miscalculation. So we have put forward proposals for what we call "confidence-building measures." They cover a wide range of activities. In the Geneva negotiations, we have proposed that the U.S. and Soviet Union exchange advance notifications of missile tests and major military exercises. Following up on congressional suggestions, we also proposed a number of ways to improve direct U.S.-Soviet channels of communication.

These bilateral proposals will be broadened at the conference in Stockholm. We are working with our allies to develop practical, meaningful ways to reduce the uncertainty and potential for misinterpretation surrounding military activities, and to diminish the risks of surprise attack.

Arms control has long been the most visible area of U.S.-Soviet dialogue. But a durable peace also requires us to defuse tensions and regional conflicts. We and the Soviets should have a common interest in promoting regional stability, and in finding peaceful solutions to existing conflicts that permit developing nations to concentrate their energies on economic growth. Thus we seek to engage the Soviets in exchanges of views on these regional conflicts and tensions and on how we can both contribute to stability and a lowering of tensions.

We remain convinced that on issues like these it is in the Soviet Union's best interest to cooperate in achieving broad-based, negotiated solutions. If the Soviet leaders make that choice, they will find ~~the United States~~ us ready to cooperate.

Another major problem in our relationship with the Soviet Union is human rights. ~~It is~~ Soviet practices in this area, as

Page 10

much as any other issue, ~~that~~ have created the mistrust and ill will that hangs over our relationship.

Moral considerations alone compel us to express our deep concern over prisoners of conscience in the Soviet Union, over the virtual halt in the emigration of Jews, Armenians, and others who wish to join their families abroad, and over the continuing harrassment of courageous people like Andrei Sakharov.

Our request is simple and straightforward: THAT The Soviet Union ~~must~~ live up to the obligations it has freely assumed under international covenants -- in particular, its commitments under the Helsinki Accords. Experience has shown that greater respect for human rights can contribute to progress in other areas of the Soviet-American relationship.

Conflicts of interest between the United States and the Soviet Union are real. But we can and must keep the peace between our two nations and make it a better and more peaceful world for all mankind.

These are the objectives of our policy toward the Soviet Union, a policy of credible deterrence and peaceful competition that will serve both nations and people everywhere for the long haul. It is a challenge for Americans. It is also a challenge for the Soviets. If they cannot meet us half way, we will be prepared to protect our interests, and those of our friends and allies. But we want more than deterrence; we seek genuine cooperation; we seek progress for peace.

Cooperation begins with communication. We seek such communication. We will stay at the negotiating tables in Geneva

Page 11

and Vienna. Furthermore, Secretary Shultz will be meeting with Soviet Foreign Minister Gromyko in Stockholm. This meeting should be followed by others, so that high-level consultations become a regular and normal component of U.S.-Soviet relations.

Our challenge is peaceful. It will bring out the best in us. It also calls for the best from the Soviet Union. No one can predict how the Soviet leaders will respond to our challenge. ~~But~~ [THE PEOPLE OF] our two countries share with all mankind the dream of eliminating the risks of nuclear war. It is not an impossible dream, because eliminating those is so clearly a vital interest for all of us. ~~We~~ [OUR 2 COUNTRIES] have never fought each other; there is no reason we ever should. Indeed, we have fought alongside one another in ~~the past~~ [2 WORLD WARS]. Today our common enemies are hunger, disease, ignorance and, above all, war.

More than 20 years ago, President Kennedy defined an approach that is as realistic and hopeful today as when he announced it:

> "So, let us not be blind to our differences --" [HE SAID] "but let us also direct attention to our common interests and to the means by which those differences can be resolved."

I urge the Soviet leadership to move from pause to progress. If the Soviet government wants peace then there will be peace. The journey from proposals to progress to agreements may be difficult. But that should not indict the past or despair the future. America is prepared for a major breakthrough or modest advances. We welcome compromise. In this spirit of constructive competition, we can strengthen peace, we can reduce greatly the level of arms, and, yes, we can brighten the hopes and dreams of people everywhere. Let us begin now.

Those differences — are they not differences between govt's. differences in pol. philosophy and policy? The common interests are those things that peoples of different countries share. If THE people of the Soviet U. and the United Stat could visit together with no language barrier to hinder them would they debate the differences between pol. philosophies?

Well those differences would turn out to be differences in governmental structure & philosophy. The common interests would have to do with the things of everyday life for people everywhere.

Leave this in

Suppose Ivan & ANYA found themselves in a waiting room, or sharing a shelter from the rain with Jim & Sall and there was no language barrier to keep them from getting acquainted. Would they debate the differences between their respective govt's? Or would Anya & Sally find themselves comparing notes about their children, while Ivan & Jim found out what each other did for a living.

Before they parted company they would probably have touched on ambitions, hobbies, what they wanted for their children and the problems of making ends meet. And as they went their separate ways Anya would be saying to Ivan, "wasn't she nice, she gave me a new recipe." Jim would be telling Sally what Ivan didn't like about his boss. They might even have decided they were all going to get together for dinner some evening soon.

Above all they would have proven that people don't make wars. People want to raise their children in a world without fear, and without war.

They want to have some of the good things over & above bare subsistence that make life worth living. They want to work at some craft, trade or profession that gives them satisfaction and a sense of worth. Their common interests cross all borders

(over)

~~Anger, hom, simplicity could be Ruins, Luing, Hand, Tra~~

If the Soviet Govt. wants peace than there will be peace. Together we can strengthen peace, reduce the level of arms and know in doing so we have fulfilled the hopes & dreams of ~~people~~ those we represent and indeed of people everywhere. Let us begin now.

NOTES

Introduction: "Two Spiders in a Bottle"

1. This, at least, was the scenario envisioned during the NATO Command Post Exercise Able Archer 83, conducted from November 7 to 11, 1983. "Exercise Scenario," Undated, NATO Unclassified.

2. Air Force Seventh Air Division, Ramstein Air Base, "Exercise Able Archer 83, SAC ADVON, After Action Report," December 1, 1983, Secret NOFORN.

3. Air Force Seventh Air Division, Ramstein Air Base, "Exercise Able Archer 83, SAC ADVON, After Action Report," December 1, 1983, Secret NOFORN.

4. On November 4, 1981, President Reagan's secretary of state Alexander Haig, who had previously served as the Supreme Allied Commander Europe, testified to the Senate Foreign Relations Committee that "there are contingency plans in the NATO doctrine to fire a nuclear weapon for demonstrative purposes to demonstrate to the other side that they are exceeding the limits of toleration in the conventional area, all designed to maintain violence at the lowest level possible." David Abshire, who served as the U.S. permanent representative to NATO, recalled that the "targeted" city could have been Kiev; he also recollected that he had always wanted to tell Reagan during a drill that Soviets were launching a retaliatory single-weapon nuclear attack on Boston but not to worry, "It's only signaling." Abshire reiterated that he was "was not a M.A.D. man." Bernard Gwertzman, "Allied Contingency Plan Envisions a Warning Atom Blast, Haig Says," *New York Times*, November 5, 1981; David Abshire interview conducted by author, February 29, 2008; "Exercise Able Archer 83: Information from SHAPE Historical Files," March 28, 2013, NATO Unclassified.

5. A declassified CIA *Studies in Intelligence* article, "The 1983 War Scare in U.S.-Soviet Relations," described Gordievsky as "number two in the London residency."

6. Christopher Andrew and Oleg Gordievsky, *Comrade Kryuchkov's Instructions: Top Secret Files on KGB Foreign Operations, 1975–1985* (Stanford: Stanford University Press, 1993), 87.

7. Christopher Andrew and Oleg Gordievsky, *Comrade Kryuchkov's Instructions: Top Secret Files on KGB Foreign Operations, 1975–1985* (Stanford: Stanford University Press, 1993), 88.

8. UK Ministry of Defence, "Soviet Union: Concern About a Surprise NATO Attack," May 8, 1984, Top Secret, UMBRA GAMMA, US/UK Eyes Only.

9. The President's Foreign Intelligence Advisory Board, "The Soviet 'War Scare,'" February 15, 1990, Top Secret, UMBRA GAMMA WNINTEL NOFORN NOCONTRACT ORCON. The classifications markings indicate: Communications Intelligence (UMBRA), Signals Intelligence (GAMMA), Sources and Methods (WNINTEL), No Foreign Nationals (NOFORN), No contractors or consultants (NOCONTRACT), and Originator Controlled (ORCON).

10. The President's Foreign Intelligence Advisory Board, "The Soviet 'War Scare,'" February 15, 1990, Top Secret, UMBRA GAMMA WNINTEL NOFORN NOCONTRACT ORCON.

11. Averell Harriman, "Memorandum of Conversation with Andropov," June 2, 1983, W. Averell Harriman Papers, Library of Congress, Manuscript Division, Box 655. For the Russian version, see Soviet notes of a meeting between General Secretary Yuri Andropov and Averell and Pamela Harriman, June 2, 1983, RGANI [Russian State Archive of Contemporary History], F 82, OP 1, D 36, R 27-55, LL 33-44.

12. Ronald Reagan, *An American Life* (New York: Simon & Schuster, 1990), 257.

13. "Ronald Reagan's talking points for Conversation with Soviet Ambassador Hartman," Ronald Reagan Presidential Library, Matlock Files, Chron March 1984, Box 5.

14. Robert Gates, *From the Shadows: The Ultimate Insider's Story of Five Presidents and How They Won the Cold War* (New York: Simon & Schuster, 2007), 273.

15. Fritz Ermarth, "Observations on the War Scare of 1983 from an Intelligence Perch," for the Parallel History Project on NATO and the Warsaw Pact, November 6, 2003.

16. Mark Kramer, "The Able Archer 83 Non-Crisis: Did Soviet Leaders Really Fear an Imminent Nuclear Attack in 1983?" Also in German, "Die Nicht-Krise um Able Archer 1983: Fürchtete die sowjetische Führung tatsächlich einen atomaren Grossangriff im Herbst 1983?" in: Oliver Bange und Bernd Lemke (Hrsg). Wege zur Wiedervereinigung (München: Oldenbourg, September 2013). Thorsten Borring Olesen, "Truth on Demand: Denmark and the Cold War," in Nanna Hvidt and Hans Mouritzen, ed., *Danish Foreign Policy Yearbook 2006*, Danish Institute for International Studies, 105; see also Beth Fischer's review of Vojtech Mastny's "How Able Was 'Able Archer'?" at H-Diplo.

17. The author is the Director of the Freedom of Information Act Project at the National Security Archive. For more information about the Archive, visit its website, www.nsarchive.org.

18. Copies of the originals and further analysis of these documents can be found at the Able Archer 83 Sourcebook, http://nsarchive.gwu.edu/nukevault/ablearcher/.

Part I: "Standing Tall," the "Mirror-Image," and Operation RYaN

1. *American Cryptology During the Cold War, 1945–1989, Book IV: Cryptologic Rebirth, 1981–1989,* Thomas Johnson, National Security Agency Center for Cryptologic History, 1999, Top Secret COMINT UMBRA/TALENT KEYHOLE/X1.

2. Vladislav M. Zubok, *A Failed Empire: The Soviet Union in the Cold War from Stalin to Gorbachev* (Chapel Hill: The University of North Carolina Press, 2008), 265.

3. Ronald Reagan, Remarks at a Meeting with Republican Congressional Candidates, East Room, White House, Washington, D.C., October 6, 1982, available at the Ronald Reagan Presidential Library's online Public Papers of President Ronald W. Reagan.

4. Alexander M. Haig Jr., *Caveat: Realism, Reagan, and Foreign Policy* (New York: Scribner, 1984), 105.

5. Ronald Reagan, Address Before the Japanese Diet in Tokyo, November 11, 1983, available at the Ronald Reagan Presidential Library's online Public Papers of President Ronald W. Reagan.

6. The "Paradox of Ronald Reagan" was expanded upon at a December 3, 2015, Miller Center on the Presidency talk entitled "The Reagan Paradox: How the 40th President Baffles His Biographers (And His Aides, His Children, Even His Wife)," delivered by National Security Archive director Thomas Blanton; notes are in author's possession.

7. Anatoly Dobrynin, *In Confidence: Moscow's Ambassador to Six Cold War Presidents* (Seattle: University of Washington Press, 2001), 606.

8. General Secretary Andropov made a similar quip to Ambassador Dobrynin: "'I am unlucky to get exactly this American president to deal with. Just my bad luck,' he said to me lightly, but there was a measure of bitterness in his words." Anatoly Dobrynin, *In Confidence: Moscow's Ambassador to Six Cold War Presidents* (Seattle: University of Washington Press, 2001), 551. Ronald Reagan, *An American Life* (New York: Simon & Schuster, 1990), 14.

9. Jack Matlock Jr., *Reagan and Gorbachev: How the Cold War Ended* (New York: Random House, 2004), 6.

10. Alexander M. Haig Jr., *Caveat: Realism, Reagan, and Foreign Policy* (New York: Scribner, 1984), 102–109; Raymond Garthoff, *The Great Transition: American-Soviet Relations and the End of the Cold War* (Washington, D.C.: The Brookings Institution, 1994), 45–46.

11. Letter from Brezhnev to Reagan, March 6, 1981, Ronald Reagan Presidential Library, Executive Secretariat, NSC: Head of State File, box 38, ID 8190198.

12. Letter from Reagan to Brezhnev, April 24, 1981, Ronald Reagan Presidential Library, Executive Secretariat, NSC: Head of State File, box 38, ID 8190204.

13. Raymond Garthoff, *The Great Transition: American-Soviet Relations and the End of the Cold War* (Washington, D.C.: The Brookings Institution, 1994), 46.

14. Letter from Reagan to Brezhnev, April 24, 1981, Ronald Reagan Presidential Library, Executive Secretariat, NSC: Head of State File, box 38, ID 8190204.

15. The two leaders continued to correspond with each other through October 20, 1982, but the letters were sterile communications, drafted by the Department of State and the Ministry of Foreign Affairs, largely dealing with international incidents. These included the imposition of martial law in Poland, the Israeli invasion of Lebanon, and the plight of Anatoly Sharansky, who was arrested and imprisoned for spying on the Soviet Union at the behest of the Defense Intelligence Agency. The most comprehensive collection of this correspondence can be found at The Reagan Files. http://www.thereaganfiles.com/document-collections/letters-between-president.html.

16. Letter from Andropov to Reagan, June 22, 1983, Ronald Reagan Presidential Library, Executive Secretariat, NSC: Head of State File, box 38, ID 8304209. Some have placed the date of this letter as July 4, 1983, but the copy held by the Ronald Reagan Presidential Library is clearly dated June 22. Letter from Reagan to Andropov, July 11, 1983, Ronald Reagan Presidential Library, Executive Secretariat, NSC: Head of State File, box 38, ID 8390128; Raymond Garthoff, *The Great Transition: American-Soviet Relations and the End of the Cold War* (Washington, D.C.: The Brookings Institution, 1994), 110. One opponent of Reagan meeting with Andropov was former President Richard M. Nixon. Nixon wrote a letter advising Reagan to skip a "get-acquainted meeting" with Andropov, saying that the "spirit [of goodwill] evaporates very fast" from meetings without "substance." Nixon advised Reagan to wait a year before meeting with Andropov, in 1984. At such a meeting, Nixon recommended Reagan should "work to reduce the possibility of war coming by miscalculation." Letter from Nixon to Reagan, February 25, 1983, Ronald Reagan Presidential Library, McFarlane Files, Sensitive Chron (01/07/1983–03/02/1983), Box 5.

17. Don Oberdorfer, *The Turn: From the Cold War to a New Era: The United States and the Soviet Union 1983–1990* (New York: Touchstone, 1991), 38.

18. Don Oberdorfer, *The Turn: From the Cold War to a New Era: The United States and the Soviet Union 1983–1990* (New York: Touchstone, 1991), 38.

19. According to the high-level Ministry of Foreign Affairs official, Georgy Kornienko, Reagan's handwritten letter "was received with surprise and confusion in Moscow." It coincided with another démarche from the U.S. State Department and the Soviets were unsure of which U.S. view to accept as genuine. Don Oberdorfer, *The Turn: From the Cold War to a New Era: The United States and the Soviet Union 1983–1990* (New York: Touchstone, 1991), 39.

20. Ronald Powaski, *Return to Armageddon: The United States and the Nuclear Arms Race, 1981–1999* (New York: Oxford University Press, 2000), 15. Charles Mohr, "Carlucci Calls Military Budget More 'Honest,'" *New York Times*, February 8, 1982.

21. Raymond Garthoff, *The Great Transition: American-Soviet Relations and the End of the Cold War* (Washington, D.C.: The Brookings Institution, 1994), 41; Ronald Reagan, The President's News Conference, East Room, White House, Washington, D.C., March 31, 1982, available at the Ronald Reagan Presidential Library's online Public Papers of President Ronald W. Reagan.

22. These included CIA Director William Casey, Assistant Secretary of Defense Richard Perle, and NSC Staff Expert on Soviet Affairs Richard Pipes; Ronald E. Powaski, *Return to Armageddon: The United States and the Nuclear Arms Race, 1981–1999* (New York: Oxford University Press, 2000), 15.

23. George C. Wilson, "Weinberger, in His First Message, Says Mission Is to 'Rearm America,'" *Washington Post*, January 23, 1981.

24. National Security Decision Directive Memorandum, May 21, 1982, Top Secret, accessed from the Digital National Security Archive, Presidential Directives collection.

25. National Security Decision Directive Memorandum, January 17, 1983, Secret, accessed from the Digital National Security Archive, Presidential Directives Part II collection.

26. The decision to deploy NATO intermediate range missiles to Western Europe to counter the Soviet deployment of SS-20 intermediate range missiles along its western border was made in December 1979. NATO continued preparing intermediate range missiles for deployment at the same time as they attempted to negotiate with the USSR for a reduction or elimination of intermediate range missiles in Europe; this was known as the "dual-track decision." See Leopoldo Nuti, Frédéric Bozo, and Bernd Rother, eds., *The Euromissile Crisis and the End of the Cold War* (Woodrow Wilson Center Press with Stanford University Press), 2015.

27. National Security Decision Directive Memorandum, March 28, 1983, For Official Use Only, accessed from the Digital National Security Archive, Presidential Directives collection.

28. Ronald Reagan, Question-and-Answer Session with Reporters on Domestic and Foreign Policy Issues, March 29, 1983, available at the Ronald Reagan Presidential Library's online Public Papers of President Ronald W. Reagan.

29. "Replies by Yu. V. Andropov to Questions from a Correspondent of Pravda," *Pravda*, March 27, 1983. Translated by Tass.

30. Unpublished Marshal Sergei Akhromeyev interview conducted by Don Oberdorfer, 1990 Mudd Manuscript Library, Princeton University.

31. "Deception, Self-Deception and Nuclear Arms," by McGeorge Bundy for the *New York Times Book Review*, March 11, 1984; Thomas Cochran, William Arkin, and Milton Hoenig, *Nuclear Weapons Databook: Volume I U.S. Nuclear Forces and Capabilities* (Cambridge: Ballinger Publishing Company, 1984), 292.

32. "Gorbachev's Instructions to the Reykjavik Preparation Group," October 4, 1986, in Svetlana Savranskaya and Thomas Blanton, *The Last Superpower Summits* (Budapest/New York: Central European University Press, 2016), 163.

33. David Hoffman, *The Dead Hand: The Untold Story of the Cold War Arms Race and Its Dangerous Legacy* (New York: Doubleday, 2010), 61.

34. Anatoly Chernyaev, *My Six Years with Gorbachev* (University Park: University of Pennsylvania Press, 2000), 9.

35. See chapter five of Aleksander Savelyev and Nikolay Detinov, *The Big Five: Arms Control Decision-Making in the Soviet Union* (Westport: Praeger, 1995).

36. Zasedanie politbyuro TsK KPSS (Meeting of the Politburo of the Central Committee of the Communist Party of the Soviet Union), August 4, 1983, Library of Congress, Manuscript Division, Dmitrii Antonovich Volkogonov Papers, Container 26, Reel 17.

37. John Kohan, "The KGB: Eyes of the Kremlin," *Time*, February 14, 1983.

38. Vojtech Mastny, "How Able Was 'Able Archer'?: Nuclear Trigger and Intelligence in Perspective," *Journal of Cold War Studies*, Vol 11 No 1 2009, 120–121. McFarlane believed Soviet bureaucracy "nurtured the idea" of a dangerous Ronald Reagan in an attempt to "drive a wedge between the U.S. and Europe," but also acknowledged genuine fear within some sectors of the Soviet Union. Robert McFarlane interview conducted by author, April 22, 2009.

39. See "Soviet Thinking on the Possibility of Armed Confrontation with the United States," December 30, 1983, Reagan Presidential Library, Matlock Files, Chron January 1984 [2 of 3], Box 90887; Gerhard Wettig, "The Last Soviet Offensive in the Cold War: Emergence and Development of the Campaign against NATO Euromissiles, 1979–1983," *Cold War History*, 9 no. 1 (Feb. 2009), 79–110.

40. Interview with Colonel General Varfolomei Vladimirovich Korobushin with participation by Senior Defense Department Advisor Vitalii Kataev by John Hines, December 10, 1992, in *Soviet Intentions 1965–1985: Volume II Soviet Post-Cold War Testimonial Evidence*, by John Hines, Ellis Mishulovich, of BDM Federal, Inc. for the Office of the Secretary of Defense Office of Net Assessment. Unclassified with portions "retroactively" classified.

41. Raymond Garthoff, *The Great Transition: American-Soviet Relations and the End of the Cold War* (Washington, D.C.: The Brookings Institution, 1994), 173.

42. For a comprehensive discussion of the danger of Launch on Warning, see Bruce G. Blair, *The Logic of Accidental Nuclear War* (Washington, D.C.: Brookings, 1993), especially chapter seven; Benjamin Fischer, "The Soviet-American War Scare of the 1980s," *International Journal of Intelligence* (Fall 2006), 480–517.

43. Interview with Viktor M. Surikov, Deputy Director of the Central Scientific Research Institute, by John Hines, September 11, 1993 in *Soviet Intentions 1965–1985: Volume II Soviet Post-Cold War Testimonial Evidence*, by John Hines, Ellis Mishulovich, of BDM Federal, Inc. for the Office of the Secretary of Defense Office of Net Assessment. Unclassified with portions "retroactively" classified.

44. Valentin Varennikov, *Nepovtorimoe, (Unique) Volume 4* (Moscow: Sovetskii Pisatel', 2001), 168.

45. Benjamin Fischer, "The 1983 War Scare in U.S.-Soviet Relations," *Studies in Intelligence*, Undated (circa 1996), Secret.

46. Other sources vary the spelling of RYaN. Soviet Ambassador to the United States Anatoly Dobrynin spelled it "ryon." Another spelling includes the word "surprise": "VRYAN" *"vnezapnoe raketno yadernoe napadenie"*—surprise nuclear missile attack. Czech Intelligence referred to the operation as NRJAN. One document shows that the Bulgarians monitored "VRYAN indicators" as late as June 1987. These East German documents confirm that the operation continued until at least April 1989. "The 1983 War Scare, Part One," http://www2.gwu.edu/~nsarchiv/NSAEBB/NSAEBB426/; Anatoly Dobrynin, *In Confidence: Moscow's Ambassador to Six Cold War Presidents* (Seattle: University of Washington Press, 2001), 523; Oleg Kalugin, *The First Directorate: My 32 Years in Intelligence and Espionage Against the West* (New York: St. Martins, 1994), 302; "Bulgarian Ministry of

Interior; MVR Information re: Results from the work on the improvement of the System for detection of RYAN indications," March 9, 1984, AMVR, Fond 1, Record 12, File 553, provided by Jordan Baev; Peter Rendek, "Operation ALAN—Mutual Cooperation of the Czechoslovak Intelligence Service and the Soviet KGB as Given in One of the Largest Leakage Cases of NATO Security Data in the Years 1982–1986."

47. Christopher Andrew and Oleg Gordievsky, *Comrade Kryuchkov's Instructions: Top Secret Files on KGB Foreign Operations, 1975–1985* (Stanford: Stanford University Press, 1993), 67. A quasi-official history of Russian foreign intelligence states that the goal of Operation RYaN was to counter "the real threat to the security of the USSR and Warsaw Pact countries" caused by Western military developments and the introduction of new weapons systems. A.I. Kolpakidi and D.P. Prokhorov, *Vneshnyaya razvedka Rossii* [The Foreign Intelligence Service of Russia] (Saint Petersburg: Neva, 2001), 80.

48. Ministry of State Security (Stasi), "Note About the Talks of Comrade Minister [Mielke] with the Chairman of the KGB, Comrade Chebrikov, in Moscow," February 9, 1983, http://www.wilsoncenter.org/publication/forecasting-nuclear-war.

49. KGB Chairman Yuri Andropov to General Secretary Leonid Brezhnev, "Report on the Work of the KGB in 1981," May 10, 1982, http://nsarchive.gwu.edu/NSAEBB/NSAEBB426/

50. "Report on the Work of the KGB in 1982," March 15, 1983, http://nsarchive.gwu.edu/NSAEBB/NSAEBB426/. Recently, Benjamin Fischer has introduced an additional potential source of East German fear: CANOPY WING, purportedly a U.S. military research project to exploit a vulnerability of Soviet Warsaw Pact command and control communications to launch a "decapitation/surgical" strike. Benjamin Fischer, "CANOPY WING: The U.S. War Plan That Gave the East Germans Goose Bumps," *International Journal of Intelligence and Counterintelligence*, 27:3, 431–464.

51. "Deputy Minister Markus Wolf, Stasi Note on Meeting with KGB Experts on the RYAN Problem, 14 to 18 August 1984," http://digitalarchive.wilsoncenter.org/document/115721. It is possible that this new coordinating division was created as a reaction to the false alerts generated by Operation RYaN in response to Able Archer 83.

52. Months earlier, *WarGames*, a film about a boy who inadvertently hacks into and engages a U.S. military computer programmed to win a nuclear war, was released. President Reagan watched the movie and subsequently discussed it with members of Congress. Scott Brown, "WarGames: A Look Back at the Film That Turned Geeks and Phreaks into Stars," *Wired*, July 21, 2008. For more information on the RYaN computer system, see Nate Jones, "The Vicious Circle of Intelligence," for the Cold War International History Project, November 13, 2014, https://www.wilsoncenter.org/publication/forecasting-nuclear-war#nate and Sean Gallagher, "WarGames for Real: How One 1983 Exercise Nearly Triggered WWIII," *Ars Technica*, November 25, 2015, http://arstechnica.com/information-technology/2015/11/wargames-for-real-how-one-1983-exercise-nearly-triggered-wwiii/.

53. The President's Foreign Intelligence Advisory Board, "The Soviet 'War Scare,'" February 15, 1990, Top Secret UMBRA GAMMA WNINTEL NOFORN NOCOTRACT ORCON.

54. The President's Foreign Intelligence Advisory Board, "The Soviet 'War Scare,'" February 15, 1990, Top Secret UMBRA GAMMA WNINTEL NOFORN NOCOTRACT ORCON.

55. "Deputy Minister Markus Wolf, Stasi Note on Meeting with KGB Experts on the RYAN Problem, 14 to 18 August 1984," http://digitalarchive.wilsoncenter.org/document/115721.

56. "Ministry of State Security (Stasi), About the Talks with Comrade V. A. Kryuchkov," http://digitalarchive.wilsoncenter.org/document/119320.

57. "Ministry of State Security (Stasi), Report on Development and Achieved State of Work Regarding Early Recognition of Adversarial Attack and Surprise Intentions (Complex RYAN)," http://digitalarchive.wilsoncenter.org/document/119334.

58. "Ministry of State Security (Stasi), Report, Indicators to Recognize Adversarial Preparations for a Surprise Nuclear Missile Attack," http://digitalarchive.wilsoncenter.org/document 119338. A partially declassified CIA document shows that Operation RYaN had an analogue in U.S. intelligence gathering. The CIA was also working with the DIA, and presumably allied intelligence agencies, to create a list of indicators—including the defense industry—for its chiefs of station to monitor, in an attempt to "emphasize greater early warning cooperation with intelligence services." Other parallels to RYaN date back to 1961, when the Soviets also instructed embassies in all "capitalist" countries to collect and report information during the Berlin Crisis. In 1991, one might have deduced the January 16 Desert Storm campaign by monitoring the influx of pizza deliveries to the Pentagon, according to current U.S. Army Operational Security (OPSEC) training materials. In October 1983, justifying the KGB's difficulties, Kryuchkov stated, "Even in the United States they have not completed this [a RYaN equivalent] yet." "The 1983 War Scare, Part One," http://www2.gwu.edu/~nsarchiv/NSAEBB/NSAEBB426/.

59. "Report, Ministry of State Security (Stasi), About Results of Intelligence Activities to Note Indicators for a Surprise Nuclear Missile Attack," http://digitalarchive.wilsoncenter.org/document/119909. For more on continuity of government, see James Mann, "The Armageddon Plan," *The Atlantic*, March 2004.

60. Descriptions of a still-classified report by the British Joint Intelligence Council and the U.S. President's Foreign Intelligence Advisory Board have confirmed Gordievsky's accounts. See "The 1983 War Scare, Part Three," http://www2.gwu.edu/~nsarchiv/NSAEBB/NSAEBB428/, and "British Documents Confirm UK Alerted U.S. to Danger of Able Archer 83," https://nsarchive.wordpress.com/2013/11/04/british-documents-confirm-uk-alerted-us-to-danger-of-able-archer-83.

61. Ronald Reagan, The President's News Conference, Room 450 of the Old Executive Office Building, Washington, D.C., January 29, 1981, available at the Ronald Reagan Presidential Library's online Public Papers of President Ronald W. Reagan.

62. Raymond Garthoff, *The Great Transition: American-Soviet Relations and the End of the Cold War* (Washington, D.C.: The Brookings Institution, 1994), 56–57.

63. Ronald Reagan, Address to Members of the British Parliament, Royal Gallery at the Palace of Westminster, London, June 8, 1982, available at the Ronald Reagan Presidential Library's online Public Papers of President Ronald W. Reagan.

64. Ronald Reagan, State of the Union Address to Joint Session of Congress, Washington, D.C., January 25, 1983, available at the Ronald Reagan Presidential Library's online Public Papers of President Ronald W. Reagan.

65. Ronald Reagan, Interview with the President, December 23, 1981, available at the Ronald Reagan Presidential Library's online Public Papers of President Ronald W. Reagan.

66. Anatoly Dobrynin, *In Confidence: Moscow's Ambassador to Six Cold War Presidents* (Seattle: University of Washington Press, 2001), 526.

67. Roy Guttman, "Bad Tidings: The World According to Haig," *Newsday*, August 12, 1984, 18.

68. Raymond Garthoff, *The Great Transition: American-Soviet Relations and the End of the Cold War* (Washington, D.C.: The Brookings Institution, 1994), 85.

69. Ronald Reagan, Remarks at the Annual Convention of the National Association of Evangelicals in Orlando, Florida, March 8, 1983, available at the Ronald Reagan Presidential Library's online Public Papers of President Ronald W. Reagan.

70. Only 28 percent of Americans polled stated they believed the Reagan administration's defense policies had brought the United States "closer to peace." In a separate question, 40 percent of Americans felt it "very likely" or "fairly likely" that the United States would "get into a nuclear war within the next ten years." George Gallup Jr., *The 1983 Gallup Poll* (New York: SR Books, 1984), 265–266.

71. For a possible Soviet analogue, see Gorbachev advisor Aleksandr Yakovlev's account of their "walk that changed the world" at a Canadian farm. "Shaping Russia's Transformation: A Leader of Perestroika Looks Back—Interview with Aleksandr Yakovlev," Institute of International Studies at the University of California, Berkeley. November 21, 1996, http://conversations.berkeley.edu/content/alexander-yakovlev.

72. Don Oberdorfer, *The Turn: From the Cold War to a New Era: The United States and the Soviet Union 1983–1990* (New York: Touchstone, 1991), 16.

73. The Soviet diplomat responded: "'let me put it bluntly. We regard the huge rearmament program in the United States now under way amidst political tension between the two countries as a real threat to our country's security. Do the American people want a war? The answer seems clear to us: it does not, no more than any other people. As for us, every family in the Soviet Union knows what a war is like and what disasters it can bring to us all. We proceed from the belief that the American president clearly realizes that.'" Anatoly Dobrynin, *In Confidence: Moscow's Ambassador to Six Cold War Presidents* (Seattle: University of Washington Press, 2001), 518.

74. Ronald Reagan, Diary, April 6, 1983.

75. *American Cryptology During the Cold War, 1945–1989, Book IV: Cryptologic Rebirth, 1981–1989,* Thomas Johnson, National Security Agency Center for Cryptologic History, 1999, Top Secret-COMINT-UMBRA/TALENT KEYHOLE/X1.

76. Ronald Reagan, *An American Life* (New York: Simon & Schuster, 1990), 267.

77. Anatoly Dobrynin, *In Confidence: Moscow's Ambassador to Six Cold War Presidents* (Seattle: University of Washington Press, 2001), 482.

78. Speech by Yuri Andropov to Political Consultative Committee in Prague, January 4, 1983. From VA-01/40473, Bundesarchiv-Militärarchiv, Freiburg; translated by Svetlana Savranskaya for the National Security Archive.

79. KGB to London Residency, February 17, 1983, No. 373/PR/52 in Christopher Andrew and Oleg Gordievsky, *Comrade Kryuchkov's Instructions: Top Secret Files on KGB Foreign Operations, 1975–1985* (Stanford: Stanford University Press, 1993), 69.

80. Interestingly, reliance on human intelligence to detect a first strike was a strategy not exclusively employed by the Soviets. A February 1, 1985, CIA memo from the U.S. National Intelligence Officer for Warning to the U.S. Director of Soviet Analysis entitled "Warsaw Pact Early Warning Indicator Project" indicates that the United States also used human intelligence to warn of a Soviet nuclear attack. The memo stated, "NIO/Warning has prepared a selected set of indicators for use by our Chiefs of Station in [redacted] to emphasize greater early warning cooperation with intelligence services." The attached fifty-page list of indicators has been redacted. February 1, 1985, "Warsaw Pact Early Warning Indicator Project," CIA Memorandum, in CIA Records Search Tool, National Archives and Records Administration NARA, College Park, MD; February 17, 1983, KGB to London Residency, No. 373/PR/52 in Christopher Andrew and Oleg Gordievsky, *Comrade Kryuchkov's Instructions: Top Secret Files on KGB Foreign Operations, 1975–1985* (Stanford: Stanford University Press, 1993), 71–73.

81. Regrettably, *Comrade Kryuchkov's Instructions* includes a facsimile reproduction of only the first page of this document. The additional pages were translated and typeset into English with no Russian corroboration of their authenticity.

82. Oleg Kalugin, *The First Directorate: My 32 Years in Intelligence and Espionage Against the West* (New York: St. Martins, 1994), 302.

83. Gordievsky describes Soviet leadership in 1983 as "self-isolated, self-indoctrinated," and "under the influence of their own propaganda." House Military Research and Development Subcommittee of the Committee on Armed Services, *Russian Threat Perceptions and Plans for Sabotage Against the United States*, 106th Cong., 1st sess., 1999, 13; Anatoly Dobrynin, *In Confidence: Moscow's Ambassador to Six Cold War Presidents* (Seattle: University of Washington Press, 2001), 522.

84. Memorandum for Deputy Director of Intelligence from Deputy Director of Central Intelligence, Subject: Secretary Shultz's Comments Regarding His Meeting with Yuri Andropov, November 19, 1982, Secret, https://nsarchive.files.wordpress.com/2013/05/shultz-andropov.pdf.

85. Central Intelligence Agency, "Yuriy Vladimirovich ANDROPOV," undated.

86. He was not present at September 2, 1983, October 20, 1983, or November 15, 1983, meetings of the Politburo. At the time, there was a rumor circulating through Moscow that there had been an assassination attempt on his life. *The Dead Hand: The Untold Story of the Cold War Arms Race and Its Dangerous Legacy* (New York: Doubleday, 2010), 62; August 4, 1983, Zasedanie politbyuro TsK KPSS (Meeting of the Politburo of the Central Committee of the Communist Party of the Soviet Union); September 2, 1983, Zasedanie politbyuro TsK KPSS; October 20, 1983, Zasedanie politbyuro TsK KPSS, in Library of Congress, Manuscript Division, Dmitrii Antonovich Volkogonov Papers, Container 26, Reel 17; *Whither the Soviet Leadership*, December 12, 1983, National Intelligence Council Report, in CIA Records Search Tool, National Archives and Records Administration NARA, College Park, MD.

87. Robert McFarlane interview conducted by author, April 22, 2009.

88. Christopher Andrew and Oleg Gordievsky, *Comrade Kryuchkov's Instructions: Top Secret Files on KGB Foreign Operations, 1975–1985* (Stanford: Stanford University Press, 1993), 67; Raymond Garthoff, *The Great Transition: American-Soviet Relations and the End of the Cold War* (Washington, D.C.: The Brookings Institution, 1994), 90.

89. *Whither the Soviet Leadership*, December 12, 1983, National Intelligence Council Report, in CIA Records Search Tool, National Archives and Records Administration NARA, College Park, MD.

90. See George G. Weickhardt, "Ustinov Versus Ogarkov," *Problems of Communism* (Jan–Feb 1985), 77–82.

91. See George G. Weickhardt, "Ustinov Versus Ogarkov," *Problems of Communism* (Jan–Feb 1985), 80.

92. Markus Wolf and Anne McElvoy, *Man Without a Face: The Autobiography of Communism's Greatest Spymaster* (New York: Times Books, 1999), 222; Central Intelligence Agency Intelligence Monograph by Benjamin Fischer, "A Cold War Conundrum: The 1983 Soviet War Scare," September 1997, Unclassified.

93. Karl Koecher in *Novosti razvedki i kontrrazvedki* (News of intelligence agents and counter agents), September 1, 2006.

94. Bulgarian Ministry of Interior; "MVR Information re: Results from the work on the improvement of the System for detection of RYAN indications," March 9, 1984, AMVR, Fond 1, Record 12, File 553, Provided by Jordan Baev.

95. Peter Rendek, "Operation ALAN—Mutual Cooperation of the Czechoslovak Intelligence Service and the Soviet KGB as Given in One of the Largest Leakage Cases of NATO Security Data in the Years 1982–1986," Presented at The NKVD/KGB Activities and Its Cooperation with Other Secret Services in Central and Eastern Europe 1945–1989 Conference, Bratislava, November 14–16, 2007.

96. Markus Wolf and Anne McElvoy, *Man Without a Face: The Autobiography of Communism's Greatest Spymaster* (New York: Times Books, 1999), 299.

97. Christopher Andrew and Oleg Gordievsky, *Comrade Kryuchkov's Instructions: Top Secret Files on KGB Foreign Operations, 1975–1985* (Stanford: Stanford University Press, 1993), 69.

98. We now have access to both the American and Soviet notes of this conversation. Ambassador Harriman's notes summarize the meeting, and Harriman adds his own observations and opinions, which were no doubt read by the U.S. State Department. The Soviet notes are a more thorough verbatim transcript of the conversation, with no analysis. They include, for example, Andropov's admonition to Harriman that the current nuclear armament policies of the United States and Soviet Union "only lead to exacerbation of the difficulties and dangers. There are no productive results from it. In the final analysis, [our actions] will lose both our countries. And they [the U.S. and USSR] are not alone. After all, it is clear that every year lost to reach agreement—large or small—on arms limitation, poses new challenges, and complicates the task of curbing the arms race." Averell Harriman, "Memorandum of Conversation with Andropov," June 2, 1983, W. Averell Harriman Papers, Library of Congress, Manuscript Division, Box 655; Soviet notes of a meeting between General Secretary Yuri Andropov and Averell and Pamela Harriman, June 2, 1983, RGANI [Russian State Archive of Contemporary History], F 82, OP 1, D 36, R 27-55, LL 33-44.

99. Although he certainly did not say so to Andropov, Harriman agreed. While being briefed by Shultz before his meeting with the general secretary, Harriman concluded his preparatory meeting with the secretary of state by criticizing the president's confrontational rhetoric, opining: "I do wish the President could be more careful." Notes of a Conversation with Secretary of State George Shultz, Undersecretary of State Lawrence Eagleburger, and Averell Harriman, Undated (prior to Harriman's trip to the Soviet Union) (circa May 1983), http://nsarchive.gwu.edu/NSAEBB/NSAEBB426/.

100. Averell Harriman, Memorandum of Conversation with Andropov, June 2, 1983, W. Averell Harriman Papers, Library of Congress, Manuscript Division, Box 655.

101. Averell Harriman, Memorandum of Conversation with Andropov, June 2, 1983, W. Averell Harriman Papers, Library of Congress, Manuscript Division, Box 655.

102. Letter from John N. McMahon to Robert McFarlane, February 3, 1984, "Andropov's Leadership Style and Strategy," in CIA Records Search Tool, National Archives and Records Administration NARA, College Park, MD.

103. *1983: The View from Moscow*, November 1983, Ronald Reagan Presidential Library, Fortier Files, Soviet Project [1 of 2], Box 97063.

104. No answer from Hartman to Reagan's question has been found. "Ronald Reagan's talking points for Conversation with Soviet Ambassador Hartman," Ronald Reagan Presidential Library, Matlock Files, Chron March 1984, Box 5.

105. A declassified National Security Agency history reveals that the Reagan administration misrepresented some of the facts about the shootdown in its eagerness to "pounce on [it] and squeeze[] it dry of propaganda value." The NSA history confirms that there was an EC-Cobra Ball aircraft in the near vicinity and on a parallel route to KAL 007 monitoring the pending test launch of a Soviet SSX-24 missile, which the Soviets confused the civilian airliner for. The Reagan administration did not reveal the EC-Cobra's existence and proximity. According to the NSA's history, "No question" Soviet ground controllers thought they were tracking a second U.S. reconnaissance aircraft. "Given the paranoia that had existed since April [the U.S. had flown practice bombing runs that had penetrated deeply into Soviet territory], it was unthinkable that such a penetration could be permitted without action." After the April penetrations, Andropov issued a "shoot-to-kill order." According to the NSA history, the Soviet radar operators and pilot that shot down KAL 007 mistakenly believed it to be a reconnaissance aircraft. "It was the Reagan people who insisted that the Soviets could not have mistaken a 747 for a 707. That was their value

judgment. It was wrong, but not so wide of the mark that one can impute anything more sinister than righteous wrath. It was the height of the Second Cold War." *American Cryptology During the Cold War, 1945–1989, Book IV: Cryptologic Rebirth, 1981–1989*, Thomas Johnson, National Security Agency Center for Cryptologic History, 1999, Top Secret COMINT UMBRA / TALENT KEYHOLE / X1.

106. Ronald Reagan, Remarks to Reporters on the Soviet Attack on a Korean Civilian Airliner, Point Mugu Naval Air Station, California, September 2, 1983; Ronald Reagan, Address to the Nation on the Soviet Attack on a Korean Civilian Airliner, Oval Office, White House, September 5, 1983, available at the Ronald Reagan Presidential Library's online Public Papers of President Ronald W. Reagan.

Part II: "Thoroughly White Hot," Able Archer 83, and the Crux of the War Scare

1. Gordievsky's account incorrectly identifies the date that Able Archer began as November 2, 1983, rather than November 7, 1983, as reported by the U.S. Air Force after-action reports. Other recent research has asserted Able Archer 83 began on November 4, 1983, but this is also incorrect. Gregory Pedlow, chief historian of the SHAPE historical division, confirms that the dates in the declassified U.S. Air Force documents are correct and that Able Archer 83 began on November 7, 1983. There was however, "a written scenario (not part of the actual exercise) which began on 4 November with Orange's [the Warsaw Pact's] use of chemical weapons." According to the Congressional Budget Office, Able Archer 83 cost the United States $111 million. Eighth Air Force Strategic Air Command, *History of the Headquarters, 7th Air Division: 1 October 1983–31 March 1984. Secret.*; House Committee on Appropriations, *Department of Defense Appropriations for 1986*, 99th Cong., 1st sess., 1985, part 3, 562; "Exercise Able Archer 83: Information from SHAPE Historical Files," March 28, 2013; "Exercise Scenario," Undated, NATO Unclassified; Air Force Seventh Air Division, Ramstein Air Base, "Exercise Able Archer 83, SAC ADVON, After Action Report," December 1, 1983, Secret NOFORN.

2. Tom Kuhn, "Moving the Forces of War," *Airman* (March 1984); Eighth Air Force Strategic Air Command, *History of the Headquarters, 7th Air Division: 1 October 1983–31 March 1984.*

3. Some form of Able Archer exercise was conducted annually by NATO from 1975 until 1991.

4. These exercises included Able Archer, Reforger, Crested Cap, Northern Wedding, Brave Guy, Bold Guard, Cold Fire, Display Determination, Apex Express, Atlantic Lion, and Quantum Jump. For more information about Autumn Forge 83 and the exercises it included, see the online Able Archer 83 Sourcebook http://nsarchive.gwu.edu/nukevault/ablearcher/, especially "The 1983 War Scare Part One." An alert viewer may note that the 2015 AMC Sundance/RTL television show "Deutschland 83," which portrayed the 1983 War Scare in East and West Germany, used the names of Autumn Forge exercises as the titles for its episodes.

5. The Soviet Union also routinely conducted large-scale military exercises, including a June 1982 "seven hour simulation" of nuclear war. Ostensibly, the June 1982 exercise was less realistic than Able Archer 83. Vojtech Mastny, "How Able Was 'Able Archer'?: Nuclear Trigger and Intelligence in Perspective," *Journal of Cold War Studies*, Vol 11 No 1 2009, 115; Eighth Air Force Strategic Air Command, *History of the Headquarters, 7th Air Division: 1 October 1983–31 March 1984.*

6. Eighth Air Force Strategic Air Command, *History of the Headquarters, 7th Air Division: 1 October 1983–31 March 1984.*

7. "Exercise Able Archer 83: Information from SHAPE Historical Files," March 28, 2013; "Exercise Scenario," Undated, NATO Unclassified.

8. Air Force Seventh Air Division, Ramstein Air Base, "Exercise Able Archer 83, SAC ADVON, After Action Report," December 1, 1983, Secret NOFORN; "Exercise Able Archer 83: Information from SHAPE Historical Files," March 28, 2013; "Exercise Scenario," Undated, NATO Unclassified; The President's Foreign Intelligence Advisory Board, "The Soviet 'War Scare,'" February 15, 1990, Top Secret UMBRA GAMMA WNINTEL NOFORN NOCOTRACT ORCON. While the intent of Able Archer 83 could have possibly been misinterpreted, it was clearly an exercise. The warheads were not functional and the move through DEFCON levels was simulated, not actual.

9. Christopher Andrew and Oleg Gordievsky, *Comrade Kryuchkov's Instructions: Top Secret Files on KGB Foreign Operations, 1975–1985* (Stanford: Stanford University Press, 1993), 86.

10. *American Cryptology During the Cold War, 1945–1989, Book IV: Cryptologic Rebirth, 1981–1989,* Thomas Johnson, National Security Agency Center for Cryptologic History, 1999, Top Secret-COMINT-UMBRA/TALENT KEYHOLE/X1.

11. Central Intelligence Agency Intelligence Monograph by Benjamin Fischer, "A Cold War Conundrum: The 1983 Soviet War Scare," September 1997, Unclassified.

12. Quoted in Benjamin Fischer, "The 1983 War Scare in U.S.-Soviet Relations," *Studies in Intelligence,* Undated (circa 1996), Secret.

13. Central Intelligence Agency Intelligence Monograph by Benjamin Fischer, "A Cold War Conundrum: The 1983 Soviet War Scare," September 1997, Unclassified. The Lesser Kuril Ridge, which includes Zeleny, was also claimed by Japan.

14. Central Intelligence Agency Intelligence Monograph by Benjamin Fischer, "A Cold War Conundrum: The 1983 Soviet War Scare," September 1997, Unclassified.

15. *American Cryptology During the Cold War, 1945–1989, Book IV: Cryptologic Rebirth, 1981–1989,* Thomas Johnson, National Security Agency Center for Cryptologic History, 1999, Top Secret-COMINT-UMBRA/TALENT KEYHOLE/X1.

16. *American Cryptology During the Cold War, 1945–1989, Book IV: Cryptologic Rebirth, 1981–1989,* Thomas Johnson, National Security Agency Center for Cryptologic History, 1999, Top Secret-COMINT-UMBRA/TALENT KEYHOLE/X1; Benjamin Fischer, "The 1983 War Scare in U.S.-Soviet Relations," *Studies in Intelligence,* Undated (circa 1996), Secret.

17. Benjamin Fischer, "The 1983 War Scare in U.S.-Soviet Relations," *Studies in Intelligence,* Undated (circa 1996), Secret.

18. Benjamin Fischer, "The 1983 War Scare in U.S.-Soviet Relations," *Studies in Intelligence,* Undated (circa 1996), Secret.

19. Peter Schweizer, *Victory: The Reagan Administration's Secret Strategy That Hastened the Collapse of the Soviet Union* (New York: The Atlantic Monthly Press, 1994), 8; Central Intelligence Agency Intelligence Monograph by Benjamin Fischer, "A Cold War Conundrum: The 1983 Soviet War Scare," September 1997, Unclassified.

20. For the best accounts see David Hoffman, *The Dead Hand: The Untold Story of the Cold War Arms Race and Its Dangerous Legacy* (New York: Doubleday, 2010), 6–10 and *The Man Who Saved the World,* a documentary featuring Stanislav Petrov, by Peter Anthony, 2014.

21. The fullest explanation of Soviet command and control remains Bruce G. Blair, *The Logic of Accidental Nuclear War* (Washington, D.C.: Brookings, 1993), especially 70–72.

22. David Hoffman, *The Dead Hand: The Untold Story of the Cold War Arms Race and Its Dangerous Legacy* (New York: Doubleday, 2010), 6–10. Geoffrey Forden, Pavel Podvig, and Theodore Postol, "False Alarm, Nuclear Danger," *IEEE Spectrum,* March 2000, Vol. 37, No. 3.

23. Peter Vincent Pry, *War Scare: Russia on the Nuclear Brink* (Westport: Praeger, 1999), 37. Early Warning failures did not occur only to the Soviet Union. On November 9, 1979, U.S. national security advisor Zbigniew Brzezinski was the victim of one terrifying example, which he recounted to his aide, Robert Gates, who later served as director of Central Intelligence and secretary of defense. According to Gates, Brzezinski "was awakened at three in the morning by [military assistant William] Odom, who told him that some 250 Soviet missiles had been launched against the United States. Brzezinski knew that the President's decision time to order retaliation was from three to seven minutes. . . . Thus he told Odom he would stand by for a further call to confirm Soviet launch and the intended targets before calling the President. Brzezinski was convinced we had to hit back and told Odom to confirm that the Strategic Air Command was launching its planes. When Odom called back, he reported that . . . 2,200 missiles had been launched—it was an all-out attack. One minute before Brzezinski intended to call the President, Odom called a third time to say that other warning systems were not reporting Soviet launches. Sitting alone in the middle of the night, Brzezinski had not awakened his wife, reckoning that everyone would be dead in half an hour. It had been a false alarm. Someone had mistakenly put military exercise tapes into the computer system." In 1980 alone, U.S. warning systems generated three more false alerts. Robert Gates, *From the Shadows: The Ultimate Insider's Story of Five Presidents and How They Won the Cold War* (New York: Simon & Schuster, 1996), 114.

24. Benjamin Fischer, "CANOPY WING: The U.S. War Plan That Gave the East Germans Goose Bumps," *International Journal of Intelligence and CounterIntelligence*, Vol. 27 no. 3, 431–464. Further research is needed to determine whether the East Germans knew about the capabilities of Canopy Wing during the War Scare, or if knowledge of this program was not acquired until after.

25. Soviet notes of a meeting between General Secretary Yuri Andropov and Mayor of West Berlin Hans-Jochen Vogel, January 11, 1983, RGANI [Russian State Archive of Contemporary History] F 82, OP 1, D 37, R 27-55, LL 37.

26. "Autumn Forge 83—COMALF [Commander Airlift Forces] Briefing," September 9, 1983, from *History of the 322nd Airlift Division, January 1982–December 1983*, Volume VII Supporting Documents, Prepared by Edgar Sneed, Division Historian, Unclassified; U.S. Air Force Military Airlift Command, "Reforger 83\Crested Cap 83\Display Determination 83\Autumn Forge 83 After Act Report," December 8, 1983, from *History of Military Airlift Command: 1 January–31 December 1983: Supporting Documents Volume IX*, Confidential.

27. U.S. Air Force Military Airlift Command, "Reforger 83\Crested Cap 83\Display Determination 83\Autumn Forge 83 After Act Report," December 8, 1983, from *History of Military Airlift Command: 1 January–31 December 1983: Supporting Documents Volume IX*, Confidential.

28. Air Force Seventh Air Division, Ramstein Air Base, "Exercise Able Archer 83, SAC ADVON, After Action Report," December 1, 1983, Secret NOFORN.

29. "Exercise Able Archer 83: Information from SHAPE Historical Files," March 28, 2013; "Exercise Scenario," Undated; Air Force Seventh Air Division, Ramstein Air Base, "Exercise Able Archer 83, SAC ADVON, After Action Report," December 1, 1983, Secret NOFORN.

30. These were military operation plans (OPLANs) 10604, FANCY GIRL and 10605, GOLDEN EAGLE.

31. Air Force Seventh Air Division, Ramstein Air Base, "Exercise Able Archer 83, SAC ADVON, After Action Report," December 1, 1983, Secret NOFORN.

32. Air Force Seventh Air Division, Ramstein Air Base, "Exercise Able Archer 83, SAC ADVON, After Action Report," December 1, 1983, Secret NOFORN; British Ministry of Defence, "Soviet Union: Concern About a Surprise NATO Attack," May 8, 1984, Top Secret, UMBRA GAMMA, US/UK Eyes Only.

33. *American Cryptology During the Cold War, 1945–1989, Book IV: Cryptologic Rebirth, 1981–1989*, Thomas Johnson, National Security Agency Center for Cryptologic History, 1999, Top Secret-COMINT-UMBRA / TALENT KEYHOLE / X1; Central Intelligence Agency Intelligence Monograph by Benjamin Fischer, "A Cold War Conundrum: The 1983 Soviet War Scare," September 1997, Unclassified.

34. "Exercise Able Archer 83: Information from SHAPE Historical Files," March 28, 2013, NATO Unclassified.

35. "Exercise Able Archer 83: Information from SHAPE Historical Files," March 28, 2013, NATO Unclassified. For the likely genesis of these claims see unpublished interview with former national security advisor Robert McFarlane, undated but in 1989 or 1990, Mudd Manuscript Library, Princeton University.

36. Joint Chiefs of Staff, "Subject: Exercise ABLE ARCHER 83," December 2, 1984, Secret.

37. Joint Chiefs of Staff, "Subject: Exercise ABLE ARCHER 83," December 2, 1984, Secret.

38. The President's Foreign Intelligence Advisory Board, "The Soviet 'War Scare,'" February 15, 1990, Secret UMBRA GAMMA WNINTEL NOFORN NOCOTRACT ORCON.

39. A. Sidorenko, *The Offensive (A Soviet View)* (Washington, D.C.: U.S. Government Printing Office, 1970), 115. The United States also feared that exercises could be used as "ruses of war."

40. Unpublished interview with former secretary of defense Caspar Weinberger, 1989, Princeton University, Mudd Manuscript Library.

41. Unpublished interview with former secretary of defense Caspar Weinberger, 1989, Princeton University, Mudd Manuscript Library.

42. Christopher Andrew and Oleg Gordievsky, *Comrade Kryuchkov's Instructions: Top Secret Files on KGB Foreign Operations, 1975–1985* (Stanford: Stanford University Press, 1993), 86–87.

43. Nate Jones, "The Vicious Circle of Intelligence," for Forecasting Nuclear War: Stasi / KGB Intelligence Cooperation under Project RYaN, edited by Bernd Schaefer for the Nuclear Proliferation International History Project, Wilson Center, November, 2014.

44. "Ministry of State Security (Stasi), 'About the Talks with Comrade V. A. Kryuchkov,'" November 7, 1983, History and Public Policy Program Digital Archive, BStU, MfS, Abt. X, Nr. 2020, S. 1-7. Translated by Bernd Schaefer.

45. Christopher Andrew and Oleg Gordievsky, *Comrade Kryuchkov's Instructions: Top Secret Files on KGB Foreign Operations, 1975–1985* (Stanford: Stanford University Press, 1993), 86–87. Regrettably, no text of the November 8 or 9 flash telegram has been released or reproduced. Gordievsky's revelation of this warning is the only basis for the current historical record (though the preceding and following telegrams which he reproduced and published do serve as somewhat sturdy bona fides).

46. Christopher Andrew and Oleg Gordievsky, *Comrade Kryuchkov's Instructions: Top Secret Files on KGB Foreign Operations, 1975–1985* (Stanford: Stanford University Press, 1993), 86–87.

47. Air Force Seventh Air Division, Ramstein Air Base, "Exercise Able Archer 83, SAC ADVON, After Action Report," December 1, 1983, Secret NOFORN; The President's Foreign Intelligence Advisory Board, "The Soviet 'War Scare,'" February 15, 1990, Secret UMBRA GAMMA WNINTEL NOFORN NOCOTRACT ORCON.

48. The President's Foreign Intelligence Advisory Board, "The Soviet 'War Scare,'" February 15, 1990, Secret UMBRA GAMMA WNINTEL NOFORN NOCOTRACT ORCON.

49. Program for ACE Officer's Nuclear Weapons Release Procedures Course I-34-39,

October 17–21, 1983, The NATO School, Oberammergau Germany. In author's possession.

50. Author's correspondence.

51. Author's correspondence with Master Sergeant Tod Jennings, retired, who served as an Air Force staff sergeant during Able Archer 83.

52. David Hoffman, *The Dead Hand: The Untold Story of the Cold War Arms Race and Its Dangerous Legacy* (New York: Doubleday, 2010), 92; Don Oberdorfer, *The Turn: From the Cold War to a New Era: The United States and the Soviet Union 1983–1990* (New York: Touchstone, 1991), 65. Of the estimated 50,000 targets in the SIOP, some 25,000 were military targets, 15,000 were industrial or economic targets, and 5,000 targets were associated with the Soviet leadership. William Burr of the National Security Archive has analyzed the groundbreaking declassification of the Strategic Air Command Weapons Requirements Study for 1959 which officially confirms that U.S. nuclear targets included population centers such as Moscow, Leningrad, Beijing, East Berlin, and Warsaw. While the SIOP-6 nuclear attack plan primarily relied on missiles, rather than bombers, no doubt the majority of the 23,000 specific cities and sites that were recently declassified remained targets. The targets can be viewed at http://nsarchive.gwu.edu/nukevault/ebb538-Cold-War-Nuclear-Target-List-Declassified-First-Ever/.

53. Ronald Reagan, *An American Life* (New York: Simon & Schuster, 1990), 586.

54. Ronald Reagan, Diary, November 18, 1983.

55. Christopher Andrew and Oleg Gordievsky, *KGB: The Inside Story of Its Foreign Operations from Lenin to Gorbachev, 1975–1985* (New York: Harper Collins, 1991), 605.

56. Benjamin Fischer, "The 1983 War Scare in U.S.-Soviet Relations," *Studies in Intelligence*, Undated (circa 1996), Secret.

57. Rainer Rupp interview conducted for "Soviet War Scare 1983." Director Henry Chancellor; Exec Producer Taylor Downing; quoted with permission of Flashback Television, London, 2008. "Rainer Rupp About 'Able Archer,' His Work in NATO Headquarters, the Syrian War and the Conflict with Russia," by Karlen Vesper, *Workers World*, September 19, 2015.

58. Vojtech Mastny "Did East German Spies Prevent a Nuclear War?" for The Parallel History Project.

59. Mark Kramer, "The Able Archer 83 Non-Crisis: Did Soviet Leaders Really Fear an Imminent Nuclear Attack in 1983?" presented at The USA and the Soviet Union: Transformations of a Global Competition, 1975–1989, Eberhard Karls University, Tübingen, September 13, 2013. Also in German, "Die Nicht-Krise um Able Archer 1983: Fürchtete die sowjetische Führung tatsächlich einen atomaren Grossangriff im Herbst 1983?" in: Oliver Bange und Bernd Lemke (Hrsg). Wege zur Wiedervereinigung (München: Oldenbourg, September 2013).

60. The minutes of these meetings can be found in a donation to the Library of Congress by Soviet general-turned-historian Dmitri Volkogonov, and in "Fond 89," a collection of documents "submitted to the Constitutional Court of the Russian Federation for the trial of the Soviet Communist Party" in 1992 and published by Stanford University's Hoover Institution. One must keep in mind, however, that historians do not yet have access to the minutes of every Politburo meeting from that period. (For that matter, a set of August 4, 1983, minutes cited in this work, but not in the "The Able Archer 83 Non-Crisis" paper, describes Andropov's instructions to use "all levers" to stop the deployment of Pershing II missiles in Europe.) Most importantly, there are no accessible minutes to the key discussions during Andropov's tenure as general secretary that occurred at his hospital bedside. Roy Medvedev, *Neizvestnii Andropov* (The unknown Andropov) (Rostov: Feniks, 1999), 379–382. The Politburo minutes cited in "The Able Archer 83 Non-Crisis" are: May 26, 1983; May 31, 1983; July 7, 1983; September 2, 1983;

September 8, 1983; November 15, 1983; November 24, 1983; January 19, 1984; February 10, 1984; February 23, 1984; and March 1, 1984. They can be viewed at the National Security Archive.

61. Roy A. Medvedev, *Neizvestnii Andropov* (The unknown Andropov) (Rostov: Feniks, 1999), 379–382.

62. Conversely, the U.S. military establishment often conflated Able Archer 83 with "Reforger 83," the name for the military lift operation at the end of "Autumn Forge 83" where the United States moved its troops to Europe to prepare for a conventional war. According to the declassified Military Airlift Command after-action report, 16,044 of the 19,000 troops deployed to Europe for Autumn Forge 83 (84 percent) were deployed during Reforger 83.

63. These Soviet statements of alarm contradict Vojtech Mastny's assertion that "no high-ranking Soviet official in a position to know, including such a key figure as the first deputy chief (and later chief) of the Soviet General Staff Marshal Sergei F. Akhrome[y]ev, has been found who remembers any alarm being raised because of the NATO exercise." Mikhail Gorbachev has also stated, "Never, perhaps, in the postwar decades was the situation in the world as explosive and hence, more difficult and unfavorable, as in the first half of the 1980s." Unpublished Sergei Akhromeyev interview conducted by Don Oberdorfer, 1990, Mudd Manuscript Library, Princeton University; Central Intelligence Agency Intelligence Monograph by Benjamin Fischer, "A Cold War Conundrum: The 1983 Soviet War Scare," September 1997, Unclassified; Vojtech Mastny, "How Able Was 'Able Archer'?: Nuclear Trigger and Intelligence in Perspective," *Journal of Cold War Studies*, Vol 11 No 1 2009, 119.

64. Interview with Viktor Tkachenko, for "Soviet War Scare 1983." Director Henry Chancellor; Exec Producer Taylor Downing; quoted with permission of Flashback Television, London, 2008.

65. Interview with Viktor Tkachenko, for "Soviet War Scare 1983." Director Henry Chancellor; Exec Producer Taylor Downing; quoted with permission of Flashback Television, London, 2008.

66. Interview with Victor Yesin, for "Soviet War Scare 1983." Director Henry Chancellor; Exec Producer Taylor Downing; quoted with permission of Flashback Television, London, 2008. Yesin, who was also stationed in Cuba during the 1962 Cuban Missile Crisis, recounted that, to him, while Able Archer 83 was a time of "heightened vigilance" for Soviet missiles, the "tension was not as high as during the . . . Cuban Missile Crisis."

67. The President's Foreign Intelligence Advisory Board, "The Soviet 'War Scare,'" February 15, 1990, Secret UMBRA GAMMA WNINTEL NOFORN NOCOTRACT ORCON.

68. The President's Foreign Intelligence Advisory Board, "The Soviet 'War Scare,'" February 15, 1990, Secret UMBRA GAMMA WNINTEL NOFORN NOCOTRACT ORCON.

69. Central Intelligence Agency, Special National Intelligence Estimate, "Implications of Recent Soviet Military-Political Activities" May 18, 1984, Top Secret.

70. During a January 2000 congressional testimony, the former CIA analyst Pry asserted Able Archer 83 was "more dangerous than the Cuban Missile Crisis"; Peter Vincent Pry, *War Scare: Russia on the Nuclear Brink* (Westport: Praeger, 1999), 44; House Committee on Government Reform, *Russian Threats to the United States Security in the Post-Cold War Era*, 106th Cong., 1st sess., 2000, 70.

71. *American Cryptology During the Cold War, 1945–1989, Book IV: Cryptologic Rebirth, 1981–1989*, Thomas Johnson, National Security Agency Center for Cryptologic History, 1999, Top Secret-COMINT-UMBRA / TALENT KEYHOLE / X1.

72. The President's Foreign Intelligence Advisory Board, "The Soviet 'War Scare," February 15, 1990, Secret UMBRA GAMMA WNINTEL NOFORN NOCOTRACT ORCON.

73. "The Great Vitality of the Ideas and Cause of October," November 6, 1983, *Pravda*.

Part III: Aftermath, "One Misstep Could Trigger a Great War"

1. U.S. Army Intelligence and Security Command, "Subject: INTSUM," November 10, 1983. But the military had missed many signals. It was not until two weeks after the completion of Able Archer 83 that analysts noted and reported fully armed MIG-23 aircraft on air defense alert in East Germany. The President's Foreign Intelligence Advisory Board, "The Soviet 'War Scare,'" February 15, 1990, Top Secret, UMBRA GAMMA WNINTEL NOFORN NOCONTRACT ORCON.

2. *Soviet Thinking on the Possibility of Armed Confrontation with the United States*, Ronald Reagan Presidential Library, Matlock Files, Chron January 1984 [2 of 3], Box 90887.

3. May 1984 Central Intelligence Agency Special National Intelligence Estimate, *Implications of Recent Soviet Military-Political Activities*, in CIA Records Search Tool, National Archives and Records Administration NARA, College Park, MD.

4. Two other Soviet reactions to Able Archer 83 remain redacted in the estimate.

5. Colonel L. V. Levadov, "Itogi operativnoi podgotovki obedinennix sil NATO v 1983 godu" (Results of the Operational Training of NATO Joint Armed Forces in 1983), *Voennaya Misl'* (Military Thought), no. 2 (February 1984), 68.

6. Averell Harriman, "Memorandum of Conversation with Andropov," June 2, 1983, W. Averell Harriman Papers, Library of Congress, Manuscript Division, Box 655.

7. Memorandum of Conversation between Sergei Vishenevsky and Jack F. Matlock, October 11, 1983, Ronald Reagan Presidential Library, Matlock Files, Chron October 1983 [10/11/1983–10/24/1983], Box 2, 90888.

8. Memorandum for Robert C. McFarlane from Jack Matlock, "American Academic on Soviet Policy," December 13, 1983, Ronald Reagan Presidential Library, Matlock Files, Chron December 1983 [1 of 2], Box 2, 90888.

9. Robert McFarlane interview conducted by author, April 22, 2009.

10. Beginning on January 17, 1984, Massie met with Reagan roughly twenty times, occasionally serving as his backchannel during her visits to the Soviet Union. At the president's first meeting with Gorbachev, he carried her book *Land of the Firebird: The Beauty of Old Russia*. James Mann, *The Rebellion of Ronald Reagan: A History of the End of the Cold War* (New York: Viking, 2009), 64.

11. James Mann, *The Rebellion of Ronald Reagan: A History of the End of the Cold War* (New York: Viking, 2009), 76.

12. Memo from Director of the Bureau of Intelligence and Research Hugh Montgomery to Secretary of State George Shultz, "Subject: SNIE 11-10-1984," May 28, 1984, Secret.

13. Despite the importance of the British role discovering and warning of the danger of Able Archer 83, Britain remains far behind the United States in the declassification of this history. Most importantly, the first comprehensive report about Able Archer 83, entitled "The Detection of Soviet Preparations for War Against NATO," remains withheld at the behest of the Cabinet Office. For more information about this report and Britain's reasons for its continued withholding, see Nate Jones, "Why the Key Able Archer 83 Report Should Be Released Under UK FOIA," November 18, 2015, https://nsarchive.wordpress.com/2015/11/18/why-the-key-able-archer-83-report-should-be-released-under-uk-foia/ and Richard Norton-Taylor, "Security Chiefs Block Release of Report on 1983 Soviet Nuclear Scare," *The Guardian*, December 7, 2015. UK Ministry of Defence, "Soviet Union: Concern About a Surprise Nuclear Attack," May 8, 1984, Top Secret, UMBRA GAMMA, US/UK Eyes Only.

14. UK Ministry of Defence, "Soviet Concern About a Surprise NATO Attack," May 4, 1984, Secret; 10 Downing Street Memo, "Soviet Concern About a Surprise NATO Attack," April 10, 1984, UK Top Secret.

15. Comments of Michael Herman presented to the 15th Berlin Colloquium on Contemporary History: 1983—The Most Dangerous Year of the Cold War? Convened by Bernd Greiner und Klaas Voß, May 23, 2014. In author's possession.

16. The President's Foreign Intelligence Advisory Board, "The Soviet 'War Scare,'" February 15, 1990, Top Secret, UMBRA GAMMA WNINTEL NOFORN NOCONTRACT ORCON.

17. The Department of State did not do a particularly good job sanitizing this information. The sanitized SNIE states that there are "three main sources of uncertainty" but lists only two sources, revealing to a careful reader that information had been removed. Department of State memo from Director of the Bureau of Intelligence and Research Hugh Montgomery to Secretary of State George Shultz, "Subject: SNIE 11-10-1984," May 28, 1984, Secret.

18. The CIA continues to maintain that this account is too secret to be read by the public, denying a declassification request in 2016. The President's Foreign Intelligence Advisory Board, "The Soviet 'War Scare,'" February 15, 1990, Top Secret, UMBRA GAMMA WNINTEL NOFORN NOCONTRACT ORCON.

19. The President's Foreign Intelligence Advisory Board, "The Soviet 'War Scare,'" February 15, 1990, Top Secret, UMBRA GAMMA WNINTEL NOFORN NOCONTRACT ORCON.

20. The President's Foreign Intelligence Advisory Board, "The Soviet 'War Scare,'" February 15, 1990, Top Secret, UMBRA GAMMA WNINTEL NOFORN NOCONTRACT ORCON.

21. The President's Foreign Intelligence Advisory Board, "The Soviet 'War Scare,'" February 15, 1990, Top Secret, UMBRA GAMMA WNINTEL NOFORN NOCONTRACT ORCON.

22. Before the declassification of the PFIAB report, Fritz Ermarth, a primary author of the May 1984 SNIE, wrote an essay defending the SNIE's findings. (Fritz Ermarth, "Observations on the War Scare of 1983 from an Intelligence Perch," for the Parallel History Project on NATO and the Warsaw Pact, November 6, 2003.) He wrote: "In the late 1980s, the President's Foreign Intelligence Advisory Board (PFIAB) directed a thorough, highly classified review of the case. It was conducted by a very able young lady named Nina Stewart. It was lengthy and concluded by indicting us, the authors of the SNIE, for being dangerously relaxed. I retorted that we were being indicted for being right, alas, not the first or last time this has happened in intelligence work. If it hasn't already been, her report should be declassified as much as possible. I'll stick by the conclusions of the SNIE. But the historical work done since then suggests Nina had a point, and it is worth pursuing further."

23. At the time that this report was delivered to President Bush, the PFIAB included James Q. Wilson, John S. Foster Jr., Bernard A. Schriever, Glenn Campbell, Gordon C. Luce, John Tower, and Chairperson Anne Armstrong. It has been reported that Nina J. Stewart was the primary author of this report. On February 15, she was the acting executive director of the board. Before her role on the PFIAB she served as the assistant secretary of state for diplomatic security. After resigning from the PFIAB, she served as the deputy assistant secretary of defense for counterintelligence.

24. The analysis of the War Scare presented in the PFIAB report now appears to be the orthodox version of events accepted by government and intelligence insiders. See, for example the description of Robert Gates, who was CIA deputy director for intelligence in 1983, in his memoir: "Information about the peculiar and remarkably skewed frame of mind of the Soviet leaders during those times that has emerged since the collapse of the Soviet Union makes me think there is a good chance—with all of the other events in

1983—that they really felt a NATO attack was at least possible and that they took a number of measures to enhance their military readiness short of mobilization." Robert Gates, *From the Shadows: The Ultimate Insider's Story of Five Presidents and How They Won the Cold War* (New York: Simon & Schuster, 2007), 273.

25. Don Oberdorfer, *The Turn: From the Cold War to a New Era: The United States and the Soviet Union 1983–1990* (New York: Touchstone, 1991), 479.

26. Ronald Reagan, Diary, October 10, 1983.

27. Robert McFarlane interview conducted by author, April, 22, 2009; Beth Fischer, *The Reagan Reversal: Foreign Policy and the End of the Cold War* (Columbia: University of Missouri Press, 2000), 134; Don Oberdorfer, *The Turn: From the Cold War to a New Era: The United States and the Soviet Union 1983–1990* (New York: Touchstone, 1991), 67; Gordon Brook-Shepherd, *The Storm Birds: The Dramatic Stories of the Top Soviet Spies Who Have Defected Since World War II* (London: Grove Press, 1989), 334.

28. George Shultz, *Turmoil and Triumph: My Years as Secretary of State* (New York: Charles Scribner's Sons, 1993), 464.

29. Ronald Reagan, *An American Life* (New York: Simon & Schuster, 1990), 257.

30. Matlock ably refutes the first two of these claims in Jack Matlock Jr., *Reagan and Gorbachev: How the Cold War Ended* (New York: Random House, 2004), 75–80. McFarlane believed that Reagan's engagement with the Soviet Union was due "more by our [American political] readiness than this episode [Able Archer 83]," but also that Able Archer 83 was "timely" and "contributed to his wanting to begin to establish the dialogue and the more active mode." Robert McFarlane interview conducted by author, April 22, 2009.

31. Robert McFarlane, as cited in Beth Fischer, *The Reagan Reversal: Foreign Policy and the End of the Cold War* (Columbia: University of Missouri Press, 2000), 106–107; Ronald Reagan, *An American Life* (New York: Simon & Schuster, 1990), 278, 549.

32. For an excellent article on the Nuclear Freeze Movement through the lens of presidential politics, read Henry Maar, "A Force to Be Reckoned With: The Antinuclear Revolution and the Reagan Administration, 1980–1984," http://www.gwu.edu/~ieresgwu/assets/docs/Maar_cwc.pdf. Thanks to Martin Deuerlein and Roman Krawielicki of the Universität Tübingen for organizing "Challenges, Concepts, Ideas During the Cold War of the 1970s and 1980s," where there was vigorous debate and discussion over the end of the Cold War and the impact that the War Scare, the Nuclear Freeze Movement, and other forces had upon it.

33. Ronald Reagan, *An American Life* (New York: Simon & Schuster, 1990), 586–587.

34. See Raymond Garthoff, *The Great Transition: American-Soviet Relations and the End of the Cold War* (Washington, D.C.: The Brookings Institution, 1994), 167.

35. Robert McFarlane interview conducted by author, April 22, 2009. Though the thrust of McFarlane's various accounts of the War Scare remains consistent and illuminating, it must be noted that there has been some variation in the details and specifics that he has presented.

36. An index and, when available, documents about these NSPG meetings are available at the Reagan Files, an invaluable resource curated by Jason Saltoun-Ebin. http://www.thereaganfiles.com/. The Papers of Secretary of State Shultz and Secretary of Defense Weinberger, not currently open to the public, may also provide more insight in the future.

37. Central Intelligence Agency Memorandum for the President, Vice President, Secretary of State, Secretary of Defense, Assistant to the President for National Security Affairs, and Chairman of the Joint Chiefs of Staff, from CIA Director William Casey, "US/Soviet Tension," June 19, 1984, Secret.

38. But those claiming that there was no danger to the War Scare were nonplussed by Casey's analysis. The day after Casey warned the president of "a rather stunning array of indicators" on Soviet behavior, the chief authors of the SNIE that contained these indicators, Fritz Ermarth and David McManis, wrote to the CIA director suggesting that he walk back the thrust of his memo and report. They suggested that he tell interlocutors, "It was not my intent in sending you the memo to suggest there was any immediate danger of hostile Soviet action" and that the CIA's "best judgment . . . remains that expressed in our recent SNIE . . . that we do not believe the Soviet leadership either fears imminent conflict or is making preparations for an imminent move toward confrontation." Nonetheless, in response to these indicators, the CIA began to produce Strategic Warning Reports on a regular basis, which would "identify emerging strategic trends of more than normal concern to us." Central Intelligence Agency Memorandum for Director of Central Intelligence William Casey from Fritz Ermarth and David McManis, "Contingency Talking Points on Your Memo Entitled 'US-Soviet Tensions (Dated 19 June 1984) for Meetings with Messieurs Shultz, Weinberger, and McFarlane," June 20, 1984, Secret.

39. The President's Foreign Intelligence Advisory Board, "The Soviet 'War Scare,'" February 15, 1990, Top Secret, UMBRA GAMMA WNINTEL NOFORN NOCONTRACT ORCON.

40. Ronald Reagan, Diary, June 14, 1984.

41. According to the PFIAB report, the title of this document may actually have been: "KGB Response to Soviet Leadership Concern over U.S. Nuclear Attack," based on Gordievsky's debriefs and disseminated in October 1985. Gordon Brook-Shepherd, *The Storm Birds: The Dramatic Stories of the Top Soviet Spies Who Have Defected Since World War II* (London: Grove Press, 1989), 269–270; The President's Foreign Intelligence Advisory Board, "The Soviet 'War Scare,'" February 15, 1990, Top Secret, UMBRA GAMMA WNINTEL NOFORN NOCONTRACT ORCON.

42. Ronald Reagan, Diary, July 21, 1987; Ronald Reagan, Diary, August 5, 1987.

43. According to McFarlane, he presented Reagan in real time "everything that [Director of Intelligence] Bill Casey had from Gordievsky [who was] reporting that Soviet leadership really was concerned about [Able Archer 83]. And he [Reagan] was interested in that." Robert McFarlane interview conducted by author, April 22, 2009.

44. Ronald Reagan, Diary, November 18, 1983.

45. "Small Group Meeting, 730 AM," November 19, 1983, Ronald Reagan Presidential Library, Matlock Files, [Saturday Morning Group—Notes] (Nov–Dec 1983), Box 34, 2219; Jack Matlock Jr., *Reagan and Gorbachev: How the Cold War Ended* (New York: Random House, 2004), 75–76.

46. "Small Group Meeting, 730 AM," November 19, 1983, Ronald Reagan Presidential Library, Matlock Files, [Saturday Morning Group—Notes] (Nov–Dec 1983), Box 34, 2219.

47. Robert McFarlane, *Special Trust* (New York: Cadell & Davies, 1994), 294.

48. The first evidence of this decision is a December 3, 1983, memorandum from Matlock to McFarlane. This memorandum listed six goals Matlock wanted the speech to emphasize. The speech was ready for the president by December 20, 1983, but was delayed until January 16, 1984, on the advice of Nancy Reagan's astrologer. December 3, 1983, Ronald Reagan Presidential Library Matlock Files, Saturday Group—Notes (Nov–Dec 1983), Box 34, 2219; December 20, 1983, Memorandum from Jack Matlock to Robert C. McFarlane, Fortier Files, Soviet Project [1 of 2], 90763; Jack Matlock Jr., *Reagan and Gorbachev: How the Cold War Ended* (New York: Random House, 2004), 80.

49. Unpublished Robert McFarlane interview conducted by Don Oberdorfer, 1990, Mudd Manuscript Library, Princeton University; unpublished Jack Matlock interview conducted by Don Oberdorfer, 1990, Mudd Manuscript Library, Princeton University;

Beth Fischer, *The Reagan Reversal: Foreign Policy and the End of the Cold War* (Columbia: University of Missouri Press, 2000), 135.

50. Ronald Reagan, Address to the Nation and Other Countries on United States-Soviet Relations, East Room, White House, Washington, D.C., January 16, 1984, available at the Ronald Reagan Presidential Library's online Public Papers of President Ronald W. Reagan.

51. Ronald Reagan, Address to the Nation and Other Countries on United States-Soviet Relations, East Room, White House, Washington, D.C., January 16, 1984, available at the Ronald Reagan Presidential Library's online Public Papers of President Ronald W. Reagan.

52. Cable from George Shultz to Ray Seitz/ Brunson McKinley, "Gromyko Meeting," January 16, 1984, in CIA Records Search Tool, National Archives and Records Administration NARA, College Park, MD.

53. Cable from George Shultz to Ray Seitz/ Brunson McKinley, "Gromyko Meeting," January 16, 1984, in CIA Records Search Tool, National Archives and Records Administration NARA, College Park, MD.

54. Ronald Reagan, *An American Life* (New York: Simon & Schuster, 1990), 588–589.

55. December 15, 1983, "Address by Marshal of the Soviet Union D. F. Ustinov," *Krasnaya zvezda.*

56. Unpublished interview with Anonymous Intelligence Analyst conducted by Don Orberdorfer, 1990, Mudd Manuscript Library, Princeton University.

57. Anatoly Dobrynin, *In Confidence: Moscow's Ambassador to Six Cold War Presidents* (Seattle: University of Washington Press, 2001), 512, 527.

58. Letter from Yuri Andropov to Ronald Reagan, January 28, 1984, Reagan Presidential Library, Ronald Reagan Presidential Library, Executive Secretariat, NSC: Head of State File, box 38, ID 8490115.

59. Roy Medvedev, *Neizvestnii Andropov* (The unknown Andropov) (Rostov: Feniks, 1999), 439. Medvedev states this occurred in 1983 and does not say precisely when. The decision may or may not have been effected by Able Archer 83. Regardless, it was an important development.

60. Scott Sagan, *Moving Target: Nuclear Strategy and National Security* (Princeton: Princeton University Press, 1990), 151–152.

61. Christopher Andrew and Oleg Gordievsky, *Comrade Kryuchkov's Instructions: Top Secret Files on KGB Foreign Operations, 1975–1985* (Stanford: Stanford University Press, 1993), 90.

62. March 9, 1984, Bulgarian Ministry of Interior; MVR Information re: Results from the work on the improvement of the System for detection of RYAN indications, AMVR, Fond 1, Record 12, File 553, Provided by Jordan Baev.

63. Nate Jones, "The Vicious Circle of Intelligence," for *Forecasting Nuclear War,* ed. Bernd Schaefer, The Cold War International History Project, https://www.wilsoncenter.org/publication/forecasting-nuclear-war; Markus Wolf did not write kindly of the Soviets, or Operation RYaN, in his 1997 memoir: "Our Soviet partners had become obsessed with the danger of a nuclear missile attack," though he writes that he had not. "Like most intelligent people, I found these war games a burdensome waste of time, but these orders were no more open to discussion than other orders from above." Markus Wolf with Anne McElvoy, *Man Without a Face: The Autobiography of Communism's Greatest Spymaster* (New York: Random House, 1997), 222.

64. Nate Jones, "The Vicious Circle of Intelligence," for *Forecasting Nuclear War,* ed. Bernd Schaefer, The Cold War International History Project. https://www.wilsoncenter.org/publication/forecasting-nuclear-war.

65. Nate Jones, "The Vicious Circle of Intelligence," for *Forecasting Nuclear War*, ed. Bernd Schaefer, The Cold War International History Project. https://www.wilsoncenter.org/publication/forecasting-nuclear-war.

66. Nate Jones, "The Vicious Circle of Intelligence," for *Forecasting Nuclear War*, ed. Bernd Schaefer, The Cold War International History Project. https://www.wilsoncenter.org/publication/forecasting-nuclear-war.

Conclusion: "Why Is the World So Dangerous?"

1. Meyer also wrote that the Soviets were genuinely fearful of the Pershing II missiles, believing they could hit Moscow in twelve minutes, "roughly how long it takes some of the Kremlin's leaders to get out of their chairs, let alone to their shelters." Central Intelligence Agency memo for the Director and Deputy Director from Vice Chairman of the National Intelligence Council Herbert E. Meyer, "Subject: Why Is the World So Dangerous?" November 30, 1983, CIA Records Search Tool (CREST) database.

2. *Table of Global Nuclear Weapons Stockpiles, 1945–2002*, The Natural Resources Defense Council, http://www.nrdc.org/nuclear/nudb/datab19.asp.

3. Of course, this is not to say that the USSR's security apparatus operated well. The Soviet leadership's narrow, unaccountable decision-making process led to the gargantuan, misguided, and dangerous Operation RYaN. RYaN expended scarce resources seeking out evidence of a U.S. plan for a decapitating first strike that, despite the bellicose rhetoric of the early Reagan administration, was not contemplated. The President's Foreign Intelligence Advisory Board, "The Soviet 'War Scare,'" February 15, 1990, Top Secret, UMBRA GAMMA WNINTEL NOFORN NOCONTRACT ORCON.

4. William Burr and Jeffrey Kimball, *Nixon's Nuclear Specter: The Secret Alert of 1969, Madman Diplomacy, and the Vietnam War* (Lawrence: University Press of Kansas, 2015), 42.

5. *American Cryptology During the Cold War, 1945–1989, Book II: Centralization Wins, 1960–1972*, Thomas Johnson, National Security Agency Center for Cryptologic History, 1999, Top Secret-COMINT-UMBRA / TALENT KEYHOLE / X1.

6. Michael Dobbs, *One Minute to Midnight: Kennedy, Khrushchev, and Castro on the Brink of Nuclear War* (New York: Vintage, 2009), 340.

7. See "The Underwater Cuban Missile Crisis: Soviet Submarines and the Risk of Nuclear War" by Thomas Blanton, William Burr, and Svetlana Savranskaya for the National Security Archive, October 24, 2012, http://nsarchive.gwu.edu/NSAEBB/NSAEBB399/.

8. Michael Dobbs *One Minute to Midnight: Kennedy, Khrushchev, and Castro on the Brink of Nuclear War* (New York: Vintage, 2009), 345.

9. Averell Harriman, "Memorandum of Conversation with Andropov," June 2, 1983, W. Averell Harriman Papers, Library of Congress, Manuscript Division, Box 655 and Soviet notes of a meeting between General Secretary Yuri Andropov and Averell and Pamela Harriman, June 2, 1983, [Russian State Archive of Contemporary History], F 82, Op1, D 36, R 27-55, LL 33-44.

10. Michael Dobbs, *One Minute to Midnight: Kennedy, Khrushchev, and Castro on the Brink of Nuclear War* (New York: Vintage, 2009), 345.

11. Benjamin Fischer, "The 1983 War Scare in U.S.-Soviet Relations," *CIA Studies in Intelligence*, Undated, circa 1996, Secret.

12. Reagan wrote war with the Soviet Union would be like "two spiders in a bottle locked in a suicidal fight until both were dead." Ronald Reagan, *An American Life* (New York: Simon & Schuster, 1990), 257.

13. See John Lewis Gaddis, *The Long Peace: Inquiries into the History of the Cold War* (Oxford: Oxford University Press, 1989).

14. Anatoly Dobrynin, *In Confidence: Moscow's Ambassador to Six Cold War Presidents* (Seattle: University of Washington Press, 2001), 551.

15. "The Making of a Neo-KGB State," *The Economist*, August 23, 2007.

16. Ray Sanchez, Nic Robertson, and Don Melvin, "Russian PM Medvedev Equates Relations with West to a 'New Cold War,'" CNN, February 15, 2016.

17. Memorandum for Robert McFarlane from Jack Matlock, "American Academic on Soviet Policy," December 3, 1983, Ronald Reagan Presidential Library, Matlock Files, Chron December 1983 [1 of 2], Box 2, 90888.

18. Amy Woolf, "Russian Compliance with the Intermediate Range Nuclear Forces (INF) Treaty: Background and Issues for Congress," Congressional Research Service, October 13, 2015, https://www.fas.org/sgp/crs/nuke/R43832.pdf.

19. Ronald Reagan, Address Before a Joint Session of the Congress on the State of the Union, January 25, 1984, available at the Ronald Reagan Presidential Library's online Public Papers of President Ronald W. Reagan.

20. To be sure, as long as nuclear weapons exist, so does the unacceptable risk of nuclear war. But the risk of nuclear war through miscalculation between the United States and Russia remains at a low level. Russia has even warned North Korea that its threats to deliver "preventative nuclear strikes" against the United States and South Korea could create a legal basis for countries to use military force against North Korea. Chad O'Carroll, "Russia Warns North Korea over Threats of Nuclear Strike," *The Guardian*, March 8, 2016.

21. Jen Hoffenaar and Christopher Findlay, eds., *Military Planning for European Theatre Conflict During the Cold War: An Oral History Roundtable Stockholm, 24–25 April 2006*, Center for Security Studies ETH Zurich, 161.

22. Don Oberdorfer, *The Turn: From the Cold War to a New Era the United States and the Soviet Union 1983–1990* (New York: Touchstone, 1991), 479.

Acknowledgments and Notes on Sources

1. James Hershberg, "Reconsidering the Nuclear Arms Race: The Past as Prelude," in Gordon Martel, ed., *American Foreign Relations Reconsidered, 1890–1993* (New York: Routledge, 1994), 187–210.

Index

Letters A through I refer to the image insert that follows page 66.

Nate Jones is the director of the Freedom of Information Act Project for the National Security Archive. He is also editor of the National Security Archive's blog, *Unredacted*. He lives in Washington, D.C.

Tom Blanton is the executive director of the National Security Archive at George Washington University in Washington, D.C.

Publishing in the Public Interest

Thank you for reading this book published by The New Press. The New Press is a nonprofit, public interest publisher. New Press books and authors play a crucial role in sparking conversations about the key political and social issues of our day.

We hope you enjoyed this book and that you will stay in touch with The New Press. Here are a few ways to stay up to date with our books, events, and the issues we cover:

- Sign up at www.thenewpress.com/subscribe to receive updates on New Press authors and issues and to be notified about local events
- Like us on Facebook: www.facebook.com/newpressbooks
- Follow us on Twitter: www.twitter.com/thenewpress

Please consider buying New Press books for yourself; for friends and family; or to donate to schools, libraries, community centers, prison libraries, and other organizations involved with the issues our authors write about.

The New Press is a 501(c)(3) nonprofit organization. You can also support our work with a tax-deductible gift by visiting www.thenewpress.com/donate.